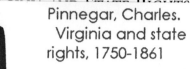

Virginia and State Rights, 1750–1861

The Genesis and Promotion of a Doctrine

CHARLES PINNEGAR

McFarland & Company, Inc., Publishers
Jefferson, North Carolina, and London

LIBRARY OF CONGRESS CATALOGUING-IN-PUBLICATION DATA

Pinnegar, Charles.
Virginia and state rights, 1750–1861 : the genesis
and promotion of a doctrine / Charles Pinnegar.
p.   cm.
Includes bibliographical references and index.

ISBN 978-0-7864-4394-9
softcover : 50# alkaline paper (∞)

1. Virginia — Politics and government — 1775–1865.
2. States' rights (American politics) — History — 19th century.
3. States' rights (American Politics) — History — 18th century.
I. Title.
F230.P56   2009   320.473'04909755 — dc22   2009009229

British Library cataloguing data are available

Cover image 2009 Shutterstock

Manufactured in the United States of America

*McFarland & Company, Inc., Publishers
Box 611, Jefferson, North Carolina 28640
www.mcfarlandpub.com*

Contents

To the memory of Patrick Henry
and the Virginia Antifederalists

Preface

Several years ago, while preparing a biography of John Buchanan Floyd, I found evidence that he was a Virginia state rights man who did not support secession prior to January 1861. However, subsequent to Lincoln's April 1861 call for 75,000 troops the Secretary heartily supported it. Either position individually was understandable but combined they cast a shadow over Floyd's ideological consistency in favor of personal advantage. Thankfully, a reread of Richard Ellis's admirable *The Union at Risk* solved the conundrum. The assumption that state rights fealty translated to a promotion of secession was incorrect. Ellis noted that two variants of the theory existed simultaneously. But, his book goals were focussed elsewhere and he allocated only a few pages to this gem. Because of the war violence, moral depravity of slavery, and post-war Southern causal explanations, historians gathered all state rights doctrinaires into the variation they blamed for the conflict. Thus, the radical state sovereigntist doctrine suffocated that of the more numerous traditionalists despite tenets that proved their doctrinal incompatibility. State rights ideology became monolithic to historians.

It was easy to promote inadvertently the latter conclusion. For example, the eminent intellectual historian Forrest McDonald in his fine *States' Rights and the Union: Imperium in Imperio* (2000) provided his readers with a chronological description of state rights disputes in the antebellum era. Still, in his trek through the decades little time was spent expanding Supreme Court or congressional decisions and southern reactions that were crucial to cementing state rights planks into the doctrine. McDonald, and most historical surveyors, operated on a level different from that required to uncover the doctrine's genesis and building blocks.

The latter aspect will take center stage in this book. Rather than attempt a national survey, it will concentrate on only one state. Except for Ulrich Phillips in his politically-centered *Georgia and State Rights*, no authors have written state rights expositions from a single state's viewpoint. What more logical choice than antebellum Virginia could be selected? The research involved two main sections. The first applied social, political, religious, and theoretical themes to establish the origins of Virginia state rights. The second concentrated on the ways concerned Virginians maintained the doctrine currency in the face of nationalistic threats to a southern interpretation of liberty.

For at least seven decades state rights were the backbone of the Old Dominion's understanding of the Union's nature. However, historical research often suffered from three defects. William Freehling reminded us forcefully that several Souths existed but modern state rights commentators usually ignored his warning. Individual rights and equality were stifled by the emphasis on extremism. Lost in the shuffle was a dynamic, expansive doctrine based on evolving Constitutional interpretations. Continually, Virginians added and deleted doctrinal planks according to historical demands.

1

The other two defects were symbiotic. Little effort had been spent uncovering either the doctrine's origins and variations — it usually arrived fully formed — or the manner in which its proponents ensured its currency. To illuminate its origins one must trace the state's social and religious background. They were incorporated with both an investigation of the state's political culture before and during the debate on Constitutional ratification and the current dominant theory. Investigation revealed that Virginians believed every dispute attacked their cherished doctrine. Thus, we must examine them closely to get a sense of the theory's hold on a powerful segment of the state's population. This methodology will spotlight any trends that account for state rights' origins and the hardening of positions between the North and South. Moreover, it will serve to correct mistaken interpretations.

We can satisfy all three requirements by making a thorough study of Virginia's responses to religious intolerance as well as political and Constitutional infringements. Its concerns were categorized during various crises that it labeled sovereignty loss. Within them one could find not only a catalyst for dispute but also its corresponding Virginia solution. Two state rights theories were produced based on either the Constitution or natural rights through compact theory.

A painstaking study of the early record unveiled another equally important impulse. If previously sovereign states amalgamated to form a single nation, a power reorganization was mandatory. Both the new national government and those of the original states were organized in different styles. A review of the initial conditions at the time of nationalization will allow the readers to predict the path state rights would take. Was it possible that multiple doctrinal versions were inevitable? What conditions would warn Virginians that events endangered their rights?

Commentators could establish doctrinal reaffirmation in two ways. One would apply the methodology employed in the first section and quote letters between famous statesmen. However, this cannot explain why the people adopted the theory so wholeheartedly and is axiomatic that its popularity was due to its resonance with them. I have adopted a second tactic. I maintain that the doctrine's popularity and longevity depended on timely public essays on the Union's nature written by state commentators or representative government institutions. Pamphlets, books, government reports, and newspapers provided a useful platform. Publicly, Jefferson answered Hamilton, John Taylor of Caroline attacked the national bank, the house of delegates denounced the assumption of state debts, James Madison laid down the Principles of '98, Edmund Pendleton listed the dangers of a nationalist policy, and St. George Tucker unveiled the basis of traditional state rights. Each pivotal period prompted a state rights reassessment instructing the people. Through the decades, William Branch Giles, John Marshall, Nathaniel Beverly Tucker, Abel Upshur and Littleton Tazewell supplied interpretations that explained current trends and their effects on Virginia. Of course, Virginia's congressional delegations and state house of delegates joined in this enterprise. Together, they ensured that Virginians had the information required to update ideals that had guided their ancestors for decades.

To recap, this manuscript's goals are to provide a basis for a state rights doctrine, separate the competing variations according to their planks, and show that Virginians had a coherent plan for keeping the nature of the Union before the public. No other work examines these aspects at the state level.

I have adopted several preconditions for material used in the writing of this book. As stated, the material promoting the doctrine was available to the public although some letters — particularly in the preratification period — from famous Virginians were selected to embellish a proven point. This achieved a dual purpose. It not only ensured that the selected passages could affect opinion within the state but also that the work avoided generalizations from one, or a few, letters.

I mined only Virginia opinion. Due to the announced breadth of the study, this restriction seemed mandatory. But how did one eliminate the most famous state sovereigntist from a book on state rights? The answer lay in the topic selection. If John Calhoun's policies were universal, some Virginia commentator would report and defend them. If not, they did not affect Virginia opinion.

This book is not Virginia or United States history. It ignored large swathes in favor of others that contain data influencing state rights doctrine. Nor do I claim that the selections were the first announcing new paths.

Usually, I have refrained from disputing commentators' comments or conclusions. If a writer wrote, "Federalists planned an elite government of the few," then it was that interpreter's opinion. For my purposes, it did not matter whether he was correct, because my focus was on what he honestly thought. Eventually, the compendium of the most popular opinions would produce a doctrinal basis. Opponents, or the reader, might consider Virginia's conclusions ludicrous, but that did not affect its doctrine.

This study concentrated on ideology, not politics or slavery, except in instances that were germane. Second, the concentration on state rights necessarily skewed opinion toward it on matters of Union. Also, the study often employed nationalistic interpretations as a foil. Advancing a proviso above, if one reads, "Marshall's decision was unconscionable" (this does not appear in the book) ,the reader must understand that the point of view was that of a Virginia state rights man. This tactic reduced the incidence of the phrase "According to...."

The electronic revolution has helped historical research significantly. Now, a researcher can use the World Wide Web in exciting ways to extend his research. If one registered with JSTOR, for example, one could read the most significant periodicals for articles relating to his study. Or, if one were unsure whether a celebrated book fit logically into an author's plan, often a copy could be found electronically. For example, several of John Taylor's books were available. After a perusal, I approached an interlibrary loan service to obtain a hard copy.

The latter function was crucial in the writing of this study. It could never have been finished without the aid of Susan Moskal and Annie Relic of the Brock University Interlibrary Loan department. Remarkably, they found copies of every request and did so with a smile. I am forever grateful for their assistance.

Charles Pinnegar
Spring, 2009

PART I

Contributing Factors Motivating Virginia's Ideological Attitudes

1

Revolutionary Era Factors Influencing Virginia's Gravitation Toward State Rights

State rights. To many, the phrase conjures up visions of sweat-stained slaves bagging cotton beneath a broiling sun; lean, battle-hardened veterans tearfully furling the Battle Flag for the last time; peaceful marchers, black and white, trudging fearfully between lines of hate-driven southerners, their snarling Alsatians straining at taut leashes; or howling Dixiecrat conventioneers intent on returning their section to an unsavory past. One cannot escape Americans' general impression: state rights and slavery, morally bankrupt twins, was the special provenance of the South.

However, from 1991, Supreme Court cases like *Gregory vs. Ashcroft, New York vs. United States, United States vs. Lopez, Prinz vs. United States, Alden vs. Maine,* and *United States vs. Morrison* have returned to state rights a modicum of acceptability. Importantly, these cases had nothing to do with slavery, and they were not South-specific. The rulings broke the mold referred to earlier. Maybe, just maybe, the commonly held position on state rights was an oversimplification. Perhaps a time and place existed when all sections recognized its reasonableness. Or, it might have been a central ingredient in the vituperative debate over federal-state power.

We will outline the origin of this theory. English precedent and Enlightenment political philosophies combined with the rise of evangelical religious sects to shape state rights doctrine. Revolutionary ideals and the nasty debate over a strong, energetic national government further sculpted state rights and helped define its major premises. Throughout this process, the concentration on liberty remained constant. By modeling Virginia we will get a clear picture of the symbiosis between liberty and state rights.

Before the Constitutional debate, two competing ideological theories were current. Some colonists found solace in the classical republican notion of a corporate society while others preferred a doctrine of self-interest and acquisitiveness. Perhaps a brief outline of several practitioners' theories will give the reader a sense of the ideological choices set before Virginians.

The radical Whig tandem of John Trenchard (1662–1723) and Thomas Gordon (?–1750) supplied some Americans with a political philosophy that applied to their condition. Their first collaboration was a collection of fifty-three essays in *The Independent Whig* that had dual foci. Both the abuses of established religion and the need for toleration drew their attention. Nevertheless, their investigation of English society after the scandalous South Sea Bubble established their reputation. In December 1720, they published the first of one hundred thirty-eight *Cato's Letters* in the *London Journal.* Named for an ancient Roman who championed virtue in the face of Julius Caesar's opposition, these republican essays extolled the Whig case for personal liberty while attacking corruption and tyranny. The duo unveiled the unhealthy alliance between some political leaders and the monied class that resulted in a well-financed pressure group able to influence the government. Because of its pre-eminent position, the people must closely scrutinize the executive branch of government.

The team did not accept any master-slave relationship and extended it to the rulers and ruled dichotomy. Trenchard and Gordon rejected any attempt to synonymize rulers with the people's representatives. Moreover, they concluded that a mixed monarchy of different classes of men was most likely to overcome man's innate self-interest, insure the people's happiness and secure liberty.

✠

They maintained their suspicion and pessimism about power in general. If the people combined Whig tenets with a mutual social compact, they could avoid its misuse. However, the guardians of liberty must be on constant alert. The law of nature, dominated by self-interest, insisted that whenever unfavorable conditions repeated so did the results.

Cato's Letters became the primary source of inspiration for the American revolutionaries. Americans republished them repeatedly in pamphlet and book form. Colonists filled speeches and newspaper editorials with allusions to the *Letters* because Americans recognized that if a corrupt government could infect England, then a similar fate awaited them unless Patriots intervened. The people must not stand idly by while their societies crumbled about them.

Charles Louis de Secondat (1689–1755), Baron Montesquieu, was the scion of a wealthy Bordeaux family. Secluded in his chateau, Montesquieu wrestled for years with one question. How did different societies form different governments? Although his aim was always to write *Spirit of Laws*, he became so fascinated with ancient Rome that it threatened to overwhelm the rest of the book. To overcome this problem, Montesquieu separated it from *Spirit*. In 1734 he published *Les Considerations sur les Causes de la Grandeur et la Decadence des Romains* (*The Causes of the Rise and Fall of the Roman Empire*). He surveyed its political institutions from its foundation until the Constantinople disaster and used them to discover the focal points that defined that era. He always examined his data with a political rather than a religious eye. In this way, he sought to escape the trap of religious prejudice.

Montesquieu planned to apply scientific knowledge and method to his collection of government forms. *Spirit's* goal was to uncover the form most likely to produce liberty and security for its citizens. To do so, he compared the tenets of various systems related to republicanism, despotism, and monarchy, and listed the pros and cons. To extend the study, he compared climates, customs, religions, and even the relationship of laws to their government.

A state would enact the laws. Its government would consist of three branches, the executive, legislative, and judicial. When each of these branches was independent of the other like that defined in the English constitution, political freedom was likely. The separation of powers ensured that one branch could not run amok and threaten the people's liberty. In addition, Montesquieu foresaw "direct, immediate participation by the people." This tenet would come under fire about 1780 because the extensive American land mass seemed to preclude direct participation. Vast territory, according to Montesquieu, favored despotism.

In addition, Montesquieu proscribed slavery and torture from a monarchy or republic, and advocated religious toleration and the separation of church and state. Rather than one institution being secondary to the other, they should work together for the good of society.

The Baron issued several guidelines for a republic. Its primary requirement was a frugal, public-spirited, unselfish citizenry that channeled its need for personal advancement into the public good and love for the republic. However, he knew that self-interest was bound to rear its head. Perhaps the pursuit of commercial gain might benefit society rather than destroy it. Americans were very comfortable with the thrust of Montesquieu's volumes. One can argue that the basis of American government can be found in *Spirit*. However, it also became a cornerstone for the argument for small state aristocratic domination. Eventually, the notion of self-interest sublimated by societal needs came under attack after the Revolution. Tocqueville considered Montesquieu's adherence to civic humanism in the face of American materialism to be a serious flaw in the theory. Were not the English, the authors of his model constitution, busy earning profits?[1]

Before we turn our attention to the next authorities, we must understand two terms that they employed. Our philosophers believed that a state of nature existed before the advent of government. "Society" was merely a congregation of individuals, each following his own course of action. Of course, this revealed certain unhappy characteristics. For example, there existed the potential for the domination of the weak by the strong. Still, rational individuals could recognize and overcome difficulties by creating a form of government. However, the form promoted could differ depending on the community's state of nature experience.

The social contract was between the state of nature individuals who had rationally chosen to organize their society. Each must accept certain minimum rules and regulations and eventually cede some power to an authority that enforced them. Note that the authority's power rested on individual consent and that this consent was based on the decisions of rational individuals, absent duress.

The progenitor in this field was the monarchist Thomas Hobbes (1588–1679). His magnum opus, *Leviathan*, was the first to apply empiricism to the field of human activity. A keen student of the physical sciences, Hobbes concluded that the current political theory based on religion and ethical interpretation caused disputes between king and Parliament. His replacement thesis proposed natural law as the model for human law and advised the people to consent to sovereign rule. He argued that if a community ignored his model, humanity would pay a terrible price.

How did he arrive at these conclusions? According to Hobbes, all state of nature humans were equal. On the surface, this appeared to be a positive trait, but Hobbes interpreted it differently. Because individuals were equal, they often quarreled due to a competition for resources, a mistrust of others' motives, or a desire to maintain or enhance one's reputation. As a result, mankind was in a state of constant conflict. Life was brutal and lawless, with each man adopting whatever measure that preserved his life. In other words, civil society, under this view, was impossible.

Hobbes adduced that selfishness motivated individuals. Seeking their own success and avoiding failure was natural for them. To combat this proclivity, humans banded together for protection. This mobilizing led to the construction of a social contract whose tenets encompassed the members' rules of behavior. Obviously, based on the central trait of selfishness, the social contract must contain clauses that introduced authority. To be successful, all contract signatories must obey the individual or group wielding authority. Although Hobbes was a lesser light in the construction of an American political philosophy, John Locke (1632–1704) expanded some of his ideas.

The political struggle leading to the Glorious Revolution motivated Locke's *Two Treatises on Government*. His ambition was to stamp out any conviction that a monarch had divine and absolute rights. Moreover, he planned to replace it with a theory in which political order would result in the liberty of individual citizens. According to Locke, there existed a natural law, driven by reason, that governed an individual's actions in a state of nature. Within that law every man was free to pursue his own agenda without interference from others. All men were equal in this state, and they defined this equality as "life, health, liberty, or possessions." Yet one must be aware that undiluted liberty did not follow an individual into society. Once he left a state of nature for a society, he assigned his power, and could not retrieve it unless that society failed.

Locke realized that his theoretical model — he gave one weak example of an actual state of nature — produced several "inconveniences." It was prone to war; "full of fears" based on uncertainties regarding the preservation of "lives, liberties and estates"; populated by men who were naturally corrupt; and contained no legal mechanism to judge disputes, carry out sentences or protect property. Despite these obstacles, all men, according to reason, would remain in a state of nature until they consented to join in a society.

When a group of individuals united to form a society, each member gave up his "equality, liberty, and executive power" to a defined legislative authority better equipped to protect the individual rights of its members. Note that this meant each ceded his power to the legislative entity. Thus, its power was the cumulative sum of the powers of its members. In addition, when the individual left the state of nature for a proposed society he recognized majority rule unless a specific reference in the compact relieved him of that duty. As a result, majority-sponsored laws bound the whole society. The residents called this the "consent of the people."

The members protected this right through a supreme legislative body. Its duty was to preserve their property from any corrupt grasp. The legislative body received its legal boundaries from a constitution, the "first and fundamental act of society." Of course, the legislature had restrictions. Its laws had to reflect the people's will and could not be an affront to the laws of nature. For example, since the end of government was the preservation of property, the legislative body could not strip it from an individual. Most important, it could not terminate its compact with the people.

This contract could be considered political and/or social in scope. It created both power and obedience classes. As we will see later, the federal version, due to its nature, required its governmental creature to strictly construe its delegated powers while the social type protected individual liberty and the right to hold private property.

One of the government's main tasks was to decide what laws best served society. It could not transfer this duty to others because only the people had that power. Locke judged that the few laws necessary for the protection of society's property would take little time to pass. Thus, the legislature need not be in session for extended periods. Because a governmental body must be available to oversee the laws, Locke invented another, labeled the executive.

Whatever type of government society chose, it must enumerate the duties and powers of its officers. Locke attributed "sovereign" only in relation to God. However, he inferred the political sense in his description of the government form the society would have after leaving the state of nature. In a democracy, the legislative body, the repository of power, would be sovereign. Man could not abandon his freedom because it was too closely aligned with self-preservation, a fundamental law of nature. Others easily expanded this from self-preservation to personal liberty.

The people of the society had certain governmental restrictions placed upon them. Anyone who lived within society's confines and enjoyed its benefits was liable to its laws and must obey the will of the majority. Certain rights balanced these restrictions. If an enemy conquered the society, its citizens had the right to fight the oppressor. Moreover, they did not have to obey any government to which they had not given consent. If they withdrew it, thus dissolving government, they might start again and build a new one. To those who argued that this would mean constant rebellions, Locke posited that the people would always do the right thing.

Perhaps surprising, Locke argued that men did not have to wait for tyranny to strike them. If it foresaw the danger, society could take preemptive action. To wait implied tyranny would take place. Once this happened, the chance for repelling it was lost.

Last, the people, through their legislative body and its constitution, had the inalienable right to direct the society. If anyone passed laws inimical to the people, they did not have to obey them. They may even use force against the perpetrators of the law.

John Locke spent considerable time examining threats to the commonwealth. Any despotic power was unnatural because it could kill at pleasure. Usurpation was "domestic conquest" and could "never have right on [its] side." It involved the attempt by an individual or group to steal and apply the power legally assigned to another. Tyranny advanced the danger one step. It was "the exercise of a power beyond right, which no body can have a right to." It included the extension of power for personal gain but generally presumed some illegal manipulation to achieve it. Notice that Locke did not stipulate the body that usurped or tyrannized. Any form that replaced the preservation of property through other acts was tyrannical. Specifically, Locke's legislative body could become tyrannical if it ignored its role as the protector of the public trust. According to his theory, the people could resume its power after removing it from the legislative branch.

From the above, one could predict that, to Locke, the usurpers or tyrants were the true rebels. The people, as we know, had the natural right to fight tyranny. Nevertheless, the enumeration of these rights should not lead one to conclude that rebellion was the answer to all disputes. Locke firmly believed that the whole of the people could adjudicate them whenever a difference of legal opinion arose.

Interpreters of Locke's compact faced several obstacles. The first was the definition of "state." It could be the geographical area occupied by a society, the institutions, agencies, and people of the government, or the people that populated the society. One might even attempt to combine two or more of these possibilities. Second, who were the participants of the compact? A theorist could choose from the states but not its citizens; the states and their citizens; the state governments; the people who first agreed to form a government and the constitution upon which they agreed; two mystical minds, state and popular; states and the federal government; the rulers and ruled; the rulers and people; a compromise between governmental powers and personal liberty; the people; and the people of state governments. Moreover, who were the people? It could be a consolidated national community; the members of a state of nature that formed each state and delegated their power to it; or a Virginia elite best situated by power and circumstance to direct the state. Last, the interpreter would be stymied by Locke's imprecision on the effects of government dissolution. In one section, he claimed that a dissolution of the government did not result in a similar fate for its society. Yet, later he implied the opposite.

Due to the Whig stress on balanced government and liberty, the commentator above would have few problems with the written compact. It would protect liberty against power while recognizing that government must have authority to function; reflect a contractual sense while avoiding the ruler-ruled model; achieve status as fundamental law by popular ratification;

12   I. Contributing Factors Motivating Virginia's Ideological Attitudes

and establish the recognized sovereign. It could be the consolidated people, the states or the people of the states. One thing was certain. Any Locke explication must deal with the compact's rational justification for governmental overthrow under certain conditions.

One final caveat. When we listed the possible compact participants above, the similarities some bore with others was striking. As a result, Americans had a working knowledge, but not an intimate understanding of the intricacies of the original theory compared with an interpreter's translation. However, they understood two notions. They had the right to replace a tyrannical government and consent had formed it. For most, that was enough.

To conclude this brief study, one should stress that Locke's *Treatise* was theoretical and written shortly after the Glorious Revolution. Moreover, he must have known that its application would be by analogy. Mankind had advanced society too far to revert to a state of nature. This interpretive caveat would lead to a curious situation. Proponents of mutually antagonistic systems would use it as a citation for the promulgation of their ideas. Also, some would advance their notion of government while ignoring or suppressing Locke's societal concerns while others did the reverse. Thus, when ostensibly quoting Locke, one must be sure to do so. Too often, either a Lockean interpretation by someone with a hidden agenda or one that selectively appropriated specific sections fooled readers.

John Locke's *Two Treatises* was a smashing success in America. Publishers printed and reprinted pamphlets extolling his principles of natural rights throughout the colonies. They reinterpreted, rehashed and rewrote his theory. Finally, Americans could study Locke's ideas within myriad colonial tomes. Saying that they were an essential element in the Declaration of Independence was safe.[2]

Most literate Americans, as with John Locke's theories, were familiar with Adam Smith's theses although few might be considered experts. Their interest did not translate to action during the Revolution since his *The Wealth of Nations* was contemporaneous with the war, but its tenets certainly drifted into the American conscience before the Convention of 1787. During the intervening years, the primary economic group that found solace in its conclusions was the Virginia squirearchy. Smith's theories melded nicely with its vision of an agrarian-led society. Below, we will show several instances in society and government that coincided with planter experience.

Perhaps the most attractive feature of Smith's tome for Virginia planters was his advancement of the thesis that self-love, ie: self-interest, was the most relevant motivator of human behavior. According to Smith, private individuals gave little thought to promoting society's interests. Instead, their support of local rather than foreign products, for example, was aimed at securing a cheaper product for themselves. An unintended consequence of this decision, his "invisible hand" characterization, was the promotion of society's good. If everyone bought a cheaper local product, that industry would flourish and provide economic impetus to the society.

Because mankind had an insatiable drive to better its own condition, and a resort to self-interest often produced the corollary of a benefit to society, business could produce economic benefits despite the corrosive effects of governmental intervention. "The natural effect of every individual," said Smith, "to better his own condition" could overcome "one hundred impertinent abstractions with which the folly of human laws too often encumbers its operations." Unfortunately for some Virginia planters, adherence to a theory of a self-loving man driving the society's economy would necessarily conflict with others' comfortable belief in corporate republicanism.

Smith recognized that a modern society would encompass several different social classes.

It was his surmise that the differences between them were not natural. "Habit, custom, and education" would surely be discriminating. These could be augmented by personal qualifications such as beauty, strength, virtue, and wisdom. However, the two most important were "the superiority of fortune" and the "superiority of birth."

These class differences defined the competing economic classes. When he examined a nation's produce, Smith discovered three generators, rent from tenants, wages from labor, and profits from investing in stocks. These led naturally to the occupations of farmer, wage earner, and merchant. Smith considered the first pair essential to economic viability, but labeled the third an "unproductive class." He knew that private economic gain never prostrated a nation economically whereas government mismanagement might do so. This happened if the "public revenue" was turned over to "unproductive hands" that produced nothing concrete themselves while benefiting from the labor of others. It was possible that the drain on the public purse from such unproductive people might overwhelm the "frugality and good conduct" of the society and lead to economic chaos. Merchants mirrored this definition perfectly. They were consumed by their own interests rather than those of society and were guided by "avarice rather than virtue." Yet, Smith did define one path of redemption for this self-interested, unproductive class. Perhaps they could work hard at their profession, save capital, and eventually reach an economic position from which they could join the planter gentry.

The gentry perched atop the status ladder. Not only were they freeholders but also their land produced rents from its tenants. Strangely, Smith lauded planters because the collection of rents required no physical labor whereas merchants, who operated similarly, were castigated for their method of earning capital. The difference seemed to be that the gentry neither formed an economic plan based on rent collecting nor did it visit the marketplace.

Smith's view was that any hierarchy of job classes must have agriculture at its apex. There was, he said, a "natural order of productive and socially desired capital investment led by agriculture then commerce and last manufacturing." Without government interference, individual capital would "naturally fall into those channels in this sequence." It was mandatory for the successful economic state to ensure that its agricultural segment was fully developed in order to produce capital that could, in turn, grow its commercial sector. Only then should the state turn to manufacturing. Because the farmer must constantly meet changing conditions, he probably had more individual skills than the tradesman, but the latter had the advantage of faster technical improvements. This advantage would prove crucial once the society turned to manufacturing. At some future date, it was probable that all arable farmland would be occupied. Then, men would be forced to move to the cities and adopt the factory worker's life. Until this occurred, agriculture had one great advantage over commerce or manufacturing. Times of national stress, like war, were less likely to destroy agriculture compared to its two competitors. It would take "violent commotions" lasting "a century or two" to destroy a nation's agricultural system.

Government could either help or hinder business. It was clear that civic government must precede any acquisition and development of property. Smith reiterated that despite the "exactions of government," businessmen would gradually accumulate capital that improved their economic position. Government could secure this dynamic if it protected the businessman by positive laws and at the same time refrained from infringing his liberty.

Some governments could stunt capital growth by directing the investment of capital. This authority "could safely be trusted, not only to no single person, but to no council or senate whatever, and ... would nowhere be so dangerous as in the hands of a man who had folly and presumption enough to fancy himself fit to exercise it." Smith, extending his criticism, warned even the sovereign, who presumed to understand the market, against interfering. After all, it was evident that government officials were "the greatest spendthrifts in society." For example, bounties on some items had become so out of control that they were more valuable than the product the bounty protected. Despite these government intrusions, Smith admitted that, so far, government had been unable to retard "the natural progress of England toward wealth and improvement."

It was the state sovereign's duty to supply the nation with a judiciary separate from the executive. Historically, the executive had performed the duties of a judicial administrator but as they became more onerous, he appointed an officer to perform them. In a modern state that cozy relationship had to be broken, otherwise justice would often be "sacrificed to, what is vulgarly called, politics." In addition, the nation must ensure that no man or government infringed the private rights of others. The only way to protect them was to make the judiciary both separate and independent from the executive. To secure independence, the "charge should not be liable to be removed from his office according to the caprice of power."

How could Smith's concentration on self-interest benefit the state? Surely, the prospect of Virginians single-mindedly pursuing their individual self-interests was unpalatable. No, said Smith, the opposite was the case. Man's natural desire for economic improvement through commercial activity forced him to marshall his resources wisely. Competition would benefit society because, for example, it would reduce prices.[3]

Not only political and social theory but also religious dissent played a major role in Virginia's favorable opinion of state rights theory. Before we focus on Virginia's evangelical religious dissent, we will describe the institution at its center. The established church was the Church of England and it was considered part of the London diocese. Although one might expect its leadership to be in either the Colonial Office, or even in London, the real power fell on the local church vestries.

Geography partitioned early Virginia into two sections, the privileged Tidewater and the hardscrabble back country of those seeking their fortune. Not surprisingly, the affluent, socially homogeneous, easterners dominated the established Church of England. Sadly, the extension of gentry influence to the church yielded poor results. The Anglican Church served only one constituency, the planters, and over time its immediacy dimmed. Its spiritual message was lost while respect for its clergy drifted away. Church attendance often became merely a venue for discussing business or political affairs. One might guess correctly that the declining established church had no currency in the back country.

Tidewater and Piedmont emigrants, driven by the promise of cheap or free land, usually followed the river systems westward. Because of their settled mores and established Church connections, they were unlikely to settle among foreigners. Although the first dissenters were Quaker immigrants who settled near the Virginia coast, their numbers were eclipsed in the early 1730s, by an important immigration of Pennsylvanians into the Shenandoah Valley. Scotch-Irish and German settlers planted a society of dissenters directly on the likely emigration path to the rich Shenandoah lands and beyond to the Southwest. The small farms, variety of crops, independence from slave labor, and lack of defining social structure made democracy particularly appealing to these farmers. Frugality, lack of ostentation, and simplicity of style increased the likelihood that they would accept a dissenting religion. The Scotch-Irish were devotees of John Knox (1505-1572), individualistic, and immersed in the Old Testament. They preached democracy and religious liberty.

These settlers had a more important role in the future of Virginia. Significantly, the Scotch-Irish dissenting tradition and hatred of England and its concomitant battles with authority prompted one historian to label them "republican by instinct." As a result, they could not abide "privilege and inequality whether in Church or State." Liberty, unfettered liberty, which to them was tantamount to religious freedom and toleration for other creeds, drove these individualistic immigrants to seek their goals in another colony. Politically, the rule of the majority not the rule of property holders was paramount and any constitution must reflect the ideal of equality. To them, government was the result of a compact among the people. Of course, any successful application of these beliefs would require an overhaul of Virginia's existing institutions.

During the 1740s, an initial evangelical wave of religious fervor, commonly called the Great Awakening, surged over Virginia. Evangelistic sects elevated the individual and promoted simplicity and purity. Doctrine was not the prime attraction although it fomented dissatisfaction with the role of the stodgy established church. The Awakening eventually encompassed three successive, clearly delineated, phases. The Presbyterians led, followed by the Separate Baptists, and then the Methodists. Because of the nature of the Virginia Awakening, one group waxed and waned and another replaced it, continuing the revival. Finally, after the Revolution, all three sects experienced a simultaneous resurgence that added thousands of Virginians to their ranks.

The first evangelical wave followed the Scotch-Irish and German immigrants into the Valley. Like a great wedge, the settlers thrust themselves southward into colonial Virginia. About 1738, the Pennsylvania Synod assumed responsibility for its Virginia back country adherents. In this first stage, the Presbytery concerned itself with both the religious welfare of its existing members and funding a few itinerant preachers to spread the word.

The Germans found the tenets of evangelism immediate. The claim that each individual could have a personal relationship with God fascinated them. However, the Scotch-Irish aggressiveness against privilege and religious persecution marked them as the leaders of the first dissenting wave. Governor William Gooch rewarded the immigrants with a grant of toleration. Surely, a dissenting religion so far from the capital could not affect the established church. He was wrong. Itinerant Presbyterian ministers ignored the laws designed to prevent the spread of evangelical religions and drifted into the Anglican communities to the east. Driven by the moral degeneracy of both the clergy and doctrine, Hanover County dissidents withdrew from the established church and organized a new religion.

Unfortunately for their sect, the Presbyterian revival foundered for two reasons. First, it lacked a dynamic leader. Second, the siren call of virgin lands triggered another emigration westward. Nevertheless, the early evangelists left their mark on Virginian society. Their rejection of established church ritual and challenge of the existing social order lit a flame of revolution among the lower classes. The Great Awakening would provide many Presbyterians — and later sects — with common goals. An elevation of the group as a social class, religious liberty, the abolition of an established church, and the building of a constitution founded on democratic ideals became legitimate goals.

Following closely on the Presbyterian heels were the Baptists. They wanted a church whose goal was the promotion of individual good conduct with the Bible as the center of theology. Their most recognizable quality was their dogged pursuit of religious liberty. Because God, not men, called them, Baptists often broke the law and preached in Anglican parishes. Seeking to avoid confrontation, they stoically ignored occurrences of violence, ridicule, and social disorder against them. The colonial government had decreed that all ministers must obtain a license to preach, but if one considered himself guided by the Almighty, such earthly rules were specious. These religious convictions mirrored the rising tide of liberty in Virginia. Baptist refusal to follow established custom in church affairs reflected the colonial rejection of British taxation policies. Natural rights must take priority. Thus, the Baptist challenge was indirect but still damning. However, its influence began to recede by 1774 and the next wave eclipsed it.

The Methodist revival had three significant impacts. Unlike the Baptists who supported the Patriot movement, the Methodists remained neutral. But, these Revolutionary pacifists, by the nature of their revival, added another voice to the attack on the *status quo*. In addition, it thrust deep into the power center of the established church.

The successive waves of dissident evangelism that swept Virginia in the pre–Revolutionary decades paused, and then re-emerged into one coincident statewide Awakening of all the sects about 1785. The result of the new wave of enthusiasm was a democratization of the established churches that catered to the lower and middle classes. This sensitization to democracy in the new churches prepared their parishioners for the idea of self-government while maintaining their emphasis on the value and equality of individuals. The example set by the churches' organizations continued that of the previous Awakening and emphasized to the middle-class yeoman that he need not accede to the gentry's definition of leadership. This was particularly true of the Baptists, a dissenter church that was completely democratic.

How did the Great Awakening affect the Revolution? Initially, it introduced the virtue of democratic government. Slowly, their disciples began to consider this form of government the norm. Additionally, these evangelicals transferred the focus of their dissent from the established church, to the mother country. For example, taxation reform and religious toleration became Revolutionary goals.

One cannot ignore the spirit of independence engendered in its followers by the Great Awakening. Their conviction that they had a personal relationship with God made it easy for them to imagine separating from England. The Baptists, particularly, were not loath to speak and act against any perceived threat. They had fought legal strictures placed on their churches and personal attacks against their theology and were stronger than ever. It was evidence enough for them that one should fight for one's rights.[4]

The preferred post–Revolutionary government style was molded by two symbiotic factors. Most Virginians concluded that the Articles of Confederation, if upgraded, suited their requirements because it spelled out their basic particularistic viewpoint. By particularism we mean the tendency of every state of a federation to retain its laws and promote its interests.

According to one eminent Virginian, circumstances inextricably entwined American liberty and government. "Liberty," claimed Woodrow Wilson, "has never come from the government. Liberty has always come from the subjects of the government. The history of government is the history of resistance. The history of liberty is the history of the limitation of government, not the increase of it." Government limitation would be enhanced by a particularistic populace.

Virginia's particularistic bent, a precursor to state rights, was the product of English resistance to government usurpation and a certain autonomy based on Empire neglect. Moreover, the Revolution stamped defiance into the Virginia psyche and proved that a determined populace could bring even kings to heel. In addition, the religious dissenters had demonstrated that well-organized pressure groups could not only elicit change from a controlling society but also provide a model of local self-government.

Locke's compact theory was ubiquitous in Virginia's political discussions. The Presbyterians considered its tenets a requirement of government, not just a debating theme. Its precepts were often incorporated into important Virginia and national documents. One of these, the Articles of Confederation, declared that each state of the Union was sovereign. Furthermore, every power not expressly assigned to the central government, remained with the state. This assertion melded nicely with Virginia's insistence that local self-government was the type most likely to govern best. Any suggestion that the Articles were unequal to its task would likely produce consternation among Virginia's particularists.

Three examples can synthesize its relationships. John Leland, a fervent Baptist and eventual Antifederalist, publicized localist concerns that most traditional state rights men would recognize. He verified the centrality of Locke's theory and from it divined several principles. Virginians must give up part of their liberty and property to ensure the remainder; the people were sovereign; everyone, including the rulers, was responsible to the law; government was a compact; citizens could ignore any law inconsistent with the constitution; the citizenry could replace a government unable to protect the people's liberty or property; only the people, not the legislators, could alter the constitution; and every individual within society maintained his right of conscience and did not surrender it to the laws of his society.

Besides these tenets, Leland held several familiar opinions. The Legislature should promote short sessions and pass as few laws as possible. The ideal government taxed equitably and spent frugally on government expenditures, paid all debts on time, promoted commerce to ensure a balanced budget, advanced agricultural opportunities, and remained dependent on the people.

Virginians had little interest in continental matters and a sense of union was ephemeral in the American colonies. Royal charters governed New York, Massachusetts, Virginia, New Jersey, North and South Carolina, Georgia, and New Hampshire. Others were proprietary — Pennsylvania, Delaware, and Maryland — and two, Rhode Island and Connecticut, had charters. Religion, economics, and regional differences further separated them. A brief examination of one event highlighted the separation.

In 1753, the supervising body of the American colonies was the London Board of Trade. It viewed the French courting of the Six Nations confederacy, and Indian relations overall, with trepidation. Therefore, it ordered the governor of New York, James DeLancey, to convene a conference between the representatives of seven colonies and the tribes. In 1754, at Albany, New York, these representatives met to design a single treaty — rather than one with each tribe — in the name of the king. Benjamin Franklin proposed an extension of this agenda and persuaded the colonial representatives to accept a plan of union. The Crown would appoint the executive and designate him President-General. The people of the colonies would control the legislature, the Grand Council, through representatives chosen by their assemblies or by special conventions. Interestingly, it included neither a provision for a judiciary nor any provision for amending the formula. Despite the support of the Albany conventioneers both the king and several colonies rejected the plan. As a result, the colonies began the French and Indian War (1756–1763) divided. Obviously, the separated colonies, prior to the Revolution, distrusted both each other and the Colonial Office. Richard Ellis described the situation accurately. "Attempts to unite them," he wrote, "or to get them to cooperate all ended in failure, foiled by political jealousies, commercial rivalries, petty hostilities, and a variety of other problems, both real and imagined."

The tendency toward particularism survived even the ravages of the Revolution. In 1782, the Virginia General Assembly overturned a law that authorized Congress to tax imports. Why? Only the General Assembly had the power to levy taxes within Virginia. To allow an outside agency to do so would be "injurious to its sovereignty" and "may prove destructive of the rights and liberty of the people."

However, these incidents insinuated that Virginia particularism may have evolved. During the Albany conference it was concentrated on the evils of a strong central government, an institution that was just a replacement for the Revolutionary English monarchy. Particularism by 1788 had expanded to include the dangers to Virginia institutions from another section. Virginians would have to be very careful that this paranoid view did not dominate their calculations.[5]

The Articles of Confederation became a touchstone for dissent. The men who had stitched it together were mainly small farmers living an isolated country life. They had developed an affinity for low and few taxes and frugal government that did not interfere with their constituent's lives. The Virginia county court was such an example.

Nevertheless, there was another sizeable group of Articles' supporters who did not fit the agrarian mold. They had determined that by one means or another, they could control the burgeoning democratic spirit within the state, but were doubtful about the ability of their neighbors to do the same. Rather than chance a new national government inimical to their interests they chose to support the Articles.

A smaller group, evident in Virginia, supported the Articles simply because it certified their local influence. No national figure would challenge their power.

Initially, the states had designed the Articles to provide for "common defense, security of liberty and general welfare." However, they did not create a government that ensured these ideals. Instead, they initiated "a league of friendship" similar to a treaty. Some may consider the Congress based on the Articles to be nothing but a collection of state representatives who congregated occasionally to sort out mutual problems. Others might argue that the Articles represented a hastily cobbled together association of states. Were it not for the British peril, Americans might never have considered it a blueprint for federal government.

Unfortunately, the Articles had several built-in weaknesses. As a league of sovereign states, it had no overriding sovereign power. Suppose one state refused to follow an article. By the most popular political theory of the day, the analogy to John Locke's compact, the other members could leave the union. Similarly, some disputed the interpretation of the "perpetual" union. One group considered it an indicator that the states met as equal sovereigns. Another contended it referred only to the constancy of the Union, not to the specific words contained in the Articles. Congress could not force its member states to comply with a ruling; the unanimous consent rule made it impossible to pass laws even in the presence of a majority; and often member states negotiated separate agreements, particularly those dealing with trade. Whenever Congress passed a law, its implementation was at the mercy of the individual states. Occasionally, the result was "the usurpation of private rights under constitutional cover."

Besides those listed above, several other defects were evident to James Madison. In April 1787, on the eve of the Constitutional Convention, he gathered his objections in a pamphlet

Vices of the Political System. The states often ignored orders that requisitioned material; arrogated federal powers to themselves; trespassed on each other's laws and rights; ignored necessary projects like canals and commercial laws that would benefit their constituents; accepted that they might be unable to protect their citizens from the rule of a militant minority with superior military skills than the majority; and passed laws that contradicted both their own and other state's decrees.

As indicated earlier, the basic problem, according to the opponents of the Articles, was one of power. Specifically, the congressional delegates who struggled with the Articles deficiencies daily recognized they must strengthen the central government. James Madison, who constantly defended his state's prerogatives, slowly came to realize that a major change was necessary. His opponents argued that the Articles needed revision, but that its core was still relevant. Perhaps the only requirements were extensions of power over trade and tariffs. The idea had been common from the outset, although never consummated.

More often than not, these power struggles revolved around state sovereignty. It had been a problem since its introduction in 1777. The sovereignty, freedom, or independence, argued Thomas Burke, "and every power, jurisdiction and right[s], which [are] not by this confederation expressly delegated" to the Union as represented by Congress belonged to the states. Notice that whereas the Articles delegated power, jurisdiction, and rights to Congress, sovereignty, freedom, and independence were not. For years, delegates favoring a stronger central government would fight to reverse this implication. For example, John Quincy Adams argued that state sovereignty had usurped that of the people defined by the Declaration of Independence and confirmed by the Revolution. Also, both Madison and James Wilson realized that if state sovereignty remained the hallmark, the necessary congressional power to veto any state legislation was impossible. Moreover, the Articles form of government, because it was only a league, could never ensure the preservation of the Union. However, even a less offensive plan that gave Congress power to regulate commerce and set tariffs was anathema to Virginia if it placed the South at the mercy of the North.[6]

The aggregate of the above factors sculpted Virginia's political culture, shading it toward state rights. However, the dynamics of Constitution-building raised fears among Virginians about its effects on their native state. Could they trust the new national government to protect Virginia's interests? Unfortunately, the first act of the ratification play must have persuaded many that their concerns were well founded.

In 1787 American representatives met at Philadelphia supposedly to hammer out some much needed changes to the Articles. Most Virginians expected a specific outcome. But, the Convention was essentially concerned with variations on the theme of national government rather than an informed debate between disciples of opposing views. By shunting aside the New Jersey Plan early in the proceedings, the Federalist delegates forced the opposition Antifederalists to concentrate on ameliorating the proposed Constitution's effects rather than defeating its intent.

These conditions were not duplicated in the Continental Congress or the Virginia assembly. They each contained a powerful Antifederalist faction prepared to dispute the necessity or contents of the Constitution. In Congress, Richard Henry Lee labeled his Antifederalist colleagues "Patriots" and stigmatized the opposition as "Monarchy men, Aristocrats, and Drones" as well as predatory businessmen. A member of the latter faction, Edward Carrington of Virginia, warned James Madison that Lee, and another respected Virginian William

Grayson, were organizing opposition in New York. However, Henry Lee "warmly recommended" the new document and expected Congress to transmit it to the states with a supportive resolution.

For parts of three days beginning September 26, Congress debated its role in the ratification process. The tactics of the opposing sides were clear. The Federalists sought to dispatch the document to the state legislatures quickly and express their recommendation for passage in a covering resolution. Antifederalists would counter by building constitutional roadblocks to that strategy. Due to an agreement to omit some items from the journal, recreating a verbatim debate was impossible, but enough evidence remained to give us the flavor of the arguments.

Although many attempts to postpone motions fragmented discussion, four resolutions, two from each faction, framed the dispute. Nathan Dane of New York began. He reviewed the Convention's implementation process and followed it by characterizing the new Constitution as "an entire system in itself" and not an "alteration in the Articles of Confederation." Constitutionally, the Articles did not extend to Congress a role in the amending process. Thus, its members could not offer any opinions "respecting a System of Government no way connected with these forms." Because of these considerations, Dane's resolution said that, in good faith, Congress should send the Constitution plus inclusions to each state legislature without comment. In turn, Richard Henry Lee resolved that the Constitution should be forwarded to the state legislatures but contain two additions based on constitutional law and precedent. Article XIII of the existing constitution required unanimous approval for amendments while an earlier Virginia resolution indicated the convention's object was simply to revise it. The Federalist Abraham Clark of New Jersey also moved to send a copy of the Constitution plus inclusions to the state legislatures. Unwisely, Clark's motion directed those bodies to take certain actions that were beyond the scope of Congress. No power permitted the Convention to direct state action. Edward Carrington attempted to repair Clark's mistakes but, he too ran into trouble. He assumed that Congress had the power to consider the Constitution and, more important, that it agreed with the contents of that document. He recommended that state conventions adopt, ratify, and confirm it. All these resolutions forced Congress to answer two interrelated questions. According to the Articles, could it examine the Constitution and report a recommendation to the state legislatures? If so, could Congress also amend it before transmission?

Clearly, R. H. Lee did not think Congress had the right to categorize the Convention document. His resolution spoke to the question and during debate he emphasized the unconstitutionality of its genesis. He correctly reminded his colleagues that they could not study the Constitution as it subverted the very document that defined Congress's power. Later, in a letter to George Mason, Lee made his point succinctly. "Upon this consideration of the Constitution under which we now Act," he wrote, "some of us were clearly of the opinion that the 13th article of the Confederation precluded us from giving an opinion concerning a plan subversive of the present system and eventually forming a New Confederacy of Nine instead of 13 States." However, he admitted that Congress had misapplied its power in the past, particularly in the field of trade agreements.

After digesting his colleague's reasoning, Henry Lee, a Virginia Federalist, decided that examining the question had merit. Discussion could illuminate not only whether an opinion was proper, but also throw light on the introduction of amendments. William Grayson supported Lee's interpretation because it was clear to him that it would not affect the ratification process in Virginia. He surmised that its citizens would realize Congress could not support either view but would have approved ratification if it could have done so. Edward Carrington, we know, suggested Congress abbreviate the process and append a resolution supporting ratification. James Madison provided a different tack. He reminded Congress that the resolution cited earlier as a barrier against congressional opinion had included a phrase that made a national government a goal of the convention. Still, the extension of his argument went too far. He proposed that "the powers of the Convention were defined by their Commissions in nearly the same terms with the powers of Congress delivered by the Confederation on the subject of alterations." As a result, Convention powers mirrored those of Congress. If Congress refused the Constitution, one must conclude that the Convention did not follow its mandate. However, to benefit the country, acting unconstitutionally was common for Congress, and this was another of those instances. What did he mean by "nearly" the same terms? Had he forgotten that Congress must follow the dictates of a complete constitution and not just one article? The specter of unconstitutional acts piled one atop the other to achieve a new constitution must have disheartened delegates.

Perhaps the best indicator of Congress's opinion on the form of the document transmission can be found in their constant objections about the manner in which putative resolutions were drawn. Whenever one side offered a resolution, an opponent would complain that the choice of language, or organization of ideas, contained subliminal indicators of the true opinion of Congress on ratification. For example, Pierce Butler of South Carolina labeled Dane's resolution as "calculated to disapprove." Madison argued that if Congress did not specifically endorse the Constitution, Americans would assume it did the opposite but Richard Henry Lee looked at the same scenario and came to the opposite conclusion. Since Congress did not usually send out material it disapproved, then a forwarding of that opinion was tantamount to an approval of the Constitution by Congress. These examples demonstrate two trends. First, the parties did not trust each other. Second, forwarding the Constitution to the states without comment might be best, but there was a clear inference that the delegates assumed they could offer an opinion.

Of course, any conclusion that Congress could append an opinion to its transmission brought Henry Lee's earlier judgment into play. If Congress were going to judge, it must examine the document. This would require a clause-by-clause debate and pry open the Pandora's box of amendments. To the Federalists, this scenario was anathema because it stalled the debate and prevented a quick transference to the states. Richard Henry Lee, who had earlier invoked Article XIII to dispose of any ratification attempt, now posited that Congress had every right to amend the Constitution to protect the liberty of the people. Shockingly, the Federalists did not try to dissuade their opponents from that position. Instead, they adopted a variation on R. H. Lee's constitutional argument against examining the Constitution. Such an amending dynamic was inexpedient since Congress was merely a way station on the road to the state legislatures. Debate in Congress would be superfluous since it was just a seconding body. In any case, the Convention could not reexamine amendments since it had disbanded. Most important, constitutionally, a document amended by Congress became its creature. Thus it followed that only the state legislatures could ratify it. But, this inferred different states might ratify different versions of the document, a constitutional nightmare. Of course, Lee would avoid these problems by sending the document plus amendments to a second constitutional convention.

With the opposition argument in mind, Lee tested it by offering amendments to the Constitution. Overall they consisted of those one might expect in a Bill of Rights but it did contain some interesting additions. There would be free and frequent elections, an independent judiciary, an eleven-member Council of State to replace the Vice President, and an increase in the size of the House of Representatives. Also, representation by population, Madison's original idea, would define the Senate. After Congress studied these amendments, Lee applied the clincher. He demanded that Congress record the ayes and nays on each amendment in the journal. Abraham Clark, stunned by the implications of a negative vote among some constituencies, commented that to do so "will cause injury by coming on the Journal." As a compromise, the house agreed to forward the Constitutional package from the Convention to the states without comment. The Antifederalists had apparently derailed any opposition attempt to skew the state results by adding descriptive language implying congressional acceptance of the Constitution.

Nevertheless, the Federalists had some success. When the congressional authors wrote the resolution, they craftily organized the word "unanimously" so that an unwary reader might conclude that it referred to congressional agreement on the Constitutional contents rather than on its transmission. Moreover, they did manage to get the Constitution before the people in good time. Without support for amendments within Congress, the Antifederalists were merely fighting a rear guard action hoping to slow the Federalist steamroller.[7]

Shortly after Congress's sparring over the fate of the Constitution, Governor Edmund Randolph received Virginia's copy. As a delegate, he had temporarily rejected the Convention's handiwork, seeking a protocol by which a Virginia convention could discuss and either accept or reject amendments. Thoughtfully, he urged George Mason to adopt the following agenda in the legislature as a solution. First, the house should legitimize a state convention. To examine the national popularity of some amending procedure, the delegates should approve a list of revisions and transmit them immediately to the other state legislatures. Significantly, this process should be completed before any conventions met. If the states rejected the amendments and ratified the Constitution then it took affect immediately. However, if nine states agreed, then Virginia's ratification would depend on the inclusion of those revisions in the Constitution.

By October 16, the legislature had received the Constitution and enclosures and was prepared to deal with them. Surprisingly, Patrick Henry, the expected leader of any Antifederalist opposition, "declared it transcended" the House of Delegates' legal power to judge its contents. A convention of the people must perform that task. The house accepted his reasoning and it scheduled a further consideration by the Committee of the Whole on October 25. Of course, this agreement short-circuited Randolph's tactic.

The Federalist Francis Corbin opened the procedural debate. He offered a set of resolutions governing the process. Henry and Mason immediately rejected one whose purpose, they claimed, was to deny the introduction of amendments from the convention floor. To emphasize their opposition, they offered a resolution specifically condoning amendments. George Nicholas, a formidable Federalist, disputed both their interpretation and resolution since they suggested that the Constitution required amendments. Pointedly, neither Corbin nor Nicholas denied that such a right existed. John Marshall, Federalist and future Chief Justice, urged that the legislature adopt the same solution as had Congress when faced with a similar roadblock. They should send the documents to the convention with only an admonition for "free and ample discussion." The legislature adopted his compromise.

Although we now understand the process governing the Constitution's transmission from Congress to the Virginia Convention, we should realize that outside forces might affect its deliberations. This was the goal of an Antifederalist clique whose aim was to form a Virginia-New York axis of opposition. On December 12, 1787, the Virginia General Assembly passed legislation reserving funds for delegates who wanted to correspond with those from other states. Following instructions, Governor Randolph transmitted the act to the other states. By early March, Governor George Clinton of New York reported its receipt but after two months, he complained about the lack of follow-up. On May 18, a Federal Republican Committee dispatched to Virginia a circular letter proposing that Antifederalists pool their ideas. Randolph now faced a dilemma. Was it a private or public communication? His advisory Council of State informed him that it was a public letter and should be forwarded to the legislature and not to the convention then in session. By the time the convention tabled it in late June, the delegates had completed their work, blunting an organized resistance.

Another attempt by individual Antifederalists met a similar fate. The Federal Republican Committee of New York sent letters to individual Antifederalists residing in other states. The purpose was to set up a mechanism to amend the Constitution before the states ratified it. A New York courier carried one to Virginia and returned by June 16, 1788 with responses from Patrick Henry, George Mason, and William Grayson. Their synthesis was that a New York delegation meet its counterpart from Virginia and draft a strategy for introducing amendments. By June 21, its proponents shipped the possible New York amendments south, but it was too late for Virginia's consideration.[8]

2

The People's Preratification Estimate of the Constitution

We have noted the role of European Enlightenment political theory, Great Awakening religious fervor, and home-grown particularism in Virginia's state rights dogma. One cannot question their cumulative effect but a fourth — constitutionalism — took precedence. It was local and produced a wave of on-the-ground disputatious commentary. All bands of the doctrinal spectrum chipped in opinions that might enlighten the delegates to the upcoming ratification convention. Primary among them was the federal/state distribution of power, issues associated with republican government, and elections. By surveying these reactions closely in the next few chapters, the reader will sense the background and progression of Virginia's trek toward a state rights doctrine. Could it trust the central government to protect its liberties?

Another rationale dictated the methodology applied to these chapters. It was the author's contention that state rights was a poorly understood doctrine often misinterpreted. If this were the case, simple assertions would never persuade readers that the author's contentions were valid. His other avenue was to prove his case by presenting a mass of data that was impossible to misunderstand. Since the latter was more historically acceptable, it was chosen. The sequel was a study, including some repetitious argument, of the passage of the Constitution through ratification.

Virginia commentators on elections concentrated on either the articles defining the process or the type of representation they could expect. Whereas Virginia usually had annual legislative elections, the Constitution designated biennial federal contests. Alexander White preferred the transfer of the state methodology to the Constitution, but he saw no danger in the replacement. Candidates must come to grips with two issues. They had to travel great distances and constantly upgrade their knowledge of other states to be effective. Because of these challenges, few good men would consider the position attractive if they had to repeat the election process every year. James Madison suggested that frequent elections would induce some representatives to argue they were not responsible for the results of legislation. Suppose a bill began its journey through Congress during their term but was finalized after they left. How could the electorate hold them responsible for its results? In *The Federalist* No. 63, Madison offered a second interpretation to the same facts. He linked the two-year term of the House to the six-year term of the Senate. A representative who faced replacement in two years might not have the time to implement a complex legislative program whereas a senator, in triple the time, might do so.

Debaters proffered two other reasons for a two-year term. Disputed elections militated against a one-year term. Thorough investigation took longer. Moreover, little chance existed that the electorate, every two years, would select representatives that did not reflect its concerns. Since tyranny appeared unlikely, as some argued, a limited federal government like that defined in the Constitution did not require annual elections.

Naturally, Virginians examined the election process associated with various government branches with Congress receiving the most attention. The Federal Farmer believed he had uncovered a major flaw in election proceedings. Did the Constitution require a successful candidate to get a majority or would a plurality suffice? Such a scenario might occur in elections among several candidates. An initial plurality might lead to a runoff to achieve a majority. The Farmer hoped that pluralities would never become usual as they carried with them several negative aspects. They reduced the number of voters; introduced corruption to the process; and produced a poor result if the government did not uniformly distribute voting boundaries. However, his solution was not viable. He proposed a process similar to that held in Virginia's counties. All the voters would assemble at one site and cast their ballots. They would elect the candidate who earned a majority.

The Old Dominion's citizens had a broader criticism of Congress's power over elections. Why did it have any input into the time and place of elections held within Virginia's borders? Moreover, it was not clear to some, like the Baptist leader John Leland, why Congress should have any control of Virginia's choice of representatives. Would not such a power abrogate the promise of republican government if its application forced people to travel an unconscionable distance to vote? As interpreted facetiously by the *Kentucky Gazette*, the Constitution gave Congress the power, if it chose to use it, to force Georgia voters to travel to Boston in the depths of winter just to vote.

Federalists sought to alleviate these fears. Alexander White insisted that any supposed state power to organize elections would necessarily result in Congress being subservient to it. In a national system this was unthinkable. Also, Congress could not be more specific about the election process because, inevitably, states would make geopolitical changes that would render obsolete a fixed date and time. Another Virginian listed a more sinister reason. If a state could edit the election criteria, it could use it to "impede[d]" the federal government.

Writers scattered other election criticisms and rebuttals. Obviously, the state legislature's venue must be the site of its Senate election but that might result in a hierarchical system. Madison perceived that the Senate would be the home of sober thought unlike the democratic passion expected from the House of Representatives. Therefore, it should be smaller and serve a longer term to expend on thorny issues. Moreover, the longer limit would attract competent men who otherwise would not serve.

Should not the people of Virginia have the opportunity to elect the nation's chief executive? Rather than this natural process, the Constitution expected Virginia electors to vote for an individual about whom, in all likelihood, they knew nothing. Republicus extended this concept. He considered the method of presidential electors tantamount to the people sacrificing their suffrage rights to those who had no data on the candidates. Just examine the case in which the election devolved on Congress. It deteriorated into a case of electors of electors choosing the executive. Surely this was an antirepublican process.

Electoral restrictions galled some Virginians. Thomas Jefferson predicted that, without a clause defining rotation in office, the man first elected president would become president-for-life. Similarly, the Federal Farmer advocated a system that would allow states to recall their senators. Such a power would remind them that their constituents retained the power to censure them. George Lee Turberville argued that time limits were a natural product of republican government. It seemed logical that the people's representatives return periodically to their roots.

The character of representation stimulated furious debate. Edmund Pendleton was comfortable with the mode of agency representation promoted by the Constitution since Virginians did not expect their representatives to be "Angels from Heaven." Even one or two bad apples should not drive one to burn the barrel. Madison offered some advice for choosing them. Most Virginians accepted that the Constitution foresaw representatives who were virtuous and held the good of society in esteem. However, not ensuring they remained so would be foolish. Virginians could expect that they would have "a temporary affection at least to their constituents." Once in office, they would become adjusted to its "honor and distinction." If representatives wanted to maintain them, they must get reelected which required the good offices of the people. Thus, biennial elections defined in the Constitution ensured the efficacy of agency government. Furthermore, one must remember that any law Congress passed would also operate on its members. Thus, it would be self-defeating purposefully to pass a bad law.

Three practical considerations drew the attention of Antifederalist critics. They were unnerved by the ramifications associated with the number and social class of the prospective representatives and whether they would truly understand their constituents. A few positive aspects were associated with the methodology. With so few representatives, tracking their performance would be easy and the cost for maintaining them would be small. Interestingly, the *Virginia Independent Chronicle* calculated that under the new system Virginia's percentage representation would increase while its taxation decreased. James Madison contended that sixty or seventy representatives could govern adequately while either six or seven, or six or seven hundred, were unacceptable. The first placed too much power in the hands of a few representatives while the second was just a "mob." Remember, he cajoled, when the results of the census took effect, the number of representatives would increase dramatically. He then focused on the opposition notion of a mandatory, immediate, increase in representation. Yes, he acknowledged, it was an "important principle" that a delegate knew his electors, but one must be careful not to carry the requirement too far. Surely, he could not know everything. Being familiar with any legislation affecting his district was sufficient for a representative. That narrowed his field of concern to "local knowledge" of "commerce, taxation, and the militia." Another Virginian applied a practical rule. If his fellow statesmen truly delegated some of their power to an agent then the number of agents was insignificant. Why not just have ten?

Complaints about the number of representatives were common. Richard Henry Lee considered the choice of artificial numbers to be invalid and raising them was mandatory. The Federal Farmer also demanded increased representation. It seemed natural that a federal republic like that planned in the Constitution required many representatives. If America started with just a few, eventually, power would devolve to one man, a tyranny. For example, if the House of Representatives remained small, it was possible that a few members could control the taxation bills. The Farmer also offered a theoretical argument. If the agreement between the people and the government was a true compact, the number of representatives should be fixed. Unfortunately, the scheme proposed in the Constitution promoted variable numbers.

The third major debate examined the relationship between representatives and their constituency. Comment, led by the Federal Farmer, was overwhelmingly negative. He began by assuming that the new government would promote a situation in which the people's representatives would be chosen from "the elevated classes in the community." Naturally, this translated into a gentry-controlled legislature. Thus, the people would have no opportunity to vote for someone like themselves. Of course, the result would be a national legislature with two components containing representatives from the same social class instead of a House of Representatives dominated by the people. Apparently, the Farmer was more comfortable with the familiar mixed government than the new representative government promoted by the Federalists. For example, Madison assumed that the people's representatives would be a cut above their constituents.

Three other election items were worthy of mention. The *Kentucky Gazette* complained that the House and Senate should both follow Madison's cherished rule of proportional representation. The Farmer concluded that despite Congress's putative lack of representation compared with the Virginia General Assembly, it reserved most of the power. This would lead to the "annihilation" of the states. Madison considered the relationship between representation and the three-fifths rule. Each state defined its own suffrage rules so the southern states could argue that slaves were inhabitants despite their absence from other states. To avoid unnecessary dispute, the Convention agreed on a rule "which regarded the *slave* as divested of two-fifths of the *man*."[1]

✠

Unsurprisingly, debate over power issues was lively. To begin, everyone agreed that a government must have power to fulfill its mandate. But, Madison warned that its necessary application would increase the likelihood of corruption. However, Virginians would be satisfied if a check attended each assignment to prevent it. Antifederalists estimated that these dangers would be associated with the allocation of excessive congressional powers. Harry Innes, An Old Planter, William Grayson, and even James Madison's cousin agreed with this conclusion. William Russell and the eminent Federalist jurist Edmund Pendleton joined them. The latter inferred that the Convention had strewn powers in the Senate's path "improperly" thus promoting "great confusion." Richard Henry Lee and A True Friend joined the negative chorus. The former predicted "the great unguarded powers" assigned to the "Rulers" would challenge the "Civil Liberty and the happiness of the people." A True Friend, in an inflammatory remark, wrote,

> Let us then, in the first place, agree on a few preliminary positions. You, Gentlemen, the preachers up of the new Constitution, will not surely contest a fact proved by the records of all ages and of all nations, that is, *that the liberties and the rights of the people have been always encroached on, and finally destroyed by those, whom they have entrusted with the powers of government;* these have continually abused the confidence reposed in them; and whether this confidence was placed in a single magistrate, or in a body of magistrates, the authority ceded to them by the people has been constantly turned against themselves; has subjected; and in fine enslaved them.

Reverend Madison adopted a similar position. He reminded his cousin that the Constitution broke a "fundamental Axiom in Politics." When "Powers are united, Govt. must soon degenerate into a Tyranny." Benjamin Harrison offered a gloomy prediction on the Union's future due to the excessive powers assigned the president and Congress.

Perhaps we should classify the powers so roundly condemned by Virginia Antifederalists. James Madison

> reduced [them] into different classes as they relate to the following different objects — 1. security against foreign danger — 2. regulation of the intercourse with foreign nations — 3. maintenance of harmony and proper intercourse among the States — 4. certain miscellaneous objects of general utility — 5. restraint of the States from certain injurious acts — 6. provisions for giving due efficacy to all these powers.

Powers relating to these classes were extensions of "principles" already present in the Articles of Confederation. Their amalgam led Oliver Ellsworth, and later Madison, to label the Constitution partly federal, partly national.

In order for these criticisms and rebuttals to have traction, the parties eventually had to reduce them to specifics. The Madisonian power categories impress upon us that the Federalist purpose was to outline a new government whose powers were not only delegated but also enumerated. George Nicholas, a fervent Federalist, assuaged the fears of his opponents by assuring Virginians that,

> Congress will have no powers but what are expressly given to them, and it will follow as a natural consequence that all powers which are now vested in the state legislatures will after the adoption of this government still belong to them, except such as are by that government specially given to Congress and such as the state legislatures are expressly forbidden to exercise.

Apparently, Congress had only expressed powers. Did not the Constitution enumerate them? Seemingly so, because such a list would be unnecessary if Congress had unlimited power. Madison concurred with Nicholas's assertion. "The powers delegated by the proposed Constitution to the Federal Government," he agreed, "are few and defined." Edmund Pendleton added that "in the Delegation of Power, we must be Explicit and guarded" while keeping in mind that although power corrupted, not allocating enough was a mistake. According to Alexander White, if Congress passed any law damaging the government form, the people would simply void it.

The notion of implied powers defied a consensus. The dispute had its genesis in the general welfare and necessary and proper clauses of Article I. We will refrain from expanding on the topic at this time, preferring to analyze it under the rubric of enumerated powers to follow. However, the reader must be aware that this class of powers was not new to political theory. The dispute focused on scope. Everyone agreed that Congress must pass secondary laws to implement a primary act. But, could they stand alone without reference to the primary law?

The Constitution closely allied the Supremacy Clause with the necessary and proper provision in Antifederalist minds. The Impartial Examiner asked a pertinent question. How could Congress exceed its limits if the Supremacy Clause assigned it no limits? His close reading of the clause persuaded him that it should alarm Virginians. George Nicholas disagreed. Its sole purpose was to prohibit the states from enacting laws that "defeat the measures of Congress." Remember, he advised, Congress had been given expressly delegated power to pass laws benefiting the nation. Richard Henry Lee linked this aspect to a potential Bill of Rights, and declared that

> in any government therefore, where the power of judging what shall be for the *general welfare*, which goes to every object of human legislation; and where the laws of such Judges shall be *the supreme Law of the Land*; it seems to be of the last consequence to declare in most explicit terms the reservations above alluded to.

Each party offered explanations expanding their concept of the people's sovereignty and the nature of the Union. Of course, the Antifederalists were advocates of Locke's compact theory and assigned sovereignty to the state through the people. Federalist dogma held that government power did not exist in the United States before its formation. Thus, the people did not have to "sign" a compact to retain their liberty. Constitutionally, all government power flowed from the people by delegation and they dispersed some to their state government agents and some to those in federal service, while retaining the rest. James Wilson of Pennsylvania made a crucial addition. The government's power was limited and temporary because the people did not delegate their sovereignty, in part, to any institution, but only to their agents.

Despite cavils from prominent Virginians, George Nicholas insisted that Virginia's power would be unaffected by the new Constitution.

> We do assert to you as a fact, that if the new government shall take place the people of Virginia will part with no more power than they have done already, and that Congress and the legislature of the state will together have no greater power or authority than the present Congress and the legislature of the state now possess; and the only difference will be that of the powers already parted with by the people, under the new government Congress will have a greater share and the legislature of the state less than they now respectively enjoy.

A Native of Virginia calculated that Virginia's lost powers could be categorized as those required to build a strong central government. It would still control its domestic concerns but this prediction did not assuage Reverend Madison's fears. He lamented "that Power was not distributed in such a Manner as might preserve, instead of, threaten Destruction to ye Liberties of Am[eric]a." George Lee Turberville was no less pessimistic. He foresaw the eclipse of the state legislatures. Madison, in an attempt to alleviate these fears, took pains in *The Federalist* to show that each government branch, except the judiciary, depended upon the states. When comparing state to federal power, he wrote that,

> the former [general government power] will be exercised principally on external objects, as war, peace, negotiation, and foreign commerce; with which last the power of taxation will for the most part be connected. The powers reserved to the several States will extend to all the objects, which, in the ordinary course of affairs, concern the lives, liberties and properties of the people; and the internal order, improvement, and prosperity of the State.[2]

Commentators often identified the main government branches as a potential locus of unbound power. George Mason declared that the president had too much power while the *Kentucky Gazette* warned that a president, unelected by the people, might be a villain like George III. If so, would not he seek to increase his authority? Republicus picked up this theme. The president could easily enlist "a few artful and dependent emissaries in Congress" to "perpetuate his own personal administration." The result would be an hereditary presidency. Arthur Lee added that presidential power could subvert government into an oligarchy. Even the Federalist Edward Carrington categorized the aggregate of presidential and senatorial power as a "preposterous combination."

Specific complaints accompanied these generalities. Randolph considered the power to fill vacancies when the Senate was not in session a mistake. He also rejected the clause that allowed the president to pardon individuals before a jury had convicted them. George Mason insisted that the president could avoid impeachment by pardoning all those who participated in a nefarious scheme, thus leaving no witnesses. The Federal Farmer recognized that the first president must have a term long enough to ensure a stable government, but no one should accept the idea of reelection. Any possibility of a hereditary extension would energize a villainous president to place "servile supporters" in positions to promote it. The result might be a president-for-life but a fixed term would prevent this scenario. This check satisfied Edmund Randolph.

Contending arguments refuted some of these criticisms. The *Virginia Independent Chronicle* rebutted several to indicate the lengths to which the Constitution went to check the president's power. He was elected indirectly by citizens from various states and could hold office for only four years after which he returned to his state; the people could remove him for just cause; his circumscribed powers must benefit the country; Congress could override his presidential veto; a duty to apply all laws fairly leavened his pardon power; and the Constitution required Senate approval for the implementation of many presidential powers.

The presidential veto received high marks. James Madison and Thomas Jefferson thought it mandatory. For one correspondent, acts of Congress would benefit from the president's scrutiny since, likely, he would be an experienced lawmaker. An Impartial Citizen clinched the argument by reminding his *Petersburg Virginia Gazette* readers that Blackstone's famous *Commentaries* supported presidential vetoes.[3]

According to James McClurg, accumulated Senate power was the most vigorously debated topic in Virginia. The flood of correspondence confirmed that, in some manner, the Federalists had to portray it simultaneously as a reasonable agency of state opinion and also a bulwark against central government usurpations.

A senator had to be older, and a citizen longer, than a representative to hold office. "The propriety of these distinctions," wrote Madison, "is explained by the nature of the senatorial trust; which requiring greater extent of information and stability of character, requires at the same time that the senator should have reached a period of life most likely to supply these advantages...." General attacks on the bicameral nature of the Legislature, and specific attempts to synonymize the Senate with the House of Lords did not deter him. He insisted that the nation required a legislative check on the House since it would likely "yield to the impulse of sudden and violent passions, and [to] be seduced by fractious leaders into intemperate and pernicious resolutions." The Senate, with few members and a longer term, was admirably suited for that task. The inclusion of equal state suffrage was a reasonable compromise to protect the smaller states in Edmund Pendleton's view, but not those of William Grayson and Edmund Randolph. They preferred popular representation.

Many correspondents considered the Senate a fortunate inclusion. Madison labeled it "the great anchor of the Government." A Native of Virginia saw it as the bond uniting thirteen American states of different size and interest. As we noted, it was the branch designed for long-term planning. Politically, its organization was a victory for the states since it gave them a voice in the national government and balanced individual state power. These considerations led Madison to examine other Senate contributions. We have already noted one relationship with respect to the House. However, it had another. The price of frequent House elections was the constant injection of new members. They would infuse the Legislature with new opinions and goals. The Senate would add stability. It could filter these ideas into existing or new programs. Moreover, one must not forget that frequent elections may divert a representative's focus from governing to electioneering and the interests of the people might be lost. A long-term Senate of sober, stable, men would counter this unfortunate scenario.

Claiming excessive Senate power was common among Virginians according to George Mason. He decried the vast powers assigned to a branch not elected by the people. Riding a favorite hobby horse, he claimed that the Convention could have avoided this problem by the inclusion of an Executive Council within the government structure. Edward Carrington had already expressed doubts about Senate powers and their latitude shocked others. Arthur Lee studied them and reported that although some were legislative as expected, others transgressed into the executive and judicial realms. George Lee Turberville, Joseph Jones, and the pseudonymous Republicus and Americanis all came to the same conclusion.

Federalists viewed Senate power in a different light. They were sure that the system of checks and balances would sidetrack any attempts at corruption or usurpation. The *Virginia*

Journal listed a few. Can one assume that the House would always propose the perfect appropriations bill? Would not the Senate's power to "propose and concur" ameliorate difficulties? Even if the Senate did institute money bills, the House must validate them. One should remember that Article IX, section 2, forced the Legislature to apply appropriations for lawful purposes only. Americanis supplemented these by reminding readers that the president must also agree to legislation and, usually, each power needed confirmation. For example, Virginians could expect the president to challenge any internal attempt by senators to raise their salaries. Alexander White predicted that the election of one-third of their number each year would sharply remind them of their duties.

The opponents of the new government filed many other specific criticisms. Republicus's study of the Senate convinced him that it represented no one and Edmund Randolph refused to concede its power to make treaties that were "the supreme laws of the land." According to several commentators, the impeachment procedures needed rewriting because a Senate that usually acted as a presidential counsel could not ethically judge his actions. Randolph preferred an appointed tribunal for that onerous task but A Freeholder decided that the Senate, composed of equal numbers of state representatives, was the ideal body to try the president. The Baptist leader John Leland did not expect the process to remove any senators since they would never expel one of their colleagues. Americanis promoted rotation in office as it prevented legislators from accruing power, building perpetual factions, or foisting an aristocracy on the nation. For the Federal Farmer, rotation ensured that new members with new ideas would enter the Senate and thus expose more Americans to government. Those rotated out could return home and educate their constituents.

A few Virginians voiced class supremacy concerns. Americanis noted a fear of "*an odious aristocracy* in the Senate" but A Native of Virginia rejected it. Since state legislatures chose senators, one could assume that they would properly investigate candidates. Also, every two years, the election process eliminated one-third of its members. Surely this was a filter against an aristocratic Senate. Republicus worried that Senate power would translate into an oligarchy because of its remoteness from the people. The Federal Farmer took a practical view. He would not release all the Senate powers until it proved it could operate "on equal and just principles."[4]

The process of configuring the judiciary drew little attention. Edmund Randolph could not abide the presidential nominating power and William Grayson adamantly opposed federal courts operating within Virginia. Nevertheless, James Madison considered it probable that "officers of the States will be clothed with the correspondent authority of the Union."

Several commentators stressed the positive impact of the new judicial system on the state. Edmund Pendleton offered a tentative acceptance of the scheme but linked it to the relevance of the congressional enabling legislation. "In the Judiciary," he explained, "I perceive a Plan which may in the Legal Organization of the Courts produce Oppression and great Inconvenience to the distant Citizens," but if equitably applied, it would benefit the nation. The State Soldier, who may have been George Nicholas, considered the invention of a Supreme Court a natural juridical evolution. He later noted that he could champion no other method to settle, equitably and peacefully, disputes between the states. If an argument between them required adjudication, which state would hold the trial? What set of judges would make up the tribunal? A State Soldier praised the independence of the government and the judiciary, while A Native of Virginia considered it necessary to prevent influence from both home and abroad.

Still, localistic Virginians expected the new government to continue with the procedures common in their courts. The emphasis on Virginia common law and procedure would cause a rift between its jurists and those who expected a strong federal judiciary operating under a uniform code. George Mason analogized his required system with that between the county and state courts. Local writs held locally. No uniform code was necessary.

To some, the judicial clause was impossibly vague. This raised the specter among Antifederalists that Congress could implement it to their detriment. Civis Rusticus played to this theme when he reminded Virginians that the judicial article was merely an outline waiting for Congress to flesh it out. However, this constitutional uncertainty prompted criticism. George Lee Turberville complained that its power was too extensive but A Native of Virginia riposted that such unfocussed remarks were just propaganda designed to stigmatize the Court as a "tyranny." Arthur Lee was unsure when, and if, the Supreme Court had original jurisdiction or appeal power. William Grayson had no doubt that it should hear only appeals but that assertion did not convince George Nicholas or A Native of Virginia. Each dredged up our earlier example of competing states to refute Grayson. Little did they know that a future landmark Supreme Court case would reexamine these state rights arguments.

Two other contentious issues converged on appeals. One centered on power while the other examined process. All agreed that a trial was based on facts filtered through the laws covering the action requiring adjudication. Nevertheless, the parties disputed the requirement to reexamine both facts and law on appeal. Although the Constitution included both, Richard Henry Lee surmised that the former was strictly a local matter. Joseph Jones agreed. He suspected that the facts might become skewed in a faraway Court. According to the Impartial Examiner, any review of the facts inferred that the lower court was incompetent. Simply put, the Federal Farmer concluded that the Supreme Court had power over "the law, the equity, and the fact." However, Alexander White considered one criticism invalid on its face. In civil cases, the Supreme Court would never accept, as Antifederalists contended, that a disputant could introduce new facts at the appeal level. The revered jurist Sir William Blackstone did not countenance it so litigants could never sneak it into American jurisprudence.

The second issue revolved around distance. Edmund Pendleton put it simply: the judicial clause punished "distant citizens." Richard Henry Lee expanded the thought. Article III, section 2 required any citizen involved in an appeal to travel at his own expense to the site, chosen by Congress, of the Court. Harry Innes, from far away Kentucky, found this likelihood particularly galling. His fellow citizens must undertake long journeys to seek justice. The Federal Farmer decried the extra cost to litigants and added another criticism. His experience taught him that governments changed venues constantly. The same could befall the Supreme Court. A Native of Virginia counteracted these comments by producing cases that logically required a trip to a neutral Supreme Court but George Mason disputed the connotation. Suppose the government charged a Virginian in a tax matter and it made the initial negative verdict in that state. The appellant Virginian must travel to the Court's congressionally specified "residence" for a trial that will hear both law and fact. This combination of events was tantamount, said Mason, to a denial of a promised jury trial within his vicinage.

Other fears were less concentrated. One was a jurisdictional problem. Benjamin Harrison speculated that federal courts operating within the states must not be "independent of their laws." George Lee Turberville concluded that these federal courts presaged the end of the Virginia court system and The Impartial Examiner took a similar tack. He portrayed Virginia's trial by jury system as a "bulwark[s] of civil liberty" under federal attack. Trial by jury locally before your peers drew the interest of other correspondents. Richard Henry Lee labeled it a fundamental right while George Mason reflected that only Virginians should judge Virginians. If one traveled to the Supreme Court for an appeal, who was the jury? Who were your peers on the Court? Alexander White did not accept these arguments. Trial by jury in civil cases "may with safety be left to Congress as it is to all our State legislatures." Only criminal cases required trial by jury.

Not all the effects of the judicial clause dealt with legal matters. Richard Henry Lee predicted that, since a favored few would apply the law, it would benefit the rich, not the poor. The Impartial Examiner supported his contention. Surely the Supreme Court had an aristocratic semblance. Perhaps one of the latter writer's comments might be a précis of Antifederalist opinion. "The supreme court," he wrote, "is another branch of the foederal authority which wears the aspect of imperial jurisdiction, clad in dread array, and spreading its wide domain into all parts of the continent."

The niceties of judicial review were only an adjunct to other topics. In *The Federalist* No. 39, Madison discussed government form — national vs. federal. As part of his essay, he proposed that the central government must include an agency with the power to adjudicate impartially disputes on the "boundary between the two jurisdictions." Such a tribunal, he argued, "is clearly essential to prevent an appeal to the sword and a dissolution of the compact." He expanded his point in *The Federalist* No. 44. If Congress, or a state legislature, usurped a constitutional power, the president and the Court, could intervene. Most likely, it would involve legislative acts rather than state laws.[5]

Despite its omission from the Constitutional form of government, the inclusion of a Council of State to advise the president remained a burning issue. George Lee Turberville reported it to be the second most common Antifederalist complaint. However, this was unlikely given the rancor over the inclusion of a Bill of Rights and the powers assigned to the Senate. Both Arthur Lee and George Mason decried its omission. Arthur's brother, Richard Henry, included it in his lengthy list of necessary amendments. For example, he preferred a Council, rather than the Senate, to advise the president on government appointments. Of course, a record of this advice would be kept in a Council journal. Still, a Council of State did not meet Federalist requirements. It could damage the presidential aura, stamped on the people's minds, if they misconstrued his dependence for advice in crucial areas. Practically, the dominating presence of the president would render a Council useless. Advice would not only be unnecessary but also apt to "injure" the Union. Besides, the Constitution made the president responsible for his actions. An approved Council would set in motion a process by which critics could blame it for a presidential error.[6]

The crucial debate over enumerated powers concentrated on four main issues, taxation, commerce and navigation, the necessary and proper provision, and slavery. Nevertheless, others received attention. Alexander White promoted the militia clause. If Congress controlled the nation's militia, it would reduce the need for a standing army. Also, the central government could activate it equitably among the states. Another correspondent concluded that Virginia's ability to appoint officers offset distant control. He finished by asking "Can any one seriously suppose, that Congress will ever think of drawing the militia of one State out, in order to destroy the liberties of another?" The same author made a brief comment on the accession of new states to the Union. Most would be South-oriented. Surely this certainty would lay to rest Virginia's fear of northern domination. Edmund Pendleton would have preferred the Legislature, not just the Senate, to ratify treaties and George Lee Turberville and Joseph Spencer agreed. Ignoring the people's House when ratifying treaties that governed them was not sensible. A Native of Virginia disagreed. Those who criticized the locus of power had an ulterior motive. "Protection and security" were the tasks assigned to the central government and the Constitution had best equipped it to ensure them. In any case, the Senate would corroborate the president's judgment.[7]

✠

The slavery articles elicited great interest. John Tyler and George Mason wanted importation banned forever, while the *Kentucky Gazette* leapt to the next step. Slaves should be freed. George Lee Turberville found no republican ideal that countenanced the slave trade in twenty years but not now. Of course, debaters were familiar with the compromise background that produced the importation clause, but were not sure why the other states must follow its dictates. Could not Georgia and South Carolina follow the rule while other states banned it forever?

Slave categorization, either property or person, and its implications was a valid question. George Nicholas rebutted the insinuation that the value of slave property would be reduced due to the Constitution. True, a careless Congress could produce that result by passing an emancipation act, ignoring the fugitive slave law, or imposing high slave taxes. However, the first would clash with the *ex post facto* laws of slave ownership and the second was unconstitutional on its face, but the poll tax, suggested by the third, was possible. Still, the three-fifths rule that would punish the nonslave states that paid full taxes for each resident rendered it unrealistic.

One must realize that an extension of the slaves as property discussion that followed naturally from Nicholas's contention was not just a philosophical nuance. It impacted heavily on the taxation rates of the state. This was clear to Madison. However, he seemed ambivalent initially on whether slaves were property or people. Perhaps they should be considered an amalgam of each. After all, the Constitution counted them as three-fifths of a person. He extended this conclusion to the twin pillars of taxation and representation. Speaking for southerners, he wrote: "We subscribed to the doctrine ... that representation relates more immediately to persons, and taxation more immediately to property, and we join in the application of this distinction to the case of our slaves." Since Americans insisted on the relationship between taxation and representation, slaves, who had a foot in each, could be considered both property and people.[8]

✠

The debate on the necessary and proper provision of Article 1, Section 8 was desultory in the Constitutional Convention. So too, was that dealing with the power undergirding it, the implied power allocated to Congress. That situation changed within a month. On October 6, 1787, the Pennsylvanian James Wilson set the Federalist standard. Soon, correspondents transmitted it throughout the nation.

> It will be proper ... to mark the leading discrimination between the State constitutions and the constitution of the United States. When the people established the powers of legislation under their separate governments, they invested their representatives with every right and authority which they did not in explicit terms reserve; and therefore upon every question respecting the jurisdiction of the [Pennsylvania] House of Assembly, if the frame of govern-

ment is silent, the jurisdiction is efficient and complete. But in delegating federal powers, another criterion was necessarily introduced, and the congressional power is to be collected, not from tacit implication, but from the positive grant expressed in the instrument of the union. Hence, it is evident, that in the former case everything which is not reserved is given; but in the latter the reverse of the proposition prevails, and everything which is not given is reserved.

The dispute lay in the residue of powers. What institution or group would hold them after the initial delegation? To ensure that no misapprehension results from the text, we will rewrite Wilson's thesis with a few editorial additions. When the states formed their constitutions, implication assigned every power not reserved to the people to their state representatives. In the federal constitution, every power not assigned to the representatives was reserved to the people. Interestingly, Wilson informed his audience that the reverse focus "was necessarily introduced." That necessity grew from the novel concept of the sovereignty of the people. Once Americans accepted it, the old state reservation of power dictum was impossible to maintain. The sovereign people, according to the compact, began the process with all the power, and delegated a necessary portion to its representatives. Thus, it, and not the government, must be the repository of the residue.

Many Virginians agreed with Wilson. Edmund Pendleton considered "that the people being Established in the Grant itself as the Fountain of Power, retained every thing which is not granted." Tobias Lear, writing eloquently as Brutus, reminded Virginians that

> In the formation of a political constitution it is necessary that every right and privilege which the people reserve to themselves should be particularly and individually specified; or, that the portion of their natural liberty which they give up for the enjoyment of civil government, should be expressly mentioned, in the constitution. In the former case, if in the enumeration of the rights and privileges of the people any should be omitted or forgotten, the people cannot assume them. They are lost. — In the latter, that part of natural liberty which is given up at the behest of society is fully and completely denied, and whatever is not there expressly granted remains to the people.... The powers which the people delegate to their rulers are completely defined, and if they should assume more than is there warranted, they would soon find that there is a power in the United States of America paramount to their own, which would bring upon them the just resentment of an injured people.

Yet, not all opinion was positive. Some writers did not have a firm grasp on the Wilson thesis. For example, Cassius mistakenly argued that if the Constitution enumerated the congressional powers, then the people gave up all rights not reserved. The Impartial Examiner seemed confused by the common short hand description — everything that is not reserved is given; or everything that is not given is reserved — and could see no difference between the two reserved power schemes. He was of the school that "if something is in the compact then it is retained, otherwise it is given up." A *Chronicle* writer sarcastically encapsulated his view of Virginia opinion. Wilson's exposition was

> so self-evident a principle, as to be never in danger of being questioned in future, and it will no doubt be sufficient security for posterity to know, that a Pennsylvania attorney established it; and from thence thought himself sufficiently authorised to draw the following conclusion. "Hence it is *evident* that in the former case everything which is not reserved is given, but, in the latter the reverse prevails, and every thing which is not given is reserved." Bravo J — y! this is rare security for the liberty of the press, "that sacred palladium of national freedom."

George Lee Turberville labeled Wilson's comments a "sophism." Thomas Jefferson feared that they "might do for the Audience to whom it was addressed, but is surely a *gratis dictum*, opposed by strong inferences from the body of the instrument, as well as from the omission of the clause of our present confederation which had declared that in express terms."

The result of enumerating was not clear. Suppose one attempted to list the people's rights or powers. Might not one forget some? "There the principle," Pendleton wrote, "may be turned against Us, and what is not reserved, said to be granted." An Independent Freeholder argued that Virginians would be better off accepting the implications of the people's reserved powers than placing them in a Bill of Rights. It might lead to "all powers would be considered as granted which were not expressly reserved," the opposite implication of the Constitution.

The Federal Farmer made a detour from the usual distinctions. When the people developed a Constitution, they retained the residue not delegated. Once accepted, this truth presented, to the Antifederalist Farmer, two scenarios. Either the people *and their state governments* (author's italics) retained the residue or only the people did so. Since this dichotomy would necessarily cause conflict, the Constitution should expressly list reserved government power.[9]

✠

Referring to the necessary and proper provision and its running mate the general welfare clause, James Madison offered that "few parts of the Constitution have been assailed with more intemperance than this" set. Some Virginians must have found this firestorm surprising in view of the lack of interest it evoked in Philadelphia. Nevertheless, after some study, Virginia's Antifederalists massed against it. Some, like John Tyler, recorded no overriding reason for their opposition. Others, like The Federal Farmer, were ambivalent about its specifics. Still, study convinced him that those in power, whatever their stripe, would construe the implied powers inherent in the clause to their benefit. The people needed protection since,

> It is said that when the people make a constitution, and delegate powers, that all power not delegated by them to those who govern, is reserved in the people; and that the people, in the present case, have reserved in themselves, and in their state governments, every right and power not expressly given by the federal Constitution to those who shall administer the national government. It is said, on the other hand, that the people, when they make a constitution, yield all power not expressly reserved to themselves. The truth is, in either case, it is a mere matter of opinion, and many usually take either side of the argument, as will best answer their purposes: But the general presumption being, that men who govern, will, in doubtful cases, construe laws and constitutions most favorably for increasing their own powers; all wise and prudent people, in forming constitutions, have drawn the line, and carefully described the powers parted with and the powers reserved.

To add to the air of mystery surrounding the likely interpretation, he claimed "it is almost impossible to have a just conception of their [Congress] powers, or of the extent and number of the laws which may be deemed necessary and proper to carry them into effect, till we shall come to exercise these powers and make the laws." However, it seemed likely that if one interpreted the Constitution as the home of unchecked, indefinite, implied powers, then any laws made according to its demands must be supreme.

Nevertheless, most Antifederalists had no trouble castigating the necessary and proper provision. George Mason claimed that Congress could "extend their Power as far as they shall think it proper, so that the State Legislatures have no Security for the Powers now presumed to remain to them; or the People for their Rights." George Lee Turberville, Edmund Randolph, and William Russell advanced the "infringement on state authority" theme. Can the clause not be used to "annihilate state Governments"? Will not the presence of overlapping powers presage a reduction in state power? In the extreme, was any power denied Congress? William Grayson added that "in the first place I think liberty a thing of too much importance to be trusted on the ground of *implication*."

Mason's published objections persuaded first Alexander Hamilton and then Madison and fellow Virginia Federalists to join the fray. According to the *Petersburg Virginia Gazette*, "when a power is vested anywhere, from the nature of things it must be understood to be attended by such other incidental powers as necessary to give it efficacy" while a *Chronicle* correspondent, in an intemperate response to Richard Henry Lee, argued that

> Congress can make no laws, except such, as are, essentially, necessary to carry into execution the particular powers given to them by the constitution. The clause, which follows the enumeration of these powers, invest[s] Congress with a right "to make all laws, which shall be necessary and proper for carrying into execution the foregoing powers, and all other powers vested by this constitution in the government of the United States, or in any department, or officer thereof." But, what are these powers with which Congress are invested? Are they unlimited? Are they "coextensive with every possible object of human legislation"? Divest yourself, sir, for a moment, of your violent prejudices, and, read the foederal constitution with the philosophic calmness of a man, who is in search after truth, and, unless your mind is obstinately shut against conviction, you will find, that they are not.

A Native of Virginia noted that "Congress have no further legislative authority than shall be deemed necessary to carry into execution the powers vested by this Constitution." However, he took a different route than his colleagues. He assumed the clause's purpose was to ensure that the states could never "render the Federal Government nugatory." Because of its wide interest, the Antifederalists, in a burst of tactical brilliance, attached the tag "sweeping clause" to it. Madison's task was to persuade Virginians that any fair interpretation would show that the powers derived from it were mostly incidental. He began by reminding them that in the Convention's opinion, government "jurisdiction is limited to certain enumerated objects, which concern all members of the republic, but which are not to be attained by the separate provisions of any." With this rule established, he moved in *The Federalist* No. 44 to a defense of the implicit powers concept. The Convention faced four options other than that eventually adopted. Madison systematically repudiated each to his satisfaction but it was troubling that he offered no positive reasons for including the notion of implicit powers. The reader was left with the uneasy feeling that he adopted the idea by default. Perhaps Madison expected that his audience was familiar with Hamilton's work on the same topic. If so, it was a decision fraught with danger. Since he knew Americans demanded assurance that the sweeping clause would not usurp liberty, he listed a panacea that would neutralize their fears. Redress against an unlawful application of the sweeping clause could be found in "the election of more faithful representatives."

Some had argued that the implication located in the general welfare clause "amounts to an unlimited commission to exercise every power which may be alleged to be necessary for the common defense or general welfare." Madison attacked those who "labor for objections" by "stooping to such a misconstruction." First, its objective was "to raise money for the general welfare." Note that the following enumeration involved items separated by semi-colons. The obvious interpretation, to Madison, was that the clause introduced a general defining statement that particulars later expanded. This approach mirrored that applied in the Articles of Confederation.[10]

✠

The taxation clauses, said Benjamin Harrison, were unnecessary and should be rejected. Others were more specific. George Mason and The Federal Farmer posited that only Virginians should direct tax Virginians. Since they expected an expansion of tax policies, this power should never rest with the national government. Moreover, the new government would be inexperienced and poorly-trained. Thus, Virginians could expect an inequity in taxation. Should not the states, blithely suggested the Farmer, keep the power until the government matured and then amend the Constitution? He was not finished. It was strange, he noted, that the American Revolution, fought partly because of taxation aberrations, produced a government that favored them. On another front, if taxation policy led to an increased state impost, the Farmer expected more Virginia representatives. To ensure equitable taxation, bills setting the tax rates should require a super majority of either sixty-six percent or even seventy-five percent. Last, requiring state affirmation for some taxation bills would be wise. Remember, he warned, government can control an individual's property through federal taxation.

Government necessarily would grow because tax collection required many employees. According to the Farmer, this would create "dissatisfaction" because a government tendency was to hire enough officers to enhance its importance. That would require more Virginia taxes.

Several other hot spots drew Antifederalist's ire. A suspicious George Mason reminded his readers that a useful way to "tame" a large republic like the United States was to "bit our mouths with massive curbs." Thus, the government could employ this threat to cow restless citizens. The Federal Farmer worried that it could tax citizens twice for the same necessity, or it might cancel a vital Virginia tax. Last, many Virginians feared placing the tax power in the same hands as those that controlled the army. This unappetizing scenario might result in the army forcing judicial decisions on the states.

Not all prominent Virginians feared the tax clause. Thomas Jefferson was happy that the Legislature had the taxing power because the people would control tax policy through their representatives. George Nicholas injudiciously claimed that the government would offset any direct tax applied to Virginia by a similar reduction in state taxes. Historically, the inability of Congress to tax properly had led the United States to be considered a poor investment. This injured the national "dignity as a people." Americans accepted the policy since the Constitution inextricably tied representation to taxation. In addition, it implied that taxes would be collected only for common defense and general welfare, a direction that he deemed sensible. An Old Planter surmised that, because of the three-fifths rule, Virginia taxation would be less than nonslave states. Alexander White found the crux of the matter. The collection of taxes would not be a problem as long as "justice and moderation" were its guidelines.[11]

Restrictions on trade based on the navigation article left Virginians unsatisfied. The mere majority required to pass a bill appeared to punish the agrarian South. Virginians demanded a supermajority of sixty-six percent for passage. Mason predicted that a simple majority vote combined with tariffs would result in the ruin of the "landed interest." Richard Henry Lee agreed. Because of its minority voting status, the South needed a super majority to protect its interests and prevent the formation of monopolies. The Federal Farmer was more specific. "The eastern states," he said, "will receive advantages so far as the regulation of trade by a bare majority." Richard Henry Lee agreed that a "spirit of commerce" would drive the eight eastern states to dominate and regulate trade. Caleb Wallace predicted dire results for the western states if they could not control import or export duties. It made absolutely no sense to remove the power to protect nascent industries from foreign competition on one hand, but agree that local government's role was to protect its constituents against national intrusion on the other.

Federalists disagreed. Edward Carrington categorically rejected any implication that the majority "carrying states" would pass any regulations deleterious to Virginia. Moreover, the so-called majority were not all "carrying states." New Jersey and Connecticut demonstrably did not fit, while New York and Pennsylvania were equally carrying and agricultural. Even if such a designation had validity, he could not see how it would realistically hurt Virginia. Any regulations would be general and uniform, and all states would be affected equally.

A Native of Virginia took a practical approach. If the northern states could supply the South with competitively priced goods, it made perfect sense to prohibit European competitors. Cassius, replying to Richard Henry Lee, accused him of taking his position to promote disunion. In America, the majority must rule even if Lee was correct in his assertions. What if Virginians had to pay more for their imports? Surely getting the southern trade, rather than England, would be more acceptable for the northern states. It made common sense to protect some articles to promote growth. Although he did not second Cassius's arguments, Martin Oster offered his typically jaundiced view of Virginia intent. He reported to France that it opposed the commerce and navigation laws because it had always held them in its hands, continually thwarting other state initiatives. Without naming names, Madison agreed with the gist of Oster's interpretation. The habit of some states that taxed goods in transit to others particularly incensed him.[12]

The lack of balanced government, separation of powers, or checks and balances, frustrated many Virginians. Richard Henry Lee reminded them that political theory promoted the notion of three independent branches. In particular, he argued, the executive and legislative branches must be "unconnected." Unfortunately, this Constitution concentrated all the Executive plus two-thirds of the Legislative powers in the hands of the president and Senate. George Mason, and The Federal Farmer agreed. The "united" president and Senate would make it impossible for the executive to support the House in any dispute. The Baptist leader John Leland, according to Joseph Spencer, had similar doubts. The Constitution shifted many powers previously held by Congress to a president who was "two removes from the people."

Usually, checks and balances were associated with their effect on government, but the Federal Farmer included the people and states. The former had no built-in check, like a Bill of Rights, against tyrannical acts of government. Because of this error, revolution would be the people's only redress. A similar situation existed in the latter. What check did they have against usurpations by the central government? "It leaves the powers of government," wrote the Farmer, "and the representation of the people, so unnaturally divided between the general and state governments, that the operations of our system must be very uncertain."

James Madison offered the Federalist answer to their opponent's charges. In his view, the most effective method to ensure that one department or branch did not usurp another's power was to assign, to all, powers that would permit them to resist. For example, the Convention designed the presidential veto to protect him from the legislative branch. If ambition drove one official, then that of another could counteract it. Moreover, department heads naturally rebuffed any slow accumulation of power by others. They must recognize and interweave whatever interest an individual has with the "constitutional rights of the place." Power could resist usurpation.

Remember, continued Madison, that the government designed by this Constitution did not rest on the old bedrock of separation of powers. By applying the British constitution as his model, Montesquieu made it clear that "he did not mean that these departments ought to have no *partial agency* in, or no *countrol* over the acts of each other." In other words "that where the *whole* power of one department is exercised by the same hands which possess the *whole* power of another department, the fundamental principles of a free constitution, are subverted." In fact, many states already did not have full separation of powers.

Notice that Madison expected that a department head might encroach on the powers of another. Words on paper did not offer total protection. They were a beginning. Managers must actively protect their charges. For example, he knew from experience that the state legislatures constantly usurped the power of their sister branches.[13]

Correctly, George Lee Turberville listed the lack of a Bill of Rights, an "essential" component of liberty and individual rights, as the most common complaint. These critics could be organized into two groups. Some focused on a Rights package while others separated them into individual liberties.

A crescendo of unsupported criticisms was common. Antifederalists could not conceive of a Constitution bereft of human rights provisions that would prevent illegal usurpations of the people's liberties. This fear of corruption and tyranny was a thread that ran through Antifederalist arguments. Moreover, Virginians were comfortable with the concept of a Declaration of Rights since they had embedded one in the state constitution. John Leland saw the issue in stark terms. Once men left a state of nature to form a society, they had rights that they would never give up to the new government. If the people carelessly ignored this dictum, a tyrant would invent ways to circumvent any implied right.

The Federal Farmer turned to the social compact for evidence.

> There are certain inalienable and fundamental rights, which in forming of the social compact, ought to be explicitly ascertained and fixed — a free and enlightened people, informing this compact, will not resign all their rights to those who govern, and they will fix limits to their legislators and rulers, which will soon be plainly seen by those who are governed....

Although the arguments listed above resonated with opponents of the Constitution, the implication of the Supremacy Clause on liberty was paramount. Richard Henry Lee offered a stern warning to Virginians based on his study of the new government. Since it had power incident to the general welfare and the Supremacy Clause buttressed that power, it was mandatory that the states insist on a Bill of Rights. Such a list would reduce the danger inherent in any judicial review process. As well, George Mason addressed the possibility that the Supremacy Clause could trump the current state Declaration of Rights. George Lee Turberville and The Impartial Examiner seconded his opinion.

The Antifederalist logic convinced Federalists that their own interpretation of the reserved rights process was correct. Therefore, their opponents must have another motivation for their strident opposition. Perhaps they planned to dilute national in favor of state power. In that case, Federalists were certain that they should fight any attempt at amending the Constitution with a Bill of Rights. Unfortunately, this decision eventually threatened its ratification.

After James Wilson supplied them with a debating blueprint, the proratification interest decided that they had a satisfactory rejoinder. Writer after writer hewed to his line. The *Virginia Journal* reflected their familiarity with his argument. A Bill of Rights was not only unnecessary but absurd. Either the Constitution expressly specified the people's reserved rights or the portion of their liberty extended to government. If one chose the former, any excluded rights cannot extend the list. Future "Rulers" could dispute such an extension. If, as seemed likely, the people of that time strongly objected, the Bill of Rights would promote division. In the latter case, once the people delegated a right, they could never regain it but the rest remained with them. Obviously it was the superior choice and the Convention adopted it. A *Winchester Virginia Gazette* writer, possibly Alexander White, finished this argument. Congress could not usurp the people's basic rights because they did not have the express power to do so. The sovereign people would void any congressional "attempt to exercise any powers which are not expressly delegated to them." On the other hand, Edmund Pendleton translated Wilson differently. He urged Virginians to avoid enumerations and concentrate on "Principle."

Tobias Lear repeated the dictum, introduced by John Locke, that once the people enumerated a list of delegated rights they were lost to the people permanently. Like the writer above, he included the questionable argument of forgotten rights. In any case, leaving the residue of rights to the people was safer. A Native of Virginia sailed a different course. First, he confided that, in his opinion, the scramble over a Bill of Rights had no substance. People expected one from a force of habit not necessity. Moreover, a Bill might attack liberty, not defend it. Six states had judged so and omitted it from their constitutions. These constitutions were

> the evidence of the social compact between the governors and the governed and the only proof of the rights yielded to the former. In all disputes respecting the exercise of power, the Constitution or frame of government decides. If the right is given up by the Constitution, the governors exercise it; if not, the people retain it.

Edmund Pendleton warned his protagonists that a Bill of Rights could be dangerous. If an outside agency gave it to the people, it was proof that they were not sovereign. Surely, this should deter Virginians from making enumerations of rights.

Both Antifederalists and Federalists registered other interesting disagreements. Civis Rusticus and Edmund Pendleton undercut a major Federalist tenet by stating that the sovereign — here the people — could change any Bill at will simply by ignoring the Lockean dictate. Did not any argument that revolved around the suspension of state Bills prove this contention? By this process, no Bill of Rights was immutable. Thomas Jefferson took a different approach to the same problem. While discussing tactics that one might employ to force a Bill, he suggested that the first nine states ratify the Constitution, but the next four reject it, until a Bill of Rights was added. Of course, the Constitution and any addenda to it, such as a Bill of Rights, were amendable. Thus, to some Virginians, no logical argument supported an unchangeable Bill.

Perhaps the most long-lasting effect may have been enunciated by both A True Friend and Thomas Jefferson. It dealt with trust. A True Friend specifically remarked that he did not trust James Wilson's exposition on reserved rights. In support, Jefferson implied the same inclination by asserting that no government should ever make inalienable rights subject to inference. Both writers insisted on a written Bill of Rights. A lack of trust between the federal government and the people of the states would be unfortunate.[14]

✠

Unbundled rights followed the same progression as that for the packaged Bill. Freedom of the press was mandatory in a free nation, claimed Antifederalists. Why worry, riposted Federalists, Congress has no power to restrain the press. The Constitution must extend trial by jury from criminal cases to civil as well. This was not a problem, wrote Cassius, since, obviously, a class of cases existed requiring an expert to adjudicate. Perhaps Richard Henry Lee caught the mood of Virginia's Antifederalists. The jury trial clause should mirror that of Virginia.

George Mason worried that no provision restricted a standing army. Yes, replied George Nicholas, Congress can raise a standing army but it was unlikely to do so. Last, Americans had always accepted *ex post facto* laws due to expediency and would probably continue to do so.[15]

State rights, as a coherent doctrine, was not a debate subject. Instead, snippets here and there predicted future tenets. In the following paragraphs, we will concentrate on state powers listed within the Constitution. Moreover, we will use the phrase state rights throughout this book, although the correct phrase should be state powers. However, it is unlikely that, in the future, authors will adopt the correct phraseology. In addition, we will never use the phrase "states rights" to agree with the original connotation binding individual state power to the Constitution.

No antebellum American politician would recognize a reference to state rights before ratification despite the evidence from the Articles era. Nevertheless, Madison, in *The Federalist*, made several arguments that would affect its emergence. He sought to calm state fears by implying a dichotomy of equal state and federal powers. For example, he noted that "the operations of the Federal Government will be most extensive and important in times of war and danger; those of the State Governments, in time of peace and security." Continuing in this vein, he described a government in which,

> the former [general government power] will be exercised principally on external objects, as war, peace, negociation [sic], and foreign commerce; with which last the power of taxation will for the most part be connected. The powers reserved to the several States will extend to all the objects, which, in the ordinary course of affairs, concern the lives, liberties and properties of the people; and the internal order, improvement, and prosperity of the State.

These generalized powers could lead to specific applications. Each state set the requirements for the election of representatives; caused the election of the president through the elector system; elected a Senate; and was represented in a House whose members surely would find allies in the state legislatures. Also, they had avoided any national veto, ambiguity surrounded many federal-state powers, the government seemed to have a federal tilt, and the absence of judicial review permitted the Antifederalists to claim it as a state power. Still, these victories seemed to have a shaky foundation. Although it seemed clear to Madison that these powers reflected a significant state presence in the nation's affairs, his tactic contained a flaw. While discussing equal state representation, he declared, "in this spirit [of sacrifice] it may be remarked that the equal vote allowed to each state, is at once a constitutional recognition of the portion of sovereignty remaining in the individual states, and an instrument for preserving that residuary sovereignty." Such a remark served to highlight not just the "spirit" of sacrifice but also the loss of sovereignty. The states had retreated from the lead Articles government trumpet to a second fiddle in its replacement.[16]

Because of the tactics employed by the Antifederalists, the debate over state ratification of the Constitution splintered into several related topics. Initially, Madison offered a weak motivation for the process defined in the Constitution. He admitted that the Continental Congress had incontrovertibly designated the state legislatures to perform this duty. Despite this knowledge, he proceeded to offer a justification for a different procedure that bordered on the absurd. In the face of Article XIII's requirement for a unanimous vote, he insisted that no state should have the authority to thwart the majority. To make matters worse, he added two insupportable arguments. Few Antifederalists, he claimed, had objected to the obvious unconstitutionality of the process. Thus, no further observations were required. Placing his constitutional eggs in a majority basket, he added that "the express authority of the people alone could give due validity to the Constitution. To have required the unanimous ratification of the thirteen states, would have subjected the essential interests of the whole to the caprice or corruption of a single member." His focus on one state was disingenuous. If only the conventions of the four largest states of the Union refused to ratify, they could deem that most Americans declined the Constitution despite its having met the legal requirement for success. Richard Henry Lee, for one, knew that bypassing Article XIII was unconstitutional despite Madison's questionable assertion and he would not accept the Constitution on that basis. Underlying this methodology was at least two major pitfalls for the future. How could those who expected implementation to be legally accomplished trust those who foisted it upon them? Did Madison consider the effects of his methodology if employed by future opponents of the Constitution?

Although his justification for the ratification dynamic was without merit, Madison did make a valuable contribution on the nature of the Union and the role of the states. The people acted in their capacity as people of a state. Thus, ratification was federal, not national. Recall, ratification did not require most of the people but did require most of the states. "Each state," he asserted, "in ratifying the Constitution, is considered as a sovereign body independent of all others, and only to be bound by its own voluntary act. In this relation then the new Constitution will, if established, be a *federal* and not a *national* Constitution."

The ratification debate drew fevered responses from each side. Perhaps it was the complexity of the problem or, maybe, Virginians were suspicious. For example, New Hampshire Federalists had estimated that they would lose the ratifying vote so they postponed its convention proceedings. General comments, as usual, were common. Richard Henry Lee sought amendments based on the latest government theory incorporated into the Constitution. The people, not Congress, should ratify them. Otherwise, the changes would never be considered fundamental law. George Washington rejected Lee's concern. To the general, amendments, even if necessary, could never balance the inevitable disputes against their value to the nation. How could one avoid the possibility of "Local prejudice"? George Nicholas followed the same trail. Any required changes were insignificant and not worth the effort. An Impartial Citizen echoed Washington and Nicholas,

> I, therefore, contend that though we have indisputably a right to propose amendments, yet it is unnecessary and inexpedient to exercise that right on the present occasion, and that rejection or adoption of this Constitution is the alternative.

George Mason demanded a second convention and considered subsequent amendments an "utterly absurd" concept. The Federal Farmer also dealt in an absurdity, according to his dictates. Clearly, the state convention delegates would be closer to the people than those that met at Philadelphia. Thus, any discussion predicated on the argument that the state convention cannot amend the Constitution was ridiculous.[17]

Congress had faced this question earlier and debate persuaded it that amendments were feasible. To avoid the necessity, it shipped the unamended Constitution to the states without comment. This tactic was suggested in the house by John Marshall and accepted. Edmund Randolph was sure that it should be presented to each state for either acceptance or rejection. The Federal Farmer agreed that this was the position taken by the Convention. Unfortunately, the wording of the Marshall resolution undercut their opinion. Antifederalists accepted it as a license to amend. Richard Henry Lee adopted an extralegal position as had Madison on other issues. Because "the happiness or misery of mankind depends so essentially upon government ... the right of the people cannot be questioned, of so acting with plans proposed, as to adopt them, reject them, or propose amendments to them." Considering the apparent acceptance of the concept by both Federalists and Antifederalists at the Convention, we can assume that despite some dispute, amendments were on the table. Later actions by the delegates at Richmond bolstered this opinion. Each faction openly discussed the timing of amendments while spirited debate against the concept was absent. One must realize that any instruction from the Philadelphia Convention on this important topic was spurious. It had no power to direct the states, or the people, how to proceed.[18]

Two paths presented themselves to those who decided that they could amend the Constitution. They could be added prior or subsequent to ratification. Antifederalists generated justifications for prior amendments while Federalists preferred the dynamic ratify first, amend later.

Federalists were sure that previous amendments would destroy the Union. George Nicholas, writing as The State Soldier, assured Virginians that such was the case. Amending the Constitution and disunion were Siamese twins. The Constitution contained a perfectly defined amending process. Why not use it? Edmund Randolph feared that a tendency to amend the Constitution would flourish, a fatal blow for the Union. General Washington expanded on this thesis. Probably, one state would never accept amendments offered by another. If one multiplied this prediction by a factor of at least thirteen, one could see the mortal danger to the Union. In any case, Virginians should never contemplate such a drastic step until someone proved that it was vital to the Constitution. Of course, these discussions were based on the potential Union. In case of failure, the Articles government was still intact.

Certainly, a hint of unnecessary haste pervaded the proceedings. One might argue that the Federalists attempted to push the Constitution through the ratification process before its effect on the states could be determined. James Monroe could see no justification for the Federalist assurance that prior amendments would damage the Union. Reverend Madison and the Federal Farmer foresaw the state convention enhancing the basic Constitution. Continuing, the Farmer noted that claiming that the states could not synchronize the various convention amendments was useless because such was merely speculation. Suppose it did fail? In that case, simply put the ratification before the people for a decision. Yes, this might prove time-consuming, but the opposite, a defective system, was worse. The *Baltimore Maryland Gazette* published its sense of Virginia opinion before the convention.

> You may rely, on this as a fact, that the bulk of the most respectable and independent men in this Commonwealth will not receive the new government, unless it is previously amended: they treat with ridicule and contempt the idea of first ratifying and afterward proposing amendments; they observe that only "small flies can be caught in such a web."[19]

Part of the argument for prior amendments included an action plan. It reduced to calling a second Constitutional Convention.

With few exceptions, this debate was essentially between Richard Henry Lee and James Madison, who, in a flurry of letters, sought to persuade other Virginians that their reasoning was correct. In a lengthy procedure, Lee proposed a process that might overcome the legal problems associated with ratification while providing the people a chance to recommend changes. The Virginia convention could amend the Constitution, which contained many novel ideas, and transmit them to Congress. It, in turn, would pass that package to a second Constitutional Convention that would incorporate those most wanted into the core of the Constitution. Lee knew this process was complicated, but it might ensure input from all the states through Congress; be legally responsible; and represent the people through a second convention. However, one wondered about the role of Congress considering that it had previously shown it had a power to amend.

Madison offered a litany of objections to a second convention. He could not imagine that delegates to a second convention would agree on the necessary amendments. To George Nicholas he wrote

> The circumstances under which a second Convention composed even of wiser individuals, would meet, must extinguish every hope of an equal spirit of accommodation; and if it should happen to contain men, who secretly aimed at disunion ... the game would be as easy, as it would be obvious, to insist on points popular in some parts, but known to be inadmissible in others of the Union.

If he were correct, Antifederalists might gut the new Constitution. Perhaps they would even propose a conditional ratification.

The Virginia opposition demands would place it in the unenviable position of becoming the focus of discontent. Other states could complain that they had ratified in good faith but now Virginia asked them to rethink that decision. How could this promote the "spirit of compromise" necessary for success? Madison also saw a legal problem. Inevitably, several state legislatures had passed enabling convention legislation and adjourned before Virginia's "mandatory propositions ... could be transmitted." On a personal note, he reminded Edmund Randolph that a second convention would reflect badly on the first convention delegates. Furthermore, "prudence and safety" would be challenged by a second convention.

Several other correspondents added their opinions. George Mason was adamant that the people needed a second convention to express their views. Caleb Wallace agreed but A Native of Virginia opposed them. Suppose one accepted the idea of a second convention. Would not the same argument be valid for a third and fourth? Edmund Pendleton bolstered one of Madison's attacks. If Virginia insisted on a second convention, the other states would conclude that the Old Dominion refused to "make a Common Stock" with them. It would assume the role of dictator. On the other hand, R. H. Lee advised that "to say that a bad government must be established for fear of anarchy, is really saying that we must kill ourselves for fear of dying."

Federalist criticisms against a second convention seemed contrived. Yes, dynamically, the reexamination would take more time, perhaps another year. Was there any danger that the Union would collapse within that time frame under present conditions? Arguments that other states would resist the Old Dominion's agenda ran afoul of the procedure employed for the introduction of the Virginia Plan. How could one argue on one hand that the delegates at a second convention could never agree and on the other preach the efficacy of the new Constitution? Had it not been developed by the same class of men? Moreover, the new delegates would have the benefits of both the old debate and the people's opinion. No, a sense of urgency drove the Federalist bloc. The Constitution, as written, might not stand further scrutiny.[20]

Those defending subsequent amendments assumed that each state would offer post ratification amendments. Pendleton voiced this opinion just before the convention. Madison added that "recommendatory alterations are the only ground that occurs to me." A Madison confidante, Joseph Jones, advised him that no amendments should be considered until the states ratified the Constitution. Virginians should attach their required amendments to their ratification and transmit the package to Congress. This might ameliorate the charge that Virginia took little notice of other states. Randolph saw these amendments as a chance to revisit some delegated powers and firm up ambiguities.

Earlier, we noted that George Mason had informed Jefferson that Virginians demanded amendments but Richard Henry Lee saw a problem. How could Virginians trust the amending process to the same class that had promulgated the Constitution? Remember, subsequent amendments attached to the ratification document would be merely suggestions and must pass muster with the First Congress.[21]

Since our ratification discussion concentrated on Antifederalist opinion, glancing at amendments a Federalist might consider would be informative. Edmund Pendleton advocated those "favorable to Liberty" like trial by jury, and liberty of the press, "freedom and frequency of elections, and a regulation that representatives must live among their constituents." He considered this class of amendments mandatory "to eradicate the seeds of future mischief" rather than "to remove the dangers immediately imminent in Operation." He preferred the long view over present advantage.[22]

Despite few advocates, the notion of a constitutional testing period, was interesting. Why not revisit the plan in ten years? Reverend Madison made the suggestion to his illustrious cousin. After a few years, Americans would recognize its flaws and, voting by states, repair them. Perhaps A True Friend, in a published broadside, offered the best justification.

> Sound reason and urgent necessity, lay their positive commands on us to accept the new foederal constitution; but, on the other hand prudence seems to require from us, that we should adopt it on trial only for a certain limited time, for, eight, ten, or twelve years; at the expiration of which ever of these periods may be agreed on, we will again call a general convention, in order to rectify the defects or lapses, which the unerring guides, time and experience may discover; this will then reform what our circumstances may point out for reformation.[23]

Although the statewide debate encompassed several ideas based on republican government, the two most important impacting state rights were liberty and sovereignty. Each would attract doctrinaires throughout the antebellum period.

The correlation between liberty and government was a staple of debate but a few remarks stood out from the rest. Madison, in his famous *The Federalist* No. 10, highlighted the threat of "an interested and overbearing majority" on "public and personal liberty." The American tendency was to ignore "the rules of justice and the rights of the minor party." To remedy this republican problem, one must apply a republican solution that forced not just the majority, but all the people, to remain vigilant to habitual government usurpation. However, a loss of liberty might be averted if the majority actively sought to accommodate the different interests. Liberty and the nation would expand together. Still, if the federal government challenged the liberty and authority of the states, Americans could expect united resistance. In the extreme, a Lockean revolution would be the outcome.

Madison portrayed "republican liberty" as a demanding mistress. "All power must be derived from the people" and its representatives must be kept on a short leash. Simultaneously, they must have the freedom to legislate effectively. This dichotomy emphasized "that liberty may be endangered by the abuses of liberty, as well as by the abuses of power."

Because of their role as Constitutional critics, the theme of "liberty endangered" attracted Antifederalists. Cato Uticensis considered liberty best insured by thirteen federated governments rather than one central one. Without expanding on details, the Impartial Examiner decided that the Constitution endangered liberty. Specifically, John Leland decried the absence of a clause protecting religious liberty. Perhaps Richard Henry Lee prophetically expressed the greatest fear. Any Constitution that contained the seeds of coercion was a danger to liberty. Martin Oster did not believe the Virginians' interpretations. The Vice Consul decided that the supposed attachment to liberty was just a smokescreen.[24]

✠

Three sovereignty issues received the bulk of attention. They were the sovereignty of the people, the sovereignty left to the state, and the introduction of a new theoretical construct — dual sovereignty. The concept of popular sovereignty was not clear to all Antifederalists. Even an erudite correspondent like The Impartial Examiner misunderstood its thrust. Circumstances locked him into the English model. In England, sovereignty resided in an institution — Parliament — rather than the most basic unit — the people. Thus, he complained bitterly that the Constitution transferred "the individual sovereignty from each state to the *aggregate body* of Congress." With this guide, understanding his rejection of the Constitution was easy. No power remained to Virginia. Even when correctly identified, the sovereignty of the people often did not pass Antifederalist muster. A Ploughman considered the people "the source of majesty, power and dominion." Nevertheless they "become so degenerated as to have no jealousy for their dignity, rights and privileges, [that] they never fail to find usurpers" to overthrow them. Therefore, the Constitution, with its acceptance of standing armies, was an indirect attack on liberty. An Articles-like government in which sovereignty remained with the states would better serve the nation if compared with that based on an easily-degenerated people.

Madison, as one might expect, laid the Federalist groundwork for popular sovereignty. Rather than a government based on states' sovereignty, the Constitution could "operate without their intervention on the individuals composing them." In effect, he exploded the cherished concept of state sovereignty. Alexander White picked up this thread by declaring that "the fundamental axiom ... is, that sovereignty is vested in the people, a position so plain and simple that the meanest capacity can comprehend it." George Washington made an interesting addition. "The power under the Constitution," he told a relative, "will always be in the People. It is entrusted for certain defined purposes, and for a certain limited period." This last phrase was crucial. A careful reader will understand that Washington delegated power, not sovereignty, to the government in the short term. It did not remain forever but returned to the sovereign people at its behest and remained in its hands until delegated again. Americanis confirmed the Federalist view. "That all power originally resides in the people," he expounded, was a truth "too sacred and too firmly established to require any illustrative proofs." George Nicholas made a startling foray into the sovereignty debate via the distribution of power. He saw only one difference between the present government and that proposed by the Constitution. Powers given up would shift from the state legislatures to Congress. Thus, in Nicholas's logic, the "change will only be felt by the leading men in each state, and not by the people." Surely, this definition of "the people" would have amused Madison. Moreover, Nicholas completely ignored the salient fact. Power shifted from state to general government was tantamount to a loss of sovereignty.

Perhaps as one Antifederalist — probably George Mason — suggested, sovereignty was but a "Phantom ... which is left the state." It would result in two separate governments squabbling over Virginia's tax dollars. Another scenario characterized the state "confined to interior regulations and Congress ... invested with the great objects of general administration." Because the general government was unconfined geographically, it could establish its superiority throughout the nation. James Monroe considered "state sovereignty a vain and illusory hope" although it might achieve partial sovereignty.

Many Antifederalists remained fearful of the theory of legislative sovereignty. Due to the vast territory Congress must govern, the Union would slowly slip into a consolidation that would omit Virginians from the halls of power. Such was the opinion of Cato Uticensis. He envisioned the states gobbled up by the federal government. Martin Oster confirmed the effect of consolidation and listed it as a principal reason for Virginia's opposition. Maybe, confirmed Reverend Madison, the Virginia legislature loved sovereignty's power too much to give it up.

The Federalist counterattack took several paths. Brutus could not understand the anguish portrayed by some Virginians due to a loss of sovereignty. Blithely, he posited that everyone knew "that each state must sacrifice some part of its individual advantages." The only debate concerned what powers they would sacrifice. George Nicholas, like Brutus, could not fathom the depth of feeling over a loss of sovereignty. After ratification, the states would still have the powers they now enjoyed, except those "specifically given to Congress and such as the state legislatures are expressly forbid to exercise." Thus, the Constitution would not "destroy the state governments" although it would seriously curtail their powers. This obvious sovereignty loss did not register on Nicholas but he did offer an interesting interpretation. The people of Virginia would not lose any power — sovereignty — under the new government compared with that held under the Articles. If one totaled all the powers that Congress and the state legislatures wielded presently and compared them with the same institutions under the Constitution, the only difference would be that "Congress will have a greater share and the legislature of the state less than they respectively enjoy." According to this thesis, since the combined state authorities acting on the people balanced, Virginians should be content. Unfortunately, the argument completely ignored the effect of lost state sovereignty.

Madison had a concise way of describing dual sovereignty. The new governments were a feudal system of republics "in which the sovereign, though limited, was independent." It was an admission that the states retained some sovereignty. Federalists had created a new definition of the term. The latter postulate elicited more debate than any other sovereignty issue. Could one contemplate dual sovereignty? Surprisingly, one Antifederalist, Cato Uticensis recognized early that the notion of dual sovereignty had merit. Virginians had to answer the question whether "you would be a sovereign or a sharer in sovereignty." But most agreed with The Impartial Examiner who could not countenance fuzzy thinking that accepted two coincident sovereignties over the same object. As we noted earlier, James Monroe had examined this option and applied a simple test to establish its viability. Two partial sovereignties, one national and one state, that implemented its version of a shared responsibility were bound to clash to the detriment of the latter. Thus, the notion would impair its sovereignty.

James Madison offered the Federalist position on dual sovereignty and Alexander White later confirmed it. In *The Federalist* No. 62, he persuaded his colleagues that the concept was viable despite its apparent deviation from accepted theory. An examination of the Constitution would show "that the equal vote allowed to each state, is at once a constitutional recognition of the portion of sovereignty remaining in the individual states, and an instrument for preserving that residuary sovereignty." Dual sovereignty was a reality, not just another theory. Some months later, Madison made another thrust into this minefield.

> The great desideratum in Government is, so to modify the sovereignties that it may be sufficiently neutral between different parts of the Society to controul one part from invading the rights of another, and at the same time sufficiently controuled itself, from setting up an interest adverse to that of the entire Society.

White expanded this standard Federalist view with an outwardly convincing interpretation of its application. First, he associated himself with the idea that sovereignty resided in the people. With that established, he shifted his remarks to the relationship between state and national sovereignty. "The separate states," he said, "retained all the powers of internal government." Therefore, they were sovereign locally. How could this assertion overcome Monroe's contention that it was not practical? In those cases, White argued, "two coordinate sovereignties over the same objects of dominion might be a solecism in government" but such was not so with the power distribution in the Constitution. The demarcation of powers between the two governments made it obvious that "the state governments retained their sovereignty over all objects which respect their particular States only" while the national government had sovereignty "over all objects as respected foreign nations, or equally affect all the States." However, he undercut his argument. In case of legal dispute, he added, the advantage "is evidently in the side of the State governments." This admission of future conflict negated his carefully contrived scenario of separated sovereignties.

Despite its convincing tone, this Federalist argument missed a crucial point. Once the Constitution established the sovereignty of the people, a reversion to a debate over state and federal government sovereignties was specious and confusing since it rested on institutional sovereignty. Since each institution was the creature of the people, any argument about its sovereignty, in the old sense, was internally inconsistent.

Other sovereignty issues received attention. The Frederick County Meeting claimed that history supported those who advocated a strong central government. Confederated nations whose members retained their sovereignties were notoriously weak against foreign assault. George Nicholas knew that this did not apply to the Constitution. Its form of government, and those of the states, achieved only partial sovereignty since it executed only express powers. This was obvious to Cassius. Following a different line of reasoning, he ended with the same conclusion. Because each state selected the same number of senators despite different sized populations, one must agree that the notion of retained state sovereignty was valid. James Monroe recognized that partial or reduced sovereignty was likely. Theoretically, America would benefit from a national sovereignty that united the people under one banner. Such a nation would be "elevated and sublime" as well as "benevolent and humane." However, powerful state forces would never allow it. Virginians must realize that for the powerful men of the state legislature to "make a sacrifice of their own for the good of other people ... is a degree of liberality which the human heart hath not as yet attained."

An examination of the Articles of Confederation, supplemented by his experience in Congress, had persuaded James Madison that "the objects of Union could not be secured by any system founded on the principle of a confederation of sovereign states." The Impartial Examiner rejected this conclusion. Happily, the Articles government had no coercive power on the states or its citizens. Virginia was "free, sovereign and independent" with a Declaration of Rights that was the "*basis* of government." Madison rejoined by adding that if one examined the state constitutions, one found that some, but not other, states had specifically "enshrined their adherence to the Articles." If its government consisted of equal sovereigns, then each state should record its relationship with it in the same fashion. Otherwise, the Articles of Confederation was merely a league. If the argument held, then any infraction by a member must result in the break up of the league. Since many could be listed, then one could argue that the Articles were defunct and the debate over state sovereignty must continue without benefit of any reference to the Articles. Unfortunately for those who wanted to apply this argument, it required Madison's state constitutions to take instructions from an outside entity other than the people, hardly a sovereign position.

The transfer of state sovereignty to the national government was crucial. A correspondent in the *Petersburg Virginia Gazette*, recognized the enormity of the task that had faced the Conventioneers. However, it was tempered by the knowledge that the proposed government would "secure the rights of the respective states, subject to the general controul of one sovereign authority." Nowhere did this writer contemplate a divided or partial sovereignty. A Virginian Planter agreed. In an intemperate outburst, he warned Virginians that the proposed Constitution would enslave them. Congress's unbounded powers would circumvent state authority and thus its sovereignty.

Virginians could trace much of their unease to the Supremacy Clause although George Nicholas painted it as chimerical. Complaints that Congress would have "unlimited and absolute power" were false. Following his earlier tack, he explained that members of Congress had no more power than that "expressly given to them in that constitution." Virginians must accept the distinguishing features between state and general governments or they would face the embarrassing prospect of two different laws controlling the same object. If one insisted that powers remained to the states that might supercede those of the national government, then the present exercise in constitution-building had failed. The people must understand that the Supremacy Clause simultaneously ensured the powers of the national government while not adding to Congress's power. He declared that it

> only declares those laws binding which are made in pursuance of, or in conformity to, the particular powers given by the Constitution and was only intended to prevent the different states from passing laws which might defeat the measures of Congress in such things as they have an express power given them to manage for the good of the whole.

On its face, the Supremacy Clause infringed on the sovereignty of the states. The Impartial Examiner was less charitable with respect to its intent. No doubt existed in his mind that "here the sovereignty of America is ascertained and fixed in the foederal body at the same time that it abolishes the present independent sovereignty of each state.... For the idea of two sovereignties existing within the same community is a perfect solecism." Most Antifederalists equated supreme indivisible power with sovereignty. One could not logically subdivide it. Federalists, in substance, had concocted a combination consisting of the necessary and proper clause buttressed by the Supremacy Clause to replace Madison's cherished national veto.[25]

Transitions

State rights doctrine had several roots. Using a novel methodology, European Enlightenment theorists applied scientific methods to data about familiar governments. They concluded that a social compact between individuals ensured political order and best protected liberty against power. Its basis would be an agreeable constitution defining their government's limited power to ensure it could not endanger freedom. Nevertheless, they knew that self-interest could raise havoc among the constituency unless it remained alert.

Evangelism introduced the notion that democracy was a natural condition. Its components, equality of opportunity and individual liberty, bolstered that conclusion. Compact could ensure each, said dissenters, in a Lockean government. The fight for religious liberty had transmuted into one for liberty in general and a written constitution based on compact principles would meet their criteria.

The constitutional component of state rights was based on trust. Antifederalists distrusted both human nature overall and proratification Federalists in particular. A corollary of distrust was fear. Their fealty to corporate classical republicanism encouraged them to imagine corruption, aristocracy, or tyranny behind every Article. Claims that the powerful new government would coerce the states or that consolidation would eliminate their legislatures were common. Had not the North abandoned Virginia in the late war? Surely the machinations surrounding the fateful Jay-Gordoqui treaty proved that it could not trust the northern states. Recently, congressional delegates had even manipulated the transmission of the Constitution to the states, making it appear that Congress approved it. These were not the building blocks of a trusting relationship. Virginia's localists preferred control of their own affairs.

Due to the antiratification ethos, its proponents found gremlins in almost every Constitutional Article. The breadth and depth of their concerns were amazing. However, our close examination of their nature soon uncovered their source. Although their opponents were willing to stride into the future, the past captured Antifederalists. The two factions had differing views of the nature of the Union. Antifederalist dogma was based on the work of theorists like John Locke who trumpeted the benefit of the social compact. Most Virginians favored the Articles' government that mirrored its tenets. Still, another significant group marched to Madison and Montesquieu's drumbeat. They foresaw a stable, energetic government more apt to act on individual citizens. The obvious danger was that the two sides could talk past each other. Given a specific dispute each could be correct according to its ground rules but totally wrong if one applied the other. Seeking accommodation would be difficult.

Sovereignty and reserved rights highlighted Antifederalist concerns. In time, the monarchical and aristocratic tendencies inherent in the Constitution, coupled with the powers elicited from the Supremacy Clause promised trouble for Virginia. To counter this possibility, the state required a Bill of Rights and strong checks and balances. After all, Federalists expected Virginia to diminish from a sovereign state to a second class entity in the new Union. If such was the case, it must have a list of reserved rights.

Still, each of the above conclusions only predicted a state rights doctrine. The evidence suggests strongly that Virginians were unusually well educated on the issues but nothing had yet occurred to push them into the doctrine's embrace. They were more susceptible to its blandishments but the ultimate impetus had not occurred.

3

The Virginia Ratification Convention — Issues Connected to Government

Three unresolved war irritants cried out for solution. The specter of debt repayment and tax relief, congressional power, and the effects of the peace treaty loomed over Virginians. The Revolution had devastated the state and economic depression had followed. Although its effects struck all classes, one could identify some individual patterns.

✠

Prior to the Revolution, tobacco was exchanged for British products, but seldom did the balance sheet favor the planter. Acts of 1777 and 1779 sought to alleviate this problem but the Treaty of 1783 reestablished his debt obligations. Besides Virginia's personal debt and property losses, it had incurred a large state debt and an unfortunate shortage of redeemable state funds. Farmers required new acreage to expand their farms; planters had to overcome crop failures; debtors had to pay local merchants; and British factors held thousands of pounds of planter liabilities. This economic tidal wave also swept up poor farmers, middle-class tradesmen, and even some Federalist planters who were already in arrears. Some of them argued that in this age of rationalism they had the right to ignore their wartime debts and begin clear of them. Consequently, Virginians gravitated to one of three different opinions concerning debt payment. Some, mostly Federalists, wanted to remove all legal impediments to debt collection. Others accepted that dictum but insisted on an installment payment plan. A third group decided that the only logical procedure was to wait for ratification to define the process. When the house offered a bill to make "all laws repugnant to the peace treaty" illegal, the delegates amended it with a clause that suspended the repeal until every state passed a similar act. Even the powerful parliamentarian Patrick Henry failed in his attempt to suspend the amended act. The house also defeated the notion of debt installments. After this flurry of motions, it passed the original bill amended so that it would not come into force until Great Britain lived up to its obligations.

Shortly after the Revolution, the friends of creditors, led by George Mason and James Madison, had planned the redemption of a large measure of Virginia's war debt. They accepted paper money for taxation, sold western land and confiscated Loyalist estates. After its collection, the government destroyed the paper money to prevent any reissue. Also, Virginia diverted much of its assigned congressional requisitions to a state debt sinking fund. It also collected some congressional tobacco export taxes necessary for a predicted special requisition. When Congress repealed it, the funds were diverted to debt payment. If one added land taxes to the fund, one could see that, on its own recognizance, Virginia planned to satisfy its war obligations. Unfortunately, if the federal government implemented a plan to pay state debts, Virginians might find their altruistic actions had backfired.

Many Virginians wanted to circumscribe congressional power. They recognized the logic for some increases but were unwilling to amend the basic Articles' thrust because the states were sovereign and Congress was their creature. In two instances the proposed Constitution attempted to adjust the basic relationship. First, it sought the power to raise import taxes. Second, it claimed power over commerce. In each case, Virginia delegates recognized Congress's attempts to free itself from the states' stranglehold and quashed it. When each attempt was rewritten to ensure the supremacy of the states, it passed. The Jay-Gordoqui imbroglio, while not a part of the Treaty, was a vital interest to the Kentucky and western delegates who seemed to hold the fate of ratification in their hands. The Treaty sensitized Kentuckians to the importance of sectional politics. As a result, they examined the Constitution under this rubric. One conclusion was that northerners were unhappy with the Revolution's aftermath since Congress was powerless to coerce the sovereign states into following the terms of the Treaty and had determined to change their course. The government's ineptitude was exacerbated by the constant differences of opinion on most issues. A single voice representing the United States, whether within the Articles, or in the new Constitution, seemed mandatory.

Although the above irritants annoyed Virginians, the issue that generated the greatest heat was the Treaty of Paris (1783). Each party found reasons to avoid its provisions. The mistrust between the signatories extended to the western forts, interned slaves, and the navigation of the Mississippi. The British maintained control of their frontier forts and refused to return interned slaves while Virginia would not restore property to British sympathizers and even passed laws that prevented the collection of British debts. To intensify this issue, Virginians often paid their debts with devalued paper money. Unfortunately for creditors, the Commonwealth passed an inflammatory act refusing full implementation of the Treaty until Britain returned all the forts. In addition, it had to return all captured slaves or fully compensate their former owners.

The government's lack of power to enforce treaties was a huge roadblock. As long as luminaries like James Monroe and George Nicholas disagreed on its necessity, there would be little chance of compromise. The former argued that Great Britain initiated the standoff by refusing to compensate for slave loss. The latter countered that America was the instigator because of her insistence on immediate control of western posts. Still, the continued occupation of the forts was only one burr under western saddles. Spain might shut off any expansion along the Mississippi. In addition, Indian tribes threatened emigrants who thrust westward. Thus, the continued occupation of the British fur trading posts was only one problem. As with debt payment, Virginians split over these disputes. The small group of British Loyalists urged the United States to obey the articles of the Treaty. Others, like Jefferson and Madison, supported this argument for a different reason since disobeying the Treaty seemed harmful to Virginia's honor. Westerners promoted concessions to the British, hoping that they would respond in kind. A second interest decided that the onus was on the English to act first. These split into two more groups. One considered Congress the vehicle for their demands while the other adopted a wait-and-see attitude. A last group opposed the Treaty without conditions.

So stood Virginia on the brink of the ratification debate. Debt repayment, reneged treaty terms, access to the Mississippi, and a lack of congressional power split Virginians into two competing camps. It remained to be seen whether other factors would join the list.[1]

Before we examine the debate it would be advantageous to categorize the political blocs and their attributes. By 1785, two geographically-defined factions coalesced around these issues within the Old Dominion. The first consisted principally of the counties of the Northern Neck and the James and York river basins of the Tidewater. The second, the Southside, contained the counties below the James River valley, and individual members from the Tidewater and northern Piedmont. The latter did include parts of Caroline and Essex counties, while the former included parts of the upper James plus counties over the Blue Ridge. Two satellite sections gravitated to the main players. The Shenandoah Valley usually allied itself with the Northern Neck while western Virginia typically joined the Southside. The prewar House of Burgesses had been elected during harmonious relations between the classes. Ten years later, just over 10 percent of house delegates were tradesmen or artisans whereas 20 percent were either lawyers or professional men. Interestingly, religious dissidents made up 33 percent. Most delegates were Virginia-born from English stock, lived on a farm and were home schooled. More were newly elected, owned less property, and appeared to be less able than those of the House of Burgesses. Significantly, the power center had shifted westward.

Although there remained two power blocs, their members were less consistent in their political opinions. Moreover, as many as one-third may have been non-aligned. The Southside-centered counties remained debtor rather than creditor friendly, preferred low taxes unless the law assigned the burden to others, and opposed any increase in government power. In addition, it would not protect the Loyalists or British merchants. The opposition Northern Neck coalition favored creditors, Loyalist concerns, the enforcement of the Treaty of Paris, energetic government, and the taxation of farmers but not merchants or lawyers. Kentucky leaned toward the Northern Neck position while western Virginia supported the Southside. However, either could switch depending on the issue.

Age did not act as a faction discriminator. However, house delegate occupation was crucial. At one end of a representation spectrum were the sturdy yeoman farmers while at the other stood lawyers and businessmen. Between them were the planters and others not categorized. One well-known historian refined the delegate groups above based on occupation. The cosmopolitans from the Northern Neck coalition were 37 percent lawyers and merchants, 14 percent other nonfarming individuals, 41 percent planters and 8 percent small farmers. The largely agrarian Southside localists included 9 percent lawyers or merchants, 18 percent other nonfarmers, 39 percent planters, and 34 percent small farmers.

The above data should educate readers about the issues and political blocs in the people's house prior to the ratification convention. An understanding of the state power distribution will illuminate various arguments made later in the Convention. That being said, a seminal comment made by the Federalist Henry Lee should act as a warning to those expecting organized parties. "In all local matters," he said, "I shall be a Virginian: in those of a general nature, I shall not forget that I am an American."

Now that we have a clear picture of the two issue-related factions, we must expand on the characteristics of those who formed the reorganized factions. After all, they would choose the convention delegates who would ratify or deny the Constitution.

As indicated, the Northern Neck, originally settled by the Fairfax family, encompassed the counties between the Potomac and the Rappahannock Rivers and extended west to take in the two most northern counties of the Shenandoah Valley. Over time, the Fairfaxs had sold it off in large lots. The great planters who purchased them moved upstream to open the new frontier. Because of the freeholder requirement for suffrage, the great planter's economic superiority translated into political power. The few eastern counties that mirrored the "large plantations on a waterway to the sea" design allied themselves with the Northern Neck. They were found mainly in the James and York River valleys.

A few of the initial Southside settlers benefited from huge government land grants but the majority bought a small farm and imported slaves. Few navigable rivers truncated the region, it was isolated, and in essence was still the frontier. Recall, it did not include the counties abutting the James as far as Albemarle. They exhibited the characteristics of the Northern Neck — 'major river valley' allies. A few Tidewater and northern Piedmont counties joined the Southside coalition. It was more democratic than its opponents with a reduced planter stranglehold on voting power. East of the Blue Ridge, this bloc was at least as strong as its Northern Neck opponents.

The Southside attracted mainly middle-class, provincial, farmers who were Virginia-born, of English background, and not particularly well educated. Unfortunately, it encompassed many debtors but this did not translate to severe privation. Approximately 50 percent of the adult white men were landowners. Compared with the Northern Neck, it had fewer tenants, more medium-sized farms, fewer small, and some large plantations. Because the freehold was more extensive, the great planters had less economic and political power. More than one-half the counties of the Southside contained the greatest middle-class but only one that may be considered wealthy had it equally distributed.

The Northern Neck contained the largest number of tenants, slaves, and large plantations. Thirty percent were white freeholders, but on average, their farms were smaller. Tenants and rich planters were common while the middle-class was small. Only one county of this coalition had a large middle-class. Approximately one-half the counties could be considered very wealthy but the concentration among a few planters skewed this statistic. Probably, it contained more wealthy men than the Southside but fewer small freeholders. Businessmen, merchants, and lawyers preferred life in the Northern Neck while other occupations diffused equally. The access to large navigable rivers not only offered an economic benefit but also might have been the source of the Neck's cosmopolitan outlook. They provided an access to the worlds of literature and political theory that was not common in the Southside.

Earlier, we had established that English, Scots-Irish, and German immigrants with an independent bent populated the Shenandoah Valley. In tandem with the Allegheny counties, this region replicated the Southside's large middle-class both economically and socially. However, its farm exports usually traveled east to Baltimore or Alexandria along the Potomac; it supported the collection of debts; and having Congress control commerce was not an issue. Perhaps, if the Treaty closed the Mississippi, immigration from Kentucky westward would cease. Thus, the region's eventual position was murky.

By 1780, the western counties had proliferated to such an extent that they totaled more votes than the East. Small farmers and many wealthy planters whose main focus was a free Mississippi inhabited Kentucky. Usually they supported the Southside but many western Virginia inhabitants promoted western expansion and protection from Indian depredations. Obviously, it needed a strong central government to support it. Thus, its allegiance to the Northern Neck on ratification was clear.[2]

✠

Due to the unwritten house convention that only established leaders spoke, it would be informative if we had a thumbnail sketch of their careers. Edmund Randolph (1753–1813) was born at Tazewell Hall in Williamsburg. He attended William and Mary College and later became a lawyer. Considered a distinguished scholar, Randolph also served on Washington's staff but did attend the convention that drafted Virginia's first constitution. His political career began as mayor of Williamsburg. Later, he became attorney general and finally governor of Virginia. Many of his colleagues believed he always tested the wind to see which way the political winds blew.

George Mason (1725–1792), was the master of Gunston Hall and was considered one of the richest planters in Virginia. He held the important post of Fairfax county justice of the peace and had been a member of the House of Burgesses. By 1774 he was active in pre–Revolutionary affairs, finally drafting the Virginia Declaration of Rights. However, Mason became disenchanted with the direction of Virginia's leaders. The house appointed him as a commissioner to the Annapolis Convention but he did not attend. He was considered an excellent debater, astute politician, and man of high principle. He did not foresee a static American society because inevitably, it would evolve toward his detested self-interestedness. However, by fighting the ratification of the Constitution he could slow the process to prevent unnecessary blunders.

James Madison (1751–1836) was the Federalist intellectual dynamo. A member of a large plantation family, he lived at Montpelier in Orange County. Upon graduation from the College of New Jersey [Yale] Madison immersed himself in politics. He was a member of the county committee of safety, the Virginia constitutional convention, the House of Delegates, the council of state and Congress. Moreover, he took a leading hand in the movement to amend the Articles of Confederation. He pressed for both the Annapolis Convention and the constitutional convention. Significantly, his famous *Vices of the Political System* provided a basis for constitutional reform. Unanimously, his peers recognized him as a man of stature because he effortlessly united political acumen and scholarly knowledge. Madison was not a recognized orator like Patrick Henry, but was considered "eloquent" and "convincing." On the other hand, he was stubborn and determined to have his way. Tactically, he was always prepared for debate. Considering these attributes, he was a modest man whom his colleagues found very agreeable. One correspondent reiterated that Madison was a wise, educated statesman, a good friend of Thomas Jefferson, and a staunch friend of France. In a bold prediction, the writer foresaw a future Governor Madison if his excessive modesty did not prevent it. This observation was based on Madison's previous refusal of the post of president of Congress. In two interesting asides, the observer informed his correspondent that one must study Madison for some time to get his measure. Moreover, Madison may have been a deeper thinker that Hamilton, but did not display his brilliance.[3]

George Nicholas was born in Williamsburg about 1755. He was short in stature and obese, but his skill as a debater overshadowed his physical debilities. He attended William and Mary grammar school and then the prestigious university of the same name. During the Revolution, he entered service as a captain and rose to the rank of colonel. Upon his election to the assembly he left the service. In the 1781 session, he promoted a resolution seeking an inquiry into Thomas Jefferson's actions while governor. His specialty was western land law in which he was self-taught. This expertise was crucial during the debates. Shortly after the convention, he moved to Danville, Mercer County, Kentucky and became a leading politician of the new state.

Dumfries, Virginia was the 1736 birthplace of William Grayson. He was more than six feet tall and weighed about 250 pounds, with a large head and Roman nose. Interestingly, he was a counterexample of Main's localist-cosmopolitan dichotomy. Educated at Oxford, he admired Adam Smith's work. Upon his return to Virginia, he practiced law until the Revolution began. He served as a captain in the Prince William County regiment until George Washington invited him onto his staff. Grayson continued these duties until his appointment as a Board of War Commissioner (1779–81). In 1784, he was elected to Congress. Soon, he made it clear that the government badly needed more power. However, the Constitutional allocation was excessive.

Grayson was not considered in the class of our next delegate as an orator but he was a formidable debater because of his straightforward manner. When Virginia chose her senators in 1789, Grayson defeated James Madison for one of its seats. On March 12, 1790, Grayson passed away at his estate. Significantly, his will freed all slaves born there since Independence.

Our final entry was Patrick Henry. He was born May 29, 1736, in Hanover County. His father, John, supervised his home education. However, he taught himself law. From the time he joined the legal fraternity, he was constantly in the forefront of Virginia's struggles for liberty. In 1763, during the famous Parson's Cause, he labeled the king a tyrant and expanded that theme by offering incendiary Stamp Act resolutions in 1765. By 1775, Henry was urging his fellow Virginians to take up arms against the British. It was during this time that he uttered the phrase that brought him everlasting fame. "I know not what course others may take," he thundered, "but as for me, give me liberty or give me death." In the following years he was never out of office, either as governor or delegate. Frequently, as he aged, Henry refused prestigious positions in the national government. On June 6, 1799, Henry died at his Red Hill estate.

Unfortunately, a bystander's words cannot capture the power of Henry's oratory or its effect on his audience. He seldom committed his speeches to paper. Instead, he depended upon the evangelistic style he adopted to captivate his listeners. As one might expect, the political influence of this voice of the people produced enemies. Jefferson hated him because he concluded that Henry was the behind-the-scenes instigator of Nicholas's inquiry resolution. The Lees, Richard Henry and Arthur, led one of the two assembly factions. Henry commanded the other and that fact was important enough for the brothers to dislike him. Madison and Henry clashed directly on tax collection, British debts, and the necessity for a new Virginia constitution. In each case, Henry carried the day. Apparently, the animus between these famous opponents did not deter Henry because he viewed himself as the protector of the rights, liberty, and happiness of the people. On the other hand, John Marshall, a staunch Federalist, admired Henry and recognized his power over the assembly. Perhaps a memorable Madison anecdote best illustrated his persuasive power. According to Hugh Grigsby,

> Mr. Madison, in his latter days, told Governor Coles that when he had made a most conclusive argument in favor of the Constitution, Henry would rise to reply to him, and by some insignificant action, such as a pause, a shake of the head, or a striking gesture, before he offered a word, would undo all that Madison had been trying to do for an hour before.

Of all ratification's opponents, Federalists feared Henry more than any other.[4]

Earlier, we examined the competing geographical regions and established their composition. Perhaps a closer view of their representatives would complete the picture. The New York merchant, David Henley, prior to the Virginia convention studied the list of delegates and categorized 151 by faction. He was correct in 146 of the 151 and 82 of the 85 Federalists. He did not include the remainder. Since he did not consider himself particularly astute, perhaps the categorization was not as difficult as one might think. An examination of the delegates may shine some light on his choices.

All the delegates, regardless of faction, owned some kind of property. In addition, it was about an equal value and was owned by the same class — the gentry. Despite ratification differences, they did share an immense pride in Virginia and her accomplishments. Norman Risjord applied a mathematical method called multivariate analysis to the delegate data and arrived at several interesting conclusions. He agreed that no social or economic divide existed between the two factions; the wealthiest delegates were Federalists who favored ratification, but he could not verify a direct connection between wealth, Federalists, and ratification opinion; Federalists differed from most Virginians and may have felt isolated from them; the perspective of provincialism or cosmopolitanism defined each group; and, it was likely that residence was the most important discriminator between the factions.

The gentry provided most of the delegates. They included planters, land speculators, former officers and professional men. Two factors led to their election. About 50 percent of the farmers within each county failed to satisfy the suffrage requirements. Moreover, those who qualified still voted for the same representatives that they had always supported, the gentry. In our case, Northern Neck wealthy planters slightly outnumbered those from the Southside. Since they came from the same class and had the same interests, it was more likely that ratification would have a geographic component.

The upper class exhibited certain interesting, unique attributes. They were practical men who elevated the successful businessman/planter on a pedestal. Still, they recognized that political ideals had value and were worth a struggle, particularly if they could be bent to Virginia's interests. Also, depending on circumstances, they could take on either of two seemingly contradictory roles. During the war the English viewed them as radicals. Yet, they adopted conservative opinions toward the government that had evolved in Virginia because they recognized the basis of their power and would fight to retain it. On the other hand, they willingly surrendered non-political powers such as the separation of church and state and a rewrite of the criminal code. The gentry's elevated status threatened to make a planter infallible in his own eyes, a condition that was not likely to promote compromise with his peers.

The Antifederalist bloc contained three identifiable subgroups. Patrick Henry, who opposed any augmentation of federal power, symbolized the radicals. His priorities had changed little from the days of "Give me liberty or give me death." Virginians, he believed, must preserve liberty above all. If it was secured, they could concentrate on Union. George Mason, a moderate, demanded a Bill of Rights. Nevertheless, its inclusion could not reduce his conviction that the proposed government had gathered too much power to itself. Unlike his opponents, he was uninterested in reshaping Virginia's society. James Monroe and William Grayson also took moderate positions. The latter rejected any clauses designed to engineer societal changes meant to control an unruly populace. He insisted that mankind could govern itself within a government it had designed; coercive measures were unnecessary. The former saw some benefits from a more energetic government. Still, he refused to transfer state power to the national government. In addition, he could not understand how prior amendments could affect the integrity of the Constitution. Individualists like Richard Henry Lee would countenance a small increase in government power, a taxing provision, and Madison's veto on state laws that conflicted with those of the national government. However, he was suspicious that the eight eastern states intended to regulate trade in their favor and that talk of coercing a state suggested a threat to liberty. Maybe an edit of the Articles of Confederation might be sufficient to achieve the necessary changes. His attention was on power and who would wield it. For Lee, it must be the South.

The opponents of ratification were older than their counterparts, more tuned to individual rights, and considered Virginia a unique state. They believed the proposed commerce clause punished the Old Dominion and some promoted the issuance of paper money to reduce debt. Although usually linked with the Northern Neck position, many lawyers joined small farmers, debtors, and the large middle-class from the Southside in the Antifederalist cause.

The Federalists were younger and grew up during the Revolution. As we know, they were well-to-do, often educated or even born in other jurisdictions, business-oriented, and had held significant rank in the Revolutionary officers' cadre. Despite these qualifications, they were a minority within the state. The most extreme nationalist was Henry (Light Horse Harry) Lee. He concluded that only the great men of Virginia could rule, and he invested his future with them. John Marshall agreed with Lee. To this future jurist, only the unamended Constitution could save America from the ravages of its ungovernable citizens. Madison seconded the importance of ratification to the nation, but he was not as confident as Lee and Marshall that Americans could not govern themselves. Edmund Pendleton was more moderate in his views. The potential power of the commerce clause worried him and he was certain that the Mississippi must remain an American river. Nevertheless, his study of the Constitution led him to believe that it, with all its flaws, was still the best way to preserve the Union.

As one might expect, not all the convention delegates fit nicely into the slots that we have used to organize their peers. The two major factions had to win the votes of several smaller groups and uncommitted individuals. For example, some would agree with Jefferson that the addition of a Bill of Rights might be necessary. Others were suspicious of the Madisonian concept of stability based on competing political self-interest groups. How could it supplant the corporate ideal of a virtuous citizenry intent on majority rule? This class of delegate must have found the competing models with their various corollaries very difficult to collate. Some, but not all, of one brand of government ideals, might be acceptable if joined with an equal number of those from the competition. Unfortunately, only one model, with all its foibles and visionary ideals, confronted the delegates. These uncommitted delegates were those to be courted.

These considerations suggested that we should review the Jackson Turner Main model and link our issue based parties and convention delegates. Northern Neck coalition Federalists/cosmopolitans commonly contacted the outside world while Southside faction Antifederalists/localists did not. Federalists were often business-oriented while their opponents were associated with land. The latter had little formal education while the former was well educated. During the war, Federalist delegates achieved higher rank than their opponents. Although Federalists lived next to a sizable navigable river, Antifederalists were limited to the uplands. They were often middle-class debtors whereas Federalists were upper class creditors, but wealth was not a causative discriminator for delegate selection.

George Mason held a particularly harsh view of some Federalists. He reserved his rancor for a set of ratification supporters who had publicly approved the Revolution to avoid confiscation of their estates. However, in the background, they did everything in their power to obstruct separation. They opposed the convention of 1776, the passage of the Virginia constitution, and even the Articles of Confederation until Virginia achieved independence. At that juncture, this group promoted a government mirroring that of Great Britain. Since "these persons were possessed of high position, wide family connections, and abilities, their influence was sensibly felt by those able and patriotic men who believed that the Constitution, however wisely intended by its framers, would ultimately result in impairing the liberty of the people." Mason expressed his opinion in these words,

> I have some acquaintance with a great many characters who favor this Government, their connections, their conduct, their political principles, and a number of other circumstances. There are a great many wise and good men among them. But when I look around the number of my acquaintance in Virginia, the country wherein I was born, and have lived so many years, and observe *who* are the warmest and most zealous friends to this new government, it makes me think of the story of the cat transformed into a fine lady — forgetting her transformation, and happening to see a rat, she could not restrain herself, but sprung upon it out of the chair.

There were several other potential but ultimately ineffectual reasons that might affect a delegate's vote. Virginia contained approximately 290,000 slaves circa 1789. Although the contending parties owned roughly the same number, in both raw data and relative to white inhabitants, the Antifederalists held more slaves. The delegates were commonly large slave owners on both sides. As a result, slave-holding did not affect attitudes toward ratification. The Revolutionary officers received large grants of western land in return for their faithful service. One might conclude that this economic bias might cause them to support ratification. However, they did not. About one-half voted against it. Evangelistic dissidents, residents of the Southside, concluded that the Constitution presaged a return to the days of an established church. In March 1788, the Virginia Baptist Association voted against ratification. However, one must be careful not to overemphasize this relationship. Recall that the Baptists were only about 10 percent of the population.

After Virginians collated this information, they elected their delegates. East of the Blue Ridge the Antifederalists had a majority of twelve, but the Federalists swept the Valley. This must have been a surprise to some Virginians who expected it to support the Southside. From the Valley point of view, the issues of British debt collection and congressional control of commerce counterbalanced its usual allegiance. Antifederalists seemed to control Kentucky but western Virginia leaned toward ratification. Again, this was unexpected. Usually a Southside ally, it had slipped into the Northern Neck camp. The repeal of acts that conflicted with the Treaty, a logical extension of ratification, promised a return to debt payment and a solution to British outpost issues. In essence, Virginia had chosen eighty-five Federalists, sixty-six Antifederalists, and three unknowns. The West would settle the contest. Most pundits agreed that the result would be close, only three or four votes either way.[5]

Before we concentrate on the individual debates, it might prove valuable to list probable friction points. Some Antifederalists decided that the profit motive drove Federalists. If the general government assumed the Revolutionary war debts, those holding its paper would benefit. Most expected an eventual drift toward a consolidated government, while others judged the document too vague in crucial areas. In addition, Patrick Henry argued that the substitution of the Constitution for the Articles appealed only to the gentry. The common people experienced no problems with the current system.

Tacticians agonized over the viewpoint of the western delegates. They had calculated that if Kentucky plus one county on the Mississippi voted against ratification, the likelihood was that it would fail. Of course, selection of this option would mean that George Washington could not be president. In a far-fetched scenario, it might also lead to the formation of a Virginia, Kentucky, North Carolina, South Carolina, Georgia confederacy. Each faction was bound to expend its resources persuading the western delegates of the correctness of its position. This would be difficult since the Federalists knew that the populace did not support ratification. Perhaps a roster of distinguished Virginians who would argue their case could overcome this glaring weakness.

As important as these may have been, the principal focus was on the relationship between power and liberty. Clause after clause faced the liberty test. Would it promote that ideal or infringe on it? Discussion had convinced Antifederalists that they could preserve it only if Virginia remained sovereign. Experience had taught them that the combined loss of the sword and the purse would lead to tyranny. On the other hand, Federalists knew that only an energetic government could preserve liberty. Perhaps it should be dependent, claimed Antifederalist theory, on a citizenry that was "virtuous enough to punish themselves."

Federalists' rhetoric had a different tone because their role had changed. A new system of government that favored their notions had filled the blank slate of the Philadelphia Convention. Confederacies, they said, were bad for the people. Therefore it was their task to ensure that the states did not retain their sovereignty. Moreover, the constant agitation of the Antifederalists, who equated every loss of power with tyranny, made liberty difficult to attain.

Supporters of the Constitution linked the role of government to liberty. Virginia desperately needed the new government to survive. It was a friend, a compact, designed to curb "licentiousness, factions, turbulence, and other violations of the rules of society" to preserve liberty. Rather than depending on society to prevent corruption, government would assume the task. Nevertheless, Henry, who also defined the Constitution as a compact, was happy to place liberty in the hands of "the American spirit."

The recognition of the Constitution as a compact was bound to have many corollaries. Henry voiced an important caveat. "Do you enter into a compact of government first, and afterwards settle the terms of government?"[6]

The opening Antifederalist gambit concentrated on the legality of the Convention process. They were adamant that the people of the several states had not assigned their Philadelphia delegates any power to conceive a new system of government. In addition, they would not accept that only nine states, rather than thirteen, were acceptable for ratification. To emphasize these concerns, Henry requested that the secretary of the convention read the terms of the act appointing the Virginian delegates. Realizing the potential damage to the ratification process, Edmund Pendleton quickly assumed a bold offensive. It was not the task of this convention to decide whether the Philadelphia delegates had "exceeded their powers." Breathtakingly, he ignored the continuity of the ratification process and stated that the Virginia convention's only duty was to rule on the acceptability of the new government. Yes, he admitted, the original intent of the process was to repair the Articles of Confederation. However, the Convention could not achieve it, and thus the delegates constructed another system. Extending the Pendleton axiom, he argued that the delegates' freedom to propose included a design for a new Constitution. Since the people had the power, they had the right to select the Constitution they preferred even if one or two insignificant laws were broken in the process. Therefore, finally returning to the question, no reading of the instructions was necessary. Pendleton left the convention with two linked ideas. Only the people could form a government. Moreover, the Virginia convention's duty was only to propose, not to determine.

Surprisingly, Henry accepted this illogical, unfocussed argument and the convention continued unfazed.[7]

✠

Certainly, there was a difference of opinion about the object of the Constitution. Despite
its irrelevance to the Virginia convention, we know that its thrust had convinced Antifederalists that updating a defective Articles should be the goal. Patrick Henry admitted that the
existing Articles' government "is without energy" but that was not a defect. Essentially, it was
exactly the government he wanted. As we have seen, he was sure that the Revolutionary spirit
would promote liberty.

The Federalists promoted a view diametrically opposed to this position. Government must
intervene to overcome the licentiousness of the people. Pendleton, particularly, stressed that
recent studies by eminent authors like John Locke, promoted the idea that nations required
strong governments "to preserve virtue, which they [the writers] all declare to be the pillar on
which the Government, and liberty, its object, must stand." To Federalists, society's miscre-
ants would destroy liberty unless government intervened.[8]

✠

The people's delegates were ready to scrutinize the transmitted Constitution. Originally,
the assembly designated the Virginia State House in Richmond as the convention site, but
when June 2 arrived, the huge audience forced it to move. Two days later, the convention
convened at New Academy on Shockoe Hill. After completing the initial bookkeeping tasks,
George Mason surprised the convention by offering a resolution to debate the constitution
clause-by-clause. Fathoming his motive for offering a resolution that fit nicely into Federalist strategy was difficult. Perhaps, as Lance Banning suggested, Mason concluded that the
opposition, with most delegates, might short-circuit debate on any Antifederalist arguments
supporting previous amendments. Hugh Grigsby argued that the resolution played into Federalist hands. Realistically, there existed only two ways to defeat ratification. The Antifederalists could either prove that in either its entirety it did not "attain the end of its creation" or
they must demonstrate the deleterious effects that various clauses had on Virginia. For example, they believed passionately that the Constitution threatened Virginia's liberty. However,
the resolution forced them to detect the danger lurking within one, and only one, Article at
a time. Clause-by-clause debate negated this strategy in full or in part. Thankfully, the experienced politician John Tyler alleviated part of the problem. He moved the debate to a Committee of the Whole.[9]

✠

Tactically, we can divide the formal debate into two equal time frames. The first half was
freewheeling, unstructured, and often confrontational as the debaters strung together disparate Articles to prove, to their satisfaction, general conclusions. When this methodology
threatened to both undo Federalist tactics and extend the debate endlessly, Francis Corbin
offered a resolution, which passed, to return to the natural order, clause-by-clause. The second half lacked the intensity of the first. The conventioneers, with the notable exception of
Henry, followed the new rule. As they debated each power, Federalists insisted that it was
mandatory and simultaneously checked and balanced.

Henry laid down the Antifederalist game plan. Repeatedly he challenged principles rather
than specifics. Clearly, his interest was Virginia, not the Union, and this resulted in a bunker

"we versus them" mentality. It was his rejection of the initial clause-by-clause resolution that widened debate. When he attacked generally, the Federalists were forced to respond in kind. Repeatedly, he reminded his peers that it was nonsensical for Virginia to consent to a compact and in the sequel, agree to its terms. William Grayson picked up this theme. Why the hurry? Why should the delegates allow themselves to be stampeded into ratification when Virginia could easily stand on its own? In addition, Henry often inserted positive asides on the corporate view of republicanism.

The Federalists knew they could never defeat Henry individually by pure debate, so they developed a team approach, assigning different areas to each member. The logicians were Madison and Marshall; Nicholas took charge of Virginia-centric affairs; Randolph was the infighter; Pendleton handled appeals to prestige; and Nicholas and Madison acted as whippers-in for each task. The first challenge they faced was Henry's insistence on following his own agenda. Continually, they called for proper order but he rebuffed them. Finally, after a disastrous debate on the navigation of the Mississippi, the Federalists corralled him and debate returned to a clause-by-clause examination of the Constitution.[10]

Of course, Virginians were anxious to find solutions for the three principal issues confronting the state. William Grayson and Edmund Randolph offered contrasting notions on debt repayment. Grayson could not fathom the basis of the fuss. Had not Congress passed an act on May 7, 1787, that organized the payment of state debts to Congress? Still, Randolph urged that the United States pay all debts promptly because "justice and honor require that they be punctually paid." After he insisted it was a virtuous initiative, Henry could hardly contain himself. The Constitution ensured that thousands of pounds of worthless continental money must be redeemed producing a huge state debt. How could Virginians, ravaged by war and depression, pay their share? The severe shortage of money was an economic burden. If they did follow Randolph's suggestion, how would ratification promote manufacturing in the face of a lack of capital? Henry's principal fear was that Article I, Section 10 would force Virginia to match "her share of the Continental money, shilling for shilling." The mass speculation in war certificates promoted the expectation that the new owners would recoup the face value, not the reduced rate paid by them. Madison and Mason admitted that America was rife with speculation on debt and paper money. "Many individuals," claimed Mason, "had speculated so as to make great fortunes on the ruin of their fellow citizens."

The payment of British debts had an economic corollary that made Antifederalists bristle. Recall that many Virginians considered any payment of British debts a "harsh measure." Virginia had worked hard to collect funds to assume and amalgamate its debts only to have foreign creditors claim them. Nevertheless, the Constitution might make those indebted, and sued by British citizens, travel to the faraway seat of government for trial.

Randolph had predicted the agitation over this clause. Shortly after the Constitutional Convention, he hazarded an opinion on the debt provisions to Madison. Opposition would center on the long trip litigants must take to the federal seat of government. In an aside, he told Madison that the inclusion of a similar clause in the Constitution was "odious." The likelihood of litigation moved Henry, who knew that debt payments had been withheld from the British "contrary to the Treaty." James Innes warned that Great Britain would not sit idly by while Americans deprived Englishmen of just compensation.

If the mood of Virginians on debt payment was accurate, the scenario above amounted to a double penalty. Virginia had already collected, but not dispersed, funds for this purpose.

According to Henry, "if ever a suit be instituted by a British creditor for a sum which the defendant does not in fact owe, he had better pay it than appeal to the Federal Supreme Court." Why? The Treaty debts were incurred prior to the formation of the courts that would hear them. Thus, the judiciary must issue the equivalent of *ex post facto* laws commonly frowned upon by the legal community. Also, these new courts would be unfamiliar with the state law in force when the supposed debt was initiated. The result was an uncomfortable link between debts and the judiciary.

Mason agreed that the possibility of a double payment existed, but despite its effect on some of his peers, he and Randolph insisted that Americans must pay their British debts. However, he rejected the notion that the central government could bring a state to court "like a delinquent individual." Partially negating his argument, he predicted that if the courts interfered in the debt payment problem, great swathes of the Valley would fall to British companies who would resell them at great profit.

Another Antifederalist, William Grayson, supported his colleague on the Treaty debt obligation. However, it was merely a vehicle for his attack on the court-debt-speculation linkage. "The treaty of peace with Great-Britain," he observed, "does not require that the creditors should be put in a better situation than they were, but that there should be no hindrance to the collection of debts. It is therefore unwise and impolitic to give these creditors such an advantage over the debtors." Observe the terms but refuse to feather the nests of speculators was his watchword.

Linkages were also at the forefront of Edmund Randolph's thoughts. He decried that built by the Antifederalists between Kentucky, the Mississippi, and the Treaty of Peace for political advantage. However, he realized the existence of a budding problem. If Great Britain had navigation rights prior to the Revolution, he claimed, then the United States could only assume them and no others. If Great Britain had no rights, neither did America. In any case, according to Randolph, no danger was associated with the Constitution government adopting the problem.[11]

Debate over the peace treaty and the fate of the Mississippi matched the fevered confrontation over debt repayment. Because of its influence on the crucial Kentucky votes and Virginia prosperity, the Antifederalists hammered their opponents unmercifully over the presumed threat to the navigation of the Mississippi. As usual, Henry took the lead. The new government, assisted by some delegates, was prepared to bargain away the rights to the Mississippi; reasonable men would never be convinced that forfeiting navigation rights in the short run must precede future access; America was naturally split into carrying and noncarrying states; and a glance at the list of delegates who supported the Jay-Gordoqui Treaty would persuade anyone that their motivation was their own sectional self-interest. Virginia must fight for access to the Mississippi because it was vital to its prosperity. Moreover, if they did not, Kentuckians would despise them forever for abandoning their navigation rights. Monroe replayed Jay's contention that commercial access in return for a twenty-five year ban on navigation was equitable. Congress, especially southern members, were aghast at Jay's temerity. He had proceeded with a treaty despite its order to desist. However, Monroe was hesitant to translate this single incident into a plot to "depress the growth and increasing population of the western country" and benefit the East over the South. Yet, he was sure that the charge was true in this specific case. He predicted that if the matter came before the new Senate it would follow Jay's vision and give up the Mississippi navigation rights to reduce southern power and influence. Moreover, like Henry, he decided that such an action would be in the carrying states' interests and people usually followed that path. William Grayson picked up that theme. It was natural, he insisted, for the carrying states to attempt to blunt the power of the producing states because it was in their interest to do so. Southern control of westward expansion to the Mississippi did not fit that goal. All one had to do to demonstrate the danger to the South was to perform some simple arithmetic. In a worst case scenario, the president plus ten senators, that is, five northern states, could bargain away navigation of the Mississippi. Grayson summed his translation of the northern agenda in these words:

> *Let us prevent any new States from rising in the Western world, or they will out-vote us — We will lose our importance, and become as nothing in the scale of nations. If we do not prevent it, our countrymen will remove to those places, instead of going to sea, and we will receive no particular tribute or advantage from them.* (Italics Grayson)

The Federalist response was initiated, unfortunately, by Henry Lee who admitted that he had speculated in Mississippi land. His investment had been about £8000 in gold. Nevertheless, he "united private interests to public interest" and concluded that he was "promoting the real interest of the people." Madison tried to blunt the charge of self-interest. It was not true, he claimed, that "the people at large, or the prevailing character of the Eastern States" approved of the Jay-Gordoqui Treaty. Was it not more likely that they, and not the South, would benefit more from an open Mississippi? Nicholas followed this line of reasoning.

> But we are told that we may not trust them, because self-interest will govern them. To that interest I will appeal. You have been told that there was a difference between the states — that they were naturally divided into carrying and non-carrying states. It is not reasonable to presume that the advancement of population and agriculture, in the western country, will mostly operate in favor of those states, who, from their situation, are best calculated to carry the produce of America to foreign markets.

Moreover, in a ploy intended to shift the Antifederalist focus, he claimed that the whole Gordoqui affair was the fault of the Articles Congress that had totally mismanaged it. Remember, most congressmen had represented the Atlantic seaboard. In contradistinction, the proposed House of Representatives will not be influenced similarly by commercial policy because "they are drawn from the landed interest; taken from the states at large, and many of them from the Western country."[12]

Differences of opinion over congressional power extended throughout the convention. Henry, soon after the debate started, identified a pertinent question that delegates must wrestle with if they were to assign Congress significant power. How could one trust his representative? How did the Federalist Philadelphia majority act? It ignored their well-defined task to update the Articles and instead returned home with a novel system that assigned unexpected powers to Congress. Suppose one sent the same man to the House of Representatives. Could one trust him to fulfill one's mandate? Remember that only a vague Constitution with unclear lines of demarcation between power and privilege would bind him. Perhaps fewer powers, like those delegated in the state-centered Articles, would be less likely to lead to tyranny compared with those of the government-centered Constitution.

Madison could not allow this aspersion on future representatives to pass. Logically, they were just as likely to do their duty as not. Still, the convention should not interpret his statement as a blanket acceptance that they would display "exalted integrity and sublime virtue." Instead, he reminded his audience that republican principles were predicated on an informed electorate. Also, "the security of the people" could never be threatened "unless a majority of the Representatives should concur." How this squared with his cherished view on minority rights, he did not explain.

Marshall seconded the proposition that the people had no option but to trust their representatives. If their power were truncated, how could they act in the interest of the people? Henry Lee contended that if the members of Great Britain's House of Commons could resist the king, then surely Virginians could expect their representatives to be at least as upstanding. Nicholas concurred. The supposition that Congress "from a love of power natural to all, will, in general, abuse that with which they are invested" was nonsense. On the other hand, the Federalist Francis Corbin seemed to echo the opposition view. To secure liberty, he postulated, one must limit government power by specifying it exactly. It was the people's task to insist that their representatives exercised only those powers. Returning to the party line, he noted that if one examined the powers assigned in the Constitution, one would not find any that endangered liberty.

The disposition of power was at the heart of the ratification process. Most Antifederalists recognized the need for some Constitutional expansion but refused any argument that offered only two choices, a flawed Articles or an overwhelmingly nationalist Constitution. They remembered vividly Parliament's oppression. Surely room to compromise existed between the two extremes to include, at least, a Bill of Rights and other checks on power. Mason disagreed with a Federalist proposition on comparative government powers. It assumed the Constitution government had the same powers as its predecessor. Remember, he warned, that government drew its powers from the states. Moreover, on its face, the Constitution assumed many "great and important powers" which were not the result of state transfer. Unfortunately, he bemoaned, the natural history of deliberative bodies was that in time, they would usurp power and destroy the state governments "by insidious under handed means, than such as could be openly practiced." James Monroe picked up this theme. "I only wish," he propounded, "to prevent it [national government] from doing harm, either to states or individuals; and the rights and interests of both, in a variety of instances in which they are now left unprotected, might, in my opinion, be better guarded." Also, the methodology associated with assigning representatives persuaded him that "no powers ought to be given, but such as are absolutely necessary." Patrick Henry had one query. Rather than argue about the abuse of power, should not Federalists wonder whether it was necessary? Grayson chided Marshall over the lack of checks on congressional power while Henry hammered home the point. "Can you say," he mused, "that you will be safe when you give such unlimited powers, without any real responsibility?"

Federalist proponents denied these Antifederalist claims. George Nicholas considered the argument that government must be small to be ludicrous. Obviously,

> powers, being given for some certain purpose, ought to be proportionate for the purpose, or else the end for which they are delegated will not be answered...: if they be too small, the government must molder and decay away; if too extensive, the people must be oppressed.

Edmund Randolph had earlier remarked that it had been a grave mistake to assign the Confederation power without the means to support it. He added a corollary to this generalization: "Ask if the powers be unnecessary. If the end proposed can be obtained by any other means, the powers may be unnecessary." Madison and Pendleton each reiterated a Federalist maxim. The government must have power "to make people do their duty" and protect liberty. Otherwise, one had no government at all. Poorly conceived state constitutions were a real danger to private and property rights. Edmund Pendleton reminded the convention that the system under discussion could never be mislabeled a consolidated government because it did not hold all the power within its hands. For example, Congress could not legislate on purely local Virginia affairs. Moreover, a significant part of the national government depended on the participation of the states. The irrepressible Henry Lee offered a simple test for the application of power that later motivated him to leave the Federalist party. "*Is it enumerated in the Constitution?*" If so, the power was legal, otherwise it was "arbitrary and unconstitutional." Randolph, continuing this line of reasoning, added that if the government usurped any power, the states could stop it. Perhaps George Mason delineated the crux of the dispute when he categorized the Antifederalists position.

> We wish only our rights to be secured. We must have such amendments as will secure the liberties and happiness of the people on a plain, simple construction, not on a doubtful ground. We wish to give the government sufficient energy, on real republican principles; but we wish to withhold such powers as are not absolutely necessary in themselves, but are extremely dangerous. We wish to shut the door against corruption in that place where it is most dangerous — to secure against corruption of our own representatives.

Power sharing between state and national governments, surprisingly, received only nominal attention. Monroe initiated it by assigning the federal government power over "national affairs" while the states would control "local interests." Mason proceeded one step further. He demanded "a line between the general and state governments." Ominously, he concluded that if his suggestion were not considered, the "dangerous clashing of interest and power ... must ... terminate in the destruction of one or the other." Nicholas also contemplated a division of power. Unfortunately, he left it clear that "the great national interests of the union" superseded the "local concerns [of] the state legislatures." Nevertheless, he did consider the states a natural check on the federal government. They would spread the alarm to the people if government usurped power.

One class of assigned powers had received no attention previously. It was the power of exclusive or concurrent jurisdiction and its genesis was the militia debate. During his defense of the congressional power to arm it, James Madison, supported by John Marshall, argued that although the Constitution had designated the duty to Congress it was a shared power. "The power," assured Madison, "is concurrent and not exclusive." Thus, the Constitution divided the oversight of the militia. One must assume that the states retained powers not given by implication. If so, they retained the "power to command and govern their militia ... and have it still, undeniably, unless there is something in the Constitution that takes it away." Since that document included no such restriction, the power to arm the militia remained with the state.

Henry spied an opening that would allow him to link this interpretation negatively with another festering issue. If the Federalist interpretation was relevant, should not the Constitution contain a clause, to protect the people, that prevented Congress from assuming powers not expressly listed? His colleague, William Grayson, pursued the original contention. Madison's interpretation must be false. Such reasoning led one to conclude that the states could call up the militia to suppress an insurrection although the law of nations declared that assigned power was exclusive power. To maximize their arguments, Henry added a pertinent example. Suppose insurrections broke out in two neighboring states. Congress can call the militia from the first to duty in the second whereas the governor of the first can now call them for his own use. "Which call is to be obeyed, the congressional call, or the call of the State Legislature?"

It was clear to Henry that the people gave the enumerated congressional powers exclusively. For example, if the concept that "rights not given were retained" was true, why were clauses restraining Congress included in the Constitution? Obviously, if these had not been added, "they [representatives] could have done what they [Constitutional articles] prohibit." Surely this argument negated the idea of concurrency.[13]

✠

So far, our discussion has been driven by issues festering before the Convention's advent. We will now extend our investigation to new powers it assigned to the president, judiciary, and Congress.

Madison admitted that assigning and organizing presidential powers had been the most onerous part of the Convention. However, after much debate "that mode which was judged most expedient was adopted." Henry contrasted them with those of a king. The latter, who usually had a lengthy reign, knew that his own interests must coincide with those of his people. Otherwise, revolution lurked in his realm. By comparison, the American president held office for only a few years. It was human nature that he would act in his own self-interest rather than that of his constituents. Mason criticized the lack of any rotation policy. "The great fundamental principle of responsibility in republicanism," he said, "is here sap[p]ed.... Nothing is so essential to the preservation of a Republic and Government, as a periodical rotation." This maxim, if adopted, would avoid corruption. The president would return to his state and reacquaint himself with the interests of the people.

Edmund Pendleton, Federalist, had strong reservations concerning presidential power. On reflection, he concluded that the powers assigned to the executive mirrored the British "first magistrate." It was possible that the people would lose their liberty to him because his interests were bound to differ from theirs and his wealth of powers and undefined rights would magnify this distinction. Ultimately his own interests would force him to downplay those of the people. To exacerbate matters, some careless Antifederalists demanded a Bill of Rights that translated to "this far shall you oppress us, and no farther."

Monroe, Grayson, and Mason also suspected the powers assigned to the president. According to Monroe, they required two mandatory checks and neither was present. The president must be dependent on the people for his election. Also, in case of impeachment, a panel of "dispassionate judges" should try him. Grayson shook his head at the inconsistency of the election process. Just look at the different agencies that might have jurisdiction at different times with a vote thrown into Congress. Mason decried the possibility that the Senate and president might unite to usurp government. Also, might the president command the Army in person?

Antifederalists remained fixed on the conviction that the Senate had gleaned too much power. It should not have the ability "to propose or concur in amendments to money bills" because amending was synonymous with proposing. Only "the immediate Representatives of the people" should have this power. Unfortunately, the senatorial right of reelection for consecutive six-year terms ensured that its members would become citizens of the capital city.

Federalists countered the thrust at Legislative power. State legislatures could not recall their senators because it would "impair their independence and firmness"; the withholding of the power to amend money bills would force the upper house to accept or reject the complete bill and prove time wasting; and the minimization of the number of representatives would provide a buffer that protected the electorate from corrupt candidates. The latter assertion would ensure that only meritorious men were elected to the Senate.

The article defining the national judiciary inspired more debate than its coordinate branches because of its hazy organization. Madison attempted to force a positive face on the result. "Were I to select a power which might be given with confidence," he asserted, "it would be Judicial power. This power cannot be abused without raising the indignation of all the people of the States." He agreed that Article III would promote debate, but, over time, experience had convinced him that the government would "do what is for the interest of the United States." If the convention would only take a "liberal construction" of the powers associated with the judiciary, it would realize they presented no danger. Nevertheless, he did not prevent serious dissent.

Although several irritants produced contentious differences, by far the most serious were the battles over the conflicts in jurisdiction. Pendleton was unfazed by the problem. To this learned judge, either the state or federal courts could adjudicate an issue like western land claims because, in his experience, "they will be both equally independent, and ready to decide in strict conformity to justice.... I should no more hesitate to trust my liberty and property to the one, than the other." Madison refused to follow that lead. "Controversies affecting the interest of the United States," he said, "ought to be determined by their own Judiciary, and not be left to partial local tribunals." Upon second thought, Pendleton endorsed this standard Federalist position.

It did not convince Antifederalists. Grayson reminded his colleagues that the Court power to rule in all cases under the Constitution or laws of the United States "is of stupendous magnitude" due to its lack of definition. Who could guess how the future would affect local jurisdictions? Henry feared that the federal government would build courts in every county. If it did, it would strip the state courts of their power. William Grayson championed the idea that inconsistencies in the Constitution would produce conflict between the federal and state judiciaries. He predicted that the federal judiciary "will interfere with the State Judiciaries"; sufficient checks had not accompanied the separation of judicial powers; concurrent jurisdictions would result in "ludicrous consequences"; and the result would be an inferior state court. "This Court," he intoned, "has more power than any Court under Heaven." Patrick Henry agreed. The Constitution provided no clear line of demarcation between several crucial powers. In fact, one might conclude that the Philadelphia delegates purposely avoided precise terminology.

Importantly, any suggestion that state judges could also sit on the federal bench would badly affect the South. An independent Virginia judiciary was the Old Dominion's only defense against tyranny. Trial by jury in the defendant's vicinage was in danger unless Congress passed regulations to affect that end. Judges unacquainted with Virginia's circumstances could reverse local, impartial decisions. However, Congress might not choose to pass acceptable directives. George Mason feared that the clash between the courts would leave the state judiciary with no task.

The roadmap defining possible appeals' litigants, except for land claims by citizens of the same state claiming grants in another, was improper. What was the process, Mason demanded, if the Court made a judgment against the state? Would one "put the State's body in jail"? It seemed probable that the Philadelphia delegates had organized the judiciary "to weaken the State governments, to make them contemptible, and then destroy them."

James Monroe, seconded by Grayson, expanded the concept that judiciaries with authority over the same subject would clash, forcing one to supersede the other. Virginia's Antifederalists, with a tilt to localism, expected to maintain their own court procedures. Its courts had developed their common law precedents and federal additions were unwelcome. Patrick Henry also attacked this notion. Ignore the words written in the Constitution he warned. The general government could interpret or apply them in a manner foreign to Virginia practice. Because of its widely dispersed population, mountainous barriers, and difficulty of travel, Virginia needed a court system that it could trust. Overall, Antifederalists foresaw a future in which Congress would expand the brief list of Article III powers to the detriment of the South's judiciary.

John Marshall objected to any insinuation that the Supreme Court would always rule against the states. This was constitutionally impossible because that document had no clause on, for example, property or contracts. Obviously it could not overrule a state on these issues. "If they [government] were to make law not warranted by any of the laws enumerated, it would be considered by the Judges as an infringement of the Constitution which they are to guard." The courts would declare all such laws void.

Randolph assigned the Judiciary the task of preventing usurpation, both by states and individuals. With respect to trial by jury, he explained that the Constitution could protect it in criminal cases but not civil, because the state systems were different. Moreover, he and Marshall agreed that any constitutional defects could be corrected when Congress wrote the regulations controlling the Court.

The appellate clause drew equal criticism. Long journeys incident to the process received almost unanimous condemnation. Pendleton labeled the enforced trip to the capital city a "great hardship." Mason painted a portrait in which a litigant traveled "a thousand miles from home" to find out that proving his case was impossible. Randolph could not abide the whole section, particularly the appeals process, its "greatest evil." Yet, he was willing to set aside his criticism for the good of the Union and Pendleton joined him. Neither the clause that forced people to travel hundreds of miles to litigate appeals nor the "law and fact" provision favored the people. Maybe Virginians could trust the constitutional amending process or a guiding regulation to allay their fears. Mason agreed and James Madison seemed to concur. Perhaps, he concluded, the convention could trust Congress to correct this error and remedy "vexatious appeals."

Madison did attempt to redirect the debate to a positive tack. He admitted that danger lurked in a system in which one branch of government had power to define the authorities of the others. The constitutional policy of submitting cases for the jurisdiction of American federal judges was a novel idea. He concluded that they "will as readily do their duty as deviate from it."[14]

Judicial review of state or congressional laws had not been a prime Convention topic. Because the Constitution contained articles that might result in powers claimed by either state or national governments, it was natural that Virginians should consider judicial intervention. The delegates did not identify judicial review specifically as a topic of debate but did allude to it several times in passing. Thomas Jefferson, from abroad, had signaled his acceptance of the idea when associated with the presidential veto, but preferred the Court have the power. The State Soldier had viewed it as a corollary of Congress's laws being the supreme law of the land. "Any laws made in contradistinction to any ... clause" would be void. In the convention, Pendleton agreed. The clauses "arising out of the Constitution" and "in pursuance of those" assured that the national courts must have a review power. Logically, the court must have it as protection from outside encroachments. Still, initial usurpations could be limited by Congress. John Marshall extended the idea to judicial review of congressional laws. If Congress passed a law objectionable to the enumerated powers, the court would rule it void.

Not all the delegates were as confident that judicial review was necessary or legal. Patrick Henry, as usual, wrapped his argument in terms of liberty. What would Virginians do if the Supreme Court ruled a federal law "paramount" to a state law? Historically, the Virginia Court of Appeals had never feared opposing Articles' legislation. Will the new judiciary be as independent? Grayson agreed with the implication. No other branch whose tasks would mirror those of the Virginia judiciary was necessary. Interestingly, Edmund Pendleton had been involved in a classic case concerning an unconstitutional Assembly law just recently.[15]

Attention was not restricted to only power issues. A host of other attributes affecting republican governments reached the convention floor. Often, delegates associated liberty and aristocracy scenarios with other topics. Federalists identified licentiousness as the principal danger to liberty. As usual, they presented an energetic, strong, government as the panacea to any attack on that ideal. Pendleton reminded the convention that "the most respectable writers ... recommended making the ligaments of government firm." If coupled with "a rigid execution of the laws" American freedom would be safe. However, this government must actively reflect the people's ongoing interests. It must not become a shell dedicated to protecting rights but forgetful of its obligation to govern.

The proratification faction was careful, it assured Virginians, to circumscribe government power so that its energy would not challenge freedom. "Liberty is secured," stated Francis Corbin, "by the limitation of its powers; which are clearly and unequivocally defined, and which are to be exercised by our own Representatives freely chosen. What power is given that will endanger liberty?" In addition, the Constitution provided a road map that would encourage lawmakers to return to their roots. "Good conduct" only would ensure their reelection. This model secured liberty from tyrants. In the extreme, Pendleton suggested that Virginians could recall their delegated powers, or change them, to prevent the abuse from recurring.

Patrick Henry led the Antifederalist response. Hosannas to liberty seemed to echo throughout the hall each time he spoke. In a magnificent display of oratory he set out to snatch the title of liberty's savior for his faction. Repeatedly, he pinioned Federalist arguments with sharp counterexamples. Still, he recognized that the concept of liberty had taken on a new connotation. While the object of the Revolution had been liberty for all, consolidation seemed to have overcome it in some quarters. The end of government, he demanded, should still be liberty. It would not simply be a list of rights that government could not ignore. The people must control government for two related reasons. They were not only the source of power but also they were the most likely body to accept limitations on its power. The model government for inclusive liberty was already in existence — the Articles of Confederation. Thus, ratification of the Constitution would succeed only after the convention convinced him that it did not endanger Virginia's liberty.

Why did Federalists, asked Henry, assume that a dynamic government would protect liberty? Obviously, if the new government failed in its promises, it would endanger liberty "and tyranny must and will arise." Moreover, the Federalist goal of an energetic government bent on national glory would not affect the average American if the Constitution oppressed him and his liberty was lost. "But I will submit to your recollection," he reminded the convention, "whether liberty has been destroyed most often by the licentiousness of the people or by the tyranny of rulers."

The lack of a Bill of Rights convinced Henry that liberty was lost. His experience with the Virginia equivalent convinced him that such a document was mandatory. Particularly, Henry demanded guarantees for trial by jury and freedom of the press and religion, but his interest expanded to reserved rights and the necessary and proper provision.

He could not see how the surrender of state powers, a staple of the Constitution, could possibly reflect any republican ideal. Surely it was counterintuitive that the elimination of long held rights could protect liberty. For example, the Virginia judiciary would lose power under the Constitution. Presently it was "the sole protection against any tyrannical execution of the laws" and its reduction in status would signal oppression. Henry, that incomparable wordsmith, left us with another memorable phrase. "Liberty," he exhorted, "the greatest of all earthly blessing[s] — give us that precious jewel, and you may take every thing else."

Henry applied a reality check to Edmund Pendleton's recipe for dealing with government usurpation. Did anyone believe they would curb tyrants with a piece of paper? Had tyrants ever willingly desisted from usurpations? No mere convention would stop them. Only revolution could prevent a loss of freedom. This scenario was doubly dangerous because Henry assumed that the new government would overstep its bounds. Thus, Pendleton's model, while theoretically interesting, was unlikely to prevent tyranny.

Federalists realized that they must trump some of Henry's assertions or cede the liberty debate. John Marshall claimed that his party held "the title of being firm friends of the liberty and rights of mankind." Henry Lee joined in. "I conceive," he added, "that I may say with truth that the friends of this paper are true republicans, and by no means less attached to liberty than their opponents." While these may have been fair comments, they were dominated by Henry's persuasive rhetoric.

The theme of aristocratic government influence played out within the convention. George Mason insisted that the Constitution made it certain that the aristocracy would control Congress and Henry echoed his colleague's apprehension. "Will the Honorable Gentlemen say it," he queried, "that a poor man, as enlightened as any man in the land, has an equal chance with a rich man to be elected? He will stand no chance though he may have the finest understanding of any man in the shire."[16]

✠

Each faction was aware of the interrelationship between self-interest, human nature, political theory, and republican government. Henry put it nicely for the Antifederalists. "But," he said, "the depraved nature of man is well-known. He has a natural biass (sic) towards his own interest which will prevail over every consideration unless it be checked." William Grayson seconded that opinion. "Considering the corruption of human nature, and the general tendency of mankind to promote their interest, I think there is great danger." Henry Lee believed that Rhode Island would eventually adopt the Constitution "unless she departs from the primary maxims of human nature, which are those of self-preservation."

Each party applied its conclusion to disparate articles of the Constitution. Obviously, they linked taxation schedules to self-interest. For example, the president, whose power was short-lived, would "seek his own self-interest." Previously, we identified the Antifederalist position on the aborted Mississippi treaty and the role of the carrying states in it. The immediate past provided another example. Had not the delegates in the late Convention sought to aggrandize their own states? Their self-interest was legendary in Virginia. Generally, they were disposed to thwart the interests of the "productive states."

Experience convinced the Antifederalists that local interests would absorb the attention of the nation's congressmen. One announced scenario predicted that they might even attempt to set regulations to fix their number. If so, they would be following the example set by a series of Virginia burgesses. Self-interest had driven crucial political decisions.

George Nicholas denounced these negative connotations. He considered it mandatory that representatives "attend to the interests of their constituents." Failure to follow this axiom would result in defeat at the polls. Pendleton's solution to self-interested government usurpations would require Virginians to "assemble in Convention; wholly recall our delegated powers, or reform them so as to prevent such abuse; and punish those servants, who have perverted powers designed for our happiness to their own emolument." Henry was more succinct. "All checks," he warned, "founded on any thing but self-love will not avail." Where were the checks that would keep representatives from "ruining us"? If one contrasted the danger to reelection with "personal interest, their ambition and avarice" it was clear the latter would predominate.

Henry offered an interesting example to support his self-love contention. The English government form included houses of lords and commons and a king. The self-interest of the lords kept the other two branches in check. Otherwise the House of Lords would author of its own demise. Similarly, it "stimulated" the king to ensure the welfare of the people represented by the commons. If he did not, revolution was the result. Extending the argument, Henry contended that the lords would prevent a commons' encroachment on the king's power. Its self-interest would lead it to conclude that, otherwise, a rebellion would swiftly bring a reduction in its power. The Constitution contemplated none of these scenarios. "Tell me not of checks on power," he fumed, "but tell me of checks founded on self-love." To be successful, the new government required a virtuous man to occupy every position, an unlikely occurrence. If not, "virtue will slumber" because "there are only ideal balances" in contrast to the English system. On the other hand, if your rulers "can stand the temptations of human nature, you are safe. If you have a good president, senators, and representatives, there is no danger. But can this be expected from human nature...? Without real checks it will not suffice that some of them are good.... Where is the rock of your salvation?"[17]

Virginia's delegates split over the benefits associated with majority rule. For example, the four smallest states in the Union could defeat any amendment. Henry was adamant that this did not reflect "the spirit of republicanism." It demanded "that a majority of the community have a right to alter Government when found to be oppressive." Still, Monroe labeled majority rule "the security of republicanism."

Federalists agreed. Randolph knew that "refusing to submit to the decision of the majority is destructive of every republican principle." For example, the people's representatives would set taxation rates and their majority decision must stand. Francis Corbin leavened these remarks. He listed the three millstones around republicanism's neck as "faction, dissension, and consequent subjection of the minority to the caprice and arbitrary decisions of the majority." Often, they followed some partial or local advantage rather than representing the interest of the collective community. "To avoid this evil," he concluded, "is perhaps the great desideratum of republican wisdom; it may be termed the philosopher's stone."[18]

Madison's extended republic notion convinced Federalists of its viability. The classical argument was that one government could never rule a geographically large country like the United States because it contained too many competing interests. This truism did not convince Francis Corbin. Exactly how small, he asked, must the country be to consider republican government viable? Henry added a clarification. Only a despotic government could rule such a country. Madison disagreed and restated his new theory of the extended republic. "We may therefore conclude," he said, "that our representatives, being chosen by such extensive districts, will be upright and independent. In proportion as we have security against corruption in representatives, we have security against corruption from every other quarter whatsoever." However, some Antifederalists were adamant that the two contending geographical sections were homes to wildly different cultures and could never amalgamate into a single state.[19]

Sovereignty debate made it clear that the two parties had unsolvable differences. Historically, theorists had insisted that, within government, one, and only one, locus of sovereignty existed. The Federalists now rejected this maxim. Sovereignty not only resided in the people, but also it was divisible. This difference in opinion lay behind the dispute over the American form of government.

Although the dichotomy seemed clear on the surface, a significant problem lurked below. Who were the people? Madison attempted to answer the question. "The general government," he said, "derived its authority from [the state] governments and from the same sources from which their authority derives, that is, from their sovereign peoples." Thus, both the central and state governments derived their power from the same source, but when it acted on the central government it acted as a state. Madison emphasized this interpretation. "Should all the states adopt it, it will be then a government established by the thirteen states of America, not to the intervention of the legislatures, but by the people at large." Therefore, in either state or central government, all power resided with the people. John Marshall expanded the idea. "The state governments did not derive their powers from the general government; but each government derived its powers from the people, and each was to act according to the powers given it." Still, this did not clarify the question. As one historian wrote:

> In the debate over ratification, Federalists stressed the division of authority between the state governments and the general government under the sovereignty of the people. Glossing over the conflicts that were bound to arise in a state system based on dual and concurrent distribution of power, they were content to allow the precise character of "the people of the United States"—and hence of the nature of the Union—to remain ambiguous.

Lesser issues were publicized. The loss of Virginia's sovereignty coupled with the absence of a Bill of Rights translated to the endangerment of "our rights and privileges" and presaged a consolidated government; the agents of this contract were unclear; according to one translation, a litigant might haul the sovereign state of Virginia before the Supreme Court to answer charges; a division of sovereignty raised a serious question about government conflicts; and the agency that would adjudicate them was not specified?[20]

To this point, we have alluded to compact theory in several instances but refrained from expanding on its effects on the delegates. Because it played a central role in Antifederalist dogma, and guided some Federalists in their view of federal-state relations, we will expand on its nature. First, we will make some general comments. Convention-specific debate will follow.

Although the preamble to the Constitution prepared one for a subsequent compact, it was not that which one would expect. We know that Madison's theories adopted not only Oliver Ellsworth's "partly federal, partly national" designator but also identified two compacts defining societal, and then governmental relationships. He concentrated on two broad issues — government must protect individual rights and the people should curb government power. The familiar notion of a compact between rulers and ruled was supplanted by "a compact between political societies."

What, then, was the nature of the Antifederalist Union? Was the government based on society's deliberate action or had it evolved organically? Obviously, the former, that contemplated a compact, mirrored Antifederalist goals while Federalists like James Wilson and Alexander Hamilton favored the latter. Compact assumed that the states had created both the Constitution and the Union. After all, conventions organized by the state legislatures and witnessed by state citizens ratified the Constitution. Thus, the Union was democratic because the amalgam of the state governments represented all Americans.

Unfortunately for Federalists, they never came to grips with defining the people of the United States. One historian, Herman Belz, referred to sovereignty of the people as "a clever theoretical invention." On the other hand, social contracts were common within the states. Just before the convention the *Virginia Independent Chronicle* reminded its readers that a contracted free government must follow the will of the people. One fact was clear. Despite disputes over sovereignty's location and divisibility or the contract's signatories, compact theory dominated its competitor, organic evolution of government.

The translation from theory to practice in government produced a laundry list of Antifederalist consequences designed to assure liberty by limiting government. It was by the people's consent; its powers, both state and federal, were delegated by the people; majority rule was mandatory; suffrage qualifications must be realistic; the right of revolution to combat government usurpations followed Locke's theory; and government should never contemplate coercion of either an individual citizen or a state. Richard Henry Lee, focusing on the requirements for liberty, concluded that a social compact would include freedom of religion and the press, trial by jury in both civil and criminal cases, a small peacetime standing army, frequent elections, an independent judiciary, the prohibition of excess punishment, bail, or fines, the right to assemble peacefully and petition the government, a ban on search and seizure, and an Executive Council.

Society's acceptance of a social contract unleashed other questions. Who were the ratifying agents? Had the people ratified "as separate political communities" or as a "single encompassing community"? For our study, the debate produced the "compact — strict construction — state rights" continuum that bubbled until 1861.

Considering the social compact's relation to federal-state concerns and the liberty vs. power dichotomy, perhaps its popularity should not surprise us. Surely compact theory fulfilled it's promise. Nor should one consider state rights arguments based on compact to be opportunistic. The danger, as described by Madison, was that unsophisticated interpreters of the theory would analogize it incorrectly and make a crucial misstep that introduced unintended consequences.

From the evidence, Antifederalists seemed to be comfortable with the ideals of classic corporate republicanism. Local self-government, personal liberty, civic virtue, and limited government power bound them together. Loosely, it appeared that the Federalists had adopted the liberal implications of Locke's theory while their opponents concentrated on the benefits of compact. However, events of the 1780s predicted that this set of values would be replaced by one in which personal liberty triumphed over corporate equality.

Last, we must examine the concept of state secession. Southern states claimed this reserved right. However, they did not get this notion from Locke. We know that his theory insisted that once a member joined a society he remained within its bounds until it, of its own volition, ceased to exist. Instead, southerners claimed Locke's right of revolution from that same theory.

This raised another problem. Locke wrote his thesis at the time of the Glorious Revolution of 1688. Revolution was his only bulwark against tyranny. Thus, he cited it as his recipe for the reestablishment of a popular government. But, the term "secession" was not common politically until the following century. Might Locke have employed it within his theory if it had been available? Therefore, those who argue that Locke demanded revolution as his answer to tyranny were literally correct but possibly, suffered from tunnel vision. Simply put, he was not the arbiter of the necessity of secession since he never considered it.[21]

Virginia's delegates sought a sense of legitimacy for their Revolution. One could readily be found in a theory that delineated circumstances in which revolution was acceptable. Since it had been successful, it was natural to apply compact theory afterward.

Contract dynamics were important to Antifederalists. Recall Henry's cogent remark about the proper debate order. All delegates had to understand the Constitution's terms and thrust before accepting them. If so, few would ratify the Constitution without a Bill of the Rights. He warned the convention that its failure to demand a Bill's inclusion ignored John Locke's proviso that the signatories to a contract "cannot by any compact deprive or divest their posterity." Edmund Pendleton recognized the compact's role. Consequently, he offered earlier a method for avoiding conflict in the face of a usurper. Most Virginians, he knew, saw the Constitution as a compact. "What was it," he asked, "that brought us from a state of nature to society but to secure happiness? And can society be formed without Government? Personify Government: Apply to it as a friend to assist you, and it will grant your request. This is the only Government founded in real compact." The government's duty was to secure the people's happiness. Still, the originators of the compact were unspecified. Were they the people or the states? Antifederalists preferred a dichotomy of rulers and people in which the latter were those of the states. They meted out power to the central government and withdrew it for cause.

Some Virginia Federalists would not accept the compact notion of government. They perceived that the Constitution broke the mold of a classic compact. James Madison's novel theory of concurrent compacts prompted such a decision. He defined two. The first was unwritten and existed among the people in a state of nature as they agreed to form a society. Next, they produced a written contract that defined the people's government. The reader can see that compact theory had arcane features. As one historian remarked, even its expositors were unlikely to understand its import thoroughly. In day-to-day terms, Americans understood well enough, but were liable to concentrate on the government contract rather than that in a state of nature.[22]

4

The Virginia Ratification Convention — Constitutional Power and Rights

Although the last chapter concentrated on correcting past errors, it introduced briefly the Constitution's dispersal of power and rights. The congressional enumerated powers, election articles, and the crucial debate over reserved rights are the focus of this section.

✠

Due to the last clause of Article I, Section 8, Federalists felt constrained to assure Virginians that the Constitution's enumerated powers were well checked and not expansive. Madison promised his colleagues that they "can only operate in certain cases." Power spread among the three branches reduced chances of usurpation. Also, Virginians could expect that local issues would remain in local hands. "Federal representatives," he said, "could be responsible only for those great and national matters — few and carefully defined — on which they [Virginians] could trust them to reflect the people's needs and will." Henry Lee returned to basics. Although the people were the source of power, he lectured, their agents could apply only the enumerated powers. If faced with a legal question concerning an assumed congressional power, his test was plain. Was it enumerated? John Marshall ignored his earlier view on concurrent powers, remarking that Article 1, Section 2 listed all restraints on state power except those that they exclusively gave to Congress.

The weakness in the above contentions was tunnel vision. Federalists assumed that the enumerated powers excluded the sweeping clause. Perhaps it was merely an adjunct to those listed above it. Because of its importance, we will study its effect separately.[1] But first, we will cycle through many of the enumerated powers plus one that antiratificationists coveted.

✠

Antifederalists objected bitterly to the treaty clause because it circumvented the House of Representatives in the ratification process. After all, the Constitution defined treaties as supreme law. Should not the representatives of the people have a voice in such an important process? Also, reverberations from the Mississippi debate still lingered. The Constitution would alleviate two southern anxieties if treaty ratification required both Houses to participate. Not only lost Mississippi navigation rights but also concern over northern trade domination would disappear. Yet, William Grayson continued to pound away at the Mississippi predicament. Future ratification of that defunct treaty, by the terms of the Constitution, would amount to the dismembering of the Union. If Americans considered the western territories part of their heritage, the Constitution ought to provide expressly, he warned, "that no dismemberment should take place without consent of the Legislature." Keeping up the pressure, Henry reminded the convention that, according to his interpretation, the Spanish treaty, under the Constitution, would have cost America navigation of the Mississippi.

Francis Corbin discerned no danger from the treaty power. Certainly it would be unwise to give it to the president alone. That would be repugnant to republican ideals. Consequently, the Convention delegates checked the president's power by insisting that the state representatives, the Senate, consent. Additionally, treaties had a special relation for the nation. Either America must respect them completely or they should not ratify them. Otherwise, the United States would be perpetually at war.

Madison could not understand Antifederalist quibbles. Essentially, he claimed, the Constitution made few changes compared with the Articles protocol; treaty powers applied only to their objects; as an external power it applied only to foreign nations; time and circumstances would alter the relationships between the United States and other countries; and the impeachment provisions could deal with any presidential treaty usurpation. Edmund Pendleton agreed with Madison that there was no appreciable difference in the two government forms with respect to the treaty power. For those who predicted usurpations through the manipulation of minimum Senate numbers, the Judge offered a dose of reality. He assured the convention that for such an important vote as a Mississippi treaty, every senator would be present. It would require two-thirds of that number from nine states to ratify. That was a significant hurdle.[2]

Both direct and indirect taxation conjured up other issues for Virginia Antifederalists. Any acceptance of the principle of direct taxation, they preached, was tantamount to consolidated national government and would demolish the familiar, comfortable confederation. Of course, the loss of the tax power would translate into a loss of prestige. They would become "contemned and despised." If, as expected, the proposed government lived well, the cost would be onerous. Grayson extended this prediction. "Giving the right of taxation," he predicted, "is giving a right to increase the miseries of the people."

George Mason, despite Federalist claims, anticipated that the governments could each tax Virginians for the same reason. Based on that prediction, he warned that no one would agree to such a collection by two different agencies. He offered the simple poll tax to highlight his contention that his inference was correct. Patrick Henry agreed. The new form of government made double taxation certain. Moreover, if the convention ratified the scheme, general government taxes would supercede those of the states. Virginia would get only the leftovers. Remember, he argued, even if different government agencies taxed Virginians now, they all came from one place — the people.

Constructing the taxation schedules equitably would be impossible for the sixty-five federal representatives. Realistically, they knew little about other states and could never compute their share. Unfortunately, once Congress recognized the difficulty, it would likely just adopt the easiest method and apply it. Not only did the states differ in their ability to pay, said Grayson, but also they had different interests. The government would tax southerners on their slaves while northerners would be immune. Thus, those who initiated any slave tax would neither pay it nor account for their actions to their constituents for it. According to Henry, this translated into a higher direct tax on the southern states.

A complementary issue was each section's role in trade. The northern states were carrying states while the southern were noncarrying, agricultural producers. This division highlighted the natural American split in interests. Virginia Antifederalists concluded that the Constitution favored the carrying states at the expense of the producers. Again, the North could obviously benefit from its ability to organize the taxation schedules.

Despite Antifederalist loathing for the taxation scheme, Henry did offer some scenarios under which he might accept direct taxation. He would never condone it unless the system of requisitions remained in force and Virginia defaulted. In such a case, Congress should severely punish it. Possibly, Congress could expel it from the Union. Still, Virginia held its fate in its own hands under his proposal. Surely, it knew its own ability to pay better than outsiders. Perhaps James Monroe enunciated the finality of the Antifederalist position. "My attachment to the Union and an energetic Government," he intoned, "is such, that I would consent to give the General Government every power contained in that plan, except that of taxation."

The Federalists, as one might expect, found little common ground with their opponents. They decided that government would not contemplate direct taxes until it finished its national enumeration; it could never resort to coercing a state in a nonrepublican requisitions' system; taxes collected from the Articles era would match those arising from the Constitution; a direct tax was synonymous with Union and a "necessary evil"; the United States might require a direct tax in time of war; and only a majority of the people's duly elected representatives could implement it. Moreover, if the general government started a direct tax, each state would decide which article to tax.

Madison provided two cases to emphasize the protection aspect of a direct tax. In wartime, imports and imposts would decline. Also, when the country became fully populated, imports might not be as necessary. If one looked to the future, direct taxes might provide a buffer against fiscal disaster.

Straining logic, Edmund Pendleton would not agree that governments could tax an item twice. If they could, it would be for two distinct, separate reasons. Randolph would not go this far. Because it would be in their best interest, the state and federal governments would avoid taxation for identical reasons. Madison reminded the convention that multiple taxations were common in Virginia. At that time, the government collected parochial, county, and state taxes. In any case, all taxes came from the people.

George Nicholas scotched any insinuation that there would be two separate sets of tax collectors operating in Virginia. In addition, indirect taxes would account for at least 90 percent of the government's requirements. Randolph agreed with his colleague and added that the use of one common set of collectors would save money. Also, the people were familiar with the state collectors and would feel more comfortable with them. Returning to his previous point, Pendleton saw this as a good solution since "both lay taxes, but for different reasons."

Madison and Francis Corbin may have made the most telling arguments. Unless an emergency intervened, Congress was unlikely to resort to direct taxes. Pendleton chided Monroe on this point. The latter had doubted its necessity. The former wondered why there was a difference of opinion if that were true.[3]

Congress's militia power, according to the Antifederalists, was excessive. Remember, Virginians had forged their opinion on decentralization during the Revolution. It led them to believe that they must protect their rights from a strong government. George Mason feared that granting excessive militia powers to Congress "would finally destroy the state governments more effectively by insidious, underhanded means, than such as could be openly practiced." In addition, Henry was astonished that Congress would now have control over both taxation and the militia. "We started with the purse," he bemoaned, "and now we are required to part with the second." He also attacked the continuum of power. The state could not achieve its goals if Congress neglected its duty to initiate the process. Of course, this opened the door for eventual debate on the exclusivity of Congress's militia powers.

John Marshall assumed a lead role for the Federalists. He stated that each government derived its powers from the people and applied them accordingly. Since the people retained any power not given, and their agents, the state legislatures, had not given up "power to command and govern their militia," they retained it. Only an "incompatibility" could prevent the state legislature from retaining this power. Thus, the power over the militia was concurrent, not exclusive. Henry found this argument incompatible with reality. A plain reading of the militia article led him to conclude that the states could not call the militia in case of insurrection. The Constitution gave that power exclusively to Congress and did not contemplate the Legislature sharing it with the states. In an example designed to move his audience, he supposed two concurrent events. America was at war, but the enemy had not invaded, and a southern state experienced a slave revolt. Clearly, the state must rely on Congress to call out the militia. Article 4, Section 4, required Congress, on the application of the state legislature or executive, to protect the states. Simultaneously, Article 1, Section 8, assigned power to call the militia "to quell insurrections." At what point will the state call the militia? Since these powers were all congressional in nature, we can see that the idea of a concurrent power over the militia would not stand scrutiny. Grayson took this position one step farther. He asserted that the states could not "command the militia" except by implication. Henry supported this position.

Madison tried a different line. Much angry debate had surrounded the role of an energetic central government since the publication of the Constitution. He proposed that the militia clause would mitigate any fears on that topic and be "an additional safeguard to our defense." It would be particularly important to the southern states. Moreover, they could accomplish it without reducing state power one iota.[4]

George Mason continued his crusade, begun at Philadelphia, against the continuation of the slave trade. He labeled it "odious" and "disgraceful to mankind." Mason, like Henry and John Tyler, had concluded that the trade harmed Virginia's society. Nevertheless, they could see no way to eliminate slavery because of its economic importance and consequently, there was "no security for the property of that kind which we have already" in the Constitution. Northerners bent on manumission, would attack it. Madison objected to that suggestion. According to his reading, no clause in the Constitution could support an attack on state slavery. Henry was not as sure. He predicted that future generations would "search that paper to see if they have power of manumission."

Several other slavery issues reached the floor. Henry presented a scenario based on implied powers that could "if we be engaged in war, liberate every one of your slaves if they please. And this must and will be done by men, a majority of whom have not a common interest with you." Beware, he warned, that they could apply the general welfare clause of the Constitution to free the slaves. All that was necessary was a government that considered the institution deleterious to the best interests of the nation. In an emergency, the central government might even arm them. The possibility that fugitive slaves, fleeing to the capital city because it was not a state, would be freed struck Grayson. Nicholas assuaged this fear by reminding him that the states would form the capital from land they donated and would insist on provisions to counteract this possibility. Madison reminded his peers that the convention could not have agreed on the Constitution without the slavery clauses. The fugitive slave law protected owners against loss of property. Also, "since tax is the partner of representation, the states cannot be taxed on their slaves."[5]

Familiar arguments dominated the debate over checks and balances. Still, convention-eers presented a few twists and one new major idea. Antifederalists still claimed that no check existed to prevent government branches from uniting to tyrannize the people and challenge liberty. In counterpoint, Federalists reminded them that "the primary right of power in the people" with frequent elections was the best check on government usurpation. However, it was left to Patrick Henry to take the argument to a new level. Recognizing the influence of modern theory on many delegates, he surprised the convention by declaring that self-interest was the most potent check on government usurpation. Virtue would be shunted aside. Some members of the convention must have blanched at Henry's appeal to self-interest. Typically Federalists expected individuals to pursue it. Still, Henry employed it against ratification of the Constitution and Federalist ideology simultaneously. See, he inferred, if one assumed your maxims, this would be the result.

Henry extended the examination of checks on the Court. A study of Article 3, Section 2 would find that the only effective check on the Court was self-restraint. However, each faction in the ratification debate disparaged human nature. During times of internal stress, the disputants might expect a Court bias.[6]

Election dynamics and its soul mate representation invited close scrutiny. Federalists dominated the short debates on suffrage. Francis Corbin intimated that property was the basis of suffrage and Madison added that land owning Virginians would support that rule. Those who argued that only property holders should have the suffrage offered no size distinction. This raised a red flag. On one hand, the "inherent right" of suffrage might be reduced since its universality would "defeat the admirable end of the institution of representation." On the other, theorists had proclaimed that the state protected liberty if it prevented few citizens from voting and insisted on voting equality. Thus a man with a large property holding should have the same rights as did one with a few acres.[7]

Overwhelmingly, the election clause that drew the most interest was that which allowed Congress to assign the time and place of federal elections. George Nicholas explained that the federal government must have the power to defend itself against state intrusions. In one script, the states refused to set the date and shattered the Union. In another, they might space out the elections so widely that the House of Representatives would not be full. Henry had a variation on that theme. Congress had the power to organize the polls to disenfranchise voters. If it did, the people would have contempt for their representatives because their suffrage had been abused.

Monroe extended the argument to the election of the president. Could not Congress arrange elections serially so that interests could organize behind a second candidate if the first were failing? They could easily throw elections into Congress. This would be a disaster for the people who would be disenfranchised. As we know, William Grayson decried the methodology of electing the president because it had no conformity. Differing agencies voted for him under different circumstances. George Mason was even more severe in his criticism of the dynamics highlighted by Grayson. It was just a sop to the people to fool them into thinking that they had elected a president. The Constitution, he argued, defined a procedure that ensured that multiple candidates would run and made the chance of a majority vote — in which they might say that the people participated — unlikely. The selection by the House from the five highest vote getting candidates also separated the successful candidate from the people. Perhaps only the top two in the list would ameliorate this defect.

The debate introduced other issues. The Constitution would bypass republican ideals if a small state like Delaware had as many votes as Virginia. Henry noticed that the Constitution did not account for the election ground rules. How did one count the votes? Would property owners have an advantage? Randolph and Nicholas would not go down that path. Virginians, they concluded, would not consider the suffrage requirements a benefit to rich property owners because the rules were the same as they had been before the Constitution. Any man who owned twenty-five acres, for example, could vote in the federal election. Madison fielded a Monroe query concerning Senate elections. The reason that the Convention delegates did not fix its election dynamics was to avoid forcing the state legislatures to travel to a site not of its choosing. Over time, it might change.[8]

George Nicholas opened the debate on representation by presenting the Federalist agenda. Virginians need not fear that their representatives would have little knowledge of their constituent's local interests. The Virginia General Assembly would attend to that task. In any case, federal representatives would get their data in the same way as did delegates — from the people. Moreover, the two levels of government were sure to express their concerns to each other. The secret of good representation was to elect virtuous men who would be immune to corruption. Otherwise, the government form would have no effect. Corrupt officials would defeat the intentions of any form.

Two years service was mandatory for complete representation. Sending a man home just as he became familiar with his duties was nonsensical. Surely if one allowed his state delegate a one year term his federal equivalent should get two. The people need not fear that term length because federal powers began in the states and their representatives would be on guard to "sound the alarm to the people" if the government usurped state rights. In a dispute, Virginians could be assured that its 160 delegates would have "more influence than the ten members of Congress." Moreover, the crassest federal self-interest ensured that they would follow their constituent's dictates since reelection loomed. Unrealistically, Nicholas pronounced that all the representatives would be virtuous and would sublimate their base interests. Edmund Pendleton found common cause with his colleague. Antifederalist insinuations about the quality of representation flabbergasted him since Virginians would elect men who instilled confidence, as they had always done. They need not fear that other government branches would fatally corrupt them. Examine the British House of Commons. Despite its weaknesses and scandals, it still could "contend with the executive of that country." The American Congress would act similarly.

Other Federalists chimed in with disparate opinions on the expected quality of representatives. Returning to the Mississippi theme, Madison posited that the new House of Representatives would not bargain away the commercial rights because they were representatives of the landed interest. Randolph supplemented Nicholas's stress on officeholder virtue. Would not Virginians be more secure if represented by ten virtuous men rather than an unknown crowd since they had always preferred virtue and ability over virtue and connections? Moreover, the Constitution provided a guarantee of virtue since all laws passed in Congress operated mutually on their representatives. Randolph played a Pendleton theme. He could not understand the opposition's continual harping on the scope of representation. The sixty-five would represent not just Virginia, but the nation. Surely, they would realize the need for upgrading their knowledge and do so in the nation's interest.

Shifting emphasis, Randolph remarked that a numerical cap should accompany any increase in the number of representatives. Too many would likely lead to corruption and shattered secrecy in negotiations. The insinuation that representatives might be corrupt surprised John Marshall. Since all Virginians could not go to Congress, an agency system was mandatory. Therefore, one must trust it and give one's representative the power to do his job. Madison developed that theme. "We may therefore conclude," he said, "that our representatives, being chosen by such extensive districts, will be upright and independent. In proportion as we have security against corruption in representatives, we have security against corruption from every other quarter whatsoever."

Antifederalists rejected this optimistic script. Large congressional districts were a focus of their discontent because that faction promoted the notion of more, not fewer, representatives. For a Virginian familiar with 160 elected delegates to represent one state, sixty-five for the nation seemed ludicrous. Grayson agreed that to trust "our liberty and property" to so few representatives was an error. Thus, only some interests would be met. "But sure I am," Henry complained, "that the dangers of the system are real, when those who have no similar interests with the people of this country are to legislate for us — when our dearest interests are left in the power of those whose advantage it may be to infringe them." How could an unknown localist compete with a rich gentryman whose reputation was wide? Surely, well-known but not necessarily better qualified large property holders would fill the federal positions. As usual, Henry synthesized the Antifederalist position. Analogizing Great Britain with Virginia, he questioned, "will the Honorable Gentlemen say it, that a poor man, as enlightened as any man ... has an equal chance with a rich man to be elected? He will stand no chance.... It will be so here."

Overwhelmingly, Antifederalists insisted that Madison's government by interests translated to a claim that each district's representatives reflect the people's demographics. Despite Federalist claims, George Mason refused to budge from his assertion that the gentry could never represent the people adequately. Instead, they would represent their own interests. Proper representation required the official to immerse himself in his constituents' lives. For example, how will he know what the correct tax will be on each state?

Arguments claiming that public men will all be virtuous were not realistic. Some would be, and some would not. Mason feared that man's "natural lust of power" would eventually lead to a loss of liberty. William Grayson made one ominous prediction. It was clear to him that the present system would result in "unequal, grievous, and oppressive" representation. It would pit "a fraction of one part of the Union against the other." He did add another concern. Unless they highly compensated them, Virginians could expect their representatives to be corrupt.

History had taught Henry that rulers had always "been actuated by individual interest" differing from that of the people. Would they, the few, have the power to defend Virginia's rights? Could one trust them? Did they earn one's trust by their actions at the Philadelphia convention? In fact, it would be a "novelty" to find a government not in this mold. Henry's assertion raised an interesting proposition. He expected self-interest to drive his "rulers" whereas classical republican principles, like civic virtue, guided the people.[9]

Discussions about elections and representation led naturally to an examination of republican government. It reduced to two related questions. What was each party's understanding of the basis of republican government? Would its implementation produce consolidation? If the latter were true, southerners feared the annihilation of their section. Patrick Henry synthesized the Antifederalist position.

> The honorable gentleman said that the two judiciaries and legislatures would go in a parallel line, and never interfere: that, as long as each was confined to its proper objects, there would be no danger of interference: that, like two parallel lines, as long as they continued in their parallel direction, they never would meet. With submission to the honorable gentleman's opinion, I assert that there is danger of interference, because no line is drawn between the powers of the two governments, in many instances: and, where there is a line, there is no check to prevent the one from encroaching upon the powers of the other. I therefore contend that they must interfere, and that this interference must subvert the state government, as being less powerful.

Edmund Pendleton reminded his fellow delegates that republican government could flourish in many forms, even a monarchy. The Constitution guaranteed a republican government because it was the basis of the political philosophy behind it. For Pendleton, this reduced to "liberty in his [even poor men] person and property." Madison added another Federalist component. The will of the majority must dominate that of a "trifling minority." Francis Corbin expected this government "to protect, defend, and strengthen the United States."

James Madison acknowledged that republican governments had not always thrived. Some had allowed majority rule to cloud their judgment regarding abuses against the minority. This mistake led to factionalism and ultimately discord and tyranny. Often this abuse took the form of stamping out "local considerations" and endangering liberty. Thus, the citizenry of the republic must be constantly on the lookout for indications of government usurpations.

Antifederalists considered the Articles' government the perfect republican vehicle. They accepted the concept that the people should delegate power to their representatives, but insisted that it return after a short period. They could not understand how the Constitution government could represent all the people, particularly the less affluent. Henry concluded that "this Constitution ... squints toward monarchy...." George Mason predicted that the government might begin with a republican goal, but it would deteriorate to a consolidated state. For Henry, "such a government is incompatible with the genius of republicanism."

It was this prediction and its corollary, southern annihilation, that burdened Antifederalist supporters. Henry entreated,

> I beg gentlemen to consider: lay aside your prejudices. Is this a federal government? Is it not a consolidated government for almost every purpose? Is the government of Virginia a state government after this government is adopted? I grant that it is a republican government, but for what purposes? For such trivial domestic considerations as render it unworthy [of] the name of legislature.

Even a friend of a "firm, federal, energetic government" like John Dawson could not abide a shift from "a confederation of independent states" to a "consolidated government." Did not the accepted theory on government enshrine the idea of legislative sovereignty? Everyone knew that every state had only one sovereign, and that was the supreme legislative power. Surely, the Constitution would annihilate the state legislatures since the new government could act directly on the people without reference to the states.

The debate that crystallized the importance of consolidation to Antifederalists took place immediately. After George Nicholas's opening salvo on June 4, Patrick Henry rose to reply for the opposition. "My political curiosity ... leads me to ask who authorized them to speak the language of 'We, the people' instead of 'We, the states?' States are the characteristics and soul of a confederation. If the states be not the agents of this compact, it must be one great consolidated, national government, of the people of all the states." Several interesting interpretations stood out. One would note that he applied John Locke's theory twice, once by analogy. Henry analogized the "states" to Locke's "people." Moreover, the consolidation he discovered was Lockean. Last, Henry assumed that the United States was a confederation founded on a compact with all its philosophical baggage. One was the notion of the sovereignty of the states.

Edmund Randolph replied for the proratification delegates. He posited that the Articles' government did not provide an agency for the people's ideas. Assuming his point, he then retorted that it was only natural to consult the people on a contract that bound them. According to Hugh Grigsby, Randolph misunderstood the thrust of Henry's declamation. The governor ignored the shift from sovereign states to sovereign people. Edmund Pendleton tried a different route. He declared that only the people could form a government or delegate powers. "What have the states to do with it?" he queried. Pendleton also referred to a Lockean concept. He returned to the transition from a state of nature to the Constitutional compact.

Henry recognized that the convention had misconstrued his opening gambit and referred it to the genesis of the Constitution. If the partial statement "We, the states" had prefaced it, the document would have been a compact defining a confederation with all its nuances. Otherwise, the government must be considered consolidated. So, his thrust was not on Union but on the type of government expected by the fathers of the Constitution. Madison recognized Henry's conundrum. Still, he had a ready-made solution. He cast off the shackles of the past and declared, as he had in *The Federalist*, "I conceive myself that it [government] is of a mixed nature, it is in a manner unprecedented.... In some respects it is a government of a federal nature; in others it is of a consolidated nature." Not surprisingly, Henry could not concur with what he considered Madison's evasion. Everyone agreed, he argued, that for all purposes affecting the whole Union, the government was consolidated. The states would handle only "trivial cases." George Mason added some bite to Henry's argument. He postulated that the Federalists, in the Constitution, had purposely organized a consolidated government to destroy the state legislatures and judiciary.

Unfortunately for Federalist explanations, John C. Calhoun later proved conclusively that the phrase "We the people of the United States" did not refer to the collective people without state boundaries. An examination of previous drafts of the Preamble showed that the debates included state enumerations whenever the people were included.

Madison offered an explanation for the derivation of the republic's power. The general government could not consider itself independent of the state legislatures. That road led to usurpation. At this point, Madison offered a corollary to his earlier theory. Both the general government and the state legislatures had the same power source — the people. It insured that the new republican government, at one instant, could be considered federal as the people acted federally, and on another consolidated, as the people acted in that manner. This theory depended on the acceptance of the notion that the parties to the contract are "the people — but not the people as composing one great body; but people as composing thirteen sovereignties." Such a definition backstopped the partly-partly notion and permitted the states to act locally in their own interest.[10]

The ratification process itself separated the factions. John Tyler knew that learned men, who had declared wildly different interpretations of almost every article of the Constitution, stocked the convention. If such was the case, how could they contemplate ratifying it anyway? Edmund Randolph attempted to answer this conundrum. He feared that without Virginia's support, the Union would disband, leaving the Old Dominion isolated. Moreover, the document contained the means for correcting any defects and virtuous men would ensure that they repaired them. For example, congressional legislation or regulation would circumscribe the despised appellate judicial powers. If that did not happen, surely the amending process would swing into action.

Randolph offered an opinion on another contentious issue. What were the parameters of ratification? According to the governor, "Wholly to adopt or wholly to reject, as proposed by the [Philadelphia] convention, seemed too hard an alternative to the citizens of America." James Madison explained another issue. Why must the people ratify the Constitution? If the state legislatures performed this task, the document would be considered a treaty between sovereign states. As such, any single breach of its provisions negated the complete treaty. Still, could not Congress poll every American? Unfortunately, this solution immediately encountered two roadblocks. According to Locke, upon Independence, the state "political societies" remained viable. Moreover, each state had its own constitution that required amending to agree with the federal Constitution. Thus, Virginians might argue successfully that Americans in other states were changing both Virginia's constitution and "political society." Only one solution existed. Each "political society" must ratify the Constitution. Thus, the people of the several states acting in that capacity and not as the people of the United States, would ratify the document. Of course, a corollary to this dynamic was that since sovereignty rested in the people of the states, any powers not assigned to government remained with them.[11]

The issue of reserved rights was at the nexus between the contending theories of government's nature. Before continuing, the reader should recall two salient points. The Tenth Amendment defining the authorities associated with reserved rights was not yet in effect. Also, Virginians inevitably linked them with the Declaration of Rights and particularly trial by jury, freedom of the press, and freedom of religion.

Until Parliament proclaimed the English Bill of Rights in 1688, the king and people could never agree on the location of the power residue. Finally, it limited the king's power and defined those of the people. Thus, according to Patrick Henry, Federalist claims that Virginians need not fear any loss of their rights were specious. History proved that they must be stipulated. It was particularly crucial because of the loss of state sovereignty defined in the Constitution.

The most obvious target would be the Virginia Declaration of Rights. A national Legislature that had no checks on its power would puncture its protection. Moreover, without some specific coverage, one left one's inalienable rights to the whim of Congress that "will construe it as they please." In an amusing exchange, Henry challenged, "a bill of rights may be summed up in a few words.... Why not say so? Is it because it will consume too much paper?"

Federalists countered this insinuation. Since the people retained all powers not given up, they said, a Declaration (Bill) of Rights was superfluous. However, both George Nicholas and Edmund Randolph displayed one weakness in that argument. Each referred to an obvious location of the power residue. This led naturally to a discussion of the three reserved rights listed in Virginia's Declaration of Rights. Madison insisted that this list was not discriminating. One must always be careful of an enumeration, he warned, because if one assumed it was exhaustive, one would give all powers not listed to the government.

Henry was prepared for Nicholas's and Randolph's weak argument. No, he lectured, the location of the power residue was not clear. In Europe, and particularly Great Britain, the people relinquished all the rights not expressly reserved to Parliament. Grayson agreed wholeheartedly. After all, even the despised Articles included a clause defining the location of the residue. If declaring the location specifically in that instance had been necessary, why not in this? A quick glance at the state constitutions would confirm that the states had followed the European model. That residue fell to the governments.

The Federalists realized this was a losing argument. Everyone could see that the combination of the Supremacy Clause and the necessary and proper provision made the contention untenable. Therefore, in the ratifying document the convention included clarifying language. Driven by Antifederalist complaints, it asserted that trial by jury and liberty of the press and religion were not endangered by the Constitution. That claim perked up Henry's attention. How would one interpret the finite list? Since it reserved some rights, all others must be relinquished. The ratified document must contain an admission that powers not granted remained with the people. Addenda offered no assurance since Congress might ignore them. George Nicholas promised the convention that the companion paper contained the Antifederalist interpretation of reserved rights. Now, Madison could crow that his interpretation was correct. Still, the addenda was too late and was not part of the Constitution. Had not the Federalists insisted on an up or down vote with no amendments?

Henry Lee revealed another error in Federalist dogma. He agreed that state constitutions reversed the location of the residue rights compared with Federalist claims although the Constitution corrected this procedure. If that were so, questioned Henry, why did the Constitution contain clauses that restrained congressional power? He answered his own query: "Is not the clear implication this — that if these restrictions were not inserted, they could have performed what they prohibit?"

The role of implication occurred several times during these debates. Here, it was crucial. Patrick Henry claimed that it was a target of the Revolutionaries. Since power change was a zero sum game, augmentation of congressional power diminished that of the people. Most dangerously, the implication clause of Article I, Section 8 had no bounds.[12]

The debates on a Bill of Rights and the necessary and proper provision ranged widely and often overlapped. For our purposes we will treat them discretely.

Antifederalists considered a Bill indispensable to liberty. They required a constitutional compact that was an unambiguous declaration of the locus of powers or rights. It must include every power the people delegated to the government and avoid implication. In addition, the states must retain any powers not assigned to the central government. If a Bill did not fulfill these basic requirements, Antifederalists predicted a long list of scenarios redounding negatively on Virginia. Incident to its loss of sovereignty was the sacrifice of the protections defined by the Declaration; the Supremacy Clause negated those same inherent rights; the existence of the Virginia Declaration proved that Virginians would never trust their rights to strangers; the poor, uneducated farmer could never plough through the voluminous, scholarly treatises enunciating his implied rights, but he could grasp a straightforward list containing them; a

Bill of Rights would leaven any inclusion of the concept of judicial review; an unconstrained federal judiciary would endanger the Virginia common law system built over decades; and ratification without a Bill would ensure that consolidation and the loss of liberty would follow ratification.

Federalists considered many of these complaints mere exaggerations. They had decided that the tidal wave of complaints was an Antifederalist tactic designed to weaken the idea of a national government. After all, some American states had no Bills of Rights. Even that in Virginia gave little protection to the people as its provisions were merely recommendatory. Moreover, the Antifederalist argument based on compact theory and specific constitutional provisions was a sham. The people did not contract with their government to assure their liberties. Instead, they were the source of government and granted it all its powers. Therefore, a Bill of Rights was unnecessary and redundant. If deviations did occur, the obvious solution was the "primary right of power in the people." Elections would be more useful than a "Paper-Bill of Rights." Despite this rejection of a portion of compact theory, the most popular Federalist argument was based on another familiar implication. The basic Lockean compact insisted that after the sovereign people delegated certain powers to their government, the residue remained with them. Since the people had never surrendered trial by jury and the other named rights, they retained them. Some added that all powers eventually returned to the people while others replaced "the people" with "the states." Thus, Randolph's curt "a bill of rights, therefore, accurately speaking, is quite useless, if not dangerous to a republic" was an accurate assertion of the Federalist position.

The opposition assumed that corruption was sure to occur. Therefore, Randolph's maxim did not move it. Obviously, some check must balance the powers of the sweeping clauses. Monroe offered a brief scenario to alert the convention to the need for a Bill of Rights to counteract the general powers. Suppose a demand for a direct tax accompanied the lack of a Bill. To put it into effect, Congress abrogated trial by jury, a right not specified within the Constitution. What clauses in the Constitution prevented the scenario? With the implication dam breached, further debate revealed dangers inherent in a standing army, *ex post facto* laws, and to freedom of the press and trial by jury. Nevertheless, the most telling was one proposed by George Mason. Suppose oppression beset America and a heroic writer exposed it. What check prevented Congress from claiming that he was a threat to the "general peace, encouraging sedition, and poisoning the minds of the people," and bringing him to justice? Patrick Henry added another nail to the coffin of the Federalist interpretation. Examine Article I, Section 9. One could view it as a weak Constitutional Bill of Rights. By implication one could argue that Congress had power to take every action not expressly forbidden. Henry then examined *habeas corpus* and concluded that "if it had not said so, they could suspend it in all cases whatsoever." If one accepted the initial premise, this argument was a counter example to the Federalist claim concerning the locus of the residual rights and stressed the necessity of a Bill of Rights. When one appended these dramatic examples to the dangers to liberty inherent in the combination of the Supremacy Clause and the necessary and proper provision, one can see that the Federalists fought an uphill battle.[13]

Strangely, the sweeping clause — George Mason's appellation for the necessary and proper provision — received little attention in the Constitutional Convention. In Virginia, Federalist apologists offered several disparate secondary reasons for this clause's inclusion. For example, the Constitution must ensure that Congress had powers proportionate to the needs of legislation even if other means of arriving at legislation might make its use unnecessary. Also, Americans must trust their representatives to apply the power judiciously. Once this was established, they soon moved to other arguments. Chief among them was the constant assertion that the clause "does not in the least increase the powers of Congress. It is only inserted for greater caution, and to prevent the possibility of encroaching upon the powers of Congress." George Nicholas, in one of his characteristically informative speeches, laid out the Federalist interpretation.

> The Committee will perceive, that the Constitution had enumerated all the powers which the General Government should have but did not say how they were to be exercised. It therefore in this case tells *how* they shall be exercised. Does this give any new power? I say not. Suppose it had been inserted at the end of every power, that they should have power to make laws to carry that power into execution: Would this have increased their powers? If therefore it could not have increased their powers, if placed at the end of each power, it cannot increase them at the end of all. This clause only enables them to carry into execution the powers given to them, but gives them no additional power.

James Madison reminded his colleagues that the application of a delegated power necessarily implied the "authority to make laws to execute it." Obviously, listing those powers delegated to Congress or left to the states was physically impossible so this was the best solution. Pendleton agreed. The "plain language of the clause is to give them power to pass laws in order to give effect to the delegated powers." In any case, the people and states need not worry about usurpations. When they identified one, the state governments would swing into action and present a "bold and active opposition." Also, the judiciary would have the power to make any tyrannous laws void "or else the people will have a right to declare it void."

Antifederalists remained unconvinced. Behind these arguments, reinforcing their fear that Congress could assume undelegated powers lay implication. These usurpations would not occur immediately. Instead, they would play out over time and would "finally destroy the State governments more effectively by insidious underhanded means than such as could be openly practiced." This prophesy would occur, asserted Henry, if the Supreme Court proved friendly to Congress. James Monroe could find no limits like those described by Federalists in the clause. Exactly where were the limits or qualifications? In Henry's words, the sweeping clause delegated Congress "the power to do every thing." Again, Mason demanded some clause that declared "that rights not given to the central government were retained by the states."

Examples of the harmful effects of a combination of the sweeping clause and delegated powers were common. Monroe linked direct taxation and the sweeping clauses to an abrogation of trial by jury; Henry, as we know, linked the sweeping clause to a simultaneous call for the same state militia; Mason, earlier, had linked taxation and the clause to freedom of the press; and most important, the association of the Supremacy Clause to the necessary and proper provision was a dagger aimed at the people's liberty and reserved rights.

Edmund Randolph adopted a conciliatory position. It appeared to the governor that each side had exaggerated its position to such an extent that neither was believable. He blamed neither side for the discrepancy. The fault lay in the clause's construction. It was too vague.[14]

Randolph had a narrow view of the power residue in the general welfare clause, also called a sweeping clause by some. Congress could collect only enough taxes "to pay the debts and provide for the common defence and welfare of the United States." Internally, it enunciated that the collection of taxes backstopped its inclusion. Moreover, it did not foresee "a substantial power to provide for the general welfare of the United States." George Nicholas agreed. Any insinuation that the clause could extend other delegated powers was false. Public debts were the focus. Unfortunately, this was exactly the interpretation assumed by Antifederalists. William Grayson labeled the general welfare clause one of "indefinite power." Randolph again condemned this view. "No man who reads it can say," he assured his fellow conventioneers, "it is general, as the Honorable Gentlemen represented it. You must violate every rule of construction and common sense, if you sever it from the power of raising money, and annex it to any thing else."[15]

One did not have to study the clauses above deeply to sense the importance of implication within their interpretations. Unfortunately, future agents, not those so sure of the current meanings, would interpret the implications buried within the clause. Patrick Henry sensed this acutely. "Implication is dangerous," he expounded, "because it is unbounded: if it be admitted at all, and no limits be prescribed, it admits of the utmost extension." Again, he attacked the Federalist assumption that "every thing that is not given is retained." Could not one use implication to arrive at the reverse proposition?[16]

✠

The basic underpinning of state rights lay in the federal-state power sharing arrangements. Within this debate its two most important supplements were a raucous discussion on the amending process and an appended list of reserved rights known as Virginia's reservation. George Mason suggested that "we ought to give power with a sparing hand to any Government thus imperfectly constructed." However, Henry Lee intimated that, as Madison defined it, power could be split between the two governments. Grayson agreed but registered the opinion that in every dispute, the state government would be overruled. The result would be an emasculated state legislature. George Nicholas rejected this interpretation. Virginia's 160 delegates would sway ten congressmen. These conclusions highlighted a common exaggeration by modern critics of state rights. Its adherents were not opposed universally to government power. However, federal power must be limited. Nicholas reminded the conventioneers that the states had originally held each power now assumed by the general government. Therefore, they would guard carefully against usurpations on the rights of the states.

When the debate encompassed state rights, a change in the role of the people was evident. From the beginning, Henry rejected any assumption that the people had given the Philadelphia delegates the "power to use their name." Conventioneers had obviously "exceeded their power" because they were simply state deputies not agents of the people. The Federalists would never accept this interpretation. Repeatedly, Nicholas, Marshall, and Madison highlighted the sovereignty of the people and their central position in preventing usurpations and tyranny. Madison even defined the people's highest sovereign capacity as its role as "the states." Surely they could challenge any unconstitutional government actions. These assertions were unlikely to move Henry. He had already reminded the convention that any negative on state laws was likely to proceed in the opposite direction. Could not the new government veto state laws at will?

Several other issues cropped up. According to Federalists, only the people, not the states, could ratify the Constitution. Parroting Lockean theory, Henry rejected this interpretation. Basing his observations on his requirement that the Constitution must form a confederation, he then argued that the people had no role in building "leagues, alliances, or confederations." The sovereign states were the proper agents. In answer to a question on the state right to have slaves, Madison asserted that "no power is given to the general government to interpose with respect to the property in slaves now held by the states."

As usual, Patrick Henry encapsulated the Antifederalist' state rights dilemma. While discussing the power of treaties, Henry reminded the delegates that they could infringe on the basic rights of a Virginian. In florid language, he argued, "We are told that the state rights are preserved ... I ask and demand, how do the rights of persons stand, when they [Congress] have power to make any treaty, and that treaty is paramount to constitutions, laws, and every thing?"[17]

Not only did the delegates recognize that they must be able to adjust the powers of the central government, but also they sought guarantees for both state and individual rights. Amendments would achieve each. Edmund Randolph knew that the Convention had erred in its suggestion that ratification required solely an up or down vote. Maybe corrections could be made before ratification but Edmund Pendleton concluded that the process defined in the Constitution could correct any defects and George Wythe agreed. Mason admitted that if they enshrined the amendments he insisted on "I shall most heartily make the greatest concessions and concur in any reasonable measure to obtain the desirable end of conciliation and unanimity." Randolph cited the appellate provision of the judiciary clause as a perfect example of a mistake that needed adjusting. Henry, concentrating on republican ideals, unearthed another. Despite constant Federalist claims that the Constitution could amend its own defects, Henry proved it specious. If the majority wanted to employ the Article, the four smallest states, with the overwhelmingly smallest population, could defeat the amendment. Benjamin Harrison offered the political background to Henry's remark. During the debate in Philadelphia, the small states had received every concession they sought, so they would never accede to amendments.

Eventually, three amendment issues surfaced. Two were familiar. Antifederalists continued to insist on previous amendments while Federalists lampooned them. The possibility of disunion convinced Randolph that their consideration so late in the process was dangerous. Francis Corbin reminded his colleagues that the inclusion of previous amendments would require those states that had already ratified to reexamine their decision. John Marshall predicted that they would encourage the delegates opposed to ratification to flood the document with strictly local amendments to defeat it. James Innes alleged that the concept of previous amendments removed the people from the debate since they had not had an opportunity to study them.

Henry warned of the dangers of subsequent amendments. To accept the idea was tantamount to "leaving it to the casual opinion of the Congress" for debate and inclusion. Moreover, the reserved rights listed in the reservation, which we will examine later, would be left to opinion. Recall his query: "Do you enter into a compact of Government first, and afterwards settle the terms of the Government?" After Madison posited that other states would not accept Virginia's previous amendments, Henry reminded him that to argue now that the same states in Congress would accept them later was naive. Harrison raised the question of trust. Did the North help Virginia during the Revolution? Would the small states help Virginia?

Late in the debate, the delegates introduced another amending procedure. Due to Federalist uncertainty about ratification, they agreed to add some proposed amendments and guarantees to the ratification package. We will label it Virginia's reservation.

It contained various reserved rights' stipulations. Historians have generally accorded it little importance but Virginians lauded it for decades and quoted it in their eventual seces-

Figure 4.1: A Comparison of Resolutions Leading to Virginia's Reservation Statement

Randolph's Model

If it be not considered too early, as ratification has not yet been spoken of, I beg leave to speak of it. *If I did believe ... that all power not expressly retained was given up by the people, I would detest this Government. But, I never thought so, nor do I now.* If in the ratification we put words to this purpose,—that all authority not given, is retained by the people, and may be resumed when perverted to their oppression; and that *no right can be cancelled, abridged, or restrained, by the Congress, or any officer of the United States;* I say, if we do this, I conceive that as this stile of ratification would manifest the principles on which Virginia adopted it, *we should be at liberty to consider as a violation of the Constitution, every exercise of a power not expressly delegated therein.*

Wythe's Resolutions

WHEREAS the powers granted under the proposed Constitution are the gift of the people, and every power not granted thereby, remains with them, and at their will: No right therefore of any denomination, can be cancelled, abridged, restrained or modified by the Congress, by the Senate or House of Representatives, acting in any capacity, by the President, or any department or officer of the United States, except in those instances in which power is given by the Constitution for those purposes: **And among other essential rights, liberty of conscience and of the press cannot be cancelled, abridged, restrained or modified by any authority of the United States**:

AND WHEREAS any imperfections which may exist in the said Constitution ought rather to be examined in the mode prescribed therein for obtaining amendments, than by a delay with a hope of obtaining previous amendments, to bring the Union into danger:

Resolved, That it is the opinion of this Committee, **THAT THE SAID CONSTITUTION BE RATIFIED.**

But in order to relieve the apprehensions of those, who may be solicitous for amendments,

Resolved, That it is in the opinion of this Committee, That whatsoever amendments may be deemed necessary be recommended to the consideration of the Congress, which shall first assemble under the said Constitution, to be acted upon according to the mode prescribed in the fifth article thereof.

Engrossed Version

WE the Delegates of the people of Virginia ... *DO, in the name and in behalf of the people of Virginia, declare and make known that the powers granted under the Constitution, being derived from the people of the United States may be resumed by them whensoever the same shall be perverted to their injury or oppression, and that every power not granted thereby remains with them and at their will: That therefore no right of any denomination, can be cancelled, abridged, restrained or modified, by the Congress, by the Senate or House of Representatives acting in any capacity, by the President or any department or officer of the United States, except in those instances in which power is given by the Constitution for those purposes:* **And among other essential rights, the liberty of conscience and of the press cannot be cancelled, abridged, restrained or modified by any authority of the United States.**

With these impressions; with a solemn appeal to the searcher of hearts for the purity of our intentions, and under the conviction, that, whatsoever imperfections may exist in the Constitution, ought rather to be examined in the mode prescribed therein, than to bring the Union into danger by a delay, with a hope of obtaining amendments, previous to the ratification:

We the said Delegates, in the name and in behalf of the People of Virginia, do by these presents ASSENT TO, AND RATIFY THE CONSTITUTION....

sion declaration. Perhaps Madison's description of it as "a few declaratory truths not affecting its [Constitution] validity" and Albert Beveridge's notation that it was "some claimed & general matters" persuaded readers that it was simply a piece of boiler plate. However, James Monroe wrote Jefferson that the proceedings "terminated as you will find in a ratification which must be considered, so far as a reservation of certain rights go, as conditional, with the recommendations of subsequent amendments." Madison admitted it contained "truths," while Monroe indicated that it should be considered in the same manner as amendments. By comparison, the *New York Journal* commented on its uniqueness. Thus, enough uncertainty existed to warrant further examination.

Any study will quickly run aground on two issues unless it solved them. Who were the people? Did the reservation reflect just an interesting preamble or was it a warning from the conventioneers about future federal-state relations?

Participants had no doubt that the reservation was the positive result of convention dynamics. James Madison, in a letter to Alexander Hamilton, admitted that his faction had to trade some "highly objectionable" amendments for ratification. If such was the case, the argument that it was boiler plate lacked validity. The Antifederalist insistence on a Bill of Rights fuelled the reservation.

On June 21 Edmund Randolph prepared the convention for a possible reservation and amendments (See Figure 4.1). As the convention concluded, Patrick Henry would evidently offer such a list. To intercept this probability, George Wythe, on June 24, proposed that the convention, sitting as a Committee of the Whole, ratify the Constitution and recommend selected amendments. His two resolutions, based on Randolph's model (see Figure 4.1), proposed that the people retained the residue of powers, and that the central government could not infringe the people's rights. Specifically mentioned was "liberty of conscience and of the press." Henry immediately objected. He preferred to transmit a list of objections and amendments to the other states for further consideration. Nicholas sought to placate the opposition. In an amazing speech he laid out the consequences of a Virginia reservation.

> Mr. Nicholas contended that the language of the proposed ratification would secure every thing which Gentleman desired, as it declared that all powers vested in the Constitution were derived from the people, and might be resumed by them whensoever they should be perverted to their injury and oppression; and that every power not granted thereby, remained at their will, no danger whatever could arise. For, says he, these expressions will become a part of the contract. The Constitution cannot be binding on Virginia, but with these conditions. If thirteen individuals are about to make a contract, and one agrees to it, but at the same time declares that he understands its meaning, signification, and intent, to be, what the words of the contract plainly and obviously denote; that it is not to be construed so as to impose any supplementary condition upon him, and that he is to be exonerated from it, whensoever any such imposition shall be attempted, — I ask whether in this case, these conditions on which he has assented to it, would not be binding on the other twelve. In like manner these conditions will be binding on Congress. They can exercise no power that is not expressly granted them.

He posited four important themes. First, the ratifying process included a state's right to amend the proposed Constitution. Also, to this Federalist spokesman, the people mentioned in the reservation were Virginians, not the consolidated people of the United States. Moreover, the former retained the residual rights. Last, Nicholas constructed a justification for Virginia protest in federal-state disputes. The rights, and the reservation that contained them, defined conditions under which Virginia joined the Union. If Wythe's amendments were a part of the ratification, so too would be other similar additions. For example, the other states, by accepting Virginia into the Union, accepted its reservation. Due to these assertions, one might understand the Antifederalist's faith in their credo. The rights, and the reservation that contained them, defined conditions under which Virginia joined the Union.

In the compromise's spirit, the convention met the next day to finish the process. Still to be refined were the Wythe resolutions, Henry's amendments and ratification. Antifederalists, with no success, recommended a process in which they would circulate a declaration of rights and previous amendments among the states. Shortly afterwards, the convention ratified the Constitution.

Next, it turned to Wythe's introductory resolutions and stripped the preamble from his second resolution but passed the remainder. Five notable Federalists, Randolph, Nicholas, Madison, Marshall, and Corbin, produced a form of ratification to replace the deleted preamble. Another group, comprising eleven Federalists and nine of their opponents prepared the compromise amendments.

We have already indicated that the notion that the reservation was merely a few truths was questionable. Although no other state had included an extended reservation as did Virginia, both New York and Rhode Island did after that fact while others commented on reserved rights. A comparison (see Figure 4.1) of Randolph's model, Wythe's resolutions, and the engrossed form will persuade the reader that its genesis was within the convention and that the delegates produced a document that reflected its concerns. Randolph asserted the right of the people to the residual rights and specifically laid a restraint on government with respect to those rights. Wythe built on this outline and identified specific protected rights. He added an important proviso concerning previous amendments, a call for ratification, and a recommendation on the inclusion of amendments. The committee's final version included references to each of these. However, the second Wythe resolution that the First Congress consider the amendments was unnecessary as the convention had already passed it. Of course, the authors had updated language and phraseology, but the path from Randolph's model to the final reservation was clear. No doubt, the final form was the direct result of arguments made during the debate in the face of possible ratification defeat. It was not just "a few declaratory truths."

As we might expect from our previous discussion the committee held disparate views on whether its suggestions would be previous or subsequent to ratification. The old antagonists, Madison and Henry, spoke for the parties. Was it not clear to all that Congress would make only a "feeble" attempt to enshrine the great rights of the people? They must list unalienable rights before ratification so that Virginians would know the reservation protected them. To James Innes's contention "that you transcend and violate the commission of the people" if you insisted on previous amendments, Henry responded that Innes "admits our power over subsequent amendments, though not over previous amendments. Where is the distinction between them? If we have the right to depart from the letter of our commission in one instance, we have in the other." Madison concentrated on another dispute. He assured the delegates that the list of rights could not be exhaustive because the people had not given them up, that is "every thing not granted is reserved." Remember, if one tried to make a full enumeration, those omitted from the list would be lost.

Before we render a textual study of the phrase "that the powers granted under the Constitution, being derived from the people of the United States" (see Figure 4.1), let us restate each faction's notion about sovereignty. Federalists proclaimed the sovereignty of the people. They delegated some power to the central and state governments and retained the rest. Antifederalists also believed in the sovereignty of the people but the target of the delegation was the state government. As one might expect, allusions to the "people" or the "people of the United States" might be liable to misinterpretation. With respect to the language of the reservation, Henry Shanks, whose *The Secession Movement in Virginia, 1847–1861* is still the initial stop for Virginia researchers, claimed "it would seem from the debate on this resolution [Virginia's reservation] that the phrase 'people of the United States' referred to the people of the separate states as political entities rather than as the people of the United States as an entity." This interpretation agreed with Nicholas's earlier statement. How did they reach this conclusion and how did it affect Virginia's interpretation of the reservation?

First, the delegates knew whom they represented. The Virginia legislature had organized the convention to elicit her citizens' opinion. Moreover, the reservation clearly enunciated that it acted "in the name and in behalf of the people of Virginia." Arguments insisting that the reservation referred to the states of the United States stumbled badly. Such a view required the delegates to represent all Americans. Since New York, for example, appended a sister clause to its ratification, it also spoke for all the states. Of course, this meant that it spoke for Virginia. Patently, this was ludicrous. Similarly, North Carolina's and Rhode Island's failure to ratify was not symbolic of a national rejection but was one of individual choice. Moreover, James Madison proved that each "political society," i.e. each state, must ratify individually as a state. No, the conventions represented the states individually and no others.

Shanks translation relied on Locke's compact theory. James Madison, in his famous Report of 1799–1800, laid out the possible meanings of the word "state." Harry Jaffa agreed with Madison's assessment that the most accurate definition of state for the convention's purposes "means the people composing those political societies in their highest sovereign capacity." That capacity produced the state government compact during the transition from a state of nature. In essence, "the *states* in their highest sovereign capacity are identical with the *people of the United States* in their highest sovereign capacity." Thus, if a Virginian steeped in Lockean theory examined the crucial phrase, one could forgive him if he translated it as "that the powers granted under the Constitution, being derived from the states" and that oppression might result in a "state" resuming its power. An interesting aspect of this interpretation was that its application neatly sidestepped any charge of revolution or secession since it was neither. It was a natural right whose boundaries were self-contained.

During the final hours of the convention, the delegates examined and proposed, forty amendments. The third involved tax collecting. If accepted, it would reduce the Constitution government from a complete entity with its own taxing power to one depending on requisitions. An examination of the vote was shocking. Prominent Federalists like Pendleton, Carrington, and William Fleming voted to retain the offending amendment. Surely, this proved the uncertainty that many Federalists held with respect to the results of their deliberations. In addition, it might be a preview of a reorganization of Virginia's political blocs.[18]

Since we had a firm notion of the two constituencies contending ratification, we can also analyze voting results. Although our discussion of the issue-related political blocs prepared us for most of the vote tallies, a few mild surprises did occur. Thankfully, several eminent historians have studied and collated the results. Some referred to individuals while others reflect counties.

Jackson Turner Main's division between cosmopolitans and localists proved germane.

Most cosmopolitans voted for ratification while localists did not. Individuals who favored debt payment, were foreign born, or lived in areas devastated by the Revolution were cosmopolitans. Those who favored the return of slave property and others who distrusted any issue supported by the hated northern financier Robert Morris joined them.

The geographical grouping mirrored the preconstitution issue blocs. Generally, the counties bordering major rivers and their allies opposed those without that access. For example, the Northern Neck counties voted 24–3 in favor of ratification. They were joined by counties that equated restricted expansion and a reduction in land speculation to the continued British occupation of the western forts. Surprisingly, delegates from the Shenandoah Valley and western Virginia whom most prognosticators would expect to support the Antifederalist Southside did not do so. Some Valley delegates elevated debt payment and increased congressional power in their list of discriminators because they shipped produce east along the Potomac. Kentucky, with many small farmers and wealthy planters, needed an accessible Mississippi. Based upon the Jay-Gordoqui imbroglio, it feared northern intent and it remained an Antifederalist bastion.

With these interpretations in mind, one historian concluded that ratification would have failed if westerners had maintained their accustomed voting positions. They linked the specter of western frontier warfare to debt repayment and concluded that a successful solution of these issues might persuade the British to abandon the forts. The new national government would then provide protection and immigration would bloom.[19]

5

Government on Trial—National Policies and the State Rights Reaction

The contentious, often overheated, debate throughout first the state and then the ratification convention warned readers that support for the goals of the Constitution was spotty at best in Virginia. However, debate was only a predictor. Most Virginians would have to wait to see if the government they had supported was truly limited. Some were unwilling to take that chance.

Although prominent Virginia Federalists had assured their counterparts that the sweeping clause, consolidation, or the judiciary article did not endanger liberty, Patrick Henry would not lower his guard. According to Article V, the state legislatures could force Congress to call a convention to propose amendments. If Henry could persuade enough states to follow his lead, a significant Bill of Rights could be added and direct taxation deleted. To pressure the Legislature to action, Henry threatened to interrupt the process of organizing congressional districts. The result would be electoral chaos.

The House of Delegates, on October 30, 1788, passed a resolution demanding Congress prepare for a second convention to secure the people's "dearest rights and liberties" and prevent "those disorders which must arise under a government not founded in the confidence of the people." By November 20, amended versions had passed both state houses and in mid–February 1789 Governor Beverley Randolph transmitted them to Virginia's congressional representatives. On May 5, Theodorick Bland presented them to the House. They included a reference to Virginia's reservation and pointedly informed Congress that "the slow forms of congressional discussion" would not suit the "anxiety with which our countrymen press for the accomplishment of this important end." Instead, a convention of the states should be the vehicle of change.

Madison recognized immediately that Bland's suggestion for immediate debate was unconstitutional. He happily reminded his fellow Virginian that no discussion could occur until two-thirds of the states confirmed Virginia's request. Until then, it must "remain upon the files." Finding little support, it remained there indefinitely.[1]

Meanwhile, Congress assumed its duty to organize the national government. Two of its considerations particularly affected state rights. Early in the first session, as the House struggled with bills organizing the executive office and defining revenues, the Senate laid the basis for the national judiciary. This process confirmed the accepted tenet of Legislative authority. Since more than 55 percent of the members of the First Congress had been engaged in one role or another in the ratification process, we might predict that the dangers associated with unconstitutional acts might be few. Still, during the Articles' government, Congress only had jurisdiction over admiralty cases and disputes over state borders or land grants. State courts adjudicated all other cases. Obviously, the Constitution would seriously curtail state authority.

On June 22, the Senate, sitting as a Committee of the Whole, discussed the role of district courts. After the Committee confirmed their inclusion, Richard Henry Lee offered a motion, "nearly in the words of the Virginia amendment," that "the jurisdiction of the Federal courts should be confined to cases of admiralty and maritime jurisdiction." This circumscription mirrored amendment fourteen of the constitutional amendments prepared by the Virginia ratifying convention. Considering Lee's experience in that convention, it was surprising that his motion was immediately challenged by antiadministration Senator William Maclay of Pennsylvania. He presented a strong case that the motion would insert an unconstitutional article within the bill. Lee struggled mightily to recoup but his motion failed. In his report to Patrick Henry, William Grayson claimed that, despite its defeat, Virginia's amendment had significant congressional support. He predicted that, in time, the country would recognize the amendment's justice and demand a change in the judiciary act. "Whenever the federal judiciary comes into operation," he wrote, "I think the pride of the states will take alarm, which added to the difficulty of attendance from the extent of the district in many cases, the ridiculous situation of the venue, and a thousand other circumstances, will in the end procure its destruction."

Grayson took a central role during debate on the first clause of the act despite Maclay's suggestion that the Committee was not the proper time to harden opinion. Obviously, the total number of cases that reached the Supreme Court would be negligible, and thus fewer justices might suffice. Grayson could not see the logic of this position. He argued "that numbers were necessary to procure respectable decisions." The counterargument was not to choose more and better qualified men. The Senate adopted Grayson's view.

Friday, July 17 the Senate completed work on the Judiciary Act despite the objections of Virginia's senators. Four days later, the House finished second reading and allocated further time for the following Monday, July 27. Participants expected a southern frontal attack but the fear of judicial isolation prevented a concerted effort. True, some discussion, particularly on the Virginia amendment took place, but it never threatened the Senate version. Even James Madison seemed hesitant to criticize. Instead, he reminded his peers that "a review of the constitution of the courts in many States will satisfy us that they cannot be trusted with the execution of the Federal laws." On September 17, 1789, the House passed the Judiciary Act.

Not only did the above discussion highlight Virginia's reduction in power and prestige, but also it served to introduce two important clauses, thirteen and twenty-five. Later they would become the center of important constitutional debate. Simply put for our purposes [*Marbury vs. Madison*], section 13 on the Court's appellate jurisdiction, authorized it to issue "writs of *mandamus*, in cases warranted by the principles and usages of law." Oliver Ellsworth and William Patterson, two veterans of the Constitutional Convention, wrote Section 25 dealing with jurisdiction [*Cohens vs. Virginia*].

One would expect that the enabling of the Supremacy Clause expressed Congress's intent concerning judicial review of state laws. The Court would be the final arbiter. According to the eminent historian Leonard Levy, one expected judicial review in a federal system because the subordinate states' laws must comport with those of the federal government. Conventioneers had been aware of this requirement. On the other hand, almost no precedents extended the Supreme Court power to a coordinate branch such as Congress. We will meet these articles later.[2]

⚜

On May 4, 1789, James Madison announced his intention to introduce amendments to the Constitution in the House of Representatives. At least four motives directed his action. Federalists in the Virginia ratifying convention, fearing ratification's defeat, had promised to offer constitutional amendments and/or a Bill of Rights. Moreover, Thomas Jefferson's advice struck him as good sense. Politically, Madison must have noticed the Antifederalist streak in his congressional district. To ignore it might lead to another electoral defeat. Last, the inclusion of a Bill of Rights would signal to the people that its representatives listened to them. This would help to calm the troubled factional waters stirred during ratification. For example, John Page, the son of a wealthy Gloucester County planter, urged the House to pass the amendments speedily. His constituents had waited patiently for months for a Bill of Rights, and if none was forthcoming, he expected demands for a second convention to spike. As late as August 13, he continued to pound away at this danger.

Of course, other Federalists initially held opposing opinions on the necessity of a Bill. After all, they had just achieved a smashing victory at the polls. Did this not suggest the people's satisfaction with the existing Constitution? With so much important introductory legislation pending, it was not sensible to waste time on an unnecessary set of amendments. Almost universally, proratification advocates from James Madison and Alexander Hamilton to the Virginia convention delegates agreed that Congress had only expressly delegated powers. If so, no Bill of Rights was necessary. Of course, that phrase required clarification. Eventually, the House modified its position, but Madison had to forego two of his pet inclusions. He had insisted on a new constitutional preamble stressing the people's power. In a Lockean thrust, government must benefit them, and if it usurped their power, they could change it. Also, he would scatter the amendments throughout the Constitution rather than set them in a solid block. This tactic would reduce the possibility that they might be considered a separate, and possibly separately interpreted, document. The House refused these additions.

Virginia's congressmen held out little chance for significant amendments. Changes to government structure were not going to occur. As William Grayson predicted, "some gentlemen here from motives of policy have it in contemplation to affect amendments which shall effect personal liberty alone." Richard Henry Lee was equally sure that few of Virginia's amendments would pass. Madison, the so-called father of the legislation, admitted that he had deleted controversial articles before debate to ensure passage of the remainder. Even "proper" proposals had met that fate. Richard Bland Lee forecast passage of a few amendments "provided attempts should not be made to introduce others which would destroy the efficacy of Government."

After the usual delays, the House assigned the remaining state resolutions and potential amendments to a select committee for organization. It reported on July 28 and by August 13 the debate was in full swing. For our purposes, most of the debate was superfluous, but we will make a few comments on the article that eventually became the Tenth Amendment.

The original Madison resolution of June 8 included the suggestion that Congress insert a new Article VII, reading "The powers not delegated by this Constitution, nor prohibited by it to the states, are reserved to the states respectively." As it stood, this statement defined the location of the residual powers unless other constitutional articles intervened. Three weeks later, a House select committee reported the organization of the amendments. Madison's residual powers amendment survived intact.

After a further three weeks, the House Committee of the Whole finally found time to debate proposition eighteen, Madison's article. In a questionable parliamentary tactic, Thomas Tudor Tucker of South Carolina, brother of the famous jurist St. George Tucker of Virginia, proposed two sister amendments. The first declared that the phrase "All power being derived from the people" prefix the existing article while the second sought to strengthen this statement by inserting "expressly" between "not" and "delegated." Madison immediately objected. In light of other debates, his statement was interesting. The motion confined "the government within such limits to admit of no implied powers, and I believe ... that no government ever existed which was not necessarily obliged to exercise powers by implication." He reminded the committee that delegates had initiated such a motion in the Virginia convention and had lost. Apparently, Tucker had a different view of the meaning of "expressly" than had Madison. "He thought," he said, "every power to be expressly given that could be clearly comprehended within any accurate definition of the general power." A close reading of this interchange raised questions. What was Madison's basis for his implied powers statement? How was congressional power circumscribed by the proposal? Was expressly delegated power added? Moreover, Tucker's reply seemed unresponsive. What different interpretation could he possibly imply? Did not everyone know what expressly entailed? Perhaps a theoretical sidestep was necessary at this juncture.

Expressly delegated powers had their genesis in Article II of the Articles of Confederation but even state rights men did not foresee a return to that era's power distribution. The goal was to invoke another interpretation describing the power delegation by the sovereign people.

The Virginia convention noted two possibilities. The first, a copy of Article II, maintained that expressly delegated powers did not establish immediate incidents. Every power, without exception, that the government had was the result of a sovereign's delegation. It was summarily rejected. The second option was less restrictive. It defined expressly delegated powers to include necessary incidents. Implications whose scope was controlled were acceptable. Most accepted this theoretical replacement to Article II's restrictive power allocation. Thus, the Tenth was interpreted to begin "The powers and their immediate incidents not delegated to the United States...."

Next, the sovereign states delegated the federal government's powers, so they must be both limited and strictly construed. Otherwise, the compact parties' agreement would be shattered by a government that amended a delegated power into one not delegated. Virginians, including Federalists, commonly assumed "expressly" was inferred, because the parties to the compact, the states, insisted that the contract between them expressly announced their bargain. As a result, the Tenth Amendment must be interpreted to read "The powers and their immediate incidents not expressly delegated to the United States...." Moreover every power not expressly delegated to the government remained with the sovereign.

With these interpretations in hand, let us return to the Tenth Amendment debate and examine Madison's objection. First, he touted the extended definition of "expressly" delegated power in *Federalist* No. 44 and was familiar with its ramifications. Thus, it was fair to say that his reading made "expressly" redundant. However, future debaters might mistakenly argue for a return to the days of Article II with no implied incidents. One could easily conclude that the latter possibility was the reason for his, and the House's, rejection. Note that it did not intellectually negate Tucker's first proposal.

Tucker's main goal was defined by his order of presentation. At this stage of the debate, the House also considered placing "All powers being derived from the people" in the Preamble. Tucker did not consider this positioning constitutionally binding and preferred its inclusion in the amendment. Moreover, he understood the second of the two possible meanings of expressly delegated powers just enunciated by Roger Sherman (Connecticut) to be controlling. Madison offered a rejection based on the Article II interpretation but Tucker did not have it in mind. Express powers, to him, meant that if the sovereign delegated a power to Congress, that delegation, as described above, must imply an express delegation.

Once again, no debate on the first proposal was forthcoming, but the House's defeat of the two-part amendment consigned it to defeat. Thankfully for state rights theory, the people's sovereign power was successfully resurrected by Daniel Carroll (Maryland) who proposed that the phrase "or to the people" be appended to the proposition. Recall that in this era, Virginians commonly understood that a reference to the people associated it with the people of the several states. As noted previously, Carroll's addition ensured a limited government whose powers would be strictly construed because the sovereign states, the parties to the compact, had initiated the power delegation, and thus, expressly restricted the federal government. Thus, Tucker's goal of inserting expressly delegated powers, including some necessary incidents, was fulfilled even though the word "expressly" failed to appear in the Tenth Amendment. Strict construction contained the notion of express delegation and this interpretation was confirmed by the Ninth Amendment. We will examine the effect of the combination of these two amendments in a later section.

On August 24, 1789, the House sent its proposed set of resolutions to the Senate for approval. Senator William Maclay of Pennsylvania left a graphic description of their reception in his house. "They were treated contemptuously by [Ralph] Izard (South Carolina), [John] Langdon (New Hampshire) and [Robert] Morris (Pennsylvania)." These three Federalists attempted to postpone any debate until the next session. Despite Morris's angry denunciations, the Senate set debate for the following week. For some reason, the successful resolution to add "or to the people" was absent and the clause reverted to that originally put by Madison. Nevertheless, the Senate replaced it at the end of the proposed amendment and renumbered it Article XII.

Richard Henry Lee complained that the Senate, despite the Virginia members, had succeeded in weakening an already feeble set of proposals. Graphically, he wrote "we might as well have attempted to move Mount Atlas upon our shoulders. In fact, the idea of subsequent amendments was little better than putting oneself to death first, in expectation that the doctor, who wished our destruction, would afterwards restore us to life." Despite Virginia's disapproval, the Speaker of the House of Representatives and the vice president, on September 28, signed a document to be presented to the states for ratification.

Virginia's Antifederalist senators reacted with disgust. William Grayson informed Henry that the Senate "had so mutilated and gutted" them "that they are good for nothing, and I believe, as many others do, that they will do more harm than benefit." Richard Henry Lee agreed. The Senate "carefully culled" "the english language ... to find words feeble in their nature, or doubtful in their meaning." Patrick Henry, never one to flinch from attacks on liberty, assumed the amendments would assault that beloved tenet. "For what good can be answered by Rights," he queried, "the tenure of which must be during pleasure. For Rights, without having power & might is but a shadow." Since they contained no enforcement power within the Constitution, the rights were unlikely to prove useful. Thomas Tucker put the stamp on the process for the Antifederalist faction. Writing his brother, he claimed "you will find our Amendments to the Constitution calculated merely to amuse, or rather to deceive."

Lee and Grayson decided to make their case to the House of Delegates. They were "apprehensive for Civil Liberty" because Madison's theoretical construct of the extended sphere would not translate to America. Still, Edward Carrington's view of the situation proved correct. Because Virginians favored the process and results, the legislature refused to print the senators' report although someone leaked it several months later.

The statewide process reduced the twelve proposed articles to ten. It rejected the two affecting a change in the representation rate and congressional compensation. Reserved rights, changes to government form, and the notion of trust were the victims of the process. The Federalist dominated Congress eliminated most of the reserved rights and all of the government form proposals from the list presented to the states. To those who doubted the efficacy of the Constitution, the manner in which their counterparts handled the process was but another sharp stick poked in the eye of liberty. The Philadelphia Federalist Richard Peters emphasized it to James Madison. After studying the amendments, he quoted a relevant fable. It concerned some "Malcontents" who, after tasting a bowl of soup, could not refrain from correcting its taste, despite their overall agreement that it was delicious. Eventually,

> We'll make a *Bargain with ourselves*
> That one sha'n't poison t'other
> We are such wise suspicious elves
> That none will trust his brother.
> We'll watch our Pot with sleepless Care,
> O'er all we'll keep a tight Hand,
> For Honesty *we feel's* so rare
> Our left will cheat our right Hand.

Trust had been a much-abused quality in the run-up to the ratification of the Constitution. If it continued to deteriorate, sectionalism was bound to flourish.[3]

Obviously, there had been some dissatisfaction in Virginia with the weak Bill of Rights and its judiciary's subservience to the federal courts. However, at this early stage they were not, on their own, motives for a rush to state rights although they could signal a trend. Nor could they explain why state rights drifted south. Those answers awaited the Secretary of the Treasury's fiscal program.

Crises associated with government debt were familiar to postrevolution Americans. As early as 1780 Congress had attempted to transfer troop compensation to the states. Thus, it was no surprise that public creditors bombarded Congress with petitions demanding the earmarking of federal funds to pay the national debt. Congress, on September 21, 1789, referred the requests to Secretary of the Treasury Alexander Hamilton with instructions to organize a plan for "the adequate support of the public credit." Because of the resolution's lack of specificity, Hamilton felt free to organize the report according to his own economic philosophy.

On January 9, Hamilton, in a prodigious energetic display, informed the House that his report was ready. Five days later, it made its debut.

Hamilton had several imperatives driving his report's contents. Federalists decried the lack of public virtue in the land. Perhaps Hamilton could assist its rebirth by incorporating some monarchical tendencies. Concurrently, he sought to enhance the long-advertised stability of the nation by fostering a credit system that would lead to economic growth. If he achieved that goal, foreign investment capital would turn to America. Locally, the same policy would stir Americans to produce exports that would balance the sorry trade balance.

Hamilton observed that foreign investment would follow if the United States paid its national and state debts quickly. To do so was both honorable and economically necessary. The plan's success required innovative thought and vast government effort. During the war, the widespread use of credit by disparate agencies had flourished.

The scheme had two important corollaries. Not only would it elevate confidence in American fiscal policy but also it would tie creditors and commercial interests at the state and federal level to the Union. Also, by offering specie for payment of both a certificate's principal and interest, Hamilton introduced the country to high finance.

Hamilton's concerns did not match southern expectations. It had few large manufacturing or commercial enterprises and investors would find little of the public debt in its accounting columns. Habitually, southern states had found methods to reduce their debt. Moreover, public securities flowed steadily from their original southern holders to speculators in the North. On the surface, the South had little to gain by funding a public debt since only 16 percent of it resided in that section. Commenting that implementation could only add to sectional tensions seemed fair.

With Hamilton's motives in hand, let us examine their rationale. What were the contents of the public debt? The securities were principally loan certificates that various agencies and individuals had issued to promote the war. They amounted to about $11,000,000. After the war, the debt grew by $17,000,000 due to another certificate class that settled civilian and army accounts. By 1790, the total interest and principal ballooned to about $40,000,000.

The specifics were mind numbing. Quartermaster and Commissary-Generals had indiscriminately signed certificates, banks and governments printed devalued paper money, lottery prizes had issued certificates instead of cash, and officials had casually signed indents that represented interest paid. As one historian put it, "Hardly a means of going into debt known to the governments of the eighteenth century had been omitted by the Continental Congress: and it enjoyed the unenviable distinction of having more creditors than other governments in the world."

Virginia's debt was $2,766,017.92 of which the Continental line contributed $1,754,000. Unfortunately, Virginia's planter aristocracy viewed the Revolution locally. As a result, it mixed federal expenses with other debt. For example, they assumed both Quartermaster and Commissary certificates and showed little concern for the niceties of accounting practices. Later, as we have recorded, Virginians insisted that certificates apply to taxes. Thus, county courts recast each presented certificate in specie, replaced it with existing state certificates, and applied it to local taxes. By this method, Virginia reduced, on its own recognizance, a debt that would have been a component of Hamilton's plan.

The war's successful conclusion was the starting gun for speculation in certificates. In time, most of them gravitated to secondary investors, usually foreigners or the American gentry. Congress's instructions to Hamilton stimulated the process.

To initiate the plan, Hamilton suggested that the national government assume both state and national debts and all creditors be placed on the same footing since the same circumstances had created both debts. To implement the strategy, federal certificates with interest less than 6 percent would replace those already issued. Surely, such an ambitious goal would establish the United States's fiscal integrity. Simultaneously, it would firmly attach the bondholders to the government.

One must give Hamilton credit for his enterprise. Notice that he had to convince Americans to surrender a goal for which they had fought a Revolution. If he succeeded, he would smooth the path toward nationalism and his appeal to self-interest would not only benefit the nation but also the Federalist faction.

That was not to say that Americans unanimously accepted Hamilton's report. The notion that Congress would redeem the Continental debt at par seemed ludicrous in view of proof that it had never done so historically. Moreover, the original creditors would lose most of their principal based on the selling price. Why pay the debt in specie? Could not a less expensive method be employed? However, funding criticisms were muted.

✠

The same could not be said for the assumption of state debts. Because of the difference in debt reduction methodologies employed in the two sections, Hamilton's report was likely to benefit the North over the South. Perhaps we may sample Virginia's mood from the proratification jurist Edmund Pendleton. In a letter to his friend George Washington, he charged that Hamilton's plan was a "System out of the british Ministry" that would turn over the country's economic future to the "monied interests." It would establish Hamilton as the "American Primate" whose motive was "to give the rich Speculators at or near the Seat of Government an advantage over the distant, uninformed, unwary, or distressed Citizens." Theodorick Bland and Richard Henry Lee added their voices. The latter foresaw a continual struggle between "a vast money interest" and "the landed interest, to the destruction of the latter." By the funding act, Congress would convert the states "into mere corporations." Consolidation would result.

Surprisingly, one author of *The Federalist*, James Madison, assumed the position of floor leader for the opposition. Perhaps his motive, as E. James Ferguson stated, was "political expediency rather than a concern for the common man" but one fact was clear. Madison had left the nationalist camp. His plan to pay the debt rapidly would calm fears in Virginia that had led to his Senate rejection and a hard fight for a House seat.

The public credit plan had two main categories, funding and assumption. During debate, opponents tried to attach a major amendment to funding — discrimination — but failed. In short, funding required a holder of a security to take it to a federal agency that would pay the interest, probably in specie, although other methods were possible. Later, the creditor would receive the face value of the certificate. Of course, one must remember that over time, some of these securities, at discounted rates, had often changed hands.

There was no shortage of Virginia critics. Richard Bland Lee doubted the necessity of the process while others could not understand Hamilton's time restrictions associated with debt payment. Could not the government just sell the vacant western lands and apply the profits to the debt? John Page suggested that Congress assume only debts that the Continental Congress would have accepted. Madison disagreed. Equity demanded that all debts be paid in full. After all, various agencies had contracted them while acting in the national interest. That nation, but not government, still existed and was honor bound to pay the debt.

Madison's mention of inequities irked Virginians. Its citizens had worked assiduously to reduce its debt without federal assistance, but according to Hamilton's outline, they would receive little credit for their work. The inequality stretched to the idea of funding only existing debts. Surely some latitude was necessary to ensure the correct accounting for Virginians who had little chance to collect proper records. Moreover, once the government implemented the plan, only taxes could generate the required funds. Emigration and an overloaded tax favoring the western section of Virginia burdened the East and middle counties. Perhaps most galling, it seemed that Virginia's taxes would line British pockets despite English theft of Old Dominion slaves.

The answer to these inequities, claimed James Madison, was an amendment that he labelled discrimination. Senator William Maclay of Pennsylvania, an ardent opponent of funding, left us with a descriptive example of its necessity. £800 of certificates in Pennsylvania could be purchased for £100 and "had drawn interest on the nominal amount for four years, equal to £192. Justice and law allowed them but £24; hence they had £68 clear already, and the certificates into the bargain." Notice, however, the absence of any rebate for the original investors. Among this group were scores of Revolutionary soldiers, militia, and common people unable to cope with the blandishments of clever speculators. Madison offered a compromise. "A composition, then, is the only expedient that remains," he argued, "let it be a liberal one in favor of the present holders, let them have the highest price which has prevailed in the market; and let the residue belong to the original sufferers." By this discrimination strategy, Madison hoped to balance the scales between the original holders of the securities and the speculators. However, Madison's correspondence informed him that both townsmen and gentry refused to support the notion.

Andrew Moore favored the plan, particularly its effects on soldiers. They should be the first group compensated. Speculators who had "stripped" these ignorant men of their certificates could never claim their actions had merit. Moreover, Madison's amendment was overwhelmingly popular with the rest of the people. John Page dared the opponents of discrimination to make any argument based specifically on justice and equity. Practicality must take a back seat to justice. Alexander White reiterated the argument of states that had selflessly reduced their debts. The present scheme, minus discrimination, would ensure that they would not only pay their debts, but also have to tax their citizens to pay those of others. At least discrimination would alleviate some of their pain. Only Antifederalist Theodorick Bland offered some favorable comments about the existing undiscriminated plan. Discrimination would require extended travel to government offices. Upon arrival, a petitioner would wait uncounted hours for service. Besides, most speculators were not as bad as representatives had indicated. Nevertheless, Bland had an ulterior motive that we will encounter later. On February 22, by a vote of 13–36, the House rejected discrimination.

Critics offered several other cavils to the main plan. The people would never accept a system that overtaxed them. Even the Federalist John Page insisted that it was the wedge introducing consolidation into government. He reminded the House that his opponents in Virginia had warned its ratifying convention of this goal. However, the most common complaint was the likelihood that the plan would require the introduction of a hated tax.

Despite these criticisms, no one doubted that the funding portion of the plan would pass. As Madison admitted, "I believe that funding in any shape to be an evil; but it is an evil we are obliged to submit to in one case [funding]; but not in another [assumption]." On July 21, the plan passed with the unanimous consent of the Virginia representatives.

The debate led to several conclusions. The Federalists had initiated their program of government centralization closely tied to an economic elite. Not surprisingly, potential state rights men examined the same results but interpreted them differently. Funding was at the root of consolidation. Thus, it infringed on the rights of the states. Again, southerners found evidence that they could not trust their northern brethren.

Madison's incorporation of an argument benefiting ordinary people presaged an important plank in the future Republican platform. However, arguments about constitutionalism were not central to the House Virginians yet nor was state rights expanded. Consolidation was in the air but did not come seriously to earth at this time.[4]

Whereas Americans had expected some form of public credit, they did not foresee the assumption of state debts or the date defining their acceptability as the day of the public report. Still, the concept was not unique. As noted, the Revolutionary government, in a time of particular economic stress, had dumped some of its burdens on the states. Now it could retrieve them. Moreover, the notion of assumption had reached the floor of the Convention. Although delegates differed on its dynamic, at least they broached the subject.

Several motives, familiar from the debate on public credit, may be behind this legisla-tion. First, it was another method for Hamilton to achieve government centralization by eco-nomic means. As recipient of all national debts, the government would supplant the states as the focus of creditor activity. He would tie speculators, so roundly criticized by administra-tion critics like Senator William Maclay, to the national government. Perhaps, as Edmund Pendleton wrote, Hamilton theorized that an increase in public debt would benefit the Union. Unfortunately, to achieve it, the nation had to accept that speculators would enrich them-selves at the expense of the unsophisticated common man. Also, according to Maclay, the Fed-eralists "seriously never wish the accounts to be settled."

Opposition to the assumption of state debts emanated from all quarters. Despite it, debt ridden states like Massachusetts and South Carolina pleaded for interim relief before Con-gress settled the final accounts. Those that had accepted their obligations and organized their debts — like Virginia — would never accept this tactic. Final accounts must be prepared before a state received any compensation. Obviously, any payment of the South Carolina debt would require a deletion from Virginia's coffers.

According to Richard Bland Lee and Madison, the Federalists were on the verge of negat-ing the good will accumulated during the ratification and amending period. They seemed to delight in aggravating the large southern political bloc by their inequitable economic poli-cies. Theodorick Bland went farther. The consolidationist policies of the Hamiltonians endan-gered state sovereignty and state rights. In a statement eerily presaging future doctrinaires, he stated that "he always had supported, and should continue to support, those measures which should bind and strengthen the Union; so far as was consistent with the Constitution and the rights of the people." To emphasize his position, Bland then promoted assumption. Senator Maclay explained this contradictory line of reasoning — recall Bland's earlier remarks about the public debt. After a visit from the Virginian, Maclay reported that "he avowed his design to be a demonstration to the world that our present Constitution aimed directly at consoli-dation, and the sooner everybody knew it the better; so that in fact, he supported the Secre-tary on anti–Federal principles."

Other House representatives were hamstrung in the constitutional debate. As long as Virginia congressmen demanded that each set of debts, although different in nature, be treated as debts of the United States, their argument clashed with the Constitution. We will see later, however, that this was not a barrier to the Patrick Henry dominated state legislature.

Within the Old Dominion, opinion reflected that of its representatives. Theodorick Bland predicted Virginians were "not yet resigned for such a process [6 percent interest]." Even Federalists like Henry Lee could not continue to ignore the effect of assumption on the national debt when paired with the inequity of the plan. Monetarily, the average Virginian, according to Madison, would pay one-fifth rather than one-seventh of the total. Surely this was the definition of inequity. Assumption was just another example of the domination of the hard-working agricultural community by the northern financial speculators.

The House was riven on the main question. Voting in Committee of the Whole, it first endorsed the bill 31–26 then reversed itself 29–32. Despite many attempts to revive the idea, it was moribund. At last, the House excised assumption and passed only a funding bill. Assumption was left to either the Senate or a compromise.

The latter provided the answer. Because state rights played no significant Virginia role we will report only its essentials. Congress would build the national capital on the Potomac River and in return, Virginia lifted the barrier to the assumption clause. To compensate it further, Congress increased both Virginia's credit total against debts by $500,000 and the period for gathering claims. It extended the date to July 31, 1791.

☒

Reflecting their constituent's disapproval, the Virginia House of Delegates swung into action. When the legislature convened, it began the process of writing two resolutions condemning the constitutionalism and equity of the act. The first labelled the assumption of state debts "repugnant to the Constitution of the United States, as it goes to the exercise of a power not expressly granted to the General Government." Its stablemate, less threatening, chastised Congress for overstepping its bounds by assuming the state's right to redeem its own debt. The house, under the watchful eye of Patrick Henry, also appointed a committee of Federalists and Antifederalists to compose a thoughtful Memorial to Congress protesting the basis of the act. It must have been interesting to see Henry, Francis Corbin, and Henry Lee cooperating to beard the government.

Perhaps a letter from Senator Richard Henry Lee to Patrick Henry had sensitized the great man to the dire consequences of the path trod by Congress. Most important was "its tendency to a consolidated government, instead of the Union of Confederated states." He challenged Madison's theory of the expanded sphere and then posited an overarching state rights' tactic that would be adopted by its adherents. State rights men would pass it from generation to generation.

> It becomes the friends of liberty to guard with perfect vigilance every right that belongs to the states and to protest against every invasion on them, taking care always to procure as many protesting states as possible; this kind of vigilance will create caution, and establish such a mode of conduct as will create a system of precedent that will prevent a consolidating effect from taking place by slow but sure degrees.

Virginia based delegates were quick to answer Hamilton's assumption of state debts scheme. On November 22, 1790, the Federalist Francis Corbin reported the "Memorial from the General Assembly of this Commonwealth, to the Congress of the *United States.*" Correctly, one historian of the period has categorized it as ranking "in importance with the historic resolutions of 1798 against the Alien and Sedition Laws" because it "formulated the principle of strict construction." The first draft of the Memorial was well organized and succinct but employed descriptors like "odious," "extorts," and "deformed" that were bound to inflame the debate.

A committee organized it into three sections, policy, justice, and constitutionalism. Surely, no one could cite a republican policy that would "limit the right of the United States in their redemption of the public debt." Notice that the phrase "United States" referred to the federation of the states. Did not assumption mirror the English scheme — after its revolution — that led to enormous debts and executive influence? If "same causes produce the same effects," the United States should avoid this path. In addition, the large agrarian interest would face two evils, "the prostration of agriculture at the feet of commerce, or a change in the present form of federal government, fatal to the existence of American liberty." As usual, Virginia's representatives promoted the concept of a federal Union. Their insistence reminded Congress that influential delegates had made certain promises during the ratification process.

The Memorial continued with a criticism of "fiscal officers of Congress" whose platform "goes directly to support the exploded policy of introducing fictitious wealth through a paper medium which the general voice of America, by the adoption of the new Constitution, has already stamped with reprobation." For years, ardent Federalists had preached the gospel of paper money elimination, but now, when it suited their agenda, they embraced the notion despite probable constitutional difficulties.

Some aspects of the act defied justice. Everyone knew that Virginia's citizens had redeemed a large proportion of its Revolutionary war debt through taxation. Plans had been made to pay the balance and success seemed "not far distant." Shockingly, the act restarted the taxation process for a debt that would last until every state debt was eliminated. As a result, Congress had usurped the right of Virginia to tax her own citizens according to its requirements. Might not it be forced to pay "excesses, and other execrable schemes of taxation"? To protect its citizens, Virginia would have to lower its expectations because her citizens could not afford "double taxes." Reflecting Hamilton's motives, the Memorial complained that "holders of state certificates are forced to become subscribers to the Federal loan." Of course, this may result in "considerable loss in point of interest."

The above discussion was certainly important to Virginians economically but the last section was crucial doctrinally. "During the whole discussion of the Federal Constitution by the convention of Virginia," it reminded Congress, "your Memorialists were taught to believe 'That every power not expressly granted was retained.'" Moreover, the instrument of ratification contained Virginia's reservation that featured that clause.

> But, your Memorialists can find no clause in the Constitution authorizing Congress in express terms, to assume the debts of the states; as the guardians then of the rights and interests of their constituents, as sentinels placed by them over the ministers of the Federal Government, to shield it from their encroachments, or at least to sound the alarm, when it is threatened by invasion, they can never reconcile it to their consciences, silently to acquiesce in a measure which violates that hallowed maxim; a maxim in the truth and sacredness of which the Federal government depended for its adoption in this Commonwealth.

The Memorial ended with a constitutional bombshell. The house asserted that it had the same contract with the United States as it had during Confederation, and that "the rights of states, as contracting parties with the United States, must be considered as sacred." As a result, "the consent of the State Legislatures ought to be obtained, before the said act can assume a constitutional form." In subsequent revisions, the house eliminated or toned down some tough language, references to paper money, and Virginia's state assumption. Still, the basic elements remained.

A recap of the contents of this document revealed several important contentions. The house linked republican virtue to state rights; agriculture remained the center of the American economic experience; liberty was in danger; Virginia's reservation was consequential and in effect; the state considered itself the agent of its citizens; and the federal Union was a compact whose members should follow a strict interpretation of the Constitution. These were momentous claims and a balancing point in the nation's history. Their importance was not lost to Alexander Hamilton.

Upon receipt of the resolutions, he immediately contacted his *The Federalist* coauthor John Jay. Hamilton's reaction was spirited. "This is the first symptom," he expostulated, "of a spirit which must either be killed or will kill the Constitution of the United States.... Ought not the collective weight of the different parts of the Government to be employed in exploding the principles they contain?" In response Jay, and later William Short, advised Hamilton to sit tight. Making a fuss would only bring unwarranted attention to the Memorial and resolutions. Assumption would fight its own battles and if needed, advocates would easily be found. Benjamin Lincoln reported that he noticed little reaction in Boston surrounding the resolutions. In fact, their intensity could prove that America required a strong national government "to control the whole." Lincoln then added an interpretation about repealing the law. What would happen, he mused, if every state that questioned the equity of a law, demanded its reversal? Government would be impossible. In an aside, Lincoln doubted that Virginia had a right publicly to criticize a law of Congress. The general methodology would "keep the minds of the people in a constant state of ferment and irritation."[5]

The second plank of Hamilton's fiscal plan, presented on December 19, 1790, contained instructions for the initiation of a national bank. It began with a treatise on banking and included a recommendation for the incorporation of a national bank whose primary agent would be the government. In return, it would play a role in tax collection, assume the burden of short-term creditor and act as a depository for both emergency funds and entrepreneurial credit. Potential shareholders could purchase shares in the bank partially with government securities, and its ratio of certificates to specie was set at three to one. The result, in Hamilton's view, was a system that established one national bank note, catered to American business, and minimized the flow of specie. Confidently, he predicted that his plan would increase the movement of capital, aid government in a crisis, and ease the burden of taxes. Recent events made it easy for the bank's proponents to argue that it was indispensable during war. Tactically, Hamilton planned to make the bank permanent by tying its existence to a lasting public debt. Since it drove the economy, the government would never erase it. Neither would the bank.

This scenario was a replay of a familiar tune for Virginians and they reacted immediately. Northern commercial interests replaced British manufacturers in their minds. Had they not fought for their freedom from them? John Taylor of Caroline sadly predicted a different outcome for this battle. Now, "the Bank has a flush of trumps" but the farmers had only deuces. Soon, people would call the country "the United States of the Bank." Edmund Pendleton considered it just another scheme to promote speculation. Yet, one must examine the motives behind these criticisms. Overall, vituperative censure did not greet the act on public credit while it had done so with assumption and the national bank. What linked the latter two issues? Both affected Virginia economically and each had, to Virginians, serious constitutional flaws.

By agreement, the debate began in the Senate. As an institution, opponents charged the bank with antiagrarian and antirepublican qualities. Moreover, its formation would lead to sectional favoritism both economically and politically. Following the bill's passage, James Monroe, who had replaced the deceased William Grayson, maintained the unconstitutionality of the bill. It exceeded Congress's power because the Constitution did not enumerate it specifically.

In the House, James Madison and the newcomer William Branch Giles, who had replaced the deceased Theodorick Bland, undertook Virginia's heavy lifting. Like many of his fellow statesmen, Giles had adopted a proratification stance during the Virginia debate. However, he had not envisioned a national government that usurped power from the states or conceived that speculators could be the focus of fiscal policy. To Giles, defending the Constitution required a rejection of Hamilton's financial plan. He defined his path on the road to state rights during the debate over the militia bill. A representative offered an amendment that would result in the United States government equipping destitute Virginians. Giles took the occasion to present a general opinion on the methodology. He "was opposed to it in principle" as it was "an improper interference with the authority of the State Governments."

William Maclay left us a negative view of Giles's personality. Maclay, who had read several of his speeches and expected a lively discussion, was disappointed. Giles's "frothy manners" and his constant boasting repulsed him. The "glories of the Ancient Dominion" and personal achievement did not sit well with the Pennsylvanian. Later, Giles acerbic tongue would make him enemies in Congress. He even offered resolutions that might result in Hamilton's resignation. Interestingly, at this stage, Maclay confirmed Giles's progovernment bias. He supported the ideas of assumption and an excise tax.

The tactics of the two Virginians differed. Madison, who was thoroughly prepared, used his favored pedagogical approach. His presentation was well reasoned, dispassionate, and complete. As usual, he categorized various advantages and disadvantages of banks and applied them to Hamilton's invention. Nevertheless, constitutionalism, not mere convenience, was at the center of his presentation. He reminded the House that the Convention had rejected an attempt to charter a corporation and that the Constitution granted Congress only specific powers. A perusal of the language of the state conventions would confirm that the people had also rejected incorporation. If Congress refloated it successfully, it would endanger one of the Convention's basis ideas — limited government. Remember, he warned, whenever Virginia Federalists had explained the sweeping clause they had linked it irrevocably to the enumerated powers.

One by one, Madison attempted to demolish various Federalist attempts to link the bank to specific constitutional articles. Still, it was his attack on the sweeping clause arguments and implication that drew the most attention. He reminded the House that the ratifying conventions had agreed that the terms "necessary" and "proper" did not augment any enumerated power. To Madison, necessary was synonymous with "necessary to the end and incident to the nature of the specified powers." Because of the above conclusions, Madison, following Thomas Tucker's lead during the debate on the Tenth Amendment, was comfortable labelling the clause "merely declaratory of what would have resulted by unavoidable implication." In another flourish, Madison declared that it would be constitutional heresy to allow a government of "limited and enumerated powers" to incorporate the institution from which it would borrow. Using the same paradigm, Congress could create monopolies in a variety of fields. Most important, the constructions offered by the bill's supporters "go to the subversion of every power whatever in the several states."

Unbridled implication supported most attempts to persuade Congress that this act was constitutional. Madison attacked it frontally.

> Mark the reasoning on which the validity of the bill depends. To borrow money is made the end, and the accumulation of capitals implied as the means. The accumulation of capitals is then the end, and a Bank implied as the means. The Bank is then the end, and a charter of incorporation, a monopoly, capital punishments, &c., implied as the means. If implications, thus remote and thus multiplied, can be linked together, a chain may be formed that

will reach every object of legislation, every object within the whole compass of political economy.

Prominently, the Framers had left no important congressional power to implication. If the incorporation of a national bank resided on the enumerated list, it was mandatory. Since it was not, incorporation was not necessary.

In closing, Madison added some incidental objections. The incorporation period was too long; defining different creditor classes would inevitably favor one over the other and thus was antirepublican; the executive department should never have the power to borrow; subordinate banks within the states were anathema to state rights; and the haste of passage did not allow America's citizens to interpret the outcomes.

Stanley Elkins and Eric McKitrick argued that Madison's House strategy focussed on another audience. At least, they said, Madison hoped to amend the bill. At most, he sought to lay down arguments that President Washington might apply to veto the bill since the president had asked Madison to prepare a possible veto message. The authors' estimates seemed conceivable.

Giles took a different approach. He quickly eliminated other arguments and concentrated on the sweeping clause. However, he began by explaining his ideological conversion. Earlier, "if a bias were to influence my conduct, it would rather direct it to favor rather than to oppose the proposed measure." Nevertheless, he had "observed with regret a radical difference in opinion between gentlemen from the eastern and southern States, upon great Governmental questions, and have been led to conclude, that the operation of that cause alone might cast ominous conjecture on the promised success of this much valued government." Representatives recognized sectionalism early in the life of the First Congress.

For Giles, the proponents of the bill must demonstrate both its constitutionality and expediency. Arguments that incorporation was either expressly given or implied were specious. "Expressly," he lectured, inferred that the words "would of themselves, convey a complete idea to the mind of the authority granted, without the agent of argument or deduction." On the other hand, implication required both.

It seemed straightforward to the fiery representative that a means could not be viable unless one enumerated the end. Therefore, on its face, bank incorporation could not be a congressional power by implication because it required a previous enumeration of the power to incorporate. Since every Federalist argument reduced to one of expediency and not necessity — "a means without which the end could not be produced" — they were left with few logical alternatives. Categorizing the Federalist strategy, Giles labelled, "the present measure ... to be an unprovoked advance in this scramble for authority, and a mere experiment how far we may proceed without involving the opposition of State Governments." Moreover, the construction of a national bank subsidiary in Virginia invoked other constitutional issues. The new bank might adopt bylaws that clashed with state laws. As an aside, Giles reminded the House that such an institution would insure economic second class status for Virginia banks. Their viability was doubtful.

Giles investigated another issue. He remarked on the nature of the Union, organic vs. compact, and specified that government by compact described the American experience more accurately. He could not understand the appeal of the organic version since to do so one must accept that power flowed from "the mere creation and existence of Government."

During the debate on the representation ratio, Giles interjected a note concerning the effect of the Bank on American society. Generally, he stated, "inequality of circumstances" was likely to promote "revolutions" in government from "Democracy to Aristocracy and Monarchy." Whenever one found large disparities of wealth, one was bound to find movements for "distinctions, rank, and titles." America was at that stage. Government, and particularly the national bank, were the catalysts. Eventually, it would "corrupt this House" because some of its directors were its members.

One final comment. Several esteemed historians have remarked that the location of the seat of government drove Virginia's bank opposition. Perhaps Congress might move the national capital, located on the Potomac by the Compromise of 1790, to Philadelphia if Pennsylvanians successfully persuaded it to establish the bank there. Both Madison and Giles debunked that suggestion. One or two congressmen may have suggested the possibility, but it did not stand up to scrutiny. The present seat of government had been traded for a major component of Hamilton's fiscal plan, assumption of state debts. Without the Compromise it would never have passed the House. To now propose that the northern representatives, mostly Federalists, would renege on their agreement was to accuse them of duplicity and worse. Despite any assertions, there was never a chance that the Federalists would overturn the compromise.

On February 8, 1791, the bank act passed the House 39–20 with no Virginia support. Unfortunately for the Union, the vote was blatantly sectional. The ayes contained only one representative north of Maryland while the nays included only three south of that state. Since senators voted similarly, the outcome could be interpreted as a northern victory.

The bank debate initialized another important result. Madison completed his conversion from a proponent of an energetic, but limited, national government to one who contemplated strict construction of the Constitution. Still, we must be careful not to overplay this card. Perhaps, as one historian alleged, he adopted the latter ideology to counteract a new attack on republicanism from the Hamiltonian Federalists. If so, another swing lurked in the background. The theorist who denigrated faction was about to spearhead the formation of a national political party.

The Virginia congressional contingent's only remaining hope was that President Washington might veto the bill. He solicited opinions from Edmund Randolph, Thomas Jefferson, and Alexander Hamilton. Randolph would not include a bank incorporation among the enumerated powers, nor expand the sweeping clause to do so. Since the Twelfth [Tenth] Amendment limited the government to enumerated powers, the bill was unconstitutional. However, the main bout was between the ideological heavyweights, Hamilton and Jefferson.

Jefferson's memorandum was short and specific with no rambling phraseology. The document examined the illegal results of forming subscribers into a corporation, the unfortunate constitutional results associated with the incorporation, and the possibility that the bank was merely a convenience for American businessmen. Some of his arguments were novel, but clearly the debating points of Giles and Madison were at his fingertips.

Suppose the president did not veto the act. The formation of the corporation would break five laws. Furthermore, it would ignore one constitutional article. The laws of mortmain, alienage, descents, and forfeiture and escheat would join the republican abhorrence to monopoly. Also, the bill instituted an unconstitutional power to make laws "paramount to the laws of the States." The foundation of his constitutional argument was the Twelfth [Tenth] Amendment that reserved undelegated powers to the states or the people. Since they had not delegated incorporation, it was unconstitutional.

Rounding up several previous arguments, Jefferson reminded Washington that incorporation had no constitutional basis. It did not result from clauses designed for paying the national debt, initiating a borrowing power, or laying taxes for the general welfare. Remember, any general welfare power must comport with the laying of taxes to be constitutional. Otherwise, "it would reduce the whole instrument to a single phrase, that of instituting a Congress with power to do whatever would be for the good of the United States; and, as they would be the sole judges of the good or evil, it would be also a power to do whatever evil they please." Surely the original intent had been "to lace them up strictly within the enumerated powers." If so, the general welfare argument was specious. Moreover, necessary means, "those means without which the grant of power would be nugatory," were at the center of the Federalist argument. Earlier, he had related the danger from the sweeping clause to an unusual extension of its fundamental implication.

Jefferson then launched into the last phase of his argument, moving smoothly to a combination of the bank's constitutionality and its convenience. First, convenience alone was not an acceptable motive for incorporation and he dealt with it summarily. It could easily lead to other problems. Suppose everyone acclaimed the bank's convenience but its incorporation was unconstitutional. Congress could not form it. Jefferson examined several scenarios and proved that the Unites States could accomplish the task purportedly assigned to the bank without its incorporation. How could it be necessary? No, the incorporation of the bank was a state right. Mere convenience played no role.

Jefferson ended his essay on an interesting note. He reminded the president that unless he was sure the bill was unconstitutional, he should follow the dictates of the Legislature and refuse to veto it.

Hamilton's reply—he had read Jefferson's opinion—was more than four times as long as Jefferson's dissertation. He stated his goal in the second paragraph. Hamilton was convinced "that principles of construction like those espoused by the Secretary of State and Attorney General, would be fatal to the just and indispensable authority of the United States." Americans must sideline strict construction.

Although Hamilton's tome was lengthy, the indispensable section for his goal appeared almost immediately.

> Every power vested in a government is in its nature sovereign, and includes, by force of the term, a right to employ all means requisite and fairly applicable to the attainment of the ends of power, and which are not precluded by restrictions and exceptions specified in the Constitution.

A close reading revealed that since some entity, in this case the people, had vested power in the government, it must be a sovereign power without restriction. His implication—and implication was at the core of his argument—was clear. According to Gerald Stourzh, it was a major tool for Hamilton. "The logic of implied powers," he wrote, "impressively disposed of expedients that in the period of Confederation had been tried and found wanting." Constitutionally, the people had delegated a power to Congress, and naturally, it could extend that power. How far could it go? The government must have the means to accomplish the power's ends. This argument was no stranger to those who had studied *The Federalist*. In numbers 23, 28 and 29, he had laid out his theory. However, we must be aware that Hamilton specifically rejected the Madison chain of extensible powers example. Nor would it have been a surprise to William Branch Giles who earlier had debunked, to his own satisfaction, the organic view of the nature of government.

Hamilton considered other issues but none had the force of his government sovereignty exposition. The Twelfth [Tenth] Amendment was "nothing more than a consequence of this republican maxim, that all government is a delegation of power"; implied powers were just as powerful as those expressly given; the existence of state banks, and their presence in the dispute, was merely accidental; Jefferson's definition of necessary demanded a mental prefix of "absolutely or indispensable"; any interpretation of government's powers "ought to be construed liberally in advancement of the public good"; and the sweeping clause "gives an explicit sanction to the doctrine of implied powers." Harkening back to a cogent Federal Farmer argument during the ratification debate, the Secretary maintained that "the degree in which a measure is necessary, can never be a test of the legal right to adopt it; that must be a matter of opinion, and can only be a test of expediency." As the Farmer had warned, the interpretation of the sweeping clause would depend upon who was in power.[6]

State rights men were disappointed in the result. President Washington adopted Hamilton's constitutional interpretation. The Bank act was not vetoed.

Prompted by the president's State of the Union speech, the House on January 15, 1790, ordered the Secretary of the Treasury to prepare a report promoting commerce and manufacturing. Following his habit, Hamilton interpreted his duty in the widest terms. Almost a year later, he produced a lengthy treatise examining the nation's manufacturing sector. As we have seen, he had not been averse to promoting or partnering business interests, but this report added a regulatory role. If consumer protection would advance a manufacturer's reputation, then Hamilton favored it.

In twenty-one instances the secretary recommended increasing protective tariffs. He reduced five on raw materials and designated four for government bounties [subsidies]. A tariff commission, whose guidelines would be fixed, would adjudicate their necessity. Despite its focus on protection, not revenue production, opposition to the plan converged on subsidies.

Hamilton knew that critics would attack the constitutionalism of bounties. According to the secretary, "there is certainly no good foundation" for constitutional objections because his opponents misunderstood the general welfare clause. To give the reader an understanding of the subsequent debate, we will borrow John Miller's interpretation of the possible clause interpretations. Partially, it was its position at the head of a list of government powers that led to controversy. One could construe it "as a separate grant of substantial power to the federal government to provide for the general welfare; as a clause which merely served to introduce the enumeration of powers which followed it; or as a grant of power to tax and appropriate for ends conducive to the common defense and general welfare." Of course, Hamilton selected the last construction.

According to Hamilton, Article I, Section 8 invested the Legislature with the authority "to lay and collect taxes, duties, imposts, and excises to pay the debts and provide for the general welfare" in all but three cases. Duties must be universal and any capitation or direct tax must be proportional. Third, it could not tax state exports. Except these cases, "the power to raise money is plenary and indefinite." If Hamilton's reading of the sweeping clause during the Bank debate had been breathtaking to the Republican faction, this made astounding reading. Still, he was not finished. An examination of the Article convinced him that the phrase "general welfare" was "doubtless intended to signify more than was expressed or imported in those which preceded." In other words, by implication, Hamilton expanded the general welfare with powers different from those that preceded it by separating them in a list. Nothing in the Constitution should restrict the government in its task to attain the general welfare. Apparently, the Legislature had the absolute right, with the exceptions noted, to define that which constituted the general welfare and after its decision, appropriate funds to accomplish it. Of course, the phrase "general welfare" forbade taxation for local objects. However, if the argument became ubiquitous, anyone could apply it to a myriad of projects as widely separated as internal improvements and aiding a specific manufacturing sector.

Strangely, the factions fought the constitutional battle over bounties on a Senate fishery bill that would benefit Massachusetts almost exclusively. Again, the proratification apostate William Giles took the lead. As the first speaker on the subject, he expressed a reluctance to offer a strong opinion, but at least strict construction led him to the idea that bounties were unconstitutional. "In no part of the Constitution could he in express terms," he said, "find a power given to Congress to grant bounties on occupations." Nor could he find any power to which it could be associated. Yes, he knew that someone would resurrect the implication methodology adopted earlier in the House, but "he wished ever to see some connexion between a specified power and the means for carrying it into execution." True, Congress had power to control commerce, but its misapplication could affect competing sectors of manufacturing and agriculture by preferring one group to another making it an antirepublican practice. Why should the national revenue, sourced from all Americans, be dispersed to small groups? This was the path to monopoly and exclusive rights.

Giles moved briefly into the field of political economy protesting that government bounties devalued one man's labour by transferring its effects and enjoyment to the benefit of another. To make it a tenable theory, the proponents of the bill would have to state that "the whole product of the labor of every individual is the real property of the Government" which had the "discretion" to disperse it at its will. Unfortunately, this transformed the individual into a "slave and bondman to Government" and "would lead to a complete system of tyranny." Therefore, one should consider such a plan "bad policy" because it reduced the total wealth of the community. He suggested that the section on bounties be struck unless further arguments convinced him he was incorrect. The House would hear from Giles again.

Opposition arguments that produced unconstitutional results drove James Madison to pick up the baton from Giles. Debaters had even mischaracterized the notion of bounties. According to Madison, only two fundamental methods existed for interpreting the general welfare clause. Either it was a "general description of the specified powers, and as having no further meaning, and giving no further power than what is found in that specification; or as an abstract and indefinite delegation of power extending to all cases whatever; to all such, at least, as will admit the application of money, which is giving as much latitude as any Government could well desire."

To determine the correct interpretation, Madison returned to the Convention. No one could argue that the goal was otherwise than a limited government. Thus, it could never derive "its powers from the general terms prefixed to the specified powers." Bolstering his case, Madison reminded the House that if it promoted a broad interpretation, the carefully enumerated specific powers "must go for nothing." Moreover, in a letter to Andrew Stevenson, he insisted that history sidetracked any Hamiltonian argument for the general power. On May 29, 1787, the phrase had appeared in the Virginia Plan. It disappeared only to appear in August during a debate on debt. On August 22, a committee extended it to the collection of revenue taxes. Why did two interpretations arise? Either everyone understood that the clause referred to taxation or it slipped through in the crush of events.

Continuing in this vein, Madison uncovered some internal inconsistencies. If one argued that Congress could raise money and apply it to any purpose, one must explain why the Constitution specifically mentioned powers to raise, for example, armies and navies. A continuation in this manner must convince one that the result would be a consolidated government. To arrive at the Convention's goal, limited government, required the Constitution to chain Congress to the enumerated powers. Surely, this was the case in the Articles of Confederation, which provided the American genesis of the phrase. Moreover, "it was always considered as clear and certain, that the old Congress was limited to the enumerated powers and that the enumeration limited and explained the general terms."

Changing the focus, Madison tackled the relation between the judiciary and Congress under a general interpretation. If it did apply, "it would supersede all the restrictions understood at present to be in their power with respect to the Judiciary." Could not Congress establish courts within the United States and also jeopardize the constitutional requirement on the categories of cases allowed? If the Constitution delegated Congress both the power to appropriate for the general welfare and arbitrate its allocation, it could apply it to any cause. Specifically, the government might apply public money in the states to achieve nefarious ends.

John Page continued the Virginia portion of the debate. He quickly assured the House that Massachusetts fishermen deserved a bounty. However, he was unaware of any constitutional method to achieve it. The delegates designed the Constitution to repair obvious defects in the Articles "so far only as would secure the independence and general welfare of the Confederated States, without endangering the sovereignty and independence of the individual States." Since it gave Congress a power to tax impartially it must avoid any charge of giving one state an advantage when taxing the same object. This drew Page to the nub of his case. Any group, such as the Massachusetts fishermen, that exported its product after receiving a drawback or bounty, had by definition an advantage over those that did not receive it. "It ought to be shown," he argued, "that [bounties] can be extended to the benefit of the sailors of some of the States, and not to those of every State." Even if one could prove this point, Page was unsure whether it would benefit the Union. The solution was to have the individual states offer the bounties because not to do so would "in some degree [be] derogatory to the sovereignty and independence of the State." Otherwise, it would face one with the specter of the national government "swallowing up the powers of the State Governments, and as consolidating the different States into one Government."

The latter possibility was not a chimera to Page. Positive results could proceed from a broad general power, but human nature was weak and the bad might outweigh the good. Remember, he warned, during the ratification debate, state after state had railed against the influence of aristocracy and monarchy. Now, one faction led Congress to adopt powers that promised them. Had not "the sagacious and eloquent" Patrick Henry "foretold from his knowledge of the human heart, what would be done and said in justification of every measure which might extend the power of Congress"? If it could regulate fisheries, why not tobacco, rice, and indigo?

In closing, Page switched to the distribution of power. His remarks mirrored those made earlier by Thomas Jefferson and became a plank in the state rights doctrine. The states should have the power to legislate locally while the Legislature regulated foreign affairs. Jefferson had remarked in August 1787 that "my plan would be, to make the states one as to every thing connected with foreign nations & several as to every thing purely domestic." This prevailing attitude would prove both a strength and a weakness for future state rights men.

After considering the intervening remarks, William Giles returned to the debate. In typical style, he began by chastising the House for its loose application of the word "bounty" and followed up with its importance to the debate. Whereas drawbacks, a term introduced by some members in place of bounties, were "confined to commercial regulations, bounties may be extended to every possible object of government." Disparate subjects like *"learning, agriculture, manufactures* and even the *sacredness* of religion" might need protection. In other words, Americans must trust their government to apply this power judiciously. Possibly, according to Giles, one could make a case for commercial regulations under the regulation of commerce article. Yet, none extended this idea to regulate *"learning,* or *agriculture, manufactures,* or *religion."* In fact, the Constitution forbade this extension because it would not tolerate the extension of particular cases allowing bounties to be a generalized constitutional power under the general welfare clause. To do so would inevitably clash with a state's reserved rights. If the proponents of bounties succeeded, they could understand those who concluded that the national government was consolidated with "unlimited discretion." The sequel mirrored the reasoning presented during the sweeping clause debates. They could build a chain of powers that allowed Congress unlimited discretion.

Again Giles disputed the organic view of the formation of the Union. Robert Barnwell of South Carolina had "confidently spoke[n] of the inherent rights of this Government." Giles recognized this thrust as "a new source of authority" but it was "totally inapplicable to the Government." Delving into political theory, he reminded the House, that the sovereign people had delegated any inherent government powers, if they existed, during the state of nature transition into an organized society. Governments did not derive their delegated powers from preexisting government. To assume this connection was "an unjustifiable assumption and usurpation."

Giles appended some remarks about political parties to his oration. Behind the scenes, he discerned a sectional interest intent on influencing the House deliberations upon every important question. The *"ministerial machine"* directing Hamilton's policies would produce unintended consequences. Yes, its numerical predominance would secure his goals but its constant sectional bias would solidify political differences that were still virtual. These factions, based on "jealousies and suspicions arising from *party"* would eventually ingrain discord within the nation. Presently, he did not see the divisions as East vs. South, but agricultural vs. manufacturing. Hopefully the national interest in agriculture would leaven the divide.

In a wide-ranging letter to President Washington in September 1793, Edmund Pendleton offered his concise opinion of the application of protective tariffs. He considered the Union as one of confederated states. In such a federal Union it was bad policy to institute protective duties on some manufactures but not others. They were not only inconvenient but also produced biased results unjust to the states.[7]

In the mid–1790s the famous polemicist John Taylor, Robert Shalhope's "pastoral republican" initiated his attacks on nationalist doctrine. He was born about December 19, 1753, probably in Caroline County. Orphaned at age ten, Taylor was raised by his uncle, Edmund Pendleton, the distinguished jurist. Part of his early education was at a private school in which James Madison was also enrolled. Later, he studied law at William and Mary College.

During the Revolution, Taylor served with both Patrick Henry and the Marquis de Lafayette and rose to the rank of major. Beginning in 1779 he served four terms in the House of Delegates (1799–81, 1783–85, 1796–1800) interspersed with several caretaker periods in the United States Senate (1792–94, 1803, 1822–24). It was the first of these stints, partly overlapping the Hamiltonian policy debate, that provided the stimulus for the pamphlet *Enquiry into the Principles and Tendency of Certain Public Measures.* One might consider it the historical progenitor of its kind. They would circulate throughout Virginia educating the people to their point of view. Despite his political duties, Taylor remained a gentleman farmer at his plantation, Hazlewood.

The early Republican years found him in opposition to the policies of his former allies. He became a member of the Tertium Quids and insisted on a stricter Constitutional interpretation. Most historians consider his later writings to be a bedrock of state rights or libertarian dogma. He died August 21, 1824.

A textual analysis of the *Enquiry* revealed Taylor's target audience. Pursuing a thesis that true republicans must respond to corruption and venality, he appealed to Americans to engage the nation's aristocracy. However, several references to obscure mythical figures, long expositions on political economy, and harsh invective aimed at some commercial interests narrowed his audience to the agrarian leadership in each state. His choice was not unexpected since Virginia's powerful planters held political sway. Taylor's expectation was that they could educate the yeomanry to the dangers inherent in the administration's policies.

Taylor's presentation was often difficult to follow. His organization required readers to cache certain ideas while he skipped off to another topic. Language could be torturous, often folksy, and derivative. His sections on public finance revealed his debt to Adam Smith. Exaggeration to emphasize a point was common but his favorite tactic was to overexplain a topic to hammer his point home. Above all, he was suspicious of the Hamiltonian agenda and distrusted both its political and social thrust.

Our discussion of the congressional debate on Hamilton's plan might raise an expectation that Taylor would pursue a long constitutional harangue about its legality. Yes, he did refer to constitutionalism in passing but his target was the plan's national economic and political effects. Repeatedly, Taylor revealed his classical republicanism through his expositions of the "public good," "public obligations," and liberty through collective action. Surprisingly, he appealed to the national self-interest to achieve his goal. It could drive men to investigate the motives of their opponents and take advantage of them. Now was the time to strike. To wait invited governmental usurpation.

The stylistic criticisms above might raise questions about the validity of the pamphlet. Thankfully, the contents and not the style and organization, were paramount. Wisely, Taylor integrated a discussion on public finance with that of the Bank to emphasize the American dilemma. Hamiltonian stockjobbers were universally active. In addition, he concentrated on a different aspect of the plan. Surely Americans had already absorbed the potential constitutional problems associated with Hamilton's fiscal program. But did they fully understand how an economic program could destroy a republican community? Did they see how the aristocracy's avarice would punish individuals and even states?

Taylor's clearly enunciated goals included publicizing data on national wealth and national rights, while shedding light on the private or public morality of the Bank incorporation. To help the reader, he resorted to a series of benchmarks because "without a test for truth, self-interest and innovation, by their wily artifices, will slip out of our grasp." Unfortunately, the Constitution, due to its vagueness, was not an ideal repository of these axioms. However, one could readily recognize several such as: Republican government must depend on the people; Congress had the power to tax for the general welfare and common defence but not for the benefit of individuals; the people control the right to legislate and they periodically delegated some power to their representatives who legislated for the public good, and if they do not, the government became a usurpation.

The squire of Caroline identified several groups that challenged republican government. Uppermost was the new aristocracy. Recall, agrarians like Taylor or George Mason did not consider themselves aristocrats simply because they were rich. To fall into the aristocratic mold required one also to espouse monarchical views about the best form of government. Perhaps his contempt was best expressed during a discussion on the aristocracy's plan to control the will of the people.

> This is a design of a few individuals, exclusively to appropriate to themselves the management of the national offspring, that they may change its nature, and debauch its affections from the great object of its political duty. It is an attempt to transplant the constitution from democratic ground, in which it might flourish, to an aristocratic soil, in which it must perish.

Unfortunately for America, the aristocracy's tentacles spread into the nation's economic life. Regarding the insidiousness of its activities, he wrote,

> But, the aristocracy, as cunning and rapacious, have continued this device [interest payments], to inflict upon labour a tax, constantly working for their emoluments, whilst they also retain the chief use of the cash, and seldom part with its custody.

Significantly, the aristocracy had managed to avoid paying legal tender for their Bank stock. Instead, it traded in severely discounted old certificates at their face value and received new ones with a generous interest rate. To add insult, it argued that the government must maintain property rights, even if established by nefarious means. Taylor was aghast. No one should recognize any right unprotected by the Constitution.

The money interest, claimed Taylor, not the public good, inspired Congress. Unfortunately, rich men exploited it to accrue power. For example, senators bypassed the stricture on originating money bills and achieved their ends through taxation. They promised the people republican government but instead proposed unconstitutional acts. Where did the Constitution state that the Secretary of the Treasury could dictate to Congress?

A particular subset of Congress was especially corrupt. Its members were either directors of the bank or stockholders. This created a conflict of interest between their personal finances and their duty to their states. Bank directors had two masters, the Constitution and Bank bylaws. Could one trust these individuals to elevate the state's needs above their own? To circumvent the problem required government to reorganize so that it could never misappropriate funds lodged under its responsibility.

Two other groups raised Taylor's ire. Both the proponents of paper money and those who would form political parties injured republican government. Increasing the supply of paper was bound to increase taxation as the Revolutionary period had proven. Everyone had dismissed the concept as bad economics, but suddenly Hamilton had revived it. "It set out with a plausible pretense of curing an evil," Taylor wrote, "and it applies a worse evil. As if fire would cure a burn." Two actions would correct this abuse. The people must defeat those who supported paper money at the polls. Those elected must repeal the Bank Act.

Taylor curtly dismissed the necessity of political parties. "A party ... must signify a confederation of individuals for the private and exclusive benefit of themselves, and not for the public good." Loyal Americans who opposed their formation should be considered true patriots.

According to Taylor, the ne'er-do-wells had two goals with one corollary. They aimed to subvert the Constitution and sabotage republican government, replacing it with a consolidated state. How would they achieve their ends? They would amass great wealth among a favorite few organized into an "aristocracy and monarchy" by supporting "public abuses." This group would welcome "old tories" who sought retaliation for their ignominious defeat. Tactically, it would coopt well-known, comfortable phraseology but use it for deceitful purposes. Among them was spreading a calumny concerning sectional divisions, taking credit for positive aspects of the nation's business, labelling themselves the government, and demanding that Americans follow their lead. Citizens were encouraged to prefer a combination with a single interest rather than one dedicated to the Union, spread the notion that taxation was a minor inconvenience, and cultivate the idea that an energetic government was the positive goal of the aristocracy.

Taylor explored a particular government corruption. Treasury officers could give information to government members for their personal use. In return, the latter could ensure the viability of the Treasury agenda. This smacked of reciprocal bribes. Americans must root out such behavior early or the people would fall into the habit of considering it the cost of republican government. Venal precedents could assume an aura of respectability and live forever. To impede this process required a congressional reorganization of its own qualifications.

The Hamiltonians could shunt aside liberty, held in common with all members of society, if private interests could demonstrate the value of personal gain. It was human nature for some men to concentrate on it instead of the public good. As a result, society would suffer and interest would challenge liberty. The community should never entrust it to the hands of the "magistrates" who would surely betray their mandate. According to Taylor, "the people are the only safe guardians of their own liberty."

The bulk of Taylor's exposition on the usurper's methodology concentrated on the Bank with frequent references to public finance. He had a special hostility to the relationship between it and taxation. Bank stock must have a financial origin and the Hamiltonian scheme employed taxes. Thus, stock must be a component of the public debt that required more taxes. Moreover, bank profits were an indirect tax on the people. First, they subsidized its operations and then, through their taxes, maintained a high interest rate to produce benefits for the stockholders. Insidiously, they earned these profits at the expense of labor, whose taxes were the basis of the monetary nest egg needed to incorporate the Bank. The result was an erosion of the people's sovereignty because taxes would be collected for purposes other than the general welfare.

Taylor foresaw several results of unlimited government. Bank profits were deleterious to the community because they would never repay society for dispersed interest. Again, whenever the Bank profited, the community, the source of labor, lost. Unfortunately, no one consulted it about the dispersal of interest or bank policy. In fact, one might argue successfully that the Bank had little interest in the public good of the community.

Since Taylor linked the public debt to the Bank, it came under scrutiny. Everyone recognized that it had concentrated in a few hands. A long-term maintenance of the public debt would permit government to "control" the people's will by the application of wealth. Despite the Constitution's strictures, government would usurp the people's sovereignty. Therefore, the public debt was a sharp tool designed to dominate the people's government. "The funding system," he declared, "was intended to affect, what the Bank was contrived to accelerate." Great wealth would accumulate in a few hands and produce a party of the rich who would seek to suppress the republican states.

Inevitably, only a targeted few, including foreigners, would control all government paper. They would arrange dividend payment even if profits did not support them; control the money supply and consumer prices to produce large profits; and raise money from the public to profit themselves. They would accomplish all these through labor taxation.

Congress would support projects to produce stockholder profits if representatives forgot their obligations to their constituents. Instead, they might become creatures of the corporation and vote in their own, and the corporation's, self-interest. For example, congressmen could arrange taxation schemes to provide a Bank profit. Thus, they would reduce the state's federal representation — some would represent the Bank and not the people — and badly damage republicanism. In addition, they would compromise the impeachment process if the Bank were involved. Surely, a representative in thrall to the Bank would never impeach it.

Taylor did foray into the Constitutional issues associated with Bank incorporation but his warnings were unsurprising. He never mentioned incorporation; the Bank expanded rather than limited power; Congress had no power to apply bounties to specific industries; and the government had the power to pay debts whereas Hamilton proposed a permanent debt. Interestingly, Taylor had no faith in a balanced government since checks were merely "a confused assemblage of notions." Most important, unconstitutional, unlimited government could never take root unless it had the support of the Legislature. Americans must choose their representatives judiciously.

He did have one acidic comment about implication, the basis of Hamilton's argument for passage of the Bank Act. Incorporation was "a power tacitly ... implied, conflicting and subverting the most fundamental principles, earnestly and loudly expressed." Perhaps other institutions, for example religions, might receive the same benefit.

The purpose of this pamphlet was to sensitize American agrarians to the inevitable destruction of their republican government. To help them in their deliberations, Taylor proposed several contingencies. Hamiltonian opponents must study the inner operations of the Bank because it would provide important information in future disputes. Also, they must depend on the wisdom of the people, "the only genuine and legitimate fountain of power," to provide legislators who would remove all laws violating the Constitution. With help, they would recognize "those who invented doctrines for their own use."

The state governments were the most powerful buffers against consolidation. The people should exclude any candidate who supported paper money and "every species of artificial interest created, or to be created." Prospective senators must pass the test of republicanism from their state governments. Adopting Richard Henry Lee's tactical suggestion, Taylor proposed that in every congressional case that fathered disputed interpretations, the state must demand "explanations of the constitution" based on its spirit, original intent, and "unrestrained construction now," as well as republican principles. If a coordinated opposition adopted his agenda, Taylor had done his duty.[8]

Transitions

If the last three chapters have fulfilled their design, a reader could sympathize with state rights Antifederalists who, during the Constitutional debate, had recoiled from the expansive tendencies and attacks on liberty associated with central government power. This pair accounted for Virginians' attraction to a political dogma that promoted limited government and individual rights. Remember, we began those chapters by positing that defending limited government and liberty would legitimize the doctrine and that we would present a mass of data to support that position. True, it sometimes meant hard sledding, but surely few could now argue that Virginians, as they saw it, had little basis for their doctrinal allegiance. Specifics were not hard to find.

Ratification of the Constitution presaged several problems. Any central government application of power was bound to excite debate because the dichotomy carrying vs. noncarrying states branded the factions. Federalists promoted a strong, stable, energetic government that could act directly on the individual. Unfortunately, many Virginians considered these attributes in a faraway government to be the basis of corruption and tyranny. Moreover, power was more likely to follow self-interest rather than corporate well-being under the new Constitution. The stress on good government instead of societal benefits defined this shift away from corporate ideals. Although the Federalists had managed to carry the day, no doubt existed that a powerful particularistic Antifederalist influence, disposed toward strict construction of the Constitution, drove most Virginians.

Several specific power issues remained unsolved and potentially dangerous. Madison had urged Virginians to adopt a "liberal construction" of the Constitution. It included the concept of incidental power associated with the sweeping clause. This hardly fit the mold of government intervention expected by Antifederalists or some Virginia Federalists. Was implication to rule? Would the sweeping clause dominate the business of government? Considering local Federalist remarks, this was not the expected government role. Had not George Nicholas, a powerful influence, promoted a limited national government to vacuum away the defects within the Articles counterpart? Perhaps his faction would solve the existing constitutional problems without raising others by devolving too much state power on the central government. The new government must work within the bounds established through a plain reading of the Constitution. Yet, other parties might ignore this template, and Virginia might find itself a victim in the process.

Other clauses had avoided a significant examination. Attention to the general welfare clause was negligible while judicial review within the judiciary clause debate received short shrift. John Marshall, who would later repeat Madison's call for a "liberal interpretation" hinted that the Court would have the power to review congressional acts. However, he wrapped it in an argument that presupposed it was not in the enumerated list. As we will find later, this would not raise a barrier for the future Chief Justice.

Most important, the location of the residue of powers found no unanimity. Federalists claimed the Constitution solved that problem while Antifederalists insisted on a statement within the document assigning these rights to the states or the people that, minimally, protected its citizen's rights and its state powers. Central government supporters could placate Virginia's fears by producing a Bill of Rights. It should begin with an assertion protecting the basic natural freedoms but extend to the residual powers.

Two overarching questions controlled all Antifederalist debate concerning liberty. Would the Federalists explain how Virginia's surrender of its sovereign powers would improve its grasp on liberty? Would an unconscionable grasp for power fritter away the gains of the Revolution? Based on their allegiance to compact theory, Antifederalists constructed the following litany of liberty's demands: government should never coerce a citizen or state; individuals have certain inalienable rights; states must retain control of specific sovereign powers; and aristocracy must not plague it. Remember, implication was a sword aimed at liberty's heart. For the first time, the effects of state consolidation, a cry that would continue until 1861, ran through the state. It became a catchall for almost every grievance assumed by Virginians.

At this juncture, state rights had two prongs. The first was a legal imperative that characterized the residue of powers left to a state after the people made specific assignments to the national government. As one could easily see, this circumstance was a frightening reduction in power from the days of Articles' state sovereignty. Also, the people often forgot the second. Associated with the first, was a defence of individual rights. One could surmise, based on historical evidence, that Virginia would fight to maintain these powers.

Compact theory, the basis of state rights, had several interpretations associated with sovereignty that skewed one's definition of the Union's nature. If one adopted the traditional definition of an indivisible sovereignty, one defined the compact to be between the members of society as they left a state of nature. Therefore the people were the people of the state, and it received their power and acted for them. As a result, the Union was a confederation of states each of which represented the people. Antifederalists leaned toward this model.

Nevertheless, Madison's agile brain produced dual sovereignty. He declared that not only was the sovereignty above in play but another joined it. There existed a compact between the people of one state and the peoples of the others. This construct backstopped his famous partly national, partly federal contention of the Union's nature. It allowed Federalists to promote the idea that the Constitution defined a national government. To make matters more complicated, Thomas Jefferson's compact defined the participants to be a state on one hand and all the other states on the other. Although interesting, the latter notion attracted few adherents.

Power allocation was not obvious. Two factors clouded it. Although state rights had a legal basis within the Constitution, it also contained a Lockean extraconstitutional appeal to natural rights. Moreover, within the Constitution the Supremacy Clause and the sweeping clauses might make constitutional interpretation a function of the ruling party or Supreme Court.

Although the contents of the Constitution suggested that it was a compact, neither then nor pre–1861, was that conclusion unanimously endorsed. Many interpreters argued that the Constitution had an organic basis. Concentrating on compact theory, it would appear that the oft-proposed requirement of rulers and ruled was missing from the Constitution. This damped the argument that it was a compact. Perhaps it was neither Lockean nor that envisaged by the Articles. Instead, the Constitution said Forrest McDonald, "would be a compact among peoples of different political societies, in their capacities as peoples of the several states." The intellectual battle over the nature of the Union — organic vs. compact — had important adherents on each side. Nevertheless, the idea of a constitutional compact became ubiquitous in antebellum Virginia.

It was clear from the debate that a strong link existed between trust, government, the Constitution's benefits to Virginia, and human nature. History had proven to Antifederalists during the Jay Treaty debate that one could not expect the East [North] to desist from sectional favoritism. Moreover, they were positive that legislators, like their constituents, were susceptible to corruption. As Patrick Henry noted during debate on the possibility that a state could be a defendant before the Supreme Court, "If gentlemen construe that paper so loosely now, what will they do when our rights and liberties are in their power?" Could one trust government to protect the people's rights? For example, it was unlikely it would protect the lower, unpropertied classes.

No explanation of the ratification debate would be complete without a discussion of the link between trust and human nature. Neither party held the common people in high regard. Each doubted its ability to govern. However, the Antifederalist bloc extended its class opprobrium. It tarred the proratification faction with the aristocracy brush. Repeatedly, argument revolved around predicted Federalist corruption. No doubt, some of these assertions were simply convention tactics, but particularly prerevolution activists like Patrick Henry, William Grayson and George Mason routinely charged that the proposed government would fall prey to corrupt human nature.

Of course, the above discussion led naturally to the subject of government trust. Human nature convinced Federalists that Americans could trust the people's representatives to do their duty in the same proportion as did members of society. Antifederalists disagreed. One could not trust a member of the elite to represent a district of common folk. Instead, they would band together to dominate Congress.

The danger in this attitude lay in future laws inimical to Virginia. Radicals would surely highlight this debate for confirmation that, from the beginning, Virginians knew that they could not trust government. For example, state rights men would surely have much to say about any law or decision that seemed to negate the Virginia Federalist interpretation of the necessary and proper clause.

On the positive side, Virginia had received from George Nicholas, an assurance concerning its place in the Union and its ability to ameliorate any negative consequences of tyrannical government action. Also, if the Federalists were correct, Virginia's political elite might get the best of two worlds — power in the federal government from which to protect Virginia's interests, and continuing control of state government.

It signaled its concern with federal-state power allocations in two dramatic ways. The first was Virginia's reservation whose clauses were legal, understood by all, and supported by a Federalist leadership concerned with government power. Repeatedly, future Old Dominion stalwarts, in their Constitutional battles, referred to this document with veneration. Virginia's state rights men were sure that it was an important adjunct to ratification.

The second warning occurred in the final stages of the convention. The Northern Neck Federalist bloc had fully supported ratification. However, it could not escape the possibility that it had gone too far in allocating power to the general government. The inclusion of the proposed amendment on taxation warranted this conclusion since it would effectively truncate congressional power.

A combination of these assertions might lead one to conclude that Virginians were more comfortable with a government whose powers not only had a base but also a ceiling. If the government pierced the latter, Virginians might choose state rights in the face of danger to the Old Dominion.

Virginians did not have to wait long for a provocation that signaled the need for a state rights doctrine. Hamilton's economic program augmented the disappointment generated by the weak Bill of Rights and prompted the Virginia General Assembly's endorsement of the tenet of constitutional strict construction. The idea of limited government was clearly under attack by the proponents of constitutional implication. John Taylor of Caroline recognized it and began the pamphleteering process that became a staple of Virginia communication concerning attacks on state rights. Perhaps the Antifederalist predictions concerning the effect of ratification on Virginia had some merit. Despite these incidents, incipient state rights men regarded them as a dire warning. The final catalyst had yet to come.

PART II

Guardian of the People's
Rights — Educating the Public

6

The Principles of '98

Alexander Hamilton's nationalistic financial scheme foretold, to some Virginians, the path the opposition Federalists would trod to achieve power. As a corollary, Old Dominion activists proclaimed its misuse could only be controlled by a strict Constitutional interpretation. Still, many were willing to shelve the assembly dictates and await further defining events. Their appearance, over the space of the next few years, confirmed in Republican Virginia minds that they must have a counterbalance to the nationalistic Federalist program. State rights would be the antidote.

✠

While Virginians contested constitutional interpretations and economic disparities associated with Hamilton's program, Europe prepared for war. Conflict between France and the allies, including Great Britain, began in 1793. Although President Washington issued a proclamation that many interpreted as a position of neutrality, the combatants disregarded it. France deputized a mischievous minister, Edmond Genét, to America and, ignoring protocol, he issued letters of marque to privateers and persuaded George Rogers Clark to occupy Spanish territory. The following year, Britain began seizing American ships trading in the French West Indies. Slowly, events drew the United States into European affairs.

On April 16, 1794, President Washington nominated Supreme Court Justice John Jay as a special envoy to Great Britain. Persisting irritants between the two countries from the Treaty of 1783 plus the current war defined his agenda. If he could resolve them by treaty, the European conflict might not trouble the United States further. This design would satisfy James Madison. England, the Virginian argued in the House, must fulfill the obligations of 1783 and give the United States more liberal trade concessions. Naturally, the accomplishment of these goals would satisfy Virginia planters who would likely be the beneficiary. Just one year later, Washington transmitted the Jay Treaty to the Senate for consent.

Its contents stirred Virginian indignation. On July 29, 1795, George Wythe chaired a Richmond public gathering that angrily passed two resolutions. First, the treaty might cripple Virginia interests. It did not relax British mercantile acts associated with the West Indies, offered no indemnification for lost slaves, and established a process that allowed foreigners to own Virginia land. The latter inclusion spread alarm through the Federalist Northern Neck due to the Fairfax land cases. Second, it contained unconstitutional provisions. How could Virginia's indebted planters pay the growing $5,000,000 to $15,000,000 debt that had accumulated since the Revolution? What steps could any unconstitutional commission take to protect Virginia's commercial interests? Where were the clauses expanding neutral rights in the

127

face of the Franco-British conflict? On the other hand, the treaty seemed to contain a solution to the long-standing problem of the western forts.

Article IX proved a stumbling block. Citizens of each country who owned land within the other's territory maintained their ownership. Also, they could dispose of it "as if they were Natives" and neither country could pass a law stipulating them as "Aliens." These impositions galled Virginians. Senator Henry Tazewell offered a resolution condemning them because "the rights of the individual states are ... unconstitutionally invaded."

The next elections proved a disaster for the Federalists. The electorate severely reduced their representation in both the General Assembly and Congress. Tobacco growers in the Piedmont and south of the James River linked the spectre of debt payment to the treaty and withdrew their support.

Of course, the assembly elected a Republican governor. In anger, it approved the conduct of its senators who had opposed the treaty and suggested three Constitutional resolutions. The Constitution must give the House a role in the treaty power; reduce the Senate term of office to three years; and bar Supreme Court justices from accepting coincident government positions. In a slap at Washington, the assembly refused to state its unbounded confidence in the president.

The reaction to the terms of the treaty alerted the House to the unacceptable conditions set forth in the agreement. Virginia petitions urged their representatives to "adopt such measures ... as shall most effectively secure, free from encroachment, the Constitutional delegated powers of Congress, and the chartered rights of the people." It was within this environment that Washington transmitted a copy of the treaty to the House for its perusal.

The president could not have foreseen the storm of protest provoked by his innocuous act. Edward Livingston of New York offered a resolution requiring the president to transmit a copy of any instructions that he had issued to Jay prior to negotiations. In addition, Washington should include "correspondence and other documents relative to the said Treaty." The Virginia representatives saw no ulterior motive attached to the resolution. It was merely an innocent request for information since serious decisions required comprehensive documentation. They considered the treaty transmission an invitation to investigate it. Obviously, according to Robert Rutherford, President Washington expected the House's participation. William Giles argued that it proved that the president did not view the treaty as supreme law. Otherwise, he would never have laid it before the House. Proponents of the treaty regarded the request for information as a fishing expedition to introduce a debate over its merits. Some even argued that its enemies sought data for an impeachment of an unnamed official, probably Jay. However, John Nicholas and John Heath probably stated the undercurrent. It was their constitutional right to examine all data associated with the treaty and, considering the nation's uproar, the House must examine it closely. For one month the House struggled with the constitutional problem.

Albert Gallatin of Pennsylvania stated it simply. "The question may arise," he wondered, "whether any Treaty made by the President and Senate containing regulations touching objects delegated to Congress, can be considered binding without Congress passing laws to carry it into effect." Did the president have an unqualified power over all treaties? Were the terms of treaties unlimited? Did they contain necessary enabling powers by default? If so, they would be supreme law unchecked within the Constitution. The president would assume powers that would supersede House prerogatives.

Suppose one agreed with the argument for treaty powers. What were the outcomes? First, the treaty would be law and would require the House to obey and pass acts to initiate its provisions. Therefore, one branch, the Executive, ruled another, the Legislature. Republican checks and balances did not countenance this eventuality. Moreover, the Constitution made the House the initiator of money bills. Any requirement that forced it to surrender that power was a usurpation and unconstitutional. Did not the House, wondered Nicholas, have the power to judge the usefulness of any expenditure? William Giles expanded this notion. The power to appropriate funds was an enumerated power. Thus, it gave the House a check since the refusal of funds could short-circuit any "mischief" in a government department. John Page hammered the proverbial nail, at least to Virginians, into this version of the pro treaty argument. Yes, he agreed, the president and Senate could sign a treaty, but they could not usurp the enumerated House power and make commercial regulations "injurious to the general welfare, ruinous to the commerce of certain, and even the largest States." In other words, the Executive must keep the entire Constitution, not just one clause, in mind when separating powers.

Giles saw one aspect of the dispute in slightly different terms. True, he abominated the treaty, but he would have opposed it in any case. If constitutionalism were an issue, and it was, it was his duty to object. This was doubly important in the early days of the Union because important disputes occurred regularly given the lack of Constitutional clarity. To do his duty properly, Giles demanded the fullest information available.

According to Giles, Rutherford, and John Page, republican government demanded protection of the people's sovereignty. Remember, the Constitution enumerated Congress's powers and at least two areas, commerce and naturalization, were at issue in this debate. According to Page, time remained to establish cherished republican principles by maintaining the House's ability to make law. The Legislature must fight for the right to legislate. His colleague, Andrew Moore melded several arguments. Those who favored the treaty gave the Executive department power to supersede vested House rights subject to Senate approval. However, the Senate had equal, not proportional, representation. Therefore, its role in treaty making was not republican. The House must adopt a rule to even the playing field.

John Page recapitulated the Virginia arguments. "The treaty appears to me unconstitutional," he assessed, "because it takes from Congress that very power with which it was invested by the Constitution ... I mean the power of regulating the commerce of the United States." In addition, it infringed on the "uniform rule of naturalization" and "it interferes with the authority of the Judiciary, by establishing a Court of Commissioners ... within the United States." Moreover, it allowed the president to create government offices and salaries. The true test should have been "whatever would be unconstitutional, if done by Congress, cannot be Constitutional if done by the President and British King."

On March 8, 1796, the House easily passed a resolution asking the president for papers associated with the treaty negotiations. Seventeen days later, Livingston reported that his committee had delivered it to Washington and awaited the president's response. Within five days, the House had its answer. The Executive department would not forward any requested information because to submit to the resolution would set a dangerous precedent. Moreover, the Senate's consent obliged the House to fulfill its role by enabling the provisions. To ensure that no dispute would follow, Washington stated clearly "that the assent of the House of Representatives is not necessary to the validity of a Treaty."

A disappointed James Madison replied for the Virginia delegation. Everyone recognized that certain cases allowed the Executive to withhold information, but this was not one. Washington's opinion was without precedent and the treaty implementation infringed on House powers. Moreover, he had misread the state ratifying debates. They had discussed the treaty power under the rubric of limited power. Overall, Washington had mistaken the basis of the request for data. The original request had been benign and had no constitutional importance. To Madison, the powers of the House "had been denied by a higher authority" without sufficient cause.

The House attempted vainly to assert its independence. One day after Washington's message, it passed resolutions claiming a right to deliberate on the treaty and request information that did not relate to a constitutional matter. The ensuing debate ranged from the comparison of terms between the Treaty of 1783 and the Jay Treaty to debt payment and commercial relations. Few remarks reflected our focus but one should note that there was an emphasis on economic issues.[1]

The combination of Hamilton's policies and the oft stated differences in Constitutional interpretation during congressional debates confirmed antiratification Virginians' dire predictions. Every important debate seemed to revolve around differing constructions of government powers. Disputes over the nature of federalism and sectional politics added to the turmoil. From his spectator's seat, Thomas Jefferson labelled the combatants republicans and monarchists.

By the Second Congress, opposition to Federalist policies motivated like-minded opponents to form an antiadministration interest. The Virginia contingent placed their faith in electing more agrarians to the House and professed "strict construction, agrarianism, and republicanism." Surely, one did not have to search long and hard for the last inclusion. Had not the Federalists proven their corruption by their venal and sectional policies?

Beginning in November 1791, James Madison undertook to propagandize their goals in the *National Gazette*. Although there were moments when they reminded the reader of *The Federalist*, these efforts failed to live up to its literary style. Madison's aim was to enlighten the average person to the personal impact of Federalist policies and their effects on republican government. Moreover, he offered a party, and named it, that would protect the people. This was a huge leap. Traditionally, Virginians considered parties to be subversive to the public interest because they necessarily split the nation into competing groups and damaged the concept of an harmonious society. However, Madison decided, as he had in *Federalist* No. 10, that a balanced government could control David Hume's "necessary evil" and parties could check each other. Yet, Madison had another hurdle to cross. The new party had to sidestep any criticism of the nation's hero, George Washington. Denigrating him would be a death blow to the Republican future.

Madison did not organize his essays with a purpose. He elucidated on *Population and Emigration* and followed it by examining *Consolidation*. One on *Universal Peace* succeeded a foray into *Parties*. The impression was that Madison wrote about the topic of his interest at the moment.

He presented a literal view of consolidation. Whereas most Antifederalists foresaw an emasculation of state governments, Madison elevated the notion to include an actual abolition of states and his objections were based on this assumption. Nevertheless, he repeated Richard Henry Lee's original observation. The people must be vigilant to prevent this catastrophe.

Monarchies and aristocracies were each unsuitable for the United States. "A confederated republic," he reminded his audience, "attains the force of monarchy, whilst it equally avoids the ignorance of a good prince, and the repression of a bad one."

A government charter, since it was a compact, ensured the people's liberty because it defined benchmarks that prevented "public usurpation" of its citizens. As such, it was particularly applicable to a federal government organized into several branches and many departments. It would defend "liberty against power and power against licentiousness." Again, Madison stressed that "liberty and order will never be perfectly safe until a trespass on the constitutional provisions for either shall be felt with the same keenness that resists an invasion of the dearest rights, until every citizen shall be an Argus to espy, and an Aegeon to avenge the unhallowed deed."

Americans could not avoid political parties, but their evils could be damped. If all citizens were politically equal, had the same opportunities to enrich themselves, maintained the same property rights while reducing riches, refused to recognize laws that benefited one class over another, and defined parties to check each other, the people could accept them.

The government form was admirable. Its distribution of power checked abuses although public opinion could influence its decisions. Of course, the task of maintaining a balance of power between competing governments was difficult, but one should never ignore it. Republican principles required American citizens to maintain the boundaries between federal and state governments.

Although Madison recognized Montesquieu's government operating principles to be "fear, honor, and virtue," he preferred a triad of his own invention. Naturally, it promoted the Republicans and castigated their opponents. One of his "three species" was based on military power. However, it was the other two that drew our attention. One government, obviously Federalist, operated "by corrupt influence" in which "Private interest" supplanted "public duty." Government favorites pocketed bounties, bribes, and other benefits transforming itself into merely an "imposter." In contradistinction was a government "deriving its energy from the will of society." It was republican, "the glory of America," and "her happiness [may] be perpetuated by a system of administration corresponding with the purity of the theory."

Madison's exposition on property might remind his readers of its Lockean definition. Not only were land and possessions property but also opinions and the right to communicate them. Property was never secure in a government system "under which unequal taxes oppress one species of property and reward another species." "If the United States mean to obtain or deserve the full praise due to wise and just governments," he wrote, "they will equally respect the rights of property, and the property in rights."

The essay *A Candid State of Parties* purported to differentiate between an undemocratic party — the never mentioned Federalists — and one that embraced democratic ideals. Madison laddered his sections so an action that the latter party would have preferred rebutted one actually taken by the Federalists. Opulence attracted the opposition "division." It believed man could not govern himself, and was the home of the money interest. Although the latter were "the few" it received the greatest benefits. Slowly, this government would retreat until it "approximated to a hereditary form." Democrats suffered no such dynamic. The people, they believed, could govern themselves and considered "hereditary power as an insult to the reason and an outrage to the rights of man." Also, public measures must meet society's requirements.

Obviously, any smaller party would have two goals. It would seek to attract wealth to counteract its numerical disadvantage and attempt "to weaken their opponents by reviving exploded parties and taking advantage of all prejudices, local, political, and occupational, that might prevent or disturb a general coalition of sentiments." The Republicans — he named them — rejected these tactics. They would naturally attract the friends of democracy, and promote "a general harmony among [them], wherever residing or however employed."

Perhaps prompted by the Madisonian exposition, George Washington, unsure of the Republican interest's goals, asked Thomas Jefferson to describe them. On May 23, 1792, when Madison was almost finished his *Gazette* articles, Jefferson responded to the president. A process must be found to demark clearly the powers of the federal government and those of the states. If the latter gathered too much power, the result was "an excess of liberty." If the former slipped over the boundary, the result was monarchy. The problem was that the first case was self-correcting while the second led to stronger monarchies. Since the states must raise the barriers to usurpation, and their only tool was "wise government," Jefferson proposed several constitutional amendments. He would reduce the number of representatives and lengthen their term to make the office "a desirable station"; revisit the senatorial term of office; increase the presidential term but make him ineligible for reelection; and reduce the judiciary but increase its compensation and firm its term in office. Obviously, Jefferson's thoughts on government were bound to influence his party. Notice that he did not promote state interests above national concerns. He sought a balanced relationship between the contending governments.

The Republican congressional fight against Hamiltonian policy had been mothballed for good tactical reasons. Some, like Patrick Henry and Henry Lee, feared civil unrest if the people became too involved. More to the point, Madison, Jefferson, and Monroe had no alternative to the hated system. In a corollary to the Lee-Henry argument, an all-out war on Federalist policy might drive moderates who feared civil strife into the Federalist camp. Republicans preferred to wait for another coalescing event.

Concurrent with the rise of a Republican interest in Congress was a sister movement in Virginia. Its politics until the 1790s depended on a constant regrouping of delegates around various issues. Parties did not exist. By 1791, the Antifederalists had left the scene but several issues still rankled. Debts to British merchants, frontier instability, and the results of opening the Mississippi to commerce divided the state. As before, the solution seemed to depend on the energy of the Federalist national government.

Virginians maintained the geographic split of the ratifying period. The Northern Neck coalition had successfully switched its agricultural focus from tobacco to grain cereals. With its markets in Europe and the West Indies, it expected the national government to help expand its range. On the other hand, the tobacco-focussed Piedmont and Southside already had steady customers in Britain and France. Why should they invite a strong national government, over which they had no control, to regulate them? Despite the persistence of these issues, they were not significant enough to generate a rush toward political parties, although they could be discriminating once parties formed. Allegiances awaited another issue.

It arrived in the foreign affairs arena. Not only did the European war disclose constitutional issues we have examined, but also it hastened the formation of political parties. Relations with both the 1793 belligerents England and France provided a tipping point. Virginia Republicans had sided with radical France, while Federalists had advanced the British cause. Washington's neutrality pronouncement failed to dispel Republican concerns. Its agrarian base disapproved of the treaty although the towns accepted its wisdom.

The Jay Treaty exacerbated matters. The debt settlement clause offended Virginia's planters while the absence of neutral rights implied an acceptance of British international law interpretations. Tobacco growers rejected the treaty's handling of the western forts issue while westerners applauded it. The Virginia assembly's approval of its federal senators' treaty renunciation reflected the shrinking Federalist core. However, in 1795 Federalists saw some gains in the Northern Neck and Eastern Shore. This area had been the center of the creditor interest and it smiled on the West Indies access. Moreover, the Neck had benefited from early party organization that publicized its goals. Therefore, events in far away Europe, from which Republicans had sought to divorce themselves, provided an important catalyst for party organization in Virginia.

What disaffected groups did the moderate Republicans sweep into their new party? One segment included the agrarian Federalists who feared domination by the eastern mercantile interest. Note however that it maintained its fealty to the Union and form of government. Policy drove them into Republican arms. Some Antifederalists had no such reservations. They maintained that Americans must amend the government structure because the eastern bloc provided not only economic danger but also government usurpation. They were confident that state governments could satisfy all their requirements. Why depend on a remote government that had revealed itself to be the patron of privilege and tyranny? Unfortunately for their cause, they were shunted aside in the rush to ensure national Republican electoral dominance. However, the debtor faction of the old Antifederalist interest carried its platform with them into the new party.

Virginia's agrarian Republicans were diverse in both their rank and wealth, but their rural roots bound them. They identified with each other, the gentry leadership, and with the idea of Virginia's superiority. Whether former Federalists or Antifederalists they ported their main issues with them to the party, but sublimated them to the one that they could agree upon — an antiadministration distrust. Thus, the Republicans became a people's party representing a solid agrarian base.

This was not to say that all differences were damped. Congressional Republicans accepted government dynamics whereas many of their Virginia brethren favored a reexamination of both power sharing and the form of government. Within the state, the lesser gentry was unsure of the efficacy of either democratic government or Jeffersonian egalitarianism. Each threatened its perch on the status ladder. According to Madison and Jefferson, these men had little national vision, but they maintained a good working relationship with the natural congressional political aristocracy. Their dominance of Virginia politics ensured that Virginia's national leaders could concentrate on other matters, satisfied that Virginia was safe.

The rise of the Republican party unveiled another potential trouble spot. Elections that could conceivably match yeomen against gentry became possible. Party stalwarts agreed that class warfare must not dissolve the solid Republican majority. They must have been successful. A comparison by counties of those favoring ratification to later elections showed that of the eighty-four counties (and three boroughs), ten reversed their allegiance. Of the ten, nine shifted from Federalist to Republican. In another approximation, eighty-six Virginia delegates (plus three Kentuckians) favored the Constitution. Thirty-eight remained Federalists while twenty-three became Republicans. The rest disappeared from the historical scene. Seventy-three (and six Kentuckians) voted against ratification. Of the forty that were identifiable, thirty-eight joined the Republicans. Thus, the proconstitution interest split allegiances while the Antifederalists almost unanimously became Republicans.

The Antifederalist faction retained its belief in constitutional degradation. To prevent it, they argued, Republicans had to adopt strict construction that promoted limited federal government and state sovereignty. Moreover, the states could protect and promote individual rights better than their federal counterparts. Interestingly, future state rights advocates would share these ideals. Yet, most early Republican leaders promoted a nationalistic view. America needed an energetic government but it must not infringe on the people's liberty. Therefore, moderate Republicans maintained a central position in the power struggle. Strict constructionists like John Taylor of Caroline did not offer an agenda that a national party could follow but they could sniff out constitutional heresies.

Party organization and system changes followed. Although Virginians had established the leadership class, the rise of political parties forced a significant addition to the political requirements for that group. As well as being a gentleman, a potential candidate had to swear allegiance to a party. No longer would house delegates vote in a world of ever-changing alliances. The party's will would guide them. This would be a burden for state rights men because their fealty to state sovereignty had to be sublimated to Republican national interest.

The electoral process lost its *ad hoc* local character. Popularity contests disappeared as party identification replaced requirements of yesteryear. Seldom would a Federalist convince a Republican county that he could represent its interests. The voter, not any referral to privilege, decided which gentleman would represent him. Parties, statewide, held public meetings with specific debate topics. Some produced important resolutions that they transmitted to the General Assembly.

Perhaps the most interesting addition to the system was the invention of the caucus. Although the parties would refine it during Jefferson's terms, it set up a limited process through which it could promulgate a united agenda.

Federalist fortunes waned. As noted, Northern Neck planters and merchants began the decade supporting its cause. Shenandoah Valley and Allegheny region counties west of the Valley along with those of the western Kanawha Valley joined them. These sections had many religious dissenters who differed markedly from eastern Virginians. Still, as the decade unfolded, the opposition displaced the Northern Neck Federalists. Unlike their former allies, western support included many middle-class commercial yeomen — subsistence farmers voted Republican — who had no common cause with eastern patricians. Thus, we must be careful not to overdo the agrarian switch to the Republican party. However, we also must realize that the Federalist leadership was usually found among local merchants, lawyers, or doctors.[2]

In 1797 French declarations silenced their Republican support. France labelled American ships carrying British goods as pirates and commandeered them. Republicans, trying to recover, attempted to transfer blame to the Jay Treaty, but failed. The administration enjoyed a mini boom in popularity based on the notorious XYZ affair. French officials insulted the American commissioners, who sought relief from French depredations, by inviting them to take part in a kickback scheme.

Americans were livid at this disgraceful conduct. Taking advantage of the mood, the government prepared for war. Congress authorized an army of 20,000 in case of hostilities; began a Navy-building program; borrowed $5,000,000; and laid a direct tax of $2,000,000 on the states. One can easily predict the Republican reaction to these measures but they reserved their wrath for the Alien and Sedition Acts that were composed of an Alien, Alien Enemies, Naturalization, and Sedition Acts.

In précis, the Alien Act (June 25, 1798), assigned the president power to deport aliens that he judged dangerous to the United States by serving a warrant on them. He might allow friendly aliens, who could prove that designation, to remain under bond. If an alien ignored his warrant, he faced a possible prison term of three years, at the president's pleasure, and gave up his opportunity to become a citizen. The act would be in force for two years.

The Sedition Act (July 14, 1798), punished a conspiracy with intent that opposed any government "measure." It would charge the offending party with a misdemeanor, fine him a sum not exceeding $5000 or imprison him from six months to five years. Specifically, "false, scandalous, and malicious" publications or comments defaming the president or Congress and designed to excite the people against the government were illegal.

These acts not only struck at the core beliefs of the Republican party but also presented a political challenge. Their proponents claimed an unenumerated power that if successfully implemented would sideline any plans Republicans might have to stigmatize the Federalist government by accusing it of aristocracy and monarchy. After all, could not President Adams's huge army clamp down on dissenters? Its existence reminded Republicans of the Hamiltonian plan of the first two Congresses. Nevertheless, here, the Federalists displayed a political tin ear. Immediate national and Virginia outrage boosted the Republican standing. If the party protests were successful, the people would rally to its banner and reject the Federalist program. Coincidentally, they would elevate its compact theory as the dominant explanation of the origin of government and establish the relationship between civil and state rights.

Theoretical and constitutional opposition was diffuse. The acts struck at the underpinnings of representative government by making criticism illegal; established an unhealthy precedent that would be a guideline to future action; attacked the system of checks and balances by assigning the president legislative and judicial functions; destroyed the cherished concept of limited government; raised doubts that the government was a compact between the states; questioned the power of the Supreme Court over judicial review; and rejected a state's power to punish a crime within its sphere.

To popularize the above grievances, Thomas Jefferson and James Madison — with an assist from John Taylor of Caroline — organized two sets of resolutions. Prominent Republicans persuaded the state legislatures of Virginia (December 24, 1798) and Kentucky (November 10, 1798) to publicize the Republican response to the Alien and Sedition Laws. They were not a road map for concerted southern action but would be useful in organizing opposition against the governing Federalists. Still, one should not conclude that this was their only, or main, purpose. They clearly set out a specific theory of governance.

Thomas Jefferson wrote the Kentucky resolutions and James Breckenridge introduced a modified version to its house. An alert observer could have predicted the flavor of the content. The Constitution was a compact among the states — there was no reference to the people. Government, the result of the compact, had only certain limited powers — the residue was left to the states. If this government usurped an undelegated power, the partners to the compact could declare it void. Also, the government could never be the "exclusive or final judge" of its actions — its opinion on itself would usurp the role of the Constitution.

Jefferson was not satisfied with only one reason for voiding these abominable laws. By stacking them one above the other, he emphasized the length to which Federalists would stoop to create a monarchical government that would shatter Madison's concept of dual sovereignties. His favorite citation was the Tenth Amendment because it reserved all powers to the states or the people that were undelegated to Congress. Since the Constitution specifically listed crimes that Congress might punish, the unlisted Alien and Sedition acts were "void, and of no force" because the powers "to create, define, and punish such other crimes is reserved" to the states in their separate territories. Similarly, the combination of reserved, undelegated powers prevented Congress from controlling the freedoms of religion, speech, and press. In addition, the migration provision assigned the states the role of adjudicators of alien acceptability thus Congress did not have it. Any powers not delegated to Congress within the clause insured their reservation to the individual states.

Of course, other, more obvious, considerations existed. Because the migration law above specifically denied Congress the power, it could not prevent the migration of alien friends. Still, the Alien Act contained a clause that allowed alien removal. Obviously it inhibited migration and was unconstitutional. Other usurpations abounded. Did not an amendment forbid Congress from "abridging the freedom of speech or of the press"? Another, the due process clause, promised a right to a public trial by an impartial jury plus other basic rights. The presidential assumption of these powers was unconstitutional because it clothed him with not only executive, but legislative, and judicial powers. Perhaps the most interesting argument linked the general welfare clause to the sweeping clause and added a purposeful misconstruction of language to invest unimaginable powers in Congress. This combination

> goes to the destruction of all limits prescribed to their powers by the Constitution: that words meant by the instrument to be subsidiary only to the execution of limited powers, ought not to be so construed as themselves to give unlimited powers, nor a part to be so taken as to destroy the whole residue of that instrument.

After the Republicans delineated this shopping list of unconstitutional acts, the legislature presented its solution. The nation must understand that Kentucky remained true to the Union "for specified national purposes." However, it would never submit to a process that promised a consolidated government of undelegated powers. Boldly, it claimed that the remedy to such an assumption was "a nullification of the act." In addition, each state always had a natural right to assume powers in cases not covered by the Constitution "within their limits" and Congress was "merely the creature of the compact." If the compact partners did not protest against the Alien and Sedition Acts, the government would conclude that it had established a precedent for transferring other powers to the president.

Republicans decided that they must sensitize Virginians to the tyranny of the majority infecting Congress. These acts were probably an experiment to find the limit it might reach in duping the people. To combat them, Jefferson urged every American not to trust his representative, but to "bind him down from mischief by the chains of the Constitution." Each state was duty-bound to ensure that only constitutional acts passed scrutiny. If not, "these and successive acts of the same character, unless arrested at the threshold, necessarily drive these States into revolution and blood, and will furnish new calumnies against republican government."

The Madisonian Virginia Resolution, a compendium of resolutions, was more concise than its running mate and reiterated its specifics. It began with a general description of the compact, switched to the general reasons for a protest, and continued with the particulars against the Alien and Sedition Acts. It finished with a reminder that Virginia had been a source of "the Liberty of Conscience and of the Press" and they could not "be canceled, abridged, restrained, or modified by any authority of the United States." Virginia felt obliged to protest the usurpations of power in the set of laws because not to do so would set a dangerous precedent.

The resolution finished by appealing to the states to declare the two acts unconstitutional, and if so, they must take some unspecified action.

From the above discussion, one can mine a set of ideals, commonly called the Principles of '98, that initiated the state rights doctrine. An enterprising reader might compare them with the Virginia Address of 1790. This collection was important because it formalized a process that had developed during the decade. The Union was a compact among coequal states that produced a strictly construed Constitution that defined a limited federal government whose undelegated powers were expressly reserved to the states. Because the Constitution was a compact, a corollary that each member had the power to judge any infraction, and list methods to correct it, was logical. If a protesting state could persuade most of its costates to support it, they would bind the government within its delegated powers. Yet, if such a concurrence failed, the options were revolution or retreat. If the protesting state chose the former, natural law empowered the costates to coerce it to follow the law. Here, the first under the new doctrine, Kentucky merely sought the other states' assistance in repealing the Alien and Sedition laws. Nevertheless, the theoretical opening for more severe action was apparent.

A close reading of the above paragraph would satisfy the reader that the Kentucky Resolutions left undelegated powers to the states. Yet, it never mentioned the people. Earlier, John Taylor of Caroline and James Madison had offered their sentiments on the relationship between a state and its people. Perhaps another suggested by the eminent historian Harry Jaffa can add perspective. Consider two scenarios. First, recall that the undefined people had delegated some power to the states and some to the general government while retaining the residue. Second, according to a dominating interpretation, the original social compact united the original states, as states, to form the United States thinking these truisms resulted in the undefined people transmitted delegated power to the United States. It was a compact of states that received its powers from the signatories to the compact. Comparing the two positions, Jaffa concluded that the undefined people must be the states because the United States government received its authority in one case from the states and in the other from the undefined people. Of course, Congress should have written the Tenth Amendment "the powers not delegated are reserved 'to the States or to the people of the States respectively.'" This interpretation, reminiscent of Madison's highest capacity argument, was no more, nor less, intuitive than that offered later by John Marshall and the proponents of an organic origin for the Union. It was just different. For our purposes, it explained nicely the relationship to which Jefferson adhered. His short phrase "*each State to itself*" within the longer explanation "that the several states had constituted 'a general government for special purposes ... reserving *each State to itself* [italics added], the residuary mass of right to their own self-government'" implied a sovereignty of the people of each state.

The same reader probably noticed that the word "expressly" crept into the earlier reservation statement as it did in the Tenth Amendment. Still, Jefferson labelled the phraseology "true as a general principle" and "expressly declared" when applying it. This was bound to make a critic of the notion pause. Why would a constitutional expert like Thomas Jefferson claim an express power when that verbiage did not literally appear? Although we have offered a discussion of this topic previously, it would be germane to present a sister explanation in this context. Again, Jaffa led our discussion. We were certain that the reserved powers of the states existed before the amendment was added to the Constitution. Thus, Jaffa explained, Jefferson could argue that the powers were now "expressed" by the act of adding them to the Constitution. Otherwise, the inclusion was redundant. Of course, many did not accept this derivation, but it sufficed for state rights men.

Although we should not expect a great divergence in the two protests, a quick examination does uncover some interesting contrasts. Although these powerful men had agreed that a structured assault was necessary, they disagreed on some essentials. Jefferson applied stronger language and seemed less averse to violent action. He employed the terms "nullification" and "revolution" that Madison eschewed. Moreover, they had different visions of the organization of the compact. Jefferson conceived the parties to the compact to be each state and the aggregate of the others. Thus, he defined only two parties, destroying any implication of majority rule. Madison took a safer path. Each state was a member of the compact and therefore they could reach a majority. Also, Madison doubted Jefferson's implication that the state legislature, rather than the state itself, was the institution best suited to declare a law unconstitutional.

Not only did Jefferson and Madison disagree on the structure of the compact in 1799, but also they did not concur on the ultimate state reaction to a seizure of state power. Jefferson appeared willing to sunder the Union for a principle, while Madison sought protest and persuasion. For Jefferson, a loss of liberty trumped a collapsed Union. These distinctive opinions became the basis of different factions of future state rights men.

Briefly, one must realize that the thrust of the Resolutions was a defense of liberty, individual rights, and republican government rather than state rights and strict construction. No one urged citizens to disobey the law. That is not to say that later interpreters were incorrect if they welded strict construction and state rights to the Principles of '98. However, they were not front and center for the original authors.[3]

It remained for the house to debate the contents and motivation behind the Virginia Resolution. From December 13 to December 21, 1798, the House of Delegates scoured the resolutions. Because of their overwhelming majority, the guide offered by the house resolution, and the advantage of originating the debate, the Republican interest held the advantage. Despite the Federalist organization into debate teams they were forced into a defensive posture. The result was a fragmented approach, particularly concerning constitutionality. On the other hand, their opponents concentrated on the distribution of power predicted by the general government's agenda. Of course, each side delivered broadsides unconnected with either power distribution or the Constitution.

Blended powers, argued the Republicans, would be the result of these acts. One could count executive, legislative, and judicial functions within it. "Principles of free government" required a separation of powers assigned by the Alien Law to the president. "No oath of affirmation...; no presentment or indictment by a grand jury...; no trial by jury" were available to the alien. Instead "his accusation, conviction and punishment, were all to be announced by the Presidential officer in one breath."

Power distribution was another irritant. The Constitution had defined a system that exclusively delegated powers to each level of government plus some that each could apply. Still, the sovereign states retained the residue of powers remaining after the delegations. The people were "so fearful of the greedy doctrine of implication" that they had insisted on a clarifying amendment. After the Constitution defined the express powers of government, it left "powers not granted" to the states. Interestingly, John Taylor (Caroline) appended the contentious "expressly" to reserved powers. These acts usurped those powers.

Precedent was a menace for Republicans. If they allowed the Federalist power grab, another would soon follow. " If Congress could infringe the rights of those people [aliens], they might infringe the rights of others." Could not they apply the same procedure to place strictures on religion? What new bands will tighten around public opinion? Recall, James Madison had proclaimed it the engine that forced governmental change. Taylor transferred the argument from individuals to states. "The concentration of it [power] in an individual," he intoned, "would enslave other individuals; a concentration of it in Congress, would operate to the destruction of the state governments." Once one established presidential influence, one hastened civil strife.

Surely this relocation of power would produce a consolidated government. Because Federalists would accomplish it despite promises made during ratification, the deceit was doubly oppressive. The result, according to James Barbour (Orange) was "that the states have no check, no constitutional barrier against the encroachment of the general government."

Necessarily, a realignment of the people's freedoms would follow. Initially, it would affect the state legislators. Presently, they had sworn to oppose unconstitutional acts. Would Congress imprison them? Another would likely affect the right of petition. If the law challenged freedom of speech, that of petitioning the government would follow. Similarly, public opinion could face regulation "to detach the people from the state governments, and attach them to the general government." Whenever government invaded the sovereignty of the states, "the states have the right to communicate with each other, in the manner contemplated by the resolutions." One must always remember the Virginia reservation of rights accompanying ratification. It contained specific language protecting freedom of speech and the press. More important, it maintained a specific reservation of power to the people of Virginia.

Federalists asserted that a government must have the power to protect itself. If so, said Republicans, they could apply the argument to state governments as well. Did they not have the identical right? They must contend against laws that would destroy them. After all, the states had been sovereign both before and after ratification and "were sovereign and independent as to powers not granted." "Any attempt by Congress to legislate on this subject ... was an attack on the sovereignty" of the states.

Once the Republicans had identified the Federalist agenda for reinterpreting constitutional power, they sought to uncover its methodology. All Federalist general arguments revolved around some combination of implication and the sweeping clause. John Mercer (Spotsylvania) reminded his colleagues that implication by its nature, was unspecific, and would lead the house into an "endless discussion." Even the Virginia ratifying convention delegates had been assured that no implication was possible because "the language was so clear and its [Constitution] powers so well-defined." They were correct with respect to all the great powers. Delegates expressly listed each in the enumeration. None "depend ... upon nice construction or implication."

Each of the above, individually, perturbed the Republicans. Yet, it was the attachment of the doctrine of implication to other clauses that increased their suspicion. The sweeping clause was the chief target. According to William Daniel Jr. (Cumberland), those supporting the Alien and Sedition Laws found no solace in the exact words of the Constitution. Only a reversion to the general clauses might offer a defense of their position. Phrases like "to provide for the general welfare," "to repel invasions," and "to make laws necessary to carry the foregoing powers into effect" were ready-made for this tactic. However, any expansion of power based on this rationalization produced a conundrum. If Federalists could apply it to produce unlimited powers "the special enumeration of power in the Constitution was absurd and useless." The Framers had wasted their efforts to produce a limited government.

William Ruffin (Brunswick) added another criticism. Suppose one allowed the general welfare clause to pair with the sweeping clause. Were there any unconscionable results? Could not the present government construct a combination to extend its term to ten years, or even life? Still, he continued, such was the tyranny of implication.

Mercer offered another view of the above combination. A close examination of the sweeping clause demonstrated that it referenced enumerated powers vested in Congress. The Framers had designed the clause to allow it to execute an enumerated power, not to assume any new powers. The record of the Virginia ratifying debates would confirm this interpretation. When cornered by Patrick Henry on this exact topic, James Madison admitted that the clause "gives no supplementary power" and "is at most explanatory; for when any power is given, its delegation necessarily involves an authority to make laws to execute it."

The Republicans recognized the effects of these laws on civil rights. They endangered the Sixth through Eighth Amendments from the Bill of Rights. The president, without probable cause, could arrest an alien and deprive him "of his life, liberty, or property, without due process of law." By extension, the alien had no right to a grand jury appearance or a timely trial by jury. This was worrisome to Republican delegates who had fought hard to include a Bill of Rights.

Republican ideals, "the great end of the Constitution," were under attack. As noted, trial by jury and the extension of presidential power were "the greatest enemy which republican principals had." "'Liberty,' was to be suspended without any 'crime' being defined" while Alien Law proponents spread monarchical principals throughout the nation. Moreover, "any power which Congress should exercise, not granted by that charter, would be an usurpation upon the rights of the states, or the people." In particular, Article I, Section 9, controlling the migration of individuals, assigned Virginia, by reserved right, the control of her aliens. Now, Federalists wanted to appropriate this power to their ends.

Probably to some Republicans surprise, several colleagues challenged the import of the original resolution with respect to the origin of the Union. James Barbour repeated the Madisonian assertion that the parties to the compact were both the people and the states and Peter Johnston (Prince Edward) agreed. To confirm this opinion, Barbour listed many incidences in which the states had acted to initiate the Union. William Foushee (Richmond City) designated it a limited compact with respect to its powers. The upshot was that the convention amended the resolutions to reflect Barbour's and Johnston's concerns. This was an important inclusion for future traditional state rights men. Patrick Henry's "We the States" must be interpreted to refer to the people of the states.

As indicated earlier, the Federalist principal argument was based on implication, the sweeping clause, the general welfare clause, and combinations of the three. George K. Taylor (Prince George) laid down a basic argument. The Framers recognized that future events could not be predicted so they inserted the sweeping clause "to carry into effect the powers expressly given it by the Constitution. Whatever then necessarily flowed from these express powers, were within the scope of Congress."

Later, Taylor expanded this argument. Anyone studying the Constitution would conclude that the Convention intended "to invest every power relating to the general welfare and tranquility of the Union in the General Government." As before, future circumstances could not be predicted so powers were enumerated in general terms. Applying a common argument, he announced that a "liberal as well as candid interpretation" would force one to agree that the sweeping clause continued this interpretation.

The Republican reliance on compact did not satisfy Federalists. According to them "the people alone are parties to the compact, called the Constitution of the United States." Of course, this prevented the state legislatures from acting on the constitutionalism of the two laws. Henry Lee (Westmoreland) reminded the house that the Constitution was styled "We the People." James Cureton (Prince George) agreed with this evaluation and declared that these same people would decide through their ballots in March whether the acts were acceptable.

Like their opponents, the Federalists commented briefly on several constitutional powers. Congress could refuse to land aliens and this was tantamount to ejecting them; the president necessarily had been assigned blended powers; trial by jury was not a right extended to any aliens; only the judiciary could declare a law unconstitutional; a second convention would be "ruinous" to the Union; the correct method of protest was a congressional petition; the government had a right to protect itself; and the states, alone, never had a reserved power.

As we have done several times, we will examine voting trends prompted by the house debate to inform us about the popularity of a government position. The basic pattern established in 1788 remained steady with some exceptions. The Northern Neck, previously solidly Federalist, lost its Tidewater component with the exception of Westmoreland. The yeomen of Harrison and Ohio counties and the Southwest also withdrew their support. Now that the Indian menace had declined, they adopted the Republican cause. Similarly, the Williamsburg peninsula was lost to the Republicans.

Norman Risjord supplied the motivation for continued Federalist support. Undemocratic representation in the General Assembly burdened the merchants and farmers of the Potomac, Shenandoah, and Kanawha river valleys. Statistically, the state government ignored their needs. As a result, they turned to the federal government for support. One might hazard a conclusion that, of the two parties, the Republicans of Virginia seemed more tied to ideology than did the Federalists.[4]

About three weeks subsequent to the house debate on the Alien and Sedition Acts, it reported its deliberations publically to the people of Virginia. In addition, it rejected a Federalist attempt to append a minority report expounding its views on government. They would have to publish one separately at their own expense. Interestingly, the original authors were James Madison and, possibly, John Marshall.

Madison covered all the Republican bases, and did so with style. The acts were a pretext for usurping state power; prelude to consolidation; blatant grab for power; purposeful reordering of constitutional language to produce the opposite effect; and clumsy attempt to bypass the Bill of Rights. However, the doctrine of implication was his principal target. It was now the rule for constitutional construction. He preferred to believe that the states had not been the victim of half-truths during ratification. Had they not been assured that the preamble did not assign unlimited powers to Congress? Surely, this ran counter to the intent of the Tenth Amendment. In a nice tactical move, Madison linked the gloomy results of implication to an assault on republicanism.

> The distinction between liberty and licentiousness, is still a repetition of the protean doctrine of implication, which is ever ready to work its ends by varying its shape.... Remember that precedents once established, are so much positive power; and that the nation which reposes on the pillow of political confidence, will sooner or later, end its political existence in a deadly lethargy.

By implication, Congress could accomplish any misdeed. It might, for example, "denominate a religion to be heretical and licentious and proceed to its suppression."

The Federalist's response contained arguments that were a precursor to later Supreme Court decisions. The Framers designed the general government for the benefit of the whole nation and thus it must have the power to act on that task. "Government is instituted and preserved," the author stated, "for the general happiness and safety — the people therefore are interested in its preservation, and have a right to adopt measures for its security as well as against secret plots as open hostility." Moreover, it should expect the cooperation of the states in attaining it. Was it not logical to place the power over national affairs in the national government? Yes, the government was limited to only delegated powers. However, if one examined the Constitution for guidance, one would discover two truisms. Because it was a Constitution and not an act, it necessarily dealt with generalities. Secondly, one must not single out one clause, "we must examine the whole paper — we must examine it fairly, but liberally." Echoing the Federal Farmer from an earlier era, the author reminded Virginians that delegated power often carried with it "the particular degree or manner in which it shall be increased" and became "a question of political discretion and not of constitutional authority." Also, there were instances in which "Congress may both *define* and *punish*." Necessary implications must be made to protect the nation.

Constitutionally, the United States guaranteed to protect the states from invasion. It was obvious to the Federalist author that the power to repel invasion morphed into various congressional powers through an application of Article I, Section 8 and Article IV, Section 4. They prompted him to declare that "of these proper and necessary steps, the government possessed of the power, must judge." Thus, his methodology of applying the whole Constitution to a thorny problem supported his conclusion that a combination of Articles allowed the government to both pass constitutional laws and be the judge of the necessity. Continuing with an example, he argued that the sweeping clause obviously allowed Congress to pass "any act for the punishment of those who would resist the execution of the laws" because it "would be incontestably necessary and proper for carrying into execution, the powers vested in government." If this power was constitutional, then did it not also authorize the punishment of those acts, which are criminal in themselves, and which obviously lead to and prepare resistance?

The author followed a tortured path to give "to the legislature of the union the right to make such laws" enabling a judicial power. It rested on the common law. James Madison had stated his concerns both before and after this debate. He reminded George Washington "that the common law is nothing more than the unwritten law, and is left by all the [state] constitutions equally liable to alterations." If the common law had been part of the Constitution, it "would have broken in upon the legal Code of every State in the most material points." Expanding this notion in 1824, Madison observed that the United States government of delegated powers made it impossible "to argue that the common law be part of the 'national code'" since it was specifically limited when less important items were included. Despite Madison's opinion, the minority report author ignored its thrust.

He had a daunting task before him but found an ingenious scenario. Somehow he had to shoehorn the common law into the Constitution. Then, he had to find references to libelling the government that were germane. Recall that Article III, Section 2 defined part of the Court's jurisdiction to "all cases in Law and equity arising under the Constitution, the laws of the United States, and treaties made under their authority [and] to controversies to which the United States may be a party." Borrowing an argument from Harrison Gray Otis (Massachusetts), the author cleverly posed his crucial question. What were cases arising under the Constitution, as contradistinguished from those which arise under the laws made in pursuance thereof? This question was important, he noted, because the Article listed two classes of cases, one arising under the Constitution and the other under the laws of the United States. If they were listed separately, then they must differ substantially. The first assigned jurisdiction to cases arising from the Constitution, so he claimed that the latter must not do so. After a perusal of the legal system, he observed that the only class of jurisprudence that fit this definition was the common law.

It was time to move to the next step. Prior to the Revolution, British common law crossed the ocean to the colonies. Critically, no government change, like that brought about by the war, dissolved "obligations previously created" or "annihilated existing law." Thus, "a People passing from one form of government to another" maintained the laws of the replaced government except those specifically annulled. Therefore the common law remained a part of the legal code. As a result, "libels against the government [were] a punishable offense." Moreover, federal criminal jurisdiction was under the cloak of the Constitution since the common law was a "law of the United States."

Once the author had established the validity of the common law, he had to ascertain "whether the doctrines of the common law were applicable to libels against the government of the United States." Virginia had a state law controlling it with respect to state government. Why should there be any distinction between controlling it and libelling the federal government? If a state law bound citizens against libelling a state legislature then, sensibly, its federal counterpart should apply. Moreover, for many purposes, the federal government was that of Virginia. Therefore, even if the punishment meted out to the defendant affected the liberty of the press, "yet the act does not *abridge* that liberty, since it does not substitute a harsher or severer rule of punishment than that which before existed" by the Virginia law.

In an interesting addendum to Otis's and the minority report author's claims, Albert Gallatin (Pennsylvania), as reported by Joseph Lynch, claimed: "Even if Article III of the Constitution had provided for a common law in crime, he had yet to explain how under Article II Congress had the power to revise that law. Indeed, as Gallatin pointed out in the debates over the repeal of the Sedition Act in the Sixth Congress, the Otis position led to the anomalous situation that the federal judiciary could decide on subjects upon which Congress, for want of an enumerated power, could not legislate."[5]

The publication of these documents had mixed results in Virginia and negative reaction in the remainder of the nation. The other states insisted that the judiciary interpreted the Constitution. Mass meetings in some stalwart Republican counties belabored the acts, but when it came to the national elections shortly thereafter, the Federalist forces captured almost 50 percent of the congressional seats. One out-of-state commentator reported that the Republicans sought a revolution or secession. Perhaps it was this extreme possibility that motivated all the states responding to the Virginia and Kentucky Resolutions to reject them.[6]

Undoubtedly shocked by the negative reaction to the Resolutions, but firm in their advocacy, Jefferson contacted Madison and suggested a response. They must meet the objections squarely and justify the Resolution's content; revisit the constitutional principles that sustained the protests; ensure that America recognized Virginia's fealty to the Union while reminding it that it would never accept a government usurpation of power; and, in the extremity, offer secession as an answer.

Due to the overwhelming national rejection on grounds that Madison and Jefferson felt were a misunderstanding, the former presented a clarifying report to the Virginia legislature in December 1799 that expanded the Principles of '98. Still, one must understand that the Resolutions had another target besides the Alien and Sedition Acts. They also reminded the states of a series of laws demonstrating "forced constructions ... calculated to enlarge the powers of the Federal government." As part of his effort, he challenged many of the minority report's constitutional interpretations.

His methodology differed from that of his debating partner. While the latter dealt in broad strokes with a wide brush giving little weight to specifics, Madison presented minute detail to undercut the Federalist position. Moreover, the report's author was liable to find his constitutional solutions in combinations of articles, a bit here, and a bit there, welded together to form a cohesive whole whereas Madison generally, but not always, found his answers from within the language of the applicable clauses themselves.

Madison's first task was to clear up any erroneous interpretations of the compact. "Federal powers," he noted, "are derived from the Constitution, and ... the Constitution is a compact to which the states are parties." The first misunderstanding he faced was the definition of "state." He clarified his position by enunciating four possibilities, the territories occupied by the political societies within each, their particular governments, the societies themselves, and "the people composing these political societies, in their highest sovereign capacity," that is, the peoples of the several states in their capacities as peoples of those states. A close examination of the ratifying process would convince one that the latter was the operative definition in the United States. It reflected the notion of a compact and nicely intimated dual sovereignty, a popular argument during the Constitutional Convention. As usual, powers not delegated to either level of government were withheld from them. However, Madison extended this concept. Based on the compact's nature, it was common sense that if no greater power legitimately came into play, then only the parties to the compact — the states — could judge "whether the bargain made, has been pursued or violated." If no higher agency interfered, only the states could decide if there had been a violation of the compact and if interposition was necessary.

Interposition was never meant to be used except in cases in which "a deliberate, palpable, and dangerous breach of the Constitution" promised a usurpation of power. Moreover, it must apply only to matters "affecting the vital principles of their political system." After all, if the parties to the compact could not interpose, how could the people stop government usurpation?

Government powers were limited to those enumerated in the Constitution. Although one must read his statement carefully, he made his case by commenting that "if the powers granted be valid, it is solely because they are granted; and if the granted powers are valid, because granted, all other powers not granted, must not be valid." Remember, "the people, not the government, possess the absolute sovereignty."

The Federalists had employed several tactics and broad constitutional interpretations designed to turn the Constitution on its head. For example, they had invented a new doctrine that federal powers need not be derived from the Constitution. The claim had been, particularly in the report, that the common law "makes a part of the law of these States; in their united and national capacity." Madison went to some trouble to show that common law was local in the colonial era and was not transferred by the Articles. To repeat, when the report author examined Article III, Section 2, he concluded that the common law was a law of the United States. Thus the Constitution recognized it. "Never before," Madison remarked, "was so bad a construction applied to a text so clearly unsusceptible to it." First, no one had offered even one example to support the contention. But, most disheartening to Madison, who considered them obvious, several could be found that disproved the assumption. He then proceeded to show that judicial law could be extended without an application of common law despite the minority report argument that such an extension had only one basis — an application of common law. In fact, said Madison, "the common law never was, and by any fair construction ever could be, deemed a law for the American people as one community." If not, it could never be part of the national Constitution.

Madison extended his theory of judicial powers. First, he noted that Americans would have nowhere to turn if the judiciary was involved in usurpation. It decided, in the last resort, all questions "submitted to it by the forms of the Constitution" with respect to "the relation to the authorities of the other departments of the government" but "not in relation to the rights of the parties to the constitutional compact, from which the judicial as well as the other departments hold their delegated trusts." Otherwise, a government department that received power from another agency would have the power to "amend the authority delegating it."

Surprisingly, Madison said little about the sweeping clause. Perhaps he realized that the argument that it allowed only additional power to carry out enumerated powers, but no new grant of power, was familiar.

The Federalist tactic that riled Madison most was the application of language in a fashion to destroy its common meaning. For example, the provision for the "common defense and welfare" was borrowed from Article VIII of the Confederation and copied to Article I, Section 8. From the Confederation version neither "a general grant of power" nor authorization of taxes to the general welfare was expected "except in the cases afterwards enumerated." The Federalists purposely argued an interpretation of this phrase "so as to destroy the effect of the particular enumeration of powers by which it explains and limits them." As an example, Madison cited Hamilton's Report on Manufactures, and another of January 1797, both of which assigned Congress the power over the general welfare and thus the right to appropriate funds for each case. Remember, the general welfare clause was a part of the preamble and "cannot enlarge the enumerated powers vested in Congress" by definition. To continue in this vein would produce unlimited government in which the enumeration of powers was a waste of time. Misconstruction of language would produce a consolidated government because eventually general welfare cases would "supersede" the state sovereignties. Republican government, and liberty, would end, replaced by monarchy.

There was little in this exposition to bolster an interpretation that the Resolutions might support secession or revolution. Madison went to great lengths to assure the costates that he only wanted their support to declare the Alien and Sedition Acts unconstitutional while sensitizing them to the centralizing tendencies of the Federalist government. However, the cat was out of the bag and could never be recaptured. Future disputants could easily follow its trail.

Madison's stirring defense of basic rights enumerated in the Bill of Rights would transfer to the Republican party and later, state rights. As Adrienne Koch and Harry Ammon observed, Madison's report outlined precisely "the principles of republican self-government."[7]

Due to the many theoretical interpretations offered by sundry theorists and politicians, it would be advantageous to update compact theory. Remember, it was anchored in the sovereignty of the people and had as its corollaries the doctrines of state rights and strict constitutional interpretation.

Two versions existed. Nationalists saw the Union as a compact, if one existed, among all Americans viewed as an aggregate of individuals. Howard Belz was particularly harsh on this interpretation. He held that it "was more a clever theoretical intervention by the proponents of the Constitution." He next labelled it "legal fiction," and "a formal rather than a substantive truth." On the other hand, one could easily find contract theory in various state constitutions. If the sovereign state people could make state governments, why could they not make the new one?

State rights men reviled the nationalist version. Although Jefferson and Madison each promoted a separate state rights version — recall, they disagreed on the parties to the compact — they agreed that it involved the states. A nationalist would insist that the people must be involved, a sort of popular sovereignty. However, if one revisited the period of the Revolution, one found that it was the states, and not the Confederation government, that best resembled a republican government. Would not it make sense to recognize "the people of the United States" as the people of separate political units, that is, the states? Of course, in the former case, any dissolution led to a return to a state of nature by its followers while the latter foresaw the people governed by their states. Because the Constitution had been ratified by various state conventions, one might consider them as state representatives and conclude that the states were the parties. After all, did not the state governments represent all the people of the United States?

Who made the Union? became a central problem. Who or what was the sovereign? Could sovereignty be divided? To state rights men, the states as separate entities declared independence. Therefore, they must have preceded the formation of the United States. However, we must constantly remind ourselves of Madison's "highest capacity" argument. In this case "the states in their highest sovereign capacity" was synonymous with "the people of the United States in their highest sovereign capacity." Since the people came from a state of nature they had no higher political capacity than as people of the individual states. Due to the ambiguity of the Constitution, this interpretation was at least as valid as any other.

Two further interesting results followed. The first was a conundrum based upon the two state rights compact interpretations. Madisonian state rights men clove to a theory that many states formed the compact. This forced them to conclude that the exit from a state of nature produced a sovereign authority of the majority. Unfortunately, any individual state that attempted to decide constitutionality for all its costates usurped their power. On the other hand, Jeffersonian state rights men, who followed the two-party definition of the compact participants, had no such difficulty. They had an inbuilt "us-them" dichotomy associated with their theory. Secondly, the Union was a confederacy. It depended for its power on either the state governments or conventions of the state's people.

It would be advisable to review the notion of "the people" considering its centrality to the argument. Harry Jaffa reminded us that the sense of the word "people" caused confusion. Examine the Tenth Amendment. If, state rights men argued, the social compact was at the state level, then the Amendment referred to the aggregate "peoples" of the states and the Tenth's reservation of power should have been "to the States, or to the people of the States, respectively." This understanding was acceptable given its parameters. It was just a different "truism" than that proposed later by John Marshall. For doctrinaires, it meshed nicely with the Madisonian concept of the people.

The result of the compact was government. Naturally, this government was limited by the agreements within the compact. In no instance could it judge the extent of its own powers. An outside agency must have this power. To the state rights man, that agency was the sovereign people through the states.[8]

A student of this period must be surprised at the sudden canonization of the Constitution by a group that had aggressively fought to defeat its ratification. However, faced with reality, the Antifederalists and nascent Republicans had to reshape their ideological thinking to combat the Hamiltonian fiscal plan. A usurping government endangered republican liberty. Its defenders' principal nonviolent weapon was the Constitution. Thus, it was not the form of government that they attacked but the functionaries that had brought them to these straits.

This generalized fear could be subdivided. Some protesters concentrated on protecting the state rights that had been enunciated or interpreted in the Constitution, while others fought the baneful effects of monarchy and aristocracy on the nation. Nevertheless, it seemed that the principal motivation for defending the Constitution was the fear that the classical republican prediction of constitutional degeneration was at hand. Had not it begun already? Unless it could be stopped, or at least moderated, Virginians would suffer. The end result of degradation was usurpation and revolution.[9]

If the fear of constitutional and social degradation was the main motivation behind an Antifederalist/Republican, why did it take the form of literalism or strict construction? The Antifederalist contingent concluded that constitutions, by nature, were fragile, and degeneracy could only be sidetracked if the parties followed its terms literally. In that case, liberty would more than likely survive. The Republicans may have been driven by a reaction to the broad construction concepts of the First and Second Congresses. Broad construction's opposite was strict construction and since a large support bloc recognized its efficacy, it fit well. If latitudinarianism attacked liberty, strict construction might preserve it. However, one should not conclude from the constant application of this constitutional interpretation that Madison and Jefferson were agrarian democrats. Each had too much in common with Federalism to wear this mantle.

The above ideas could be extended to federal-state power relations. A usurpation of powers would endanger the stability of the nation. Strict construction could prevent its awful result. According to Lance Banning, "strict construction of the Constitution was an integral part of this libertarian response." It acted as a precursor, or component of several future ideals. Most important, it was the Republican basis for the arguments they advanced defending the civil rights of all Americans. Any attack on the Bill of Rights was sure to produce its invocation.[10]

Considering the information we have accumulated to this point, we can make some general conclusions about state rights. The foundation of state rights, correctly called state powers, was the Tenth Amendment. It delegated certain powers, but no rights, to each of the federal government and the states. The Constitution and Bill of Rights collected the unalienated, and inalienable, rights that were the result of the residue of power.

It appeared that Virginia's advocacy of state rights and defense of civil liberty were linked. The state, as a collection of individuals, was susceptible to the natural rights of these individuals. These rights might be found in the Declaration of Independence or in the state constitution.

First broached in 1798, traditional state rights was an interesting offshoot of the Revolutionary era's rejection of a single sovereign. The divided sovereignty that replaced it accommodated state rights and insured its legitimacy. True, it tended to localism eventually, but in the era under discussion it inferred civil liberties for all, with the exception of slaves. Arguments made in its favor were national in scope.

Our last interpretive venture involved individuals and state rights. James Madison, in *The Federalist*, warned Americans that the coexistent governments would usually not be as personally important to all Americans at all times. During war, the federal government would expand its powers while during peace, the state governments would be more popular. Harry Jaffa reminded us that Andrew Jackson was not only a strict constructionist but also a strong nationalist. The upshot was that one should be very careful when indiscriminately labelling individuals state rights men. For example, one could envision an individual who argued from a state rights point of view during peacetime but refused to do so during war. For most state rights men, defense of the nation trumped local advantage.[11]

⚹

Few would argue that the Republican concentration on individual rights and liberty was a prime ingredient in Jefferson's eventual electoral victory. Still, he required a positive agenda that the people's party could follow. On November 26, 1799, he revealed it to Madison. The nation must have peace, even with the hated English, because it needed time and resources to strengthen itself. Also, Republicans must abandon Adams's standing army as a danger to liberty and fiscal stability; be vigilant against any usurpations of power in order nonviolently to short-circuit any unhappy precedent; and, ensure that it took no action that might unite any Federalist factions against them. Noteworthy was the absence of the bombastic rhetoric of just three months earlier. Perhaps the thought of assuming the presidency of a united confederacy clashed with the idea of the secession of one of its parts.

Virginia Republicans had a firm knowledge of the Federalist base. It attracted the rich and commercial classes who found ample support from the local press. Richmond, Norfolk Borough, Princess Anne, Westmoreland, a few Tidewater and western counties like Pendleton, Rockbridge, Monongehela, and Monroe all gave them strong support. As usual, the Eastern Shore was strongly Federalist. In his camp, Jefferson counted the common people and the leadership they admired — Edmund Pendleton, John Taylor, George Wythe, James Monroe, James Madison, William Giles, and Joseph Jones.[12]

⚹

Liberty became a vehicle for sectional differences. Federalists decided that a strong, stable government enhanced their party by confronting southern localism and political excess. Their position hardened as they contemplated the events of the 1790s.

Theory divided Republicans. Some believed that the people, through their state, had positioned themselves best to protect their own liberty. Others, influenced by Federalists turned Republican, elevated individual rights and freedoms through an activist government. Each version seemed preoccupied, perhaps correctly, with the effects of power on liberty. The combination of Hamilton's fiscal policy and the Alien and Sedition Acts convinced them that corruption and conspiracy were in the air. Liberty and limited government were the antidotes.

This short exposition made it easy to understand the rift between the competing viewpoints. Northern Federalists promoted a strong national government as liberty's champion while Virginia Republicans associated such a government with corruption and licentiousness. Simultaneously, Virginia's combination of Jackson Main's localists and moderate Republicans bent on liberty through limited government was the target of northern ideologues. Accommodation was unlikely.

Virginia Republicans collected a check list of challenges to liberty. Constitutional degradation, broad construction, incipient consolidation, residual rights, and historical imperatives all convinced them that an immediate defense of liberty was mandatory. Their state government must act as a modifying force between its people and the federal government to prevent liberty from being slowly chipped away. Therefore, state rights became its guardian. The Federalist Fisher Ames drew an unintended comparison between the two versions of liberty while describing the Republicans as "new lights in politics who would not make the law but the people king ... who are more solicitous to ... expiate on some high-sounding principal of republicanism than to protect property, cement the Union, and perpetuate liberty." The Virginia representatives "see evils in embryo, are terrified with possibilities, and are eager to establish rights and to explain principles to such degree that you would think them enthusiasts and triflers."[13]

Transitions

The important lesson learned by state rights men from the 1790s was the danger of an unrestrained majority. Implication, wielded by the dominant northern Federalist party, became an unconscionable attack on liberty through deliberate misreading of both the sweeping and general welfare clauses. Even proratification Virginians like James Madison, William Branch Giles, and Edmund Pendleton could not countenance this tactic. As the Antifederalists had predicted, new interpretations challenged checks and balances. Unfortunately, the Federalist reliance on a "liberal construction," as evidenced by its attempted insertion of the common law into the Constitution, embroiled the nation in a bitter battle over authority and precedents that threatened liberty. As stated, events left state rights men with the notion that the Federalist party sought the tyranny level it could maintain without revolution.

Still, the Republican faction, with its state rights element, was a quick learner. Immediately, it understood that it required a competing party to organize and publish its ideals nationally, defeat the Federalists, and wield the power necessary to carry out its platform. Jefferson and Madison succeeded in uniting a polyglot nationalist, anti–Hamilton, agrarian party. According to Virginians, Federalists failed to pass a meaningful Bill of Rights, to carry through ratification promises, to circumscribe the Hamiltonian fiscal plan, and to refuse both Adams's army and navy increases. Moreover, they promoted the northern (or eastern) interest over that of Virginia and, therefore, commerce and manufacturing took precedence over agrarianism. With one exception, all segments of Virginia's planters and yeomen united against these "corrupt" practices. No longer could they trust a government hostile to their concerns if the plainly unconstitutional Alien and Sedition Acts were a precedent.

Strict constructionist lesser gentry, advocates of equality and a defense of individual rights, commercial farmers, and small planters joined renegade Federalists who abhorred the principle of broad construction and its running mate, implied power, to form a new national party dedicated to limited government. Federalists turned Republican joined because the government platform endangered liberty. Moderates, acting as Federalists, had previously supported ratification. Thus, it was not the government form but policy that forced their party divorce. It had proved too radical. Perhaps, they thought, a policy of moderation would heal the obvious wounds, curb wild attempts at Constitutional amendment, and swing disenchanted Federalists to their cause. Localists had a similar motivation. Nevertheless, we must not fall into the trap of portraying them as always opposing the present government. No such reaction would occur if the government trod a limited path.

One could predict that the theory behind the party's platform had to be modified to fit circumstances. Radicals like John Taylor of Caroline expected current state rights dogma to dominate but he was disappointed. Jefferson and Madison had a wider agenda and followed it rather than the blandishments of state rights men. Political reality trumped regional politics.

The shift from Antifederalism to Republicanism signaled a party tenet modification. Organized state and sovereignty rights replaced unfocussed particularism, although the reliance on compact theory remained. Party stalwarts smoothed over differences to present a united face to the people. Recall, at least two compact definitions leading to a pair of state rights groupings came into play. Still, the influx of proratification Federalists who feared both Hamiltonian consolidation and the Jay Treaty helped produce a new Republican party. It considered some Federalist theoretical tenets, but rejected those based on elitism in favor of egalitarianism. For example, traditional state rights men championed Union and accepted the government form.

The most specific catalyst toward the Republican party formation was the threat to liberty. Excessive application of implication, the threat of consolidation, incremental losses of state power to the national government through congressional action, and the blatant misapplication of familiar words and phrases to confuse the electorate challenged it. Americans were no longer sure of their representatives' position on the issues. As a result, almost every Legislative debate produced a fight over constitutional interpretation. In defense, many state rights men closely linked liberty with trust, federalism, and strict construction. They were convinced that the national government must be limited, based on the consent of the governed, dedicated to their liberty, and subject to checks and balances. The states had local powers that the national government must never usurp. Virginians, but not all Americans, were averse to government intervention in commerce. One danger lurked over the horizon. Property and individual rights might clash with government power.

Liberty was often linked to equality in Republican political theory. Fortunately for them, the decade long assaults on the Constitution and civil liberties produced a means to defend them. The Tenth Amendment with its reliance on sovereignty and reserved powers grew over the decades to become the Republican guardian against implication, consolidation, and the threat of power over liberty. By the end of the decade, this intensified struggle convinced Republicans that aristocracy might replace representative government.

Ideas had to be reexamined to forestall this result. Several of Madison's theoretical constructs had proven shaky. No one had annealed them in a real world experiment. His positions on political parties and dual sovereignty were liable to produce the opposite of his predictions. Might not this doubt extend to his notion of the expanded sphere? This might unsettle those who had considered them tactical ploys to twist debate rather than proof that the new society would be republican.

State rights (powers) was the natural product of a confederation of two or more sovereigns. The Constitution delegated some power to the new federal government and reserved the rest to the original sovereigns. However, its clauses did not necessarily spell out the power allocation exactly. Evidently, the doctrine was legal in nature, legitimate, national, and concentrated on the relation between the general government and the states rather than between equal states. Moreover, state rights men had a clear idea of the relationship between the people and their state. States were the people of the states acting in their highest sovereign capacity. In Virginia, progressively, this included not only the gentry, but also other classes, in the political process.

Taking a page from Richard Henry Lee's handbook on liberty, Virginia's state rights men actively promoted immediate state dissent to tyrannical Legislative acts. The Virginia Memorial became the prototype for state protest against central government usurpation. Its contents proved that in Virginia, its state rights faction, rather than the umbrella national Republicans, reflected local opinion. It was the first written state reaction to a congressional law, and predated the more famous Madison Report. However, its influence did not extend through the period 1805–1820 in which the traditional strict construction plank was sublimated to the nationalistic tendencies from other Republican quarters.

The combination of Virginia's Memorial and Madison's Report that bookended the decade stressed the link between individual and state rights. From this time forward, state rights doctrine would not only stress the rights of the states but also the notion of individual freedom and civil rights.

A close examination of attitudes that marked our trip through this crucial decade uncovered two interesting generalities. First, the continual attack by Virginians on government policies and the infusion of limited government Federalists produced two distinguishable doctrines. One, state sovereignty, was more radical than its counterpart, traditional state rights. Although each advocated limited government and compact theory, they contained significant differences. Like Jefferson in 1798, sovereigntists were willing to put liberty before Union and contemplate Locke's revolution/secession as an answer to constant government usurpations. The Virginia and Kentucky Resolutions publically confirmed this doctrine. Despite his later protestations, Madison's partnership with Thomas Jefferson marked his words, particularly nullification, as a sovereigntist goal in tyrannical times.

The house debate over the Virginia Resolution helped classify traditional state rights. It repeated the basic elements of the sovereigntist position, but its credo omitted nullification, the sword of sovereignty. As we noted, the traditionalists maintained that two compacts — one with the American people and one with the state — were in force. Of course, this translated that a state was not completely sovereign. Congress had submitted the Constitution to the sovereign states, and their individual peoples, through conventions, had ratified it. Importantly, this inferred that the states and the people had delegated enumerated rights. Thus, traditionalists preferred to work within the Union to achieve their aims. However, the assembly offered a strong hint in their reaction to the Alien and Sedition Laws that some act, some injustice, might radicalize them.

Students of this era should note that the doctrines of state sovereignty and traditional state rights did not depend on the institution of slavery. Its arrival as a national issue would require new additions. Moreover, the Republican ascendancy muted their differences. Sovereignty reaction required a usurpation. With a Republican Congress and Executive, this was less likely than during the 1790s.

One other issue separated the two versions. State sovereigntists were less likely to comment on the social goal of their ideology. On the other hand, traditionalists constantly referred to the importance of agrarianism to America. Because of its centrality, Americans who followed Adam Smith's philosophy should accord it a place of honor and respect withheld from manufacturing or commerce.

Although John Taylor of Caroline supported Madison's resolutions vehemently, most members of the house shied away from nullification. Not only did they prefer a more moderate line but also nullification seemed unconstitutional. Of course, one cannot ignore that they passed overwhelmingly a resolution supporting the language. Nevertheless, one would have difficulty proving Republican remarks during the debate justified claiming nullification was a party goal. It seemed that delegates would accept the premise now, work toward a national compromise, but avoid confrontation.

Our second generality involved consolidation. Every debate during this decade encouraged its inclusion because it nicely encompassed Antifederalist/Republican fears. Nevertheless, one could not imagine that real consolidation would occur. To Virginians, it signified a loss of power and prestige and promised a certain homogenization of Virginia's agrarian society toward that of the North. Could monarchy or aristocracy be far behind? Virginia's lesser gentry, local powers without a continental view, appropriated this Antifederalist convention notion, and publicized it in the 1790s. Soon, it was a staple of Republican dissent and helped integrate the old cosmopolitans with localists. With the reduction of federal support, that dichotomy lost immediacy.

The assignment of state rights fealty and apostasy by an outside agency, such as a historical researcher, raised an interesting issue. Suppose everyone recognized Virginian A as a state rights man, but for some reason, he adopted a counter position. Was any criticism for the man or the doctrine? Did one argue that the doctrine was weak or wrong because one of its believers strayed? The reader must be particularly aware that events may uncover a doctrinal weakness but that individual apostasy failed to do so.

Until this period, saying that all states had a significant state rights faction was safe. However, from this decade onward, the centrality of the doctrine as a guiding light to the defense of individual and state rights trended south. That section considered it mandatory to fight the expected tyranny of the North that had shown its true colors by its constant and consistent acts attacking southern liberty.

The antebellum period was brief. Because of this short span, participants could easily pass attitudes to the succeeding generation. For example, Governor John Floyd, a future Calhounite, was fifteen during the Alien and Sedition imbroglio. His son, John Buchanan, a reluctant secessionist and future Confederate general, was born when the governor was twenty-three.

7

Laying the Groundwork — Congressional Power and Slavery

Now that the long process of doctrinal reaffirmation had begun through publication of Madison's Report, two eminent Virginia jurists added their insights to the discussion. Edmund Pendleton identified past administration errors and defined constitutional corrections based on state rights principles. St. George Tucker sought to codify and raise the ideals' visibility by connecting them with Blackstone's classic *Commentaries* (1803).

Overwhelmingly, the American people endorsed the sentiments of Thomas Jefferson by electing him president in 1800. Thus, one might suspect the October 20, 1801 edition of the *Richmond Enquirer* surprised his joyous legions. With Jefferson's first term just underway, the cautious proratification jurist, Edmund Pendleton, opened the new decade with a governmental review and roadmap for the Republican party.

Pendleton, from Caroline county, had been a ratification proponent. Yet he had announced several reservations. He became, like Madison and Giles, a prime example of a nationalist who rejected the Federalist agenda and became a Republican.

Pendleton organized and wrote the article beautifully. Published in a popular newspaper, it was bereft of theoretical language. Thus all Virginians, whether yeomen, merchants, or planters, could understand its message. It opened with a preamble that made clear his motivation. He followed this with a list of abuses with corrective measures, and ended with constitutional issues that the nation must meet and solve. Because of the essay's impeccable organization, a product of Pendleton's experience gained by writing hundreds of legal briefs, we will follow it precisely.

Pendleton looked to the future. Activated by both a sense of responsibility to the nation and love for Virginia, he was willing to "damp the public joy." Now was the time, with a sympathetic president and Congress, to "seize the opportunity to erect new barriers against folly, fraud and ambition." One achievement would be the clarification of the dangers of government by implication.

Before establishing his agenda, Pendleton laid out the principles of government that Americans should expect. He compared them with the actual results and by doing so, hinted at his ultimate suggestions. No one intended government to be a vehicle for "avarice and ambition." Instead, its aim was the "good of the community." Thus, the present debt policy, unnecessary increases in the foreign service and judicial cadres, and preparations for a foreign war were dangerous to liberty.

Good government ultimately produced "civil liberty." However, if government officials could challenge liberty within its guidelines, then the structure must be deficient. The country did not require a standing army or an increased navy. The addition of "severe penal Laws … and a multitude of civil Officers" challenged the idea of "social liberty." If so, America must revisit the Constitution.

Peace was surely the most desirable objective for those who promoted freedom. Therefore, Virginians must expunge from the Constitution any "indirect means" that the president employed to bypass congressional authority. Both Treaties that might result in war and required legislative approval, such as the Jay Treaty, and judicial intervention that might produce the same result were examples of this constitutional defect.

Since Union would ensure "our political prosperity," the people must bind the federal government to its delegated powers. Simultaneously, state governments would have authority over local objects. Politicians must be aware that the mixture of societies amalgamated into the Union would never accept consolidated government because it promised constant strife that would rend the country. To satisfy these restrictions, the Constitution must define a clear demarcation between federal and state powers. The federal government must refrain from coopting state taxation provisions; shelve any plan to consolidate the nation; and amend the program of federal bounties and protective tariffs while maintaining state incentives. Without these changes, "the constitution has not sufficiently provided for the continuance of the union, by securing the rights of the state governments and local interests."

Republican government demanded a separation of powers. No man, or group of men, should have the power to exercise a combination of executive, legislative, or judicial powers simultaneously. The federal Senate was a particularly noxious example. It tended to "a dangerous aristocracy."

Public opinion must be free to sway representative government. Unfortunately, corrupt officials could ignore the people's sentiments because patronage, not good government, was their guide. The president could nominate legislators or judges to higher office whose loyalty was to him and not the people. This was particularly galling to trustworthy legislators whose laws corrupt judges could sidetrack. Over this whole procedure sat a Senate that rubber stamped these appointments. This tower of corruption could work inevitably toward a presidential reelection. "And thus may at length appear," suggested Pendleton, "the pheonomenon, of a government, republican in form, without possessing a single chaste organ for expressing the public will."

True, history showed that many proratification Virginians had predicted these flaws based on their negative view of human nature. Still, they had accepted them because of the perceived danger to union. Unfortunately, government had misbehaved by evading or misconstruing the Constitution. Since the people had accepted the Union, now was the time to "fix it upon *principles* capable of restraining human frailties." Pendleton's solutions followed.

The president could serve but one term and his appointing power over judges, and foreign ministers would transfer to Congress. Pendleton would also organize the minister's pay scale.

Americans must shift all executive power from the Senate, reduce its term and insist on its election by the people.

Legislators and judges, while in office, and for a definite period afterwards, could not hold another government position.

"By the concurring vote of both houses of Congress," it could remove judges from office.

Congress must fabricate a check on "the abuse of public credit." Increased armies, one of its results, were traditionally both a danger to liberty and a drain on the public purse.

A "fair mode of impaneling juries" would stifle all disagreements about their constitutional basis.

The Legislature must have the power to concur in both peace and war treaties and all implementation appropriations. Similarly, it must have the final word on any "commercial regulations."

Specifically enumerating federal powers would reduce the likelihood of a resort to implication, especially concerning the freedoms of speech, press, and religion. Congress should reduce implication by clearly stating that the common law, "in criminal cases," was not an American law. Moreover, only the Constitution, and not laws such as the Sedition Act, defined the parameters of treason.

Pendleton, completing his circle of ideas, returned to a central plea. America must find a way for "marking out with more precision, the distinct powers of the *General* and *State* Governments."

He ended his essay by warning Virginians that the Antifederalists had correctly defined the defects in human nature. He faced the "melancholy truth, That of men advanced to power, more are inclined to destroy *liberty*, than to defend it." "THE DANGER WAS NOT OVER."[1]

State rights men had divided into two wings, traditional state rights and state sovereigntists. The debate and reports promulgated by the Alien and Sedition Acts despite Madison's denunciation of the dynamic, provided the initial roadmap for future sovereigntists. Tucker's notes on *Blackstone's Commentaries* performed the same function for traditionalists.

Tucker was born July 10, 1752, in Port Royal, Bermuda. Nineteen years later, he traveled to Virginia's College of William and Mary to study law under the famous teacher George Wythe. Unfortunately, his admission to the bar coincided with the beginning of the Revolution and he went home. Upon his return in 1778, he joined the militia and served as an officer at the battles of Guilford Court House and Yorktown. After the war, he recommenced the practice of law and, in 1788, became a general court judge. By 1800, he was a professor of law at William and Mary and, three years later, Virginia appointed him a justice of its supreme court. In 1813, President James Madison elevated him to the United States District Court.

The judge was a man of many interests. Not only was he an eminent jurist but also inventor, poet, and astronomer. In 1796, Tucker penned "A Dissertation on Slavery: With a Proposal for the Gradual Abolition of It in the State of Virginia," but it failed to move his fellow statesmen. His poem, "Liberty," reviewed the events of the Revolution. Nevertheless, his notes on *Blackstone's Commentaries* solidified his reputation and earned him the sobriquet of the American Blackstone. A close reading of his exposition would convince a reader that he was not a state sovereigntist. He died November 10, 1827, at the age of 75.

In his lectures, Tucker stressed sovereignty. For example, the perpetually-sovereign people, after the Revolution, had organized themselves into a limited government to protect itself. Moreover, the federal government was the result of a compact between the states and one of its principal aims was to protect individual civil rights such as personal security and liberty and a right to private property. To do so required a strict construction of the constitution to keep the general government in check.

Tucker's opus comprised two sections. The first did not concentrate on Virginian theory, but its generalized contents held some gems that applied. We will mine them first.

Sovereigntists typically adopted more radical reactions to government usurpations than did state rights men. For example, they might threaten nullification or secession. Traditionalists chose a less combative approach. Tucker proposed that individuals should apply to the relevant court for relief. If government usurpation challenged a state power, it should "sound the alarm to the people" who should either defeat the offending representatives at the polls or demand a constitutional amendment. In the *Commentaries*, Tucker never alluded to single state secession or revolution. The Constitution would constrain both the individual and the state.

A second discriminating test involved the parties to the constitutional compact. Sovereigntists recognized only the states acting through the people in their highest sovereign capacity. Tucker accepted this as an initial position. "The acceptance of the Constitution," he wrote, "was not only an act of the body politic of each state, but of the people thereof respectively, in their sovereign character and capacity." His addendum separated his wing from the sovereigntists. "From hence," he added, "not only the body politic of the several states, but every citizen thereof, may be considered as parties to the compact, and to have bound themselves reciprocally to each other, for the due observance of it and, also, to have bound themselves to the federal government, whose authority has been thereby created, and established." To traditional state rights men, both the states, and the people were involved in compacts. Ratification was not only through the states but also the people, who bound themselves nationally.

Further indications that Tucker accepted the state rights doctrine were evident. He strongly supported the concept of equality. "All men being by nature equal," he wrote, "in respect to their rights, no man or set of men, can have any natural, or inherent right, to rule over the rest." In addition, he had faith in the Jeffersonian centrality of agrarianism. Agriculture, "the principal object of pursuit in the United States," would prevent the growth of tyranny. Because of its widespread acceptance, America could reduce its "frequent and numerous assemblies of people." Still, agrarian ideals required protection to "prevent the accumulation of wealth in the hands of the few," and return America to a feudal society. Tucker proposed "the partability of estates among all children ... and the absolute prohibition of all perpetuities in lands."

Tucker's comments unveiled a traditionalist rather than a sovereigntist. In many instances, his remarks not only translated Blackstone to the American scene, but in so doing, targeted Federalist arguments made during the debate on Madison's Report. The remainder of our discussion will show his view of the doctrine in 1803. First, he provided some basic guidelines. Afterward, he applied them to the United States.[2]

Compact occupied a central position. Any democratic government must "be founded in general consent and compact, the most natural and the only legitimate method of constituting a civil power." Tucker characterized a representative democracy, his goal, as one with frequent popular elections, limited government, and agency representatives who the people could remove for cause. Government received its power by delegated consent from its sovereigns to be used for the people's security. It should be energetic, as befit a perfect government, but society should allocate it power circumspectly. "Gradual and cautious experiment" should be the guide. Government must always be "amenable to them" and if not "a majority of the community hath the indubitable, unalienable and indefeasible right to reform, alter, or abolish it, in such a manner as shall be judged the most conducive to the public weal." Notice however, that there was no insinuation that such an action broke the compact.

An energetic compact was the "best support that freedom can desire" because its parties, at the next election, could correct Legislative errors. A constitution, the physical compact, would serve "as a beacon to apprise the people that their rights and liberties, are invaded, or in danger."

The people could respond because they were the parties to a compact. Within it, sovereignty "resides only in the people; is inherent to them; and unalienable from them."

Nevertheless, another simultaneous compact resulted in the Constitution. Its parties "still retain[ed] the character of distinct, sovereign, independent states." Since the people could resume or delegate some of their sovereign powers, they could divide it. Naturally, it followed that in neither case did the parties have limited authority. They delegated all government powers and if the government usurped sovereignty, it established a tyranny over the parties.

Tucker proposed an interesting variation on elections and candidates. As usual, he recognized the necessity of agency. However, the state should not expect "the most brilliant talents" to populate the Legislature. "A sound judgment," he propounded, "united with an unfeigned zeal for the public weal, will be more certain of promoting and procuring it [democracy]." Equality of opportunity demanded that no discrimination would "discourage modest merit from offering its services."

The form of government should have a single executive and possibly an advisory council. Electors should choose him and his term should be short. Also, he should be ineligible for reelection, censurable by the Legislature, and forbidden from other offices during his tenure. The people must take every step to prevent an overlap of powers among the three branches.

As one might expect, Tucker continually warned his readers of the dangers to liberty. Citizens must realize that "every attempt in any government to change the constitution (otherwise than in the mode which the constitution may prescribe) is in fact a subversion of the foundations of its own authority." Constitutional changes designed to assign government unlimited power would lead to despotism. Only the people, who could "alter or abolish it ... and institute ... new government" could prevent aristocratic domination. If not, the cure was revolution.

Aristocratic government, the source of tyranny, was a principal target. This government of the few, for example the Senate, could only obtain power if an agent refused his duty as a trustee and instead recognized another whose "authority is independent of the people." Still, "the most easily and successful mode in which an aristocracy commences, or advances, consists in the secret and gradual abuse of the confidence of the people, in a representative democracy."

Tucker organized power into two categories, internal and external. The former was exercised within a state while the latter was directed toward foreign nations. He had a concise list of external powers. Congress could make war in defense of the state, the executive could make treaties, and the judiciary could adjudicate intrastate controversies. In a return to an older theory, Tucker preferred the imposition of the separation of powers rather than the current checks and balances.

Any discussion of the allocation of powers in a representative government required a complementary one for individual or state rights. If a constitution foresaw a division of power that preserved the sovereignty and independence of the parties, it produced dual sovereignties. Importantly, "each of the confederates retains an entire liberty of exercising as it thinks proper, those parts of the sovereignty, which are not mentioned in the treaty of union, as parts that ought to be exercised in common." Tucker not only presented the theory of reserved state and individual rights but also defined a constitution as a treaty. To do so highlighted the sovereignty of the confederated states.

Tucker was clear about state rights. It reserved "all those branches of the supreme authority, the management of which can have little or no influence, on the affairs of the rest." Throughout this section, Tucker treated the Tenth Amendment as the citation that preserved them. His construction assumed the word "expressly" belonged to the Article. Apparently, he had accepted Jefferson's interpretation of that amendment's power.

The Judge did not shy away from the problem of a dissolution of a union. He designated the Constitution as a secession from the Articles. A legal separation could occur if all or some parties agreed by mutual consent. If most states refused to send representatives to government or for some reason an executive could not be selected, the government would fall and dissolution would follow. He did not specify any scenario for single-state secession except to quote the relevant passage from the Declaration of Independence. Because it was vague on the number of states required to abolish government, and used the terminology "they," it was doubtful if he envisioned such an event.[3]

The second section concentrated on the United States. Not surprisingly, there was an overlap in the topics examined with those of the last section. We will continue our investigation at the risk of repeating some of Tucker's theses.

For Tucker, all parties to any compact, particularly the Constitution, were political equals. They transferred nothing between them but each gave up and received the same benefits from it. Within the federal version, each of the sovereign states maintained its "perfection" within the Union. Note that Tucker acknowledged the social contract between individuals about to form a state. It protected the necessities of life, "the end of civil society," "conveniences and accommodations of life," "whatever constitutes happiness," property ownership, justice, and security. It contrasted with the federal compact that was "an act of the state, or body politic and not of an individual." Because the state, necessarily, had the power to compel its citizens, any federal power over an individual must pass through the state. Otherwise, consolidation would follow.

Still, sovereignty remained crucial. For Tucker, "when the whole body of the people are possessed of the supreme power in the state, it is a democracy." The dissolution of the colonies introduced state sovereignty and each became independent. The federation under the Articles took place "without any of them ceasing to be a perfect, independent, and sovereign state, retaining every power, jurisdiction and right, which it has not expressly agreed shall be exercised in common by the confederacy of the states; and not by any individual state of the confederacy." Of course, Tucker again appended "expressly" to his exposition. One might conclude from this constant repetition that he considered it, though unexpressed, part of the Tenth Amendment. To confirm this interpretation, he wrote that "the right of sovereignty ... in all cases not expressly ceded to the United States by the constitution, or prohibited by it to the several states, remains inviolably, with the states; respectively."

Sovereignty discussions must refer to the Constitution, the "original, written, federal, and social compact." Although Tucker recognized that each state must make significant concessions, the combination of the Ninth and Tenth Amendments ensured that powers delegated to the federal government would "receive the most strict construction that the instrument will bear." This was particularly important "where the rights of the state or of the people, either collectively, or individually, may be drawn in question." Tucker was confident that the Union's basis was a federal compact because of the act of ratification. The people, composing independent states, had accomplished it. If one examined the requirements, one found that a majority neither of the states nor of the people was mandatory. If he were correct, arguments for an organic nature were unfounded.

In order to understand Tucker's position on strict construction, we must revisit its basis, the combination of the Ninth and Tenth Amendments mentioned above. Due to the power of Madison's Tenth Amendment exposition in the Report of 1799, the importance of the Ninth in concert with the Tenth was diluted by most commentators. Originally, the Ninth was considered by Virginians as one method of circumscribing federal power. Although it did not specify any rights, it did offer a guide for future interpretations. The rights enumerated were a model for those that might be added, but those named were not exhaustive. Earlier, Madison had stipulated that the amendment combination was intentional and intended to limit federal power. The Tenth introduced enumerated powers but left those not delegated with the people. Simultaneously, the Ninth prevented new powers inimical to the enumerated list. Of course, immediate incidents were acceptable. The result was threefold. Despite the absence of "expressly," the Ninth ensured a sovereign's delegation of power; enshrined strict construction of the Constitution; and produced limited self-government.

With this background, we can better understand Tucker's theory. As might be expected, Tucker reiterated the compact basis of the Union, stressing that each state was an independent sovereign. Thus, no defined federal power could infringe on the people's sovereignty with the caveat that the people were those of the several states. He was buoyed in this opinion by the constant Federalist promises that ratification was not tantamount to consolidation. If so, Tucker felt confident that the government promised by the Convention would have limited express powers without the overt presence of "expressly." He arrived at this conclusion by examining the combination of the Ninth and Tenth Amendments.

Tucker's disquisition was similar to Madison's. The Tenth Amendment translated to a directive that federal power must be delegated by the sovereign people. Simultaneously, the Ninth Amendment provided that delegated power interpretations never usurped those left to the people. "The sum ... appears to be," he argued, "that the powers delegated to the federal government, are, in all cases, to receive the most strict construction that the instrument will bear, or the rights of the state or of the people, either collectively, or individually, may be drawn in question." The amendment combination ensured strict construction, keeping in mind that the enumerated powers included necessary incidents.

Although this interpretation would satisfy any state rights man, Tucker added another based on the Law of Nations (Vattel). Everyone agreed that Virginia had the right to self-preservation or independence. As a result, the state could not accept laws that challenged Vattel. Therefore, if the Constitution delegated a power to Congress, it did so in express terms to avoid usurpations. The result was a strict construction of the Constitution that protected the sovereign people. This interpretation was relevant because, subsequent to the Revolution, the states were sovereign and independent, retaining all powers "not expressly delegated."

As a corollary, Law of Nations' theory ensured that no treaty or agreement between sovereigns delegated away the sovereignty of one signatory. Harkening to Lockean dogma, the states must retain all powers not specifically delegated since to do so "is merely a declaration of the law of nations...."

> For no free nation can be bound by any law but its own will; and where that will is manifested by any written document, as a convention, league, treaty, compact, or agreement, the nation is bound to preserve itself as that will is expressed *in* the instrument by which it binds itself. And as every nation is bound to preserve itself, or, in other words, its independence; so no interpretation whereby its destruction, or that of the state, which is the same thing, may be hazarded, can be admitted in any case where it has not, *in the most express terms,* given its consent to such an interpretation [italics in original].

According to Tucker, the Tenth Amendment prevented any appending of the common law to the Constitution. After all, it seemed preposterous that it could assign common law powers to a state that had previously denied its application in its courts. Moreover, free, independent, sovereign states could never agree to the use of implication necessary to transport it there except in express terms.

In case one might conclude that only Republicans gravitated toward Madison's and Tucker's position, we will briefly note that of the Federalist John Page. It was his firm opinion that the combination of the two amendments necessarily forced "expressly" into their interpretation. "I say considering these things," he stated, "how could it be possible to suppose, that these two amendments taken together, were not sufficient to justify every citizen in saying, that the powers not delegated to the United States by the constitution, nor prohibited by it to the states, are preserved to the states respectively, or to the people, as thoroughly and completely; as if the word expressly had been inserted?"

Tucker must have realized that his discussion of sovereignty might prompt a federal-state power clash. To alleviate this strain, he proposed that,

> Until the time shall arrive when the occasion requires a resumption of the rights of sovereignty by the several states (and far be that period removed when it shall happen) the exercise of the rights of sovereignty by the states individually, is wholly suspended, or discontinued...: nor can that suspension ever be removed, so long as the present constitution remains unchanged, but by the dissolution of the bonds of union. An event which no good citizen can wish, and which no good, or wise administration will ever hazard.

The American government, presupposed Tucker, was a "confederate republic composed of several independent and sovereign democratic states" that retained any sovereignty not enumerated. Without them, the Union could not exist. If one accepted the notion that the constitution defined powers, the government based on it must not have any that were undefined. Moreover, unless the Legislature permitted it, these powers were never found in some standard common law.

Americans must regulate their government's operation. Because state citizens already had a social contract — their state constitutions — "it might be deemed somewhat extraordinary" to admit that the federal government, and also the states, could operate on individuals. Otherwise, the Constitution would eventually produce a consolidated government. The people of the states must deal with such a usurpation either in the courts or by defeating candidates who produced it.

Constitutional issues abounded and the coordinate branches might promulgate them. Although the Senate numbers were based on the principle of equality, the lengthy term might lead to "extending power and influence in the government." Nor should it participate in some impeachments, particularly those based on treaties. After all, it had taken part in the process. Again, Tucker was adamant that the House could refuse appropriations for a treaty.

The presidential term, like the Senate's, was too long and candidates should contest the office more frequently. The present mode of presidential selection if no candidate achieved a majority was an invitation to corruption. What were the people to think if an incumbent were fifth on the list — indicating a lack of popular support — but the House elected him?

A Constitutional amendment must reduce presidential power. He should not have the authority to deport aliens or call for volunteers thereby sidestepping the militia act. Also, the country should reexamine treaty powers. Currently, few restrictions on the subject existed and discord over the efficacy of a treaty was likely. In a shot across the bow of checks and balances, Tucker reported that they "seem not to be sufficient to restrain this department [Executive] within its proper bounds, or, to preserve it from acquiring and exerting more than a due share of influence."

The Judge offered a solution to one presidential power. To control midterm appointments, he suggested a constitutional amendment to organize a Committee of the States to perform this duty. Possibly, Tucker saw that he could use this body as a wedge toward a full Council of State.

The judiciary branch deserved high praise. It was independent from the other branches and would be a safeguard of individual rights. Nevertheless, one aspect perplexed him. Virginians had initially accepted that Congress could build tribunals inferior to the Supreme Court, but could not "demolish" them. Lately, Congress had successfully challenged this interpretation. Now, it claimed the "discretionary power to discontinue, or demolish" these courts.

Implication and its consequences caught his attention. *The Federalist* argument that, minus the sweeping clause the Constitution would still give Congress some extended incidental powers, impressed Tucker. However, they were still keyed to the enumeration and thus were limited. New powers must be incidental to those enumerated. Again, the Tenth Amendment would protect the states in case the federal government contemplated a "pretext for an assumption of any power not specified in the constitution." To repeat, Tucker assumed or inserted the word "expressly" into his considerations. "All of the powers of the federal government being expressly enumerated, or necessary and proper to the execution of some enumerated power ... "was but one instance. He extended his notion of limited powers to the Supremacy Clause. Surely it was not the product of those who extolled the benefits of liberty. Perhaps, he argued, the people were satisfied that the constitutionally limited government would be less likely to affect domestic issues. Otherwise, the Tenth Amendment would serve as a buffer.

Later, Tucker reiterated the threat of implication on reserved rights and the power of the Tenth Amendment. It was a maxim that "whatever is not enumerated is retained" and that "sovereign states cannot be deprived of any of their rights by implication" except "by their own voluntary consent, or by submission to a conqueror." The Constitution, as usual, reserved these rights through the Tenth Amendment "to prevent misconstruction or abuse" of power. Congress had not merely designed the article "to explain and secure the rights of the states, or of the people." Surely its thrust insured "that in the new government, as in the old, the general powers are limited, and that the states, in all unenumerated cases, are left in the enjoyment of their sovereign and independent jurisdictions."

Applying the treaty power for support, Tucker registered his disgust with the Federalist attachment of unbounded incidental powers to the enumerated list.

> The executive has power to make treaties, and by the treaty with Algiers, a certain tribute is to be paid annually to that regency. But the executive have no power to levy a tax for the payment of this tribute; congress, therefore, are authorized by this clause, to pass a law for that purpose: without which the treaty, although it be a supreme law of the land, in it's [sic] nature, and therefore binding upon congress, could not be executed with good faith. For the constitution expressly prohibits drawing any money from the treasury but in consequence of appropriations made by law.[4]

State rights men had always been the aggressors in the ongoing disputes between Republicans and Federalists over Constitutional interpretation. After Jefferson's election, Federalists reversed the process and scrutinized Republican policies. During the period 1800–1820 a succession of cases developed that challenged the legitimacy of the state rights doctrine and simultaneously expanded its boundaries. Two of them defined the basic misunderstandings.

Suspicious Republicans supposed that the courts had been a barrier to America's fulfillment as a free, democratic republic. National judicial appointments invariably were Federalists, promoting a misgiving that Republican views were unlikely to receive a fair hearing. A decision by President John Adams at the end of his term exacerbated this doubt. On February 27, 1801, a bill announced a revision of the original 1789 Judicial Act. During its debate, the Federalist dominated Congress posited that the Supreme Court could review congressional acts and veto those it considered unconstitutional. However, the act's contents was our focus.

At this time, pairs of supreme court justices plus a local district judge performed circuit court duties in one of three circuits. Because of the onerous travel conditions and appeal conflicts associated with this duty, the act increased the number of circuits and appointed sixteen new judges to staff them. Supreme Court justices would adjudicate only cases that reached the bench. As usual, Adams filled the circuit positions with loyal Federalists. He also reduced the number of Supreme Court justices from six to five but the government could not implement the reduction until the next vacancy. Of course, if one did not occur during Jefferson's term, it would prevent him from appointing a replacement. Most important for Virginia's myriad land claims cases, the 1801 law made it easier for litigants to transfer jurisdiction from a state to federal court.

The act also affected districts. It added ten new courts whose judges were usually the incumbents, split some existing districts while creating others, and abolished those for Kentucky and Tennessee.

After the change in government, the Republicans determined to repeal the act. The Judiciary Act of 1802 maintained the six circuit courts but assigned a justice to each. Whereas it required three judges per circuit for the implementation of the 1801 act, its replacement required only two. A circuit-riding justice would fill the third position. In addition, they made several changes to southern district courts. The remainder of the new justices had no offices or duties.

The wide ranging debate on the 1802 judiciary bill contained technical references to judges, courts, commissions, offices, and meaning of constitutional phrases like "good behavior" and "from time to time." This suggested that restating the constitutional language that controlled these references would be helpful.

> From Article I, Section 8 (The Enumerated Powers of Congress)
> The Congress shall have power to constitute tribunals inferior to the Supreme Court.
> Article III, Section 1 (The Judicial Powers)
> The judicial power of the United States, shall be vested in one supreme court, and in such inferior courts as the Congress may from time to time ordain and establish. The judges, both of the supreme and inferior courts, shall hold their offices during good behavior, and shall, at stated times, receive for their services, a compensation, which shall not be diminished during their continuance in office.
> From Article II, Section 3 (The Executive Powers)
> ... he [the president] shall take care that the laws be faithfully executed, and shall commission all the officers of the United States.

In early January 1802 both Legislative branch leaders notified their respective colleagues that they would challenge the 1801 judiciary act. Congressmen offered several concurrent arguments for its repeal or retention. Federalists doubted that the Legislature had the constitutional power to "destroy" circuit court judges by repealing the law that authorized their appointments. In any case, doing so at this time was not expedient. One thing was clear, argued the Federalist minority, if the repeal were successful every government change would signal a new court system. Republicans claimed that this position translated to a vested judicial right and that the Federalist interpretation of the good behavior clause ensured perpetual compensation. No authority would have the power to interrupt it. In essence, a Legislature could create an office that no successor could control. Republicans rejected these notions. The principal discriminator should be service to the people. Even if one considered the office property, it was "held in trust for the benefit of the people" and Congress judged its ownership.

Republicans continually stressed the role of popular opinion and elections throughout the debate. "All the departments of a popular Government," warned Senator Stevens Mason, "must depend, in some degree, on popular opinion." No government power grant allowed it to divorce itself from the nation. Remember, in a limited government the people assigned their agents power for the sovereign's benefit. In short, a republican government "makes the good of the people the paramount object of our Constitution." Thus, the people's agents must reflect the general will.

In this case, judges should hold their positions "no longer than the public welfare requires." Since the Legislature represented the sovereign people "it appears that the power that has the right of passing, without appeal, on the validity of your laws" was Congress. It had the right to constitute inferior courts and had done so "for the interest and convenience of the people." Indeed, "the revolution in public opinion had taken place before the introduction of the project; the people of the United States had determined to commit their affairs to newer agents; already had the confidence of the people being transferred from their then rulers into other hands." The people demanded the Republican solution.

Despite these claims, Federalist supporters adamantly defended a judge's vested right in his office. The Constitution, they said, supported that position. Republican detractors refused to consider this argument viable. If it were, then Congress must build the courts "not for the public benefit, but for the emolument of the judges; not to administer justice, but for their personal aggrandizement." Also, Republicans could not uncover any reference to perpetuity in office in the Constitution. It seemed that courts would exist forever for the judge's benefit, not that of the public. As a corollary, John Clopton declared that once Federalists created a court, it continued forever "merely because such abolition will affect the interest of the judges."

However, to Federalists, vesting insured judicial independence. They linked it to good behavior and inferred that the Legislature could not regulate established courts. If they accepted the idea that the Legislature could abolish courts, all independence would vanish. Successful passage of this bill would make the judiciary subsidiary to the Legislature. Republican political dominance promised to usurp power for the party and destroy a government branch.

The debate over judicial independence introduced another notion. If the Federalist vision predominated, checks and balances might be bypassed by "something like a supremacy" in the government. Now, stated John Randolph, was an excellent time to test that statement's validity. It might happen if unprincipled parties stacked the courts with their cronies. In a swipe at *Marbury v. Madison*, he suggested that the Supreme Court "may easily direct the Executive by mandamus, in what mode it is their pleasure that he should exercise his functions."

Republicans assailed these interpretations. If the office were no longer necessary, the judge who held it need not be "shielded from improper advances." Importantly, Congress intended independence "for the purpose of promoting a faithful and upright discharge of their [judiciary] duties in office." However, independence lasted only as "long as there is a necessity for keeping up the courts." By comparison with the English judges, their American counterparts were more independent.

Failure to pass the repeal bill could seriously affect precedence. Future parties, on the verge of removal from government "may pervert the power of erecting courts" to maintain their ascendancy. Any loss of control promised dire results since an unfettered court could usurp power and become a patronage host. Despite the paucity of litigation for the present courts, one could expect a perpetual increase in judges and compensation inherent in the 1801 law.

Increasing unnecessary offices and inventing useless systems was economically improper. One need only examine the demand for compensation from an abolished court to understand the judge's venality. Surely, service must control compensation. Sensible people recognized that Congress could sever a judge's salary from him for lack of service. However, Republicans did not contemplate any salary restraint for serving judges. Philip Thompson encapsulated the Republican insistence on frugality.

> The right to modify the law being conceded, but not the right to deprive the judges of their offices, our country would exhibit a spectacle which it never has yet, and I hope never will exhibit — officers without offices — judges without courts — a privileged order — out of the reach of the Constitution, (for being deprived of their offices they cannot be impeached) drawing money from the Treasury and rendering no services for their salaries.

Naturally, Republican debaters highlighted the effect of the 1801 act on the state judiciary. They must protect the "state courts from being engulfed by those of the Union." Moreover, the national judiciary threatened federal-state relations because any extension of federal court power toward individuals, for example, would endanger Virginia's citizens. The Legislature must not forget that not only its members, but also its state counterparts, followed the course of this bill carefully.

Federalists again promoted attaching the common law to the Constitution. Unfortunately, for Virginians, it appeared that any such attachment must result in a usurpation of Legislative powers by the judiciary because it challenged checks and balances. John Randolph debunked one weak opposition argument. The Federalists had emphasized the language congruence in English common law with that of the Constitution to demonstrate their symbiosis. Suppose, said the House leader, one found the phrase "direct tax" in both the Constitution and Adam Smith's *Wealth of Nations*? Did the latter attach to the Constitution also? Suppose one state's common law clashed with that of another. Which one did the court follow for guidance? No, the common law could never attach to a national document.

Legislative control and discretion was a major focus of discussion. Congress controlled compensation, the number of judges, their duty assignments and court dates but could not reduce salaries. Constitutionally, it could even postpone court sessions for years and meanwhile establish other courts to do their duties. On its face, these powers suggested a significant control over the judiciary by the Legislature.

The annulling of unnecessary courts, said Republicans, followed inevitably from the power to ordain them. Congress's power "to constitute tribunals inferior to the Supreme Court" coupled with its responsibility to the people made it mandatory that it have the power to abolish a court. Without it, Congress would have no remedy for court evils. So, Congress could annul useless offices and, when necessary, their abolition ended the judge's tenure. Remember, John Clopton found no perpetuity implication in the crucial phrase "during good behavior." In fact, argued Thompson, it was a political axiom "that an ordaining power always embraces a repealing power." Therefore, Congress had not only a discretionary power to annul courts but also could order them to have fixed terms.

Continuing Thompson's argument, Clopton reminded the House that Congress already had discretionary power to determine the number and kinds of courts. The Federalist argument that Congress had an enumerated power but could apply it in only one direction was nonsensical. Clopton, switching to the enumerated powers, reminded his colleagues that if Thompson's argument did not follow, one must extend the Federalist interpretation to every enumerated power of Article I. If so, Congress could never repeal a law to collect taxes. Clearly, the power to repeal was inherent in the positive grant.

Debate contained several other nuances in constitutional interpretation. To Republicans, the inferior courts depended on the Legislature. "From time to time," it had the power to regulate them. If it perceived an evil, it had the same power to correct the iniquity as a previous Legislature had to create it. This power was inherent in the agents of the people. William Branch Giles considered it "an invitation to revision of the courts rather than no repeal." The phrase was probably added because the novelty of the Constitution persuaded the Framers to leave room for change. As a result, establishment and abolition of courts existed simultaneously.

John Clopton expanded this idea. The Legislature had full power over the inferior courts because "From time to time" gave it discretionary power over the "number and kind of courts" including the power to abolish. He added a powerful argument. Since the good behavior clause resided in the phrase referring to judges appointed by the Executive, then it referred only to Executive-controlled appointments, not those dependent on the Legislature.

Congress, admitted Republicans, did not have the power to control a judicial officer during good behavior. However, they could abolish the office that the judge held despite good behavior. This followed from the Legislature's power to decide the need for judicial service. For example, it might not pay a judge without office.

The opposing parties had different views on the formation of the judiciary. Republicans claimed that the combination of the Legislature and Executive, that must respect the people's wishes, formed it. Federalists contended that the Constitution did so, but their opponents countered that it only declared its existence. Surely the body that established the inferior courts and one Supreme Court — Congress — was the founding agent since it defined all peripheral duties.

These disputed interpretations prepared us for an examination of the contentious 1801 judiciary act. The thrust of the various Republican allegations was that if the 1802 law had unconstitutional features, they mirrored those of 1801. Actions proved that Federalists empowered the Legislature to annul a court. Had they not featured it in their own 1801 act? In express terms, the 1801 law had separated the Kentucky and Tennessee district court judges from their courts by abolishing them. The judges had no choice but to accept their new terms of employment. They either accepted positions as circuit judges in the new system or resigned. They could not remain district court judges of an abolished court.

By transforming district into circuit courts, President Adams had created a new office on the ashes of an existing one. To exacerbate matters, he filled the new positions without the advice and consent of the Senate. Unhappily, the appointees had no special legal abilities and Randolph fulminated against "the pretensions of rendering the judiciary an hospital for decayed politicians." Giles went further. He accused the government of entrenching itself in the judiciary to insure "support of those favorite principles of irresponsibility which they could never consent to abandon." Moreover, they had begun a gradual demolition of state courts. The Republican majority planned to solve these problems by restoring all dispossessed judges to their original positions while refusing to commission Adams's coterie.

Could they vacate a court? If one argued the negative position, one encountered serious absurdities. Examine the Mississippi territory. Land claims due to its ownership by various nations were inevitable. Suppose Congress appointed an inferior court for a specific period to adjudicate the cases. What would the judges do at the end of the elapsed time? Federalists claimed they would hold the position in perpetuity. Judges without courts compensated by the people would result.

Good behavior was a discriminator for continued judicial employment. Suppose, said Mason, we extend the Mississippi example. Assume that Georgia had a claim and the United States agreed, ceding the land to the state. Subsequently, the judge's offices and duties were no longer germane. However, according to Federalists, they had a vested interest in their positions. "We hold our offices during good behavior," they would argue, "and we will behave well as long as you will let us.... Such an absurdity I am sure the Constitution never meant to justify. It is an absurdity equally repugnant to the letter and genius of the Constitution."

John Clopton took a different tack. "During good behavior" was the opposite of "during pleasure" and had no reference whatever to perpetuity. He read the defining article as a discriminator on the *office* and claimed that it depended on good behavior. If so, its term did not depend on good behavior. Therefore, the judge could hold his office, if one existed, during good behavior. Still, judges had no claim on nonexistent offices. A circuit court judgeship did not translate to an investment in the office. It could be separated from its office by impeachment and the office abolished. Any limitations, claimed Republicans, were on the office, not on good behavior.

The Federalists had argued that the right to a commission was an implied right. Without limits, the president commissioned all United States officers according to his discretion. Could the tenure be truncated? Could the officer be separated from his commission? Of course, a constitutional method was available under specific conditions. Legislative impeachment of either an officer who held an Executive commission during the pleasure of the president, or a judicial officer holding his office during good behavior was constitutional. In judicial cases, the officer could clearly be separated from his office.

The Legislative power to organize and regulate courts was by inference from the clause "to ordain and establish." The power to remove was no more nor less than other inferences. A president appointed and commissioned during good behavior, but the Legislature regulated "during the continuance in office." Thus, it may annul an office though its judge behaved. Obviously, the term limit was in the office, not on behavior, and the implication was that no service rendered meant no compensation.

A close reading of the short paragraphs above might prompt a reader to consider the role of implication in this process. Historiographically, some critics have belabored Republicans for replacing strict construction with implication during the "good behavior" argument. In particular, William Branch Giles "hitherto the most radical of strict constructionists, led the debate for loose construction, somehow making repeal into an advocacy of states' rights." To rebut these charges and fulfill a promise concerning strict construction from an earlier chapter, we will concentrate on Giles's major speech.

Before doing so, we must update our basic state rights theory. Recall, an application of implication must have a constitutional base. Its two principal sources had been the general welfare clause and the necessary and proper provision that surrounded the enumerated powers. Their applications were associated with broad construction. Nevertheless, as stated by St. George Tucker and James Madison, another source, often sublimated in the rhetoric over power extensions, existed. Implication, both camps agreed, was acceptable if it was an immediate incident to a Legislative power. Republicans had even mentioned this possibility during the struggles over Hamilton's fiscal program. Thus, Giles and his colleagues might apply implication if its target was a Legislative power and the implication augmented that power. If they obeyed this stricture, they were following strict constructionist ideals.

Giles made an initial statement that should have warned those who criticized his logic. The Federalists, he crowed, "tie down all construction to the strict letter of the Constitution" after applying the sweeping clauses for years to prop up their legislation. He would never use those articles because "he considered these words as containing no grant of power whatever but merely the expression of the ends or objects to be effected by the grants of specified powers." "It gave him great pleasure," he continued, "to meet gentlemen on this ground." Significantly, Giles announced that, like the opposition, he would apply strict construction. Of course, we will examine his words to see if he remained true to this promise.

According to Giles, Federalists contended that the Constitution vested the judicial office with its incumbent as part of his appointment, compensation depended on good behavior, and its continuance secured the office. In fact, the judge became independent and the office became his property. No authority could separate them. On the other hand, Republicans claimed that service, not good behavior, controlled compensation and that if the office were property, a judge held it in trust for the people. Since Congress represented them, it had the power to decide the fate of the office and its judge.

Giles, belatedly for the reader, laid out his plan of attack. "It is admitted that the first part of this section [Article III, section 1] expressly vests Congress with the general power to ordain and establish courts; and, if there had been no other restriction, the consequent power to unordain or abolish." On its face, Giles's stated methodology appeared to rest on implication, but further consideration would convince one that his target was an acceptable incident of the Constitutional Article. To accomplish his task, he would have to negate any restrictions on the second clause.

His first challenge was to establish that Congress's power over the judiciary was Constitutional. His colleagues had laid down its necessity, and that a combination of the Executive and Legislative branches had formed it. Moreover, the latter were responsible to the people. Therefore, Giles had a strong basis for claiming that Congress had power over the judiciary. As a result, it was dependent.

Next on his list of possible restrictions was "good behavior." His initial argument was brief. If one examined the Constitution closely, one noted that the "good behavior" required of judges was a limitation controlling the Executive branch, not the Legislative. Thus, it did not restrict the latter.

Giles was not finished. Examine "hold" of "hold their offices." Surely it conveyed the notion of tenure that required two parties, a grantor and a grantee. Who was the grantor of the Executive officer's tenure? According to Article II, sections 2 and 3, the president granted tenure at his pleasure. Thus, Congress could not control a commissioned United States officer nor a judge during good behavior except during impeachment. However, the office was another matter. The same impeachment proceeding forced Congress to treat each the same. Now, the House agreed that the office itself "is always subject to be abolished" because it fell under Legislative discretion. Therefore the power to separate a commissioned officer from his office had as an immediate incident the power to separate a judge from his court.

What was the only limit on congressional power? Congress had to pay incumbent judges a specific salary. However, Giles argued that compensation required a service. Here, the service was to the people. Since Congress represented them, it had the power to state that no services translated to no compensation. To satisfy the House that this idea was common, Giles listed many instances linking salary to service.

Giles had made his case because he had summarily dispatched all the Federalist objections to it. Congress already recognized its power to modify the courts, change their duties, and change venues, because they were all "necessary inferences" from the power "to ordain and establish." He had appended to abolish or to repeal a court to the list.

Several further arguments took Giles's fancy. While drawing up the Constitution, the Fathers had made good behavior a requirement for continued Executive office holding. But, when creating the office and compensation, they switched to continuance in office. Why did they change the focus? Giles claimed that Congress might have to discontinue an office though a judge had maintained good behavior. Thus, the Fathers limited the office but not the behavior. Still, the terminated court made it certain that its judge received no compensation.

Giles worried about Constitutional construction because his opponents had argued strenuously against an expressly stated power. Did it make sense that the Framers expected such a power to be subjected to implication? If they had assigned Congress the power to organize courts, could implication nullify it? In the same vein, a law organizing courts was repealable. Did not the Constitution invite this power? Last, Giles fell back on a truism. Whenever an act or Article listed only one limitation, no others existed. Express terminology limited Congress's compensation role. Thus, any other restriction to stop abolishment of courts required express statements.

As noted, without limiting restrictions, Giles had been successful in demonstrating that "to ordain and establish" had an immediate incident "to abolish or repeal" by eliminating other Federalist possibilities. Even if one did not agree with its tactics, he was not a strict construction apostate. The latter and implication were not mutually exclusive.

A second charge of apostasy grew from the Louisiana Purchase. In 1800, by the secret treaty of San Ildefonso, Napoleon Bonaparte persuaded Spain to cede its Louisiana territory to France. Thus New Orleans, the gateway for western American world trade, was nominally in French hands. President Jefferson, alarmed by this treaty, sent his minister, Robert Livingston, to sound out Napoleon on a possible port purchase. Taking a gamble, Livingston suggested to Napoleon that he might wish to divest himself of the complete territory. Surprisingly, Napoleon agreed. Although the government had not officially confirmed the purchase, Livingston, and James Monroe, newly arrived in Paris, could not refuse it. On April 30, 1803, for approximately $15,000,000, the territory fell to the United States. France received some commercial port privileges in New Orleans, and the United States promised territorial inhabitants incorporation into the Union with the same rights and privileges as all American citizens. Interestingly, the treaty did not define the cession boundaries. Previous ownerships by France and Spain would act as a guide.

The Purchase contained challenges both to the parties involved and the state rights doctrine. Did Jefferson have the power to consummate this treaty? Had not he argued persuasively that strict construction of the enumerated powers was his guide? Even Jefferson was unsure of his treaty powers. Perhaps the present constitutional treaty power with the advice and consent of the Senate was sufficient. If so, was not implication necessary to extend it? Its adherents appeared on the verge of violating the state rights doctrine. Nevertheless, Jefferson's optimistic outlook for future American expansion in both land and ideas overcame his ideological doubts. Agriculture would benefit from new produce that would increase trade with Europe.

On October 22, 1803, Jefferson transmitted to Congress a message outlining the legislative requirements to implement the treaty successfully. He warned that he might have to employ the army, navy, and militia to take possession of this huge territory. Congressional appropriations that the president would apply were mandatory. Moreover, he suggested that until Congress organized any civil government, all the necessary functions be placed in the hands of a presidential appointee.

John Taylor of Caroline, in the Senate and later by an election pamphlet, defended his president's decision. He attacked two opposition treaty objections. First, the United States had no power constitutionally to acquire territory. Second, the treaty stipulated that a new state be admitted despite the Constitutional absence of that power in the treaty making clause.

As usual, Taylor's facile mind found a unique, but satisfying, argument against these objections. Before confederation, each state had a sovereign power to acquire territory by either war, treaty, or purchase. Obviously, another agency had to assume this power after 1787. Either the state still possessed it, or it was forbidden to both levels of government, or the Constitution had transferred it to the general government. The Constitution forbade the first option and the second was false on its face. Therefore, the third option defined the legitimate repository of the power. Constitutionally, the government could "dispose of and regulate the territory belonging to the United States" which supposed that it could hold territory while states could not. Since the United States, but no states, could acquire and hold territory, the Constitution had transferred the sovereign power originally associated with the state to the United States. Thus, the Constitution had assigned the original state sovereign power to acquire and hold territory along with the treaty-making power to the general government.

Taylor dealt with the second argument similarly. He conceded that the treaty-making power could not build a state. However, he cleverly reminded the Senate that it could stipulate for one. Earlier, he had proved that the United States could acquire territory and, if it did, it became part of the existing territory of the United States. This territory was not part of the Union since, by definition, the United States territory included no states. Congress, the constitutional regulator, had ensured that the people of the territories had all, except political, rights. Also, the third article of the Purchase stated that the inhabitants must be incorporated into the Union. Therefore, critics suggested that the incoming territory must become a state immediately. Taylor avoided this objection. He required "that the inhabitants and their territory shall be incorporated in the Union, in the known and recognized political character of a Territory."

In summary, the Purchase was constitutional because,

> the three distinct members of the third article will be each separately and distinctly complied with; first, by an incorporation of the territory and its inhabitants into the Union, as a Territory. Secondly, by admitting them to all the rights of citizens of the United States, under some uniform rule of naturalization; and, thirdly, by protecting their liberty, property, and religion, by "rules and regulations," to be, "in the meantime," enacted by Congress, under a Constitutional power extending to territories, but not to States.

In the House, Thomas Griffin made the Virginia Federalist case with respect to the commercial regulation clause. The seventh article, he argued, defined a commercial regulation. If so, the treaty clause was unconstitutional because only Congress, not the president and Senate, had the right to set commercial regulations. Moreover, the treaty boldly set preferences for Spanish or French manufactures entering New Orleans compared with other United States' ports. Presently, Spain paid higher duties than did America at the same port. Also, Griffin enunciated the Federalist uncertainty of the political and economic effect this large territory would have on the nation. He feared

> the effects of the vast extent of our empire; he feared the effects of the increased value of labor, the decrease in the value of lands, and the influence of climate upon our citizens who should migrate thither. He did fear (though this land was represented as flowing with milk and honey) that this Eden of the New World would prove a cemetery for the bodies of our citizens.

John Randolph of Roanoke, the Republican floor leader, entered the debate during a Federalist replay of a Republican resolution introduced during the debate over the Jay Treaty. It asked Jefferson to send Congress more data on the treaty of San Ildefonso, a copy of the deed of cession accompanying that treaty, copies of any correspondence between Spain and the United States, and any documents that proved the United States had acquired title to the Louisiana territory. Randolph chastised his opponents for adopting the same position on the transmission of data that Republicans had previously decried. He agreed that instances in which the House could demand information existed. The difference was in the reaction of the people to the two treaties. They universally reviled the Jay Treaty but applauded the Purchase. Also, any demand for the Spanish correspondence might inhibit future negotiations on the Purchase boundaries.

Randolph had restrained his infamous caustic tongue to this point. However, a comment by Federalist Roger Griswold of Connecticut restored him to form. Griswold had defended his tactic of hypothetically labelling the Purchase unconstitutional and then expanding it. How, questioned Randolph, could a treaty "constitutionally ratified" be other than "constitutionally made"? If so, why did the Federalists ask for documents concerning a constitutionally ratified treaty? The only answer was political advantage. "Gentlemen profess a wish," Randolph surmised, "to debate the merits of the treaty, and yet all their arguments go to show that it is an elusive bargain, a ruinous contract; and so far, are applicable only to the question, 'Ought the laws be passed for carrying it into effect?'" For example, Federalists claimed that they were worried that Spain might reclaim the territory. How did this affect the current resolution? Information that the Treaty of San Ildefonso was secret and unpublished abruptly terminated that thread.

The following day, Randolph again countered Griswold's thrusts. Griswold had denied any government power to "acquire" territory and "by the Constitution, they were restricted to the limits which existed at the time of its adoption." Randolph easily dispatched this observation. In order for it to be tenable, the limits of the United States "must have been accurately defined and generally known at the time when the Government took effect." Since the Constitution did not lay out boundaries, and in several aspects they were uncertain, Griswold's argument was suspect. If one added the government's power to settle boundary disputes, it could clearly extend the country's borders. To emphasize this point, Randolph ended this stage of his argument with examples of boundary changes that had extended the Union.

A second Griswold cavil dealt with the extent of congressional power claiming that even if the United States could acquire territory, Congress must control the acquisition. Randolph reminded him that the president had the right to "indicate business" within Congress "by recommending particular subjects to our attention." Now, if the government had the power to acquire territory, the president, or his Executive appointee, would negotiate any treaty terms. Since Congress had the power to confirm the acquisition, the president had followed the correct protocol. He had followed the Constitutional procedure by turning the treaty over to Congress for action. "As to the initiative in a matter like this," he reminded the House, "it necessarily devolved on the Executive."

Randolph's last Griswold encounter concerned the latter's charge of port discrimination. Recall, under the terms of the Purchase, French and Spanish vessels entering New Orleans carrying their own manufactures would pay the same impost as American ships for twelve years. The exemption arose because other American ports charged foreign vessels a higher tariff than domestic ships making New Orleans a favored foreign port. Randolph insisted that the size of import duties was a matter of law and regulation and the Purchase did not contain any constitutional defect. To satisfy critics "involves the necessity of repealing those discriminating duties on French and Spanish products." Such an "inexpedient" solution was the price a country had to pay to acquire territory. Still, the House must be aware that even at that time "there are some ports entitled to benefits which other ports do not enjoy.... According to the [Federalist] doctrine of this day, this is a violation of the Constitution."

The leader's final foray into this issue's constitutionalism revolved around the "uniform rule of naturalization." Samuel Whittlesey Dana, a Connecticut Federalist, proposed that the treaty would convert Purchase inhabitants to citizens in contravention of the naturalization law. Randolph reminded him that this was not a new dynamic. A clause in the Treaty of Paris designed to solve the western forts' issue achieved the same result for local Englishmen. Once the government established its power over a territory, Congress secured its inhabitants in their liberty and property. Of course, the territorials did not reap the full benefits of citizens because, for instance, they could not self-govern. In fact, they might never get full citizenship unless the territory achieved statehood. Here, the inhabitants did not become full citizens so government did not breach the naturalization laws.[5]

The interpretations above required attention. As noted, sources have portrayed Thomas Jefferson as a doctrinal apostate. First, Jefferson acted as a nationalist Republican. Yet even if state rights principles had guided him, he was still on solid ground because in matters of national peril or importance, all state rights men were nationalists. Beneath the skin of every traditional state rights man beat the heart of a nationalist.

Such a conclusion seemed hardly credible until one examined the doctrine and historical precedent closely. Recall, particularists carved out state rights in reaction to the Constitutional power assignments. It concentrated on the relationship between America's two levels of government and the political relationships between them based on reserved and natural rights. However, the Constitution almost eliminated the states from any partnership in foreign affairs. Domestic questions were their forte. As Jefferson opined to Edward Carrington in August 1787, "My general plan would be to make the states one as to every thing connected with foreign nations, and several as to every thing purely domestic." One need only examine the period from Jefferson's first term to the Panic of 1819 to see this dynamic in action. Consistently, the Virginia Dynasty made decisions in the national interest that were anathema to radical state rights men, but not moderates. The Purchase was such an action. Despite the possible sidestep from state rights doctrine, Jefferson made the decision that benefited the nation. To recap, traditionalists were more than willing to battle nationalists over domestic policy. Nevertheless, a national peril or the attainment of an overriding national goal unsheathed the nationalist streak in moderate state rights men. However, one should be very careful about extending this conclusion indiscriminately. From the time of the Missouri Compromise, state sovereigntists contemplated a different Union.

Second, the William Branch Giles' approach to the 1802 Judiciary bill was a warning that strict construction and implication were not mutually exclusive. One could argue from a strict constructionist point of view that a Legislative power had an acceptable incident if it directly implemented that power. Later, we will see Judge Marshall coopt the idea to disprove the notion of a compact. However, strict construction still would not accept the chain of incidents famously cited by Madison. Neither Giles nor Jefferson were state rights apostates.

Early in his dissertation on constitutional law, St. George Tucker published his thoughts on the institution of slavery. "Among the blessings which the Almighty hath showered down on these states," he lamented, "there is a large portion of the bitterest draught that ever flowed from the cup of affliction."

According to Tucker, geography and climate defined slavery's location. Africans favored the southern climate to that of the North. Moreover, slaves propagated faster in that locale. As a result, they increased in the South and simultaneously decreased in the North. Also, slave values increased as they became concentrated. Since they increased the planter's profit, one might argue that it was the cause of the institution's continuation.

It was unconscionable that a country "ardent in the cause of liberty" could continue an institution incompatible with its basic tenets. Perhaps it was a "weakness and inconsistency of human nature." Otherwise, "every man who hath a spark of patriotic fire in his bosom must wish to see [it] removed from his own country." Such might have been the case if English merchants, during the colonial era, had tried to terminate "so infamous a traffic by law." Virginia's legislature attempted to curb the trade but was unsuccessful. It did not outlaw slavery, and by failing to do so earned the "acrimony" and "opprobrium ... lavishly bestowed upon her of fostering slavery in her bosom."

Unfortunately, argued Tucker, "the extirpation of slavery from the United States, is a task ... arduous and momentous." Simultaneous emancipation was too dangerous. Slaves had always obeyed and submitted to their masters' assumed superiority. This made the former unfit for freedom and the latter unable to admit equality. If one chose a mass migration of slaves to other locations, one must conclude they would likely die of famine or disease. Just as unlikely a solution was the retention of free slaves within their present communities because "they would soon become idle, profligate, and miserable."

Some considerations affected white owners. One could not disregard "the property of individuals ... in slaves." Since law had confirmed this attitude, Virginian slave owners could justly explore how it could take their property without consent or with "just compensation." In addition, worrying about their own safety was natural for them. Surely, it would be endangered by the immediate emancipation "of the *whole* of this unhappy race."

How could a Virginia abolitionist overcome these perils? Tucker noted that Pennsylvania under the guidance of Benjamin Franklin, had "begun the work of gradual abolition of slavery in the year 1780." Nevertheless, their destination was unclear. The government could not transport them to either a foreign location or American territory because it was too expensive in one case and liable to foment war in the other. Neither could they remain within the white society because, as Jefferson noted, the history of the "French colonies in the West Indies" forbade it. White prejudice had taken "deep root in our minds" and would never allow many free blacks to remain in Virginia. In a comment for the future, Tucker explained:

> The experiment [admitting slaves to full civil and social rights] so far as it has been already made among us, proves that the emancipated blacks are not ambitious of civil rights. To prevent the generation of such an ambition, appears to comport with sound policy; for if it

should ever rear its head, its partisans, as well as its opponents, will be enlisted by nature herself, and always ranged in formidable array against each other.

To solve the problem, Tucker proposed a multipart plan. All females born after its adoption were free as were their descendants but they, and each of them must compensate their masters by serving them until the age of twenty-eight. The plan denied free slaves the right to hold office, vote, own land, bear arms, or marry other than a black or mulatto. In addition, they could not be an attorney, insurer, trial witness except in cases between blacks and mulattos, executor, administrator, land trustee or capable of making a will or testament.

Tucker knew this plan smacked of racism. However, he believed that no other plan would succeed. Practically, these harsh rules might encourage freemen "to seek those privileges [civil rights] in some other climate." Perhaps the huge American territories would be their refuge to a better life.[6]

These same territories provided the first divisive flashpoint between the sections and expanded their notions of the Union's nature. On February 13, 1819, the House of Representatives moved to examine two bills enabling the territories of Missouri and Alabama to enter the Union. Congress's reaction set the Union on a path to civil war. Representative James Tallmage of New York "moved an amendment, substantially to limit the existence of slavery in the new State [Missouri], by declaring all free who should be born in the Territory after its admission into the Union, and providing for the gradual emancipation of those now held in bondage." This deviation from the usual methodology initiated a fierce debate between the slavery and nonslavery representatives.

John Tyler defined the basic dispute. Southerners expected Congress to admit Missouri immediately. Northerners rejected that idea because they had discovered, to their satisfaction, a Constitutional barrier. If so, responded their opposition, admit the state and "the Constitution of the United States will vindicate its own supremacy." Surely any disputes revolving about a republican form of government could be deliberated after Missouri's entrance to the Union. This dynamic found no northern support. Its representatives preferred to attach a rider to Missouri's constitution "that her legislature shall pass no law violatory of the Constitution of the Union." Of course, the impasse initiated a sometimes raucous debate.

The atmosphere in the initial phase mirrored others of its ilk. Constitutional arguments dominated, each side seeking advantage. However, after several uncomplimentary comments about slavery and slavers, the debate assumed a charged atmosphere. Virginians stooped to sarcasm and harsh language to rebut northern attacks. The Federalist, Edward Colston, accused a New Hampshire representative of "speaking to the galleries, and by his language, endeavoring to excite a servile war." He deserved the same fate as two Florida buccaneers intercepted by Andrew Jackson. Philip Barbour accused a Pennsylvania colleague of purposely exaggerating his slavery remarks. Sectional slurs particularly incensed James Johnson. He accused the northern states of drumming up interest "to manufacture resolutions of thanks" from citizens who had been largely disinterested. Did they think this tactic would silence opposition? A Massachusetts representative fascinated him, "a teacher of the mild precepts of the meek and lowly Jesus ... [who] talked of blood and slaughter with great *sang froid.*" Even Rufus King, a Federalist Senator, drew Johnson's ire. His sarcastic attack on King's candor must have surprised the House.

Due to the caustic language employed by some debaters, allusions to disunion were common. Barbour slyly informed the House that he had not come to Washington as "an apostle of disunion" but followed with a warning about its possibility. The Federalist James Pindall reminded his colleagues of the dire consequences engendered by "a spirit of distrust." Johnson, in full flight, announced that he was "attached to the Union; but it is a rational attachment. The moment the Union shall fail to secure and promote these objects [political rights, prosperity, tranquility] I shall detest it, as I would any other species of despotism." John Tyler compared northern demands with those of Revolutionary England and reminded his audience that America "went forth to battle, in the majesty of its strength, and achieved the victory of our independence." John Floyd worried about "the assumption of enormous powers by this House" and its effect on the states. In an interrogatory he asked, "Have they [North] not as much to hold from the continuance of this Union as we have?" Notice that none of the speakers boldly called for disunion. Instead, they left the notion to germinate.

Two territorial acquisitions acted as precedents. Each side touted the Northwest Ordinance of 1787 and the Louisiana Purchase as proof of their allegations. Virginians claimed that the former was not germane because it predated the Constitution, dealt only with a territory and not a state, contained a clause specific to territorial slavery, and had been proved, by James Madison in his *The Federalist* No. 38, to be a congressional usurpation of power. The latter, supported by the House in 1803, protected the inhabitants in their property, promised them early statehood, and was a legal contract between two recognized parties. The debate reminded representatives that, despite Congress's great power over a territory, it had never imposed a restriction on slavery. At the time, all parties knew that Spain had recognized slavery in Louisiana.

Soon, Virginia representatives concluded that the supporters of the amendment actually sought power. Johnson laid down the notion. "It is a question about power; power — that idol which has a charm, an irresistible fascination, but a human heart. It is a question calculated to test the powers of the Federal Government; to determine how much sovereignty or power is left to the States and to the people." John Tyler announced that "if we adopt this amendment, we shall be guilty of an unwarranted and most manifest usurpation of power." Later he sighed "has it come to this, that we are now to enter into this struggle for power?" If we can trust Tyler, innuendo that an individual political agenda drove some of his opponents was common. Thus, James Barbour may have been correct that restrictionists often argued at cross purposes. They could not decide whether their amendment was based on implied legislative power or on a compact. He reminded them that the states had delegated Congress power, but not the right to increase it by reducing that of the states. The main fight saw the friends of limited government clash with the purveyors of broad construction. The former maintained that, in a strange quirk, the people of Missouri would gain their rights from their servants instead of vice versa. Because the Framers had never enumerated a power to amend a state constitution, the restrictionists had to revert to implication, and "they deduce their authority to annex such conditions, through the avenue of inferences from some other delegated power." Resurrecting shades of Patrick Henry, Johnson described "this sweeping clause ... it squints not only at monarchy, but at despotism — despotism as absolute as ever wielded the sceptre over a set of crouching slaves."

As participants stated, this principal dispute was the northern majority's insistence that it could impose terms on Missouri's constitution. Congress had the power to admit a new state into the Union but Virginians translated this power as one to admit, or its opposite, to deny admission. However, nothing in the Constitution allowed Congress to admit with attached restrictions that the potential state must incorporate. It was replete with examples that bore out this contention. For example, Congress had the power to allow or deny a state's request to lay duties on imports. Could Congress add a rider that it would allow the state's request if it fulfilled another obligation? Importantly, both the Ninth and especially the Tenth Amendments foreclosed any attempt at added restrictions. The powers not delegated to the United States, and Congress, remained with the states or the people. Seemingly, to avoid this problem, any Tallmadge-like restriction would require a Constitutional amendment. Otherwise, Congress must recognize that its power over the territory of Missouri was absolute, but that over the state had to meet constitutional safeguards.

Why had Missouri suddenly to jump through these hoops? Other states, particularly Louisiana, had met only cursory opposition to their admission. John Tyler wondered if the people of Missouri could not govern themselves. Would Congress replay the same scenario if a state like Pennsylvania sought admission under a restriction that she must impose slavery in her constitution? John Floyd expressed his contempt for the notion in direct style. He would never agree to any suggestion that a state, North or South, must change or add clauses to its constitution to enter the Union. To recap, Virginia representatives agreed that the power to admit, an enumerated power, necessarily implied the power to deny admittance. Nevertheless, like Madison's famous example during the Bank fight, that power could not be the basis of further implication to set restrictions. Missourians must choose their own institutions.

John Tyler made an interesting assertion during this phase of the debate. Looking beyond the present dispute, he said "This Territory has been purchased out of the common purse: the South and the North have contributed alike. We are then the joint tenants in the estate, and, without doing an act of gross injustice, you cannot oust us of our right to equal participation with yourselves in all its benefits."

Three important tenets, equality, individual and state rights, and the right to property permeated the debate. It seemed bizarre to Virginians that the other states in the Union could control slavery but Missouri could not do so. Surely such an expectation was a direct blow to the treasured concept of republican government. Philip Barbour declared any such restriction unconstitutional and void and an assault on state sovereignty. After all, the Constitution was a compact that insured the equality of both old and new states. If a new state depended on the general government for "the faculties of her government" it would be less sovereign than its co-states because "all the states are equal in their political rights." For example, Pennsylvania passed a law banning slavery but Congress would govern Missouri on the same subject. Of course, this introduced the subject of individual rights and property. If a northerner could move to Missouri with his property, why could not a Virginian? Missouri, its citizens, and those intending to be citizens must have the same rights as those enjoyed in the original thirteen states. Only a legislative body more sovereign then the people of Missouri — a nonstarter — could impose conditions on her constitution. "Equality is all that can be asked for," intoned Tyler, "and that equality is secured to each State of this Union by the Constitution of this land." Barbour was adamant that Article IV, Section 2, clause 1 insured that "the citizens of each State shall be entitled to all privileges and immunities of citizens of the several states." If a Missourian could not hold a slave, then neither could a Virginian. "Our principle," he later announced, "does not claim for the citizens of one State greater privileges than citizens of the other States enjoyed, but the same only."

Because of the federal Fugitive Slave Law, Virginians considered slaves to be property. The Federalist James Pindall reminded the House that the Purchase had insured "*that the inhabitants should be maintained and protected in the free enjoyment of their property.*" Moreover, "a free government protects or affects the property of its citizens through the medium of its laws" and Americans must respect its treaties. The Tallmadge amendment would "violate" a term of the Purchase. "The supreme law of the land," argued Johnson, "guaranteed to them [Missouri immigrants] protection in the full and free enjoyment of their property." This declaration diametrically opposed Rufus King's declaration during the Purchase debate that the property stipulation covered only property currently within Louisiana's bounds.

John Tyler added another argument. Congress had opened the territories to immigration and encouraged planters to secure acreage at a good price. Now, it announced that the planter could not take his laborers with him and the land became useless for his plans. "Is this just?" he queried.

Barbour was anxious about the amendment's effect on future federal-state relations. Applicants to the Union might never regain lost sovereignty. The Missouri imbroglio was merely another example of government policy favoring one section of the country to the detriment of Virginia. "If you can take from any Territory a power of this kind," he railed, "when once granted what would hinder you from repealing the very act by which you would admit the same Territory into the Union?" New states, particularly those that might authorize slavery, would face restrictions from a usurping central government. A crucial extension of this notion would be the eventual "emancipation of slavery throughout the whole United States after the present generation shall become extinct." James Pindall believed the process would allow Congress serially to obliterate the states' reserved rights while John Floyd also detected the threat of precedent. Congress had "made deep inroads into the Constitution" in the past and another assumption of power made him, "as a representative of an old State," concerned about the next usurpation. Remember, said Barbour, "the States surrendered to the Federal Government no power over the subject [slavery]." States, through their constitutions, selected its existence. Without this state power, the South would have never ratified the Constitution.

Any new state constitutional restriction was sure to infringe eventually on all state rights. Everyone knew that Congress had certain legislative powers while the Constitution prohibited others to the state. "All other powers," argued Barbour, "not included in this grant, or in these prohibitions, remained with the States." Of course, we must remember that a state was the collection of its people. In a rejoinder to a New York adversary who called state rights a "new doctrine," James Johnson predicted that "conflicts of the most direful character ... may blight the hopes of the most devoted friends of liberty and self-government" if the present habit of passing unconstitutional acts persisted. Simply put, they were an "invasion of the rights of the States."

The Missouri constitution contained a clause that its citizens found necessary to protect their safety and morals. Every state had a right to exclude free blacks from immigrating into the state. For example, Missouri could prevent them from citizenship if Massachusetts could say "a black man shall not ... marry a white woman" in that state. Free men, according to Barbour, were not, and could never be, citizens of Missouri if the state opposed it. Alexander Smyth expanded on all areas of this topic. They did not meet the qualifications for citizenship, no act had ever bestowed it on them, and they had no civil rights but some freedoms. He maintained that a state could restrict a citizen from another state if he presented a danger to the former's self-preservation. William Archer seconded these claims and stressed that individual states had the power to accept or deny citizenship to any individual.

Members of the Virginia political elite traded opinions on the Missouri debate. James Madison doubted that the extension of slavery was the main reason for the uproar in Congress. He saw it as an attempt by certain interests "to form a new state of parties ... dividing the Republicans of the North from those of the South." He also made an interesting comment on the Northwest Ordinance of 1787. At its passage, he claimed, the Continental Congress had no power to prohibit slave importation. After all, if Congress really had the power, would not it have used it to forestall all slavery importation? Moreover, it was doubtful whether Congress could enforce the 36°30' line because it would act as an unconstitutional barrier to the admission of future states.

Monroe agreed that "the object of those, who brought it forward, was undoubtedly to acquire power...." They were the same class who had been willing to sell out the Mississippi navigation in 1786. Like Madison, he could not fathom the restrictions applied to future states. He closed with the ominous comment that "I have never known a question so menacing to the tranquility and even the continuance of our Union as the present one."

Spencer Roane took an extreme position on the Compromise. "The principles of 1799 are trodden underfoot, and our slaves incited to insurrection," "If driven to it, we can yet form with them [western states] a great nation," and "they [Ritchie et al.] are averse to being dammed up in a land of Slaves, by the Eastern people," were just a few of his incendiary remarks.[7]

8

The Nature of the Union — John Marshall vs. Spencer Roane

During the critical judicial period from 1819 to 1824, two of Virginia's favorite sons occupied positions destined to provide a launching pad for the debate over the nature of the Union. The Republican stranglehold on its state rights element was loosed and its Virginia doctrinaires were determined to make their theory national theory. Although other cases began the process of stamping the national rather than state rights view on the government, *McCulloch v. Maryland* and *Cohens v. Virginia* proved to be the capstones.

These cases contained myriad arguments that strained a reader's attention. Safe to say, one must read the competing arguments closely but the reward was a primer for the Constitutional dispute over the nature of the Union. It came in two mutually exclusive flavors and a recitation of their differences will prepare the reader for Virginia's concern about its place in the Union.

✠

Spencer Roane, a native of Essex County, was born April 4, 1762, and studied law both in Virginia and Philadelphia. After stints in the Virginia executive council, assembly, and senate, he became a judge in 1789. Married to Patrick Henry's daughter, he became a Jeffersonian Republican, tending to Old Republicanism and preferred a weak national government with reduced supreme authority. In 1804, he and his cousin Thomas Ritchie established the *Richmond Enquirer* to promulgate Republican ideals. From 1803 until his death in 1822, Roane made the Virginia Court of Appeals an important Republican political organization. It became his base from which to scrutinize Marshall's Supreme Court decisions.

Roane left an important legacy for Virginia jurisprudence. He single-mindedly labored to increase its power and prestige through the concept of state judicial review. Also, he promoted the notion of unanimity between judges and, unlike Marshall who was fond of natural law and rights, the importance of judicial precedents. His goal was to elevate the Virginia Court of Appeals to primacy among judicial agencies. Some might consider him the outstanding southern jurist of his time.

Interestingly, Roane supported the notion of court review of Constitutional questions, believing that the judiciary could revise any legislative act that violated either its spirit or plain words. On the surface, Roane seemed to share this conviction with Marshall. Still, Roane's preoccupation with elevating the state court could never accept Marshall's attempts to reduce its power. Independence and jurisdiction lay behind the legal disputes.

A native of the Northern Neck, John Marshall spent his early years on the frontier. He served his country during the Revolution and shared the privations at Valley Forge. The indelible impressions gleaned during the war forced the young officer to conclude that a federal government of sovereign states neither ensured the expansion of the Union nor benefited the people. After the war, Marshall held positions in the assembly and in Washington. He was secretary of war and secretary of state under President John Adams who later made him Chief Justice of the Supreme Court. Most commentators believe he reenergized the Court to meet the exigencies of a new nation with a novel constitution. He described his judicial motivation when he wrote,

> I am disposed to ascribe my devotion to the union, and to a government competent to its preservation, at least as much to casual circumstances as to judgment. I had grown up at a time when a love of union and resistance to the claims of Great Britain where the inseparable inmates of the same bosom; — when patriotism and a strong fellow feeling with our suffering fellow citizens of Boston were identical; — when the maxim united we stand, divided we fall was the maxim of every orthodox American; and I had imbibed these sentiments so thoroughly that they Constituted a part of my being. I carried them with me into the army where I found myself associated with brave men from different states who were risking life and everything valuable in a common cause believed by all to be most precious; and where I was confirmed in the habit of considering America as my country, and congress as my government.

The Chief Justice's rulings in two earlier cases set the stage for his *McCulloch* and *Cohens* decisions. John Adams had appointed William Marbury District of Columbia justice of the peace during his "midnight appointments." The correct officials had properly signed and sealed the commission, but not delivered it. Incoming Secretary of State James Madison refused to release it, so Marbury applied to the Court under a writ of mandamus, that required original Court jurisdiction, to force him to perform his duty. The situation placed Marshall in a tricky position because, as Adams's Secretary of State, he had failed to deliver the commission to Marbury. Moreover, what would be the result if Jefferson refused to honor a Supreme Court decision? It would appear impotent.

In *Marbury v. Madison*, Marshall ruled that Marbury deserved the commission, but the Court did not have the power to order its delivery. Part of Section 13 of the Judiciary Act of 1789 had unconstitutionally conferred it since Congress could not modify its own, or the Court's, powers. This decision was based on Article III, Section 2, that enumerated the circumstances in which the Supreme Court should have either original or appellate jurisdiction. Marshall ruled that,

> If it had been intended to leave it in the discretion of the legislature to apportion the judicial power between the supreme and inferior courts according to the will of that body, it would certainly have been useless to have proceeded further than to have defined the judicial power.... The plain import of the words seems to be, that in one class of cases its jurisdiction is original and not appellate; in the other it is appellate, and not original.

His decision contained the implied assertion that the Court could review executive department decisions. Nothing in the Constitution supported this contention. Nevertheless, by stringing together several Articles, Marshall arrived at this position. It became a template for his future decisions.

The second case was *Martin v. Hunter's Lessee* and its successive iterations. Due to the length of the case and changed ownerships, other individuals participated. In a business decision, Thomas, Lord Fairfax, divided his large Northern Neck properties into plantations for his personal use, lands upon which he collected quitrents, and undeveloped acres. He died in 1781 without direct heirs. Thus, the Virginia legislature assumed ownership and put much of the land up for sale. However, Fairfax's will named his British nephew Denny Martin as the property owner if he changed his name to Fairfax. Note that the conflict we discussed previously with the Treaty of 1783 guaranteeing British property, which Virginians chose to ignore, came into play. However, the courts could solve this difficulty under the terms of the Constitution that made the Treaty the law of the land.

Denny Fairfax eventually claimed all the land as his inheritance, including that sold by the state. One purchaser was David Hunter. In a bewildering array of suits from *Hunter v. Fairfax's Devisee* through *Fairfax v. Commonwealth, Hunter v. Fairfax's Devisee, Martin v. Hunter's Lessee,* and *Fairfax's Devisee v. Hunter's Lessee,* the case wended through the courts.

During this progression, Henry Lee, John Marshall, and James Marshall formed an American syndicate to purchase the land. To satisfy all parties, the assembly passed the Compromise of 1796. Two uncertainties remained. Could it repeal the act? Did the syndicate have the right to collect rent? Since the state had not confiscated the land properly before 1796 and the act might be inoperable, it decided collection was expedient. Still, the Marshall brothers ownership was tenuous.

In 1813, the Supreme Court ruled in favor of the Marshalls in *Fairfax's Devisee v. Hunter's Lessee,* revising a Virginia Court of Appeals decision. Joseph Story gave the majority decision because Marshall was ineligible to participate. Story never mentioned the Compromise of 1796, shuffled aside part of the Virginia Court of Appeals record, and introduced the Jay Treaty as new material. Despite these deficiencies the Marshall syndicate owned the land. The decision ran counter to Virginia's reliance on a federal compact that forbade one branch of the federal government to rule against a compact member. It balked at the idea that the Court had federal appellate jurisdiction over a state court because it was unconstitutional and attacked state sovereignty.

Spencer Roane's Virginia Court of Appeals reviewed the decision instead of putting it into effect. It determined that this litigation involved state, not federal law, and federal courts had no jurisdiction. Story had been incompetent to omit the Compromise of 1796 from proceedings, and the Treaty of 1783, not the Jay Treaty, was operative. Moreover, Virginia had no power to make it so. In an interesting debate started by Roane's court, the participating lawyers studied whether the Court, using Section 25 as a basis, could overturn a state law. They concluded it negated the concept of dual sovereignty and the state ignored the Court's decision.

The year 1819 proved to be a trial for Virginians. The financial panic that swept the country ruined the reputation of the Bank of the United States. Congress had begun debate on the constitutionality of its incorporation and seemed to have a jaundiced view. Moreover, we have seen that nationalistic programs like internal improvements were moribund. Southerners, initially surprised by the direction of the Missouri statehood application, were unlikely to support a Bank recharter. In this milieu, Chief Justice John Marshall, Virginia Federalist, extended national power and crippled state rights by his decision in the case of *McCulloch v. Maryland.*

Many motives colored this decision. Nationalism flagged. It required a rallying point to counter the rebirth of state rights arguments fostered by Madison's Report and the Principles of '98. If the doctrine gained popularity, government programs that might benefit the country were unlikely and state rights arguments on the nature of the Union would predominate.

Also, a festering constitutional dispute required solution. How would Congress interpret the sweeping clauses? Hamilton and Madison had theorized about implied powers, and Congress had debated the topic, but no Court ruling had disposed of it.

On what facts would the Court base its decision? Maryland had passed a law in 1818 taxing any unchartered Maryland Bank at $15,000 per annum. One such was the Bank of the United States. But, its cashier James McCulloch, refused to pay the tax, was charged, and fined. Soon, the case passed to the Supreme Court. After hearing the arguments, it decided that its incorporation was constitutional and the tax was not. These opinions surprised no one. Despite his attendance as a ratification convention delegate, Marshall's justification included questionable assertions that proved, to his satisfaction, that Congress could adopt a broad construction of the sweeping clauses, and that the Union was not a compact. To further his case, he mischaracterized Maryland's argument to enhance his own. It, he said, had argued that only the states were "truly sovereign" and the federal government's power "must be exercised in subordination to the states, who alone possess supreme dominion." Of course, Maryland made no such claim, but its presence offered Marshall a straw man to swat. Moreover, he purposefully reversed the meaning of the Ninth plus Tenth Amendments. Marshall transformed the combination from an assignment of reserved sovereign powers to a broad construction bulwark created by the absence of the word "expressly." He continued,

> Among the enumerated powers, we do not find the act of establishing a bank or creating a corporation. But there is no phrase in the instrument which, like the articles of confederation, excludes incidental or implied powers; and which requires that everything granted shall be expressly and minutely described. Even the 10th amendment, which was framed for the purpose of quieting the excessive jealousies which had been excited, omits the word "expressly," and declares only that the powers "not delegated to the United States, nor prohibited to the States, are reserved to the States or to the people"; thus leaving the question whether the particular power which may become the subject of contest has been delegated to the one government, or prohibited to the other, to depend on a fair construction of the whole instrument.

Thus, a government that most Virginians thought had only expressly enumerated powers was transmuted into one with only "expressly enumerated restrictions." Of course, these assertions dramatically affected his interpretation of the nature of the Union. No longer were the peoples of the several states the sovereigns. They were replaced by a unitary national people whose powers were limited only by specific constitutional clauses.

Unfortunately for later Federalists, George Nicholas, staunch proratification advocate, had insisted that the sweeping clause did not delegate additional powers, and Edmund Pendleton had agreed. Thus, one can understand Virginia's immediate reaction. Two pseudonymous writers, Amphictyon and Hampden, publically attacked the Court's logic, while A Friend to the Union and A Friend of the Constitution responded. The first named was likely Judge William Brockenbrough, while the second was Judge Spencer Roane. John Marshall wrote the two Friend's articles.

To repeat, Marshall realized he must stop the rising tide of state rights in Virginia before it spread nationally. He claimed that the case had reached his Court unremarkably and had not been selected to meet his ends. Remember, he advised readers, the Court was an honorable branch that Americans regarded highly. One might even argue that the prosperity of the United States connected directly to it. Thus, when one read the critics attacks, one should look for another agenda.

Amphictyon sought to impress on both the president and Congress that adopting Marshall's conclusions was dangerous. A liberal construction was bound to damage both the people and the states because it assigned Congress unlimited power. Nevertheless, the Court could never rescind a congressional act.

Roane had a different motive. He recognized that the Court had won this battle but he could salvage the war if he could rally the people to a cause. To the Virginian, principle was everything. Liberty could not be bartered. "I love the honor," he announced, "and, if you please the glory of my country, but I love its liberty better." Of course, this did not mean he was immune to practicalities. Not only had the Court delegated an unconstitutional power grab to Congress, but also it had usurped the reserved rights of the sovereign states. Thus, his goal was to rouse his fellow Republicans from their "torpor" and "apathy" by publicizing his objections. If he achieved these goals, Virginia would again lead the nation.

The *Richmond Enquirer,* edited by the moderate state rights man Thomas Ritchie, printed the Amphictyon and Hampden articles while the *Philadelphia Union* and *Alexandria Gazette* published those by Marshall. The *Enquirer* was not just any newspaper. Others commonly reprinted its contents. Interestingly, Roane and Ritchie were members of a prominent, but not controlling, Republican power group, the Richmond Junto. Marshall contended that the *Enquirer* "abound[s] with hostile attacks on this opinion." Ritchie had promised that Hampden would uncover Marshall's serious errors. In addition, he warned, one should never forget the power of the Tenth Amendment.

Amphictyon's articles were repetitive with few new ideas. He avoided legalisms and his view was moderate. A liberal construction of the Constitution was dangerous but he presented a methodology Virginia should adopt in cases of usurpation. One might read his articles like letters from an old friend. They were easy to follow, well-planned, concise, and had a clear target. His audience was the average Virginian who required a review both of the Principles of '98 and this case.

Roane's articles harshened the tone of the debate. They were sharper, less folksy. The Court decision offended him and he employed some acerbic language to make his arguments, but his writing style was excellent. He laid out his battle plan and stuck to it, constantly referred to plain Constitutional language, and listed Marshall's errors succinctly. These led to an ease of understanding. His opening warning was an attention grabber and his habit of starting each new article with a short review might persuade a reader to reexamine them. His audience was the informed Virginian who could appreciate his footnoted explanations. However, he could not escape the past. Little new exposition seized the reader's attention. His articles may be considered a good review of existing state rights doctrine.

Marshall had a similar plan but did not stick to it. He would lay out his goal but often detoured on another tangent. Still, he never bored one. His arguments reminded the reader of James Madison's innovative explosion before the Constitution debate. New interpretations flowed. True, one was never sure whether they were truly held or just ingenious inventions for the moment, but as we will see later, they were novel. Moreover, they would present nationalists with ammunition for the fight against state rights.

Language interpretation was a barrier to compromise. Almost every dispute was based on dueling definitions. Of course, each side offered the interpretation best suited to its argument. For example, Amphictyon considered "necessary" to be "those means *without which* the end *could not* be attained." Roane cobbled together dictionary definitions and concluded "necessary" meant "indispensably requisite" while Marshall was happy with "convenient or useful" or "conducive to." Roane charged that his derivation proved Marshall's habit of deviating from established custom. Similarly, the sides could not agree on the meaning of "the people" or "the states." Marshall equated "people" with "people of the United States" and "states" as designating their government. Of course, from our previous discussions, we know that his opponents would favor Madison's concept that a state was its people acting in their highest sovereign capacity. Because of these divisions, one could conclude that, since the opponents consistently applied their definitions to arguments, each was successful in making its case. Thus, two competing, equally viable interpretations of the nature of the Union and constitutional construction emerged. The one in vogue might depend on the dominant political party or partisan Supreme Court opinions.

A further comment on language was appropriate. As noted, Amphictyon's articles were tame compared with those of Roane. The latter's language was sharper, more pointed, and relentlessly attacked the Court decision. Unfortunately, Marshall's replies were unbecoming from a Chief Justice of the Supreme Court. His continual personal attacks on those who dared to criticize his opinions and his constant whining about their ability and motives distracted the reader from some powerful arguments.

The debaters adopted different tactics to make their cases. Amphictyon praised Marshall's talents, but their application to his dubious justifications for the decision disappointed him. Since they were not germane, according to Amphictyon, pronouncements on the nature of the Union and broad construction should be considered *obiter dicta* and discarded. Marshall constantly labelled his decisions "fair" while those of his opponents were "restricted." More important, he wanted to leave the reader with the impression that the objections to his decision were, at heart, political rather than constitutional. Roane insisted that established principles were under attack and their demise promised government usurpation.

The above discussions led one to categorize the two approaches. Conflicting constitutional principles and interpretations were at its core. Roane, and Amphictyon, were advocates of original intent, proffering an interpretation found "at the time of its [the Constitution] adoption." Marshall could not follow that path. He viewed the Constitution as a living document, constantly under scrutiny for changing interpretations. Thus, the debate was over original intent versus a living document.

The victor in this trial of interpretations would likely be the one who could evoke trust in his readers. Marshall did not consider his decision extreme and urged the South to trust his motives. Roane thought this approach silly. To obtain the South's trust, all the Supreme Court had to do was enforce the Tenth Amendment. Amphictyon feared the decision would ultimately lead to increased congressional power. "I cannot exclusively rely on my confidence in our representatives;" he sighed, "if that were a sufficient guarantee for the preservation of our state rights, then there would be no need for a specific enumeration of our granted powers."

Each side established its interpretation of the tenets that would color a definition of the Union's nature. Amphictyon enunciated an opinion concerning the Bank incorporation's constitutionality. Everyone agreed with Madison that it was a settled issue. Still, it was just a single case. Others might reach the Court based on a comparable process, so one must make some baseline arguments. Marshall agreed. He considered "the baneful influence of this narrow construction" tantamount to "rendering the government incompetent to its great objects." Therefore, each side regarded a debate on justification, but not the decision, a benefit to their cause.

Marshall admitted that taxation was a reserved power of the states. Nevertheless, the Constitution did forego some objects, such as imports or exports, from state taxes. Therefore, the circumstance was not novel and if a state law was repugnant to the Constitution, the Court must declare it void. "This great principle is," offered Marshall, "that the constitution and the laws made in pursuance thereof, are supreme; that they control the constitution and laws of the respective States, and cannot be controlled by them." Since "a power to create implies a power to preserve" and a state tax might destroy the Bank branch, the Maryland law was unconstitutional.

Amphictyon agreed that if one began with the assumption that the Bank was constitutional then Marshall's argument followed. His cavil was with, what seemed to him, an extension of the tax power. If the United States could tax a state institution despite the state's power to incorporate, then Congress held in its hands the future of state institutions. "Such a result," he asserted, "would destroy the sovereignty of the states within that very sphere in which it is admitted they may act without control."

Marshall was very careful with the concept of "the people." However, if one kept in mind that, at all costs, he intended to avoid Madison's "highest sovereign capacity" argument, one could see through his smokescreen. His detractors had accused him of denying that Congress's powers "were delegated by the states." Tactically, he avoided the accusation by turning the question to an affirmative statement that it was "a government of the people." After questioning Amphictyon about his definition of "people," which he had previously defined in Madisonian terms, Marshall ignored it and rambled off on his own track. The Court, which "cannot be mistaken" "not indeed in the same words, but in substance" agreed if the people he designated were those of a state. But, since Amphictyon did not adopt this definition—an erroneous pronouncement—Marshall presupposed that his opponents must mean the people were the state legislatures. Having set up the straw man, he confidently attacked it. Despite his assertion that "I cannot be mistaken" that the people were "the source from which the government of the Union derives its power," he never defined "the people," except by innuendo, as the consolidated people of the United States.

Of course, disputes over the definition of "the people" were bound to include the Preamble to the Constitution. For Marshall, "We the people of the United States" meant that the whole people defined the powers of government. No one could interpret it as "We the states." This evoked memories of Patrick Henry's famous question in the Virginia Ratifying Convention and ignored "the people in their highest sovereign capacity" as the definition of "state." Roane did not agree with Marshall's interpretation. "We the people of the United States" did not discriminate between the consolidated people and "those of the several states." Also, the Preamble was neither a functional part of the Constitution nor an assertion that the "execution" of the document was unanimous. Marshall was uncomfortable with this line of attack. He asserted that "We the people of the United States" meant only the people separated from their state governments. Under these conditions, he surprisingly agreed "that the constitution was adopted by the people acting as states."

Deliberations about "the people" led to those on ratification. During his presentation, Maryland's lawyer opened this door by arguing that ratification had been the act of sovereign states who delegated the general government's powers. Logically, the national government would be subordinate to "the States, who will alone possess supreme dominion." Yes, said Marshall, the state legislatures played a major role, but at that stage the Constitution "was a mere proposal." Remember, its submission was to the people. "Of consequence, when they act," he said, "they act in their States. But the measures they adopt do not, on that account, cease to be the measures of the people themselves, or become the measures of the State governments." Therefore, this decision bound the Articles' "state sovereignties." In any case, he agreed that the powers of the general government derived from the people of the United States, but not the states.

This dynamic met opposition. Had not the people of Virginia, when leaving a state of nature to form a constitution, delegated all their powers to the state? If so, they had no powers to deliver to the general government, having exhausted them to their state government. Marshall, without evidence, asserted that surely today this was not reasonable. The people could "resume and modify the powers granted to government" in opposition to Lockean theory.

We saw earlier that the loss of sovereign state power was foremost in state rights arguments and taxation policy was such an example. Marshall sought to characterize the dispute. States had recourse to poor tax policies. Virginians could replace their agents for instituting taxes inimical to their prosperity. However, the requirements of the general government belong, not to a particular state, but to all the people, and should be the "subject" of the government that represented every citizen. Marshall linked that power to sovereignty and concluded that the general government could tax any object that did not fall within the guidelines for state taxation.

Roane took the opportunity to employ sovereignty to challenge Marshall's assumption that the government was national in form. The Court decision concluded that although the states had not established the Constitution, Maryland was a sovereign state and a party of the government. Therefore, to Roane, the government of sovereign states must clearly be federal, not national, in form.

Amphictyon reiterated some settled state rights dogma on the preservation of reserved rights. Applying Jeffersonian logic, he affirmed the primacy of the Tenth Amendment to substantiate their retention. It was "merely declaratory" of an obvious Constitutional power. Switching to Madison's Report as an authority, the Supreme Court, said the Judge, "had no power to adjudicate away the *reserved* rights of a sovereign member of the confederacy, and vest them in the general government." Moreover, according to Virginia's reservation, part of its ratification "expressly asserted, that every power *not granted* by the constitution, remained with them (the people of Virginia), and *act at their will.*"

The concept that the Constitution was a compact dominated the nature of the Union debate. Madison's Report and Madison as Publius had ensured its preeminence for Virginians. Moreover, his notion that the people had established dual compacts satisfied most theorists, particularly Roane. Reiterating the traditional state rights view, he argued that "the constitution is a *compact* between the people of each state, and those of all the states." He proposed that an inferior tribunal like the Supreme Court could not judge the parties to the compact — the states composed of the people acting in their highest sovereign capacity. Only the original sovereigns could judge. Roane also followed Madison's lead on ratification. The "highest sovereign capacity" argument for Constitutional ratification extended to the nature of the Union so the sovereign states had formed it. This comported with Madison's assertion that the people composing thirteen sovereignties were the "parties to the government."

Amphictyon realized that any argument proving that the states had not delegated powers to the federal government must rely on "the states are not parties to the compact." If so, the state legislatures would forfeit important duties like fighting tyranny and usurpation. Marshall was not satisfied with this common assertion. In a brilliant thrust of logic, he cut the state rights cord to federalism and compact by denying the latter's existence. The Constitution was "a government created for the nation by the whole American people, assembled in convention in and for their respective states." It was the act of one, and only one, party and thus could not be a compact that required at least two parties. Compare it to Madison's dual compacts. One was among the people leaving a state of nature to form a state constitution.

Another was between the people of the state and those of the other states to form a Constitution. Each of these had a sovereign people of a state whereas Marshall proposed a consolidated sovereign people.

With this theory in hand, we can now reexamine some of Marshall's positions. Repeatedly, the informed reader noticed that he agreed with state rights positions that appeared to weaken his position. For example, he had concurred that the people of the states had delegated the general government's powers. This looked surprising at the time, but we did not comment on it. Now one can see his strategy. Without a compact, the people of a state transformed into a subset of the whole people. The statement remained true while the ramifications changed drastically.

Amphictyon declared that the success of two principles, the denial that the states had delegated federal powers and a liberal construction of the sweeping clause, would inevitably lead to consolidated government. Roane added that they would usher in "a last adieu to the state governments" because they would lose their role as constitutional watchdogs. Marshall brushed off these claims since he had not "suggested a single idea in favor of consolidation."

The Court, in its decision, repeated the principle that "the constitution and the laws made in pursuance thereof are supreme; that they control the constitution and laws of the respective States, and cannot be controlled by them." No instances existed in which a state law or court could negate a law of the general government. Roane resisted this interpretation. He refused any constitutional construction that delegated Congress power "to bind us in all cases whatsoever."

As usual, the dispersal of power between state and federal governments was at the basis of this dispute. Nationalists maintained that Congress needed all the powers necessary to carry out its functions. State rights men insisted that government "possessed only such [powers] as were expressly granted, or passed therewith as necessary incidents" while the residue remained with the states. Marshall, in a flight of rhetoric, preferred a "grant limited in its terms, but accompanied with unlimited means of carrying it into execution." This was sophistical to Roane who declared that anyone who saw any difference between it and "an *unlimited* grant of power" "must be a deplorable idiot."

Limited national government, supreme in its sphere, was a common notion according to Marshall. Did not the Supremacy Clause ensure this interpretation? Amphictyon believed this to be a noble sentiment. Still, the Court's expansive interpretation of the sweeping clause promoted the nominally limited government to an unlimited one in reality. Roane expanded this argument. Since Congress's limits were unchecked "it is in vain to talk of it as a limited government." Moreover, it was beyond him how Marshall's limited government could be supreme in the face of the sovereignty of the people.

The sphere of power attracted attention. Amphictyon invested the states with powers that controlled the people's everyday lives. Of course, a small, local government could more easily achieve this end. In addition, the people of the states were familiar with both their state legislatures and peculiar laws. If either government gathered excessive power into its hands, it "would inevitably erect a throne upon the ruins of the republic." Such an example would be the power of the federal government to tax state institutions.

According to Roane, only the people could increase power. "Subordinate agents" wielding the sweeping clause would introduce "indeterminable limits." Surely Congress must prove to its sovereign that it required an increase in power. Historically, this method had proved fruitful and had the advantage of avoiding the questionable application of the necessary and proper clause. A fair reading of the enumerated powers would satisfy anyone that the latter clause did not increase any powers that "existed in the government, before these words were used."

Roane dismissed the jurisdiction of the Court in this case because, essentially, it had not only adjudicated away the reserved rights of the states, but also it had no power to deny a state court verdict. The Union was federal, not consolidated, and the assumption that only the Court could decide constitutional issues was false. The Constitution had not "devolved that important duty" because to do so would allow the Court to amend it. "How far can a state be bound by acts of the general government violating, to its injury," he queried, "rights guaranteed to it, by the federal compact?" Since neither party could judge without prejudice, a neutral third party must adjudicate any dispute. Amphictyon agreed. It was ridiculous that one arm of the federal government — the Court — would adjudicate a dispute between the government and a signatory to the compact.

Marshall answered by reestablishing the need for a Supreme Court. If "local tribunals" judged the nation's laws, one could find no logical reason for the inclusion of the Court in the Constitution. Obviously, it was to judge national issues. Also, the clear language of the document delegated the Court power to decide. In *McCulloch*, either a congressional act was constitutional or it was not. Even *The Federalist* No. 80 proved "that the courts of the Union have, and ought to have jurisdiction, in all cases, arising under the constitution and laws of the United States." The Chief Justice ignored Roane's arbitration suggestion.

Did not this interpretation amount to constitutional amendment by the Court, not the people? Had not the Court evolved into a permanently seated Constitutional Convention? Marshall initially avoided the question by calling attention to a picayune error in Amphictyon's dissertation. Roane repeated the charge. "A new mode of amending the Constitution," he warned, "has been added to the ample ones provided in that instrument." Seemingly, the Court was blasé about which "representatives of the people" — state or federal — exercised power. Such was not acceptable to Roane. He demanded that the "adjustment of these powers ... is beyond their power, and ought not to be set aside." Only the people could amend government power. Was it not obvious that the states knew their own constituents better than the faraway federal government? Were Connecticut's representatives better equipped to make slave laws than those of South Carolina? In short, "the power of the supreme court is indeed great, but it does not extend to every thing; it is not great enough to *change* the constitution ...."

Marshall ignored these arguments. In his decision, he had reasserted the Court's power to declare congressional laws unconstitutional. "It would become the painful duty of this tribunal," he remarked, "should a case requiring such a decision come before it, to say that such an act was not the law of the land." Amphictyon rejected any premise that made the Court the "umpire" between the states and the federal government. The Chief Justice was unmoved. Again, he claimed the role of final arbiter for the Court and connected it to the need to oppose unconstitutional acts.

No other section was as highly scrutinized as the application of the necessary and proper clause. The Court initiated the debate. It proclaimed that even without the addition of the clause to Article I, Section 8, Congress had the choice of means to enhance its constitutional powers. This did not ring true for Roane. He reminded the *Enquirer's* readers that Madison's Report proved that only incidental powers attached to the clause. Amphictyon abhorred Marshall's "liberal" interpretation. He thought that the good of the country required a "restricted" construction. In reply, Marshall objected to the use of the pejorative term. He insisted that he sought only a fair ruling. After all, examine the location of the clause in the Constitution.

"The clause," he informed Roane, "is placed among the powers of Congress, and not among the limitations on these powers." Obviously, the sweeping clause did not limit power.

This grant/restriction dichotomy received close attention. Maryland's lawyer introduced it by arguing that the sweeping clause was "really restrictive of the general right, which might be otherwise implicit, of selecting means for executing the enumerated powers." Marshall thought this assertion far fetched. Constitutions designed Legislatures to legislate. If the lawyers' interpretation became popular, Congress could never select means to achieve its obvious ends. He insisted that the Convention intended this clause to "enlarge" the powers of Congress. If the Framers had wished to restrict Congress's powers they could easily have done so. Not only would any restrictive interpretation "arrest the progress of the government" but also it would reduce government benefits to the people. Soon, the states would usurp central government powers, presaging a return to the dreaded Articles' period. Counsel, and Amphictyon, insisted that one must interpret "necessary" as "indispensably necessary" to restrict its application. Marshall negated this thrust easily. He showed that a law that all considered fair could enhance tax collection although it could be done in more cumbersome ways.

Roane found the principal weakness in the constitutional placement theme. True, if the clause's thrust was a prohibition on legislation, that was its proper location. However, since "it was only contended that they create no enlargement of the powers previously given" it was placed correctly. "The words 'necessary and proper' ... did not enlarge the powers previously given, but were inserted only through abundant caution." Hammering home this point, he transported his audience back to the ratifying convention. Had not Marshall taken a different position? Yes, he had argued, Congress could not go beyond its delegated powers. Any law not warranted by an enumerated power would be void. Interestingly, "the powers not given to congress, were *retained* by the states and THAT without the aid of implication."

Amphictyon introduced a common state rights thread. If a reader interpreted each of the general welfare and necessary and proper clauses liberally, did not the rationale for an enumeration ring hollow? Did the sweeping clause not attach implication only to enumerated powers? Following a long list of obnoxious, to him, possibilities, Amphictyon appealed to the common sense of his readers. Surely the liberal construction was "inadmissible."

At this point, Marshall made another of his incredible bold leaps of invention. Recall, the Court had objected to Maryland's assertion that the sweeping clause limited Congress's powers. Simply put, the clause did not enlarge those already in existence. Mark the sequel. The Court had proven, said Marshall, that the clause did not enhance the enumerated powers. In addition, because the power level remained the same, one could not argue that the sweeping clause constricted the government's means for effecting an enumerated clause. Now, Marshall leaped to his conclusion. Since the necessary and proper clause did not restrict the means, "the court then has not contended that the grant enlarges, but that it does not restrain the powers of Congress." This opened the door to the expansion of incidental powers.

Although no clause in the Constitution enumerated a power to establish a bank or corporation, neither did it forbid "incidental or implied powers." Amphictyon construed the Constitution as conferring "on Congress the power of resorting to such means as are incidental to the express powers; to such means as directly and necessarily tend to the desired effect." Marshall cast aside the inference that the implication had to be "indispensable." Such an interpretation was "impractical" because "every case presents a choice of means." Clearly, Marshall accepted the notion that several incidents might attach to an enumerated power, none of them indispensable.

Roane sided with Amphictyon. He concluded that the inability of incorporation's friends to single out the enumerated power to which the bank attached bolstered the critic's case. Marshall realized that this requirement would strangle his view of congressional powers because an "indispensable" incident inferred an enumerated power that "cannot be executed." Perhaps it should be "natural, direct, and appropriate" to the enumerated power. Amphictyon approved a different test. First, Congress should examine a bill to confirm that the Constitution expressly granted the powers within it. If not, could the Legislature show it to be an incident *"without which"* it could not execute the power? If it could prove neither scenario, the power was reserved to the states or the people and it should reject the means and law.

Perhaps the most belabored sub-topic was the role of means and ends. Court supporters' credo insisted that Congress must have the means to achieve its ends. Marshall suggested that a legislative body entrusted "with such ample powers ... must be entrusted with ample means for their execution." Otherwise "the happiness and prosperity of the nation" might suffer. Was it not obvious that if any government had a power it must select the means to execute it? To emphasize his argument, he specified that he meant "any means calculated to produce the end." It seemed clear to him that the Framers never contemplated strict construction as a road to national benefits and success. It would change the Constitution into a law code by requiring many amendments for each case. Now, Virginians could trust the Legislature to employ the best means possible. He expressed his opinion in the oft-quoted, but still powerful phrase "Let the end be legitimate, let it be within the scope of the constitution, and all means which are appropriate, which are plainly adopted to that end, which are not prohibited, but consist with the letter and spirit of the constitution, are constitutional."

Roane employed means and ends differently. A general grant of power "carries with it all means (and those only) which are necessary to the perfection of the grant, or the execution of the power" and many law codes supported his position. Moreover, the grant of power should never impinge on the reserved rights of a compact party. His reading of Madison's Report convinced him that the onus was on the government to prove its assumption of power to be constitutional. In that case, "the dictates of reason" selected the means and the terms necessary and proper did not come into play. Of course, Roane also denied Marshall's contention that Congress must have ample means. If such was truly the case, he declared, then the government could turn to the people for permission to extend its power.

While other debaters might have proposed all these arguments, Marshall offered a special one that confirmed his innovative flair. He announced that the arguments separating enumerated powers from their incidents were superfluous because the two were not distinct. "The power to do a thing, and the power to carry that thing into execution," he proposed, "are ... the same power, and one cannot be termed with propriety 'additional' or 'incidental' to the other." So-called incidental powers were merely "the execution of one expressly granted ... and are part of the original grant." It would be a grave mistake to pretend "that such vast powers draw after them others which are inferior." As a result, "the means are appropriate, and congress may, constitutionally, select and vary them at will."

James Madison was surprised by the decision. He expressed his opinion soon after to Roane.

> But it was anticipated, I believe, by few, if any, of the friends of the Constitution, that a rule of construction would be introduced as broad and pliant as what has occurred. And those who recollect, and still more, those who shared in what passed in the State conventions, through which the people ratified the Constitution, with respect to the extent of the powers vested in Congress, cannot easily be persuaded that the avowal of such a rule would not have prevented its ratification.

Marshall's arguments won few Virginia converts to his nationalist theory of the nature of the Union. Instead, they revitalized the state rights men and provided a target for their political and philosophical attacks. But, they must bear another burden. No longer could they expect the Court to limit a power hungry Congress. Checks and balances promised a balanced government but it had proved illusory. The compact parties would have to add another weapon to their state rights arsenal to counteract the claims of the Court.

Jefferson endorsed Roane's ideas completely. "They contain," he wrote, "the true principles of the revolution of 1800." Nevertheless, he feared that the judiciary branch was intent on promoting consolidation. Roane was correct that the Constitution outlined a relationship between federal courts rather than between federal and state. Decisions like this were bound to destroy any illusion of checks and balances. Because the Court persistently introduced extraneous opinions, "the constitution ... is a mere thing of wax in the hands of the judiciary, which they may twist, and shape into any form they please."

Madison seconded Jefferson's enthusiasm for the Hampden articles. Surely, "the decision did not call for the general and abstract doctrine interwoven with the decision of the particular case." Judicial decisions should never depend on external generalities. Unfortunately, the verdict enhanced implied powers because "what is an end in one case may be a means in another." As a result, any congressional power "not expressly prohibited" might be used to bolster some specific power.

In December 1819, the legislature added its voice to the chorus of complaints. It introduced, but did not pass, two separate sets of resolutions damning the decision. The most prominent sought a Constitutional amendment establishing a separate court whose single duty was to adjudicate disputes between the general government and the states. Each jurisdiction would choose its members. Although this appeared to be an academic exercise, it provided fodder for a later attempt to limit the Court's jurisdiction.[1]

The Court announced the complicated verdict in the case *Cohens v. Virginia* during a severe economic depression — the panic of 1819 — and increasing Virginia suspicion toward its decisions. Virginians often blamed the hated Second Bank of the United States for the depression and some of its actions earned this enmity. It had been at the forefront of land speculation through its easy credit policy.

Virginia had lost much prestige earned during the Dynasty. New York had a greater population and Old Dominion congressional representation fell to third. In addition, soil exhaustion and migration rent its farming community. The new westerners demanded constitutional reforms to match its population growth forcing Richmond to modify suffrage and representation. The result was a more diverse political organization.

As we outlined, Virginia political tradition was strict constructionist, state rights, and Republican. Her citizens took pride in the Principles of '98 and the role they had played in both the election of the Dynasty and the political health of the country. The various Court decisions and public debate reawakened this proclivity because their nationalistic declarations alarmed strict constructionists.

Mimicking the past, several shifting interest groups based on family alliances, political issues, or ideological beliefs populated the House of Delegates although its members were nominally Republican or Federalist. Republicans of different stripes dominated but some traditional Federalist strongholds remained. In Washington, most Virginia representatives followed the moderate Republican theories of Jefferson and Madison, but it was true that some preferred different versions. The tendency was to fragmentation, not amalgamation. State rights men could find themselves separated from their allies politically by other issues.

The rise of the West was one instance since its economic goals differed from those of the East. Internal improvements, both federal and state, were mandatory for its development and played a central role in its political identity. Despite promises of suffrage and representation reforms, westerners decided they were second-class citizens. Their goal was to seek Virginia reform, not defend state rights from nationalist incursions.

No comments on politics in this period would be complete without reference to the so-called Richmond Junto. Historians had often portrayed it as a family compact led by Spencer Roane. Supposedly, it maintained a firm grip on Virginia policy. This was an over exaggeration. The editor of the *Richmond Whig* invented it for political purposes. The Junto purportedly voiced its opinions through Thomas Ritchie, editor of the *Richmond Enquirer*. No doubt this group wielded what power it could, but it never controlled the government. The *Cohens* case displayed its limitations. Although the *Enquirer* made its pages available for Supreme Court attacks, Justice Roane's published resolutions for constitutional amendments to limit its powers never passed the legislature.

Motivation for the attack on this decision was clear. Virginia state rights men, and Roane in particular, saw the *Cohens* case as a vehicle for both awakening Americans to a serious Constitutional crisis and reminding Virginians of their heritage. If his effort were successful, he might bind future Supreme Court justices through an overwhelming popular response. The upshot would be a federal republic with balanced state and national governments. No longer would Virginians need worry about constitutional amendments by decree. Of course, one cannot ignore the political arena. A public state rights victory was bound to benefit its political forces. Thus, Roane urged the American people to demand their constitutional rights, without violence, to protect liberty and restore constitutional integrity. In his opening address to them, Roane wrote "I address you under a solemn conviction, that the liberties and constitution of our country are endangered:— deeply and vitally endangered, by the fatal effects of that decision [*Cohens vs. Virginia*]." One last comment was necessary. Despite the importance of state sovereignty, slavery was not an issue in *Cohens*.

The reader should be warned that this was a very complicated case with overlapping arguments. They have been distilled and collated below with a minimum of legal gymnastics. Nevertheless, one must realize that the presentation below did not mirror the order of Court events.

In August 1820 the Hustings Norfolk Borough Court of Virginia fined Philip and Mendez Cohen $100 for selling lottery tickets. They thought that they had the protection of a District of Columbia statute. A Virginia act prohibited these sales because it sought to protect its own financial laws and simultaneously place a brake on gambling. The Cohens took their case to the Supreme Court on a writ of error. On March 3, 1821, Marshall announced that the Constitution assigned the Court jurisdiction and two days later, he upheld Virginia's fine. It could prevent the sale of District of Columbia lottery tickets because Congress's statute did not include a specific clause that it superseded any state law. The decision hardly seemed to warrant the year and one-half of invective that poured down on Marshall. To find its genesis, we must examine the decision and Roane's comments closely.

Tactically, Marshall simultaneously ruled for Virginia in a forgettable case and produced four *dicta* that interpreters still actively support. He defined the Court's jurisdiction, interpreted the Eleventh Amendment, reasserted the Court's power to hear appeals from state courts, and opened the door to the possibility that District laws might change state statutes. The outward appearance was a balanced decision. Nevertheless, it enhanced nationalism while striking state rights a body blow.

One may be unsympathetic to the results of Marshall's decision, but surely one must admire the tenacity with which he charged toward his goals. He made important comments on at least twelve major disputes on the Union's nature. True, several questionable passages populated his rulings. In fact he bent the truth in a few instances to fit his theory of government. However, the reader must realize that Marshall was determined, using any tool at his disposal, to remove the sovereignty plank from state rights. This case provided a means to this end.

The Chief Justice tried to muzzle Roane's criticisms. Based on information that the *American Law Journal* of Philadelphia would reproduce Roane's Court analysis, Marshall asked Justice Story to attempt to interdict it. If that did not work, he suggested Story pressure the editor to infer that publication was a favor to Thomas Jefferson, who Marshall identified as the real culprit behind Virginia's attacks on his ruling. Obviously, Marshall was willing to circumvent freedom of the press.

Virginia's counsels in the jurisdiction phase were two gentlemen familiar with congressional state rights' battles, Philip P. Barbour and Alexander Smyth. The eminent jurists David B. Ogden and William Pinkney opposed them. They examined jurisdiction under a writ of error sought by the Cohen brothers against the state of Virginia. The Court made all the lasting decisions in this phase. Although the jurisdictional disputes were often overlapping, we will treat them as discrete events for ease of handling. Hopefully, this in-depth examination will inform the reader why state rights men found the decision so devastating.

> Article III, Section 2, United States Constitution
>   The judicial power shall extend to all cases ... between a state and citizens of another state....
> Eleventh Amendment to the United States Constitution
>   The judicial power of the United States shall not be construed to extend to any suit in law or equity, commenced or prosecuted against one of the United States by citizens of another state, or by citizens or subjects of any foreign state.
> Section 25 of the Judiciary Act of 1789
>   And be it further enacted, That a final judgment or decree in any suit, in the highest court of law or equity of a State in which a decision in the suit could be had, ... or where is drawn in question the construction of any clause of the constitution, or of a treaty, or statute ... may be re-examined and reversed or affirmed in the Supreme Court of the United States upon a writ of error.... But no other error shall be assigned or regarded as a ground of reversal in any such case as aforesaid, than such as appears on the face of the record....

Barbour adamantly opposed the notion that an individual, without the sovereign and independent state's consent, could sue it. Before ratification the Articles had defined the states' sovereign authority. Nothing written in the Constitution changed it. Thus, the federal judicial power did not extend over the states. Smyth updated that view. An essential sovereign power was that "to pass and enforce" laws. Before ratification, states had that power. Afterward, it was a reserved right of the states because nothing in the Constitution delegated it to the Union.

Ogden harbored the opinion that the states had never had complete sovereignty. Instead, the sovereign people had delegated many powers and by zero sums, the states had lost them. Without total sovereignty, the states could not avoid Court scrutiny. Whenever a state exceeded constitutional restrictions, the Supreme Court, not a state tribunal, must adjudicate. In any case *Martin v. Hunter's Lessee* had settled the question whether states possessed immunity from all Supreme Court suits. In general, the Cohens' lawyers contended that "the judicial power of every well constituted government must be coextensive with the legislative and must be capable of deciding every judicial question which grows out of the Constitution and laws."

For Marshall, a case arising under the Constitution demanded that a government had denied a party a right the document conferred. If the correct decision required the Court to construe the Constitution, laws of the United States, or its treaties, it could intervene. Parroting Ogden, he reminded readers that the sovereign states had willingly surrendered some authority to benefit the American people. Whether a citizen could sue a sovereign state without consent turned on whether the Constitution recognized what was, or was not, surrendered. Occasionally it might, vaguely, be simply to "maintain the principles established in the Constitution."

The Framers knew they must delegate their preferred government "with large portions of the sovereignty which belongs to individual states." This was a fundamental of the Constitution. Within it was a clause claiming the supremacy of the Constitution and laws of the United States that defined the relationship between the general government and state legislatures. To confer "ample powers" on the government, the states had to accept limited sovereignty. If all these factors were considered — the nature of the Constitution, state subservience to it, and its relation to the Union — it was evident why "the great purpose for which jurisdiction over all cases arising under the Constitution and laws of the United States is confided to the judicial department." Did it make sense to note an exception to excuse a state from the Court's jurisdiction? In Marshall's opinion "we think a case arising under the Constitution or laws of the United States is cognizable in the Courts of the union whoever may be the parties" because a state cannot be exempted from "the spirit of the Constitution."

Roane considered this faulty logic. On their face, both the Eleventh Amendment and Article III disputed this shaky claim. Moreover, as counsel argued, the Tenth Amendment had established the correct jurisdiction as a reserved power. Virginia had not argued that it could never be brought to Court, but it did object if the plaintiff were a Virginia citizen. In addition, the Court recognized that this was true in the case in which the disputed law was a Virginia law. Why could it then claim jurisdiction under the Constitution or U.S. law? Perhaps the state court might be partial but the Court's original jurisdiction solved that problem. However, in *Cohens*, it disregarded the Constitutional restrictions by involving itself in the appeal stage. We will examine this conundrum later.

Marshall had predicted that if the Court could not reexamine a state verdict, the general government would become subservient to it. Roane reminded him that the states could also make this argument. If the Court had the power, federal courts would demolish state tribunals with no checks and balances. In other words, each argument had an equal chance of usurpation associated with it. Why not let each have a veto on the other with the people acting as arbiter? That scenario required no subservience, one to the other.

Virginia was certain that potential Court jurisdiction in a case in which a citizen attempted to appeal a state decision to the Supreme Court failed four tests. Not only did it violate specific constitutional instructions but also Court precedent and "the spirit" of the Eleventh Amendment prevented it. In addition, the Court could not review the state ruling because neither the Constitution nor United States law had been broken. The law under examination was a state law and according to Philip Barbour, the lack of constitutional jurisdiction extended to cases involving the states. Article III supported that interpretation. All other cases had appellate jurisdiction. This was exactly the distinction, as we reported, that

Marshall had made several years previously in *Marbury v. Madison*. He had rejected Section 13 of the Judiciary Act of 1789 that allowed it to "issue a writ of mandamus, because the mandamus was an original form used in a case where the Constitution gives the Court only appellate authority."

Smyth had another opinion. According to the Constitution, the federal judicial power could only correct errors made in a federal court but could never "revise" one originating in a state court. The power to "reverse a constitutional act of the state executive or legislature ... gives it no power over state courts." They could provide this function and could even declare a congressional act unconstitutional. Could one find the Constitutional mechanism that allowed appeals from a state court? Surely if the Framers had contemplated such an easy-to-accomplish end, they would have specified it. Charles Hammond, a distinguished commentator, chided Marshall for his opinion. It did not follow constitutional principles of jurisdiction and embarrassingly, opposed his *Marbury v. Madison* decision. At that juncture, he had argued the "plain words" of the Constitution separated original from appellate jurisdiction and resulted in Section 13 of the Judiciary Act being declared unconstitutional.

Marshall agreed with David Ogden that these differences had been satisfied in the *Martin* case. However, he expanded this argument. First, arguing that the federal court system was separate from that of the individual states was nonsensical. Only a misreading of the Constitution could elicit that opinion. The United States was a single nation and its judiciary interpreted the laws. If the United States adopted Virginia's suggestion, each state court would be a constitutional interpreter. Also, the people considered the United States to be a single nation. This translated to a belief that the Constitution "gave the Supreme Court power to hear cases involving the Constitution and laws of the nation, and to exercise that power by appeal."

Spencer Roane was confident that both the state courts were distinct from the general government and the states needed no constitutional exceptions to prevent a case from proceeding to the Court. The Constitution delegated government powers, including Court jurisdiction, and it could not derive them from any "remote implication." They required specific Constitutional support. The Tenth Amendment had settled that score "unequivocally." Where was the clause that defined this jurisdiction? If, as expected, one could not find it, the state's reserved powers exempted both the states and the people from the Court's jurisdiction. To sidestep this conundrum, the Court had declared itself the final arbiter, inferring that the states had no reserved powers.

Marshall and Roane could not even agree on the genesis of the Eleventh Amendment. Marshall maintained that debt servicing, not the protection of state sovereignty, initiated it. To do so, the states had tried to prevent an individual from taking a state to federal court. He was unphased by any declaration that a trial in federal court injured state dignity since the Constitution defined several instances in which a state must stand before the Court.

This characterization of the genesis of the Eleventh Amendment was evidently fanciful. It was a direct outgrowth of a Supreme Court case — *Chisholm v. Georgia* (1793) — and several Virginia assembly resolutions. Roane stressed that the Court interpretation did not comport with the understanding of those who had ratified the Eleventh. The states expected the case to initiate sovereign immunity. As early as December 3, 1793, Virginia had instructed its representatives to secure an amendment assuring immunity. The resolution declared the *Chisholm* decision was "*inconsistent with, and dangerous to, the sovereignty and independence of the individual states* as the same tends to a *general consolidation* of these *confederated* republics.[italics Roane]" Thus, Marshall had violated the Eleventh Amendment by bringing

Virginia before the Court. Unless Virginia fought this usurpation, the Court's road to jurisdictional power—"in all cases"—would be smoothed. It would circumvent the true basis of the Eleventh Amendment, the plain words of Article III, and the state's Tenth Amendment reserved powers. Make no mistake, said Roane, one could find instances in which one could sue a state, but the Eleventh Amendment contained a positive restriction. Its protection did not require Virginia to give up its sovereign rights and suffer the indignity of being dragged before the Court.

The reason that the Eleventh Amendment did not apply, said Marshall, in *Cohens* revolved around the requirements for an appeal. This jurisdictional dispute was not an appeal, although it had its features. Instead, it was a writ of error. After a lengthy, unintelligible to a layperson, comparison, Marshall concluded that it was also not a suit as usually defined by that term. Therefore, the Eleventh Amendment did not apply. A writ of error's principal function was to transmit the case from one jurisdiction to another for examination but it did not initiate a suit if no restoration of the plaintiff's property occurred. The Cohens brothers had this right because Virginia had convicted them but their defense was a law of the United States. The writ of error—transfer—allowed the Court to decide whether Virginia had violated the Cohens' Constitutional rights.

For Roane, Marshall's assertion that the Eleventh Amendment did not apply to cases like *Cohens* failed miserably because its specific language contemplated the case facts. Thus, a state could be neither a plaintiff nor a defendant. As a result, Court arguments that it must interpret the Eleventh in the "general interest" were unconvincing. Roane categorized Marshall's manipulations of the Eleventh Amendment as so slender "as only to be seen through a magnifying glass invented by the Court, in favor of their own prejudices and love of power." Charles Hammond agreed. The states had passed the Eleventh Amendment to limit any constitutional interpretation that suits could be brought against the state by an individual.

Roane floated another interesting, but undeveloped, argument. He found something untoward about the dynamics of the case transfer and Marshall's theory. Recall, the Chief Justice argued that he could examine a state case to discover whether it had unconstitutional features. However, if the Constitution and Eleventh Amendment blocked such a transfer—a writ of error—how could Marshall examine it or the documents concerning it? He had no choice but to invent paths around these barriers.

> From Article III, Section 2
>
> In all cases affecting ambassadors, other public ministers and consuls, and those in which a state shall be party, the Supreme Court shall have original jurisdiction. In all the other cases before mentioned, the Supreme Court shall have appellate jurisdiction, both as to law and fact, with such exceptions, and under such regulations as the Congress shall make.

Although we noticed a dispute concerning original or appellate jurisdiction previously, a wider ranging examination was necessary because of Marshall's inventive genius. James Barbour had initiated the discussion. The Court made Virginia a party in this case by a writ of error, "which is surely appellate jurisdiction." "But, it has only original jurisdiction since the case involved a state," thus the Court assumed prohibited jurisdiction.

Marshall applied considerable effort to disprove this contention. According to Virginia, the Constitution, in plain language, limited the Court's jurisdiction to original and not appellate forms. Moreover, these jurisdictions were mutually exclusive. On the other hand, Marshall reminded his readers that the Supreme Court had jurisdiction over cases involving the Constitution and U.S. law. Was it not true that this delegation was just as powerful as the Virginia example? If so, the Court faced a conundrum. If a state were a party, court jurisdiction was original, but if it involved the Constitution and U.S. law it was appellate. Marshall supposed that the best solution to untying this knot was to include each possibility while maintaining the Constitution's intent.

Categorizing the possible court cases might lead to a solution. They seemed to divide themselves into two groups, one defined by the character of the parties, the other by the nature of the controversy "contemplated by the Constitution." Under this division, only two extensions were possible. Either "jurisdiction is founded entirely on the character of the case, and the parties are not contemplated by the Constitution" or "on the character of the parties, and the nature of the case is not contemplated by the Constitution." If one accepted this organization, then the former explanation, in which the Constitution did not contemplate the parties, would lead to original jurisdiction while the latter, which prevented the nature of the controversy from being contemplated by the Constitution, would be appellate. Thus, Virginia was incorrect. Marshall could prove, using this construction, that the Court's jurisdiction was appellate and original.

If the above manipulations did not meet with approbation, Marshall offered two other reasons why the Court had appellate power. Cases existed in which only original jurisdiction seemed proper, but a reexamination might find a contained reference to the Constitution or U.S. law. If so, it warranted appellate jurisdiction. Also, the clause defining original jurisdiction did not forbid appeals so one could decry its adoption. Finally, Marshall declared this "tribunal invested with appellate jurisdiction in all cases arising under the Constitution and laws of the United States. We find no exception to this grant and we cannot insert one." Of course, one wondered how Marshall's gymnastic display concerning a writ of error comported with his conclusion since it was not an appeal.

References to his decision in *Marbury v. Madison* had stung Marshall because it directly challenged his interpretation in *Cohens v. Virginia*. He wrote, unconvincingly, that the *dicta* accompanying the *Marbury* case applied only to it and no one should generalize and apply it to others. *Marbury* was interested in whether the Legislature could assign the Supreme Court original jurisdiction if the Constitution had not done so. Arguments from counsel had elicited generalities from Marshall. One included the assertion that Congress had unbounded Legislative discretion to apportion power to the Court, which resulted in a Marshall *dictum*. He decided that Congress could not define its powers without Constitutional support. Admittedly, Marshall had gone beyond the bounds of the case to claim that positive words from the Constitution inferred a negative interpretation to other jurisdictional grants.

The Marshall critic, Charles Hammond, was unimpressed by this explanation. Marshall had ruled "the plain import of the words seems to be that in one class of cases its [Supreme Court] jurisdiction is original, and not appellate, in the other it is appellate, *and not original* [italics added]." Clearly, Marshall, at that juncture, considered the two jurisdictions mutually exclusive.

Roane asserted that Marshall knew he did not have jurisdiction. His ploy was to "remedy the deficiency" by scooping it up under an "all cases" condition. If the Framers had contemplated Marshall's interpretation, they could have included it in the Constitution since it would have been very easy to accomplish.

He had two other objections. It was "unseemly" for the Court to accept a case for appeal that it would never have accepted for original jurisdiction. Also, he was at a loss to understand how Marshall had managed to infer an appellate jurisdiction from the plain words of the Constitution. If the Court could achieve appellate jurisdiction in this fashion, nothing could stop it from hearing "all cases whatsoever" and "whoever be the parties." Neither of these constructions followed, according to Roane, and he supplied a comprehensive list of cases that disputed the contention that Americans could appeal all cases to the Court. Logically, this exercise defeated Marshall's notion that it could adjudicate all cases. Continuing his assertion that the state courts were independent, Roane noted one could not "appeal to the court of another government" because it had no power to force the losing party to obey.

An examination of Article III, Section 2 revealed straightforward instructions. The first clause listed the case classifications that the Court could adjudicate. The second parceled out jurisdiction, some appellate, some original. Surely this interpretation was more acceptable than the gyrations that Marshall had gone through to give himself jurisdiction. Also, it avoided the claim over "all cases" which Roane had exploded earlier.

Marshall had assumed that the Court could adjust state court judgments. Moreover, the states were not independent. Unfortunately for him, said Roane, no Constitutional words supported that claim. The Constitution's reference to inferior federal courts satisfied its need for an appellate power. Yet by ignoring the boundaries between the two systems, state and federal, the Court sought to reverse a case of another government. This was not to argue that no cases existed in which the United States formed a single entity. However, in all others, the states were sovereign and independent. As such, they had never delegated the Court the appellate power assumed in *Cohens*. To get this power, the court must amend the Constitution in the usual way.

The jurisdictional dispute seemed to be unraveling toward a contention that the Court had legal authority in all constitutional cases. James Barbour considered this unlikely because he could list several counterexamples. If one wrote "all cases" one inferred "without exception." David Ogden disagreed. When the Constitution mentioned original jurisdiction later, it was not a limit, but an extension of an existing power. Shuffling aside Barbour's examples, he admitted that yes, one might violate the Constitution without Court recourse. However, it could always intervene in cases involving the Constitution, without reference to the parties, because "every well constituted government must be coextensive with the legislature and must be capable of deciding every judicial question which grows out of the Constitution and laws."

Marshall began with the truism that the Court's role was to preserve the Constitution and laws of the United States. Originally, it could examine controversies between a state and individuals. Once a state became a party, the Court automatically got jurisdiction. Every American, according to the Constitution, had "a right to submit his case to the Court of the nation." Thus, in an expansion of that concept, a case "may truly be said to arise under the Constitution or a law of the United States, whenever its correct decision depends on the construction of either." The Court was indeed supreme.

Roane was aghast at Marshall's assertions. How could one argue for the jurisdiction of "all cases" and simultaneously ignore the exceptions? A government agency should never adjudicate a controversy to which it was a party. The jurisdiction, despite others' contentions, did not depend on a well constituted government. Although this might have some credence in a government of general powers, all United States departments had only limited power. For example, were not Congress's powers enumerated and limited? Surely Marshall's argument was interesting philosophy, but it did not belong in a legal brief.

The Court contention that the Convention had invented it primarily to preserve the Constitution and laws of the United States did not sway Roane. He fell back on a familiar argument to a Marshall unproved generality. Where was the authority that supported the assertion? What constitutional article stated this fact? "If it [Constitution] was intended to be given in so important and unreasonable a case," he asked, "would it not have been *expressly* given?"

Virginia's counsels reminded the Court that any review of such a criminal case ran counter to Court precedent because it must originate in a state court. Since the Court had no appellate jurisdiction in such a case, it was "outside the court's purview." David Ogden challenged the categorization of the *Cohens* case as criminal. Virginia had never made the selling of lottery tickets a misdemeanor. It sought only the fine. If this strange argument did not satisfy a reader, Ogden, and later Marshall, lumped it into the category of "all cases" for jurisdiction.

Roane saw a different dynamic at work. By claiming the jurisdiction over state criminal cases, the Court implied that Virginia was incompetent in her own house. Not only that, but also the Supreme Court could not trust its equivalent in Virginia to rule impartially.

> From Article III, Section 2
>   The judicial power shall extend to all cases, in law and equity, arising under this Constitution, the laws of the United States, and treaties made, or which shall be made, under their authority; — to all cases affecting ambassadors, other public ministers and consuls; — to all cases of admiralty and maritime jurisdiction; — to controversies to which the United States shall be a party; — to controversies between two or more states; — between a state and citizens of another state; — between citizens of different states; — between citizens of the same state claiming lands under grants of different states, and between a state, or the citizens thereof, and foreign states, citizens or subjects.

The juristictional question represented Roane's primary thrust. The concept of jurisdiction "whoever may be the parties" was seldom mentioned in the Virginia ratification convention although George Mason had referred to the possibility that a sovereign state could face an appeal by a citizen in a federal court. However, George Nicholas allayed his fear. The Constitution did not warrant such an interpretation and John Marshall supported this contention. According to Roane,

> Mr. Marshall, in the convention, *more* then decided this case against his *present* opinion. He denied that, even in controversies between a state and citizens of *another* state, the states could be "dragged" to the bar of the federal court. He said that the express provision in the judicial article, in relation to this case, could not be expounded so as to make a sovereign state a *defendant* in the federal courts. The opinion of this very able man was *then* governed by substance, and not by forms. Great principles then operated on his luminous mind, not hair-splitting quibbles and verbal criticisms.... So high then was the respect for the sovereignty of the states, and so strict were these great men ... that even under the express provision of the third article, and in relation to *other* states, the construction now in question was reprobated.... Every argument then used holds *a fortiori* between a state and its own citizens. That was the case under the original constitution; but the eleventh amendment to it, has put the matter entirely at rest.

Marshall's contradictory opinions gave Roane an easy target for challenging the Chief Justice's credibility. He spent considerable effort making his case against this jurisdictional assumption. Obviously, the Constitution expected the parties to any suit to be well defined — "proper parties" — and to litigate the case in the "proper court." Roane found Marshall's contention that people may be legal parties, or otherwise, and jurisdiction claimed, or not, according to only the documents or laws associated with the claim, ludicrous. "It is a novelty even in the Supreme Court itself." He listed instances in which the Court refused cases either because a previous court did not define the parties or had transferred them from an improper court. One need only read the Constitution to understand that it expected specific parties to a suit, without any exceptions. The enumeration was exhaustive.

No one, said Roane, should conclude that if the Constitution delegated some enumerated powers, then the rest automatically followed. Here, the application of that forbidden rule allowed the Court to assume that which it must prove, i.e., the general wording of the Constitutional article included this case. As a result, it was based on an ignorance and rejection of the need for proper parties because "a sovereign state cannot be made a party, in the courts of another state, without its consent."

Roane again supplied examples to highlight the exceptions to Marshall's general rule "whoever may be the parties." A particularly effective one concerned Court judges. Suppose a case involved "a cause of the judges themselves.... The great error of the Court consists, in forgetting that in a case conferring jurisdiction, the existence of necessary parties is always presupposed." Judges could not adjudicate impartially cases involving themselves.

How did Marshall, according to Roane, avoid this difficulty? If he could not, no one could define cases arising from the Constitution. Marshall's interpretation of the general clause "presupposes *cases* proper for the cognizance of the court, and those cases also presuppose the existence of the necessary *parties*."

Was it possible that a District law could apply in Virginia? James Barbour outlined the Virginia perspective against any insinuation that a District statute could supersede a state law. The Court did not have jurisdiction because the District law in question was local, not national. Both the Constitution and Section 25 of the Judiciary Act of 1789 stipulated this requirement. Article III defined Court jurisdiction to cases involving the Constitution, laws of the United States, or treaties, but did not include state law. Thus, laws of the District of Columbia did not qualify. Alexander Smyth added that Congress could establish only "local codes" for the District. Although they resembled congressional acts, they were not. Otherwise, one would have to argue that Congress had an external power over a state. Therefore, the lottery law was only a local ordinance, not United States law.

Cohens' counsel did not dispute Smyth's interpretation, but Ogden pointed out that the ultimate test was the Constitution. To examine the act and test its constitutionality the Court must have jurisdiction. William Pinkney offered a corollary. It was not the law but the Court record that might give the Court jurisdiction. The District was a Constitutional construct, thus the Court might become involved.

Chief Justice Marshall's reasoning was brief. The enumerated powers gave Congress jurisdiction over the District. Also, Congress was the legislative body, and "in legislating for the District, they necessarily preserve the character of the legislature of the Union." Moreover, Article VI, Section 2 made the laws of the United States supreme. Thus, the lottery law "binds all the states."

Flabbergasted by this assertion, Roane commented that Marshall forced the legislature of the District to act as a congressional surrogate in order for the Court to elevate one of its local ordinances to a United States statute. If he were correct, it must supersede any state law on the subject. Still, no one had presented any evidence that the Virginia law was "objectionable." Certainly a District ordinance was not applicable in Virginia and could not protect the Cohens there.

Marshall had claimed that the original court, the Hustings Court for the Borough of Norfolk, was the highest state court that could hear the case. This was incorrect. Higher courts that could hear criminal cases existed. Also, one might view it as a civil rights action. In either event, the Court should return the jurisdiction to Virginia for further examination.

> Section 22. And be it further enacted.... And upon a like process, may final judgments and
> decrees in civil actions, and suits in equity in a circuit court, brought there by original
> process, or removed there from courts of the several States, or removed there by appeal from

a district court where the matter in dispute exceeds the sum or value of two thousand dollars, exclusive of costs, be re-examined and reversed or affirmed in the Supreme Court....

Marshall and Roane had little to say on the subject. Marshall simply declared that it mirrored the *Cohens* case exactly and authorized the Court's claim to jurisdiction. Roane countered that whenever a case excluded a cause originally, it was embarrassing to apply it later in the case.

The major critic was Charles Hammond. Even if the Constitution allowed Court jurisdiction, one could not extend it to Congress assigning the Court power to review *Cohens* or every criminal case. Section 25 contemplated a writ of error from the highest state court but Section 22 limited a writ to civil suits more than $2000. Marshall had no right to ignore sections of the Act that directly rejected its application.

The Judiciary Act did not provide for criminal suits nor any mechanism for returning a case for reconsideration. Congress could make these changes, but until they did, *Cohens v. Virginia* was not a Judiciary Act suit defined by Section 25.

The Court's pronouncement that it was always the final arbiter of the jurisdiction necessarily included those cases that, according to Roane, trampled a state's reserved rights. One should never forget that the general government was partly federal, partly national, and except certain delegated powers, the states remained sovereign and independent. The confederation was a compact between two parties and neither could rule on the competency of the other. They should put all disputed cases to the people or a neutral adjudicator.

Spencer Roane was adamant about the reach of the Supremacy Clause. "The supremacy yielded by the constitution, is to that constitution, itself," he interpreted, "and the laws duly made under it, but does not extend to unwarranted expositions thereof, by the courts of *one* of the contracting parties." Considering the retention of reserved rights defined in the Tenth Amendment, labelling it supreme was a misnomer. Were not Congress's powers delegated by a sovereign power? "A government which is only entrusted with a few powers," he said, "and is acting upon these powers, by the expression of the constitution, as to such as are granted, and by the degree of necessity as to such as are implied, can scarcely be said to be supreme."

Roane posited one interesting theory. The Court had jurisdictional supremacy over only its own inferior courts defined in the Constitution and enabled by Congress. It had no power over state courts. Examine the Constitution closely. One will see the words "before mentioned" restricting appeals to those defined in the preceding article. That article does not mention state courts. Therefore, the two systems had different spheres of jurisdiction and power.

Any exposition on the Union's nature required an interpretation of the meaning of "the people." Marshall defined them as those who had given the supreme general government "ample powers" to achieve the blessings noted in the Preamble to the Constitution. There was little doubt that for the Chief Justice, the people were the one people of the United States, not the people of the states acting in their highest sovereign capacity.

Roane's people were simultaneously the people of the state and the parties to the general government. In each role they had "different rights." Since this was evident, "the interest of each state, in the federal government of the union, does not permit the administrators of that government, to encroach on the municipal rights reserved to the several states, by the confederation." The people, acting as the people of the state, decided the limits of power delegated to the "citizens of America."

Because of the breadth of the issues related to this case, we have already met some effects on sovereignty and state rights. Nevertheless, others followed.

Marshall reminded us that if a state surrendered some sovereignty, "the question whether a liability to suit be a part of this portion depends on the instrument by which the surrender is made." If an examination of the Constitution proved that a state can be sued, then one must agree that the state had surrendered the power "of judging in every case on the justice of its own pretensions, and has entrusted that power to a tribunal in whose impartiality it confides."

Also, the Union depended on the states for "large portions" of its sovereignty. For example, the Constitution designed some portions to benefit the people. The Court was one "instrument" that could insure this designation. It had the power to adjudicate "all cases of every description arising under the Constitution or laws of the United States" without excepting the states whom they could bring to Court.

The people, said Marshall, knew that the general government was supreme while exercising its delegated powers. "It can, then, in effecting these objects, legitimately control all individuals or governments within the American territory.... The states are constituted parts of the United States." Therefore, the Court could overturn state laws. Otherwise, many disparate courts could adjudicate the same issue. To a Virginia counsel's assertion that the extension of Court power defeated the spirit of the Constitution, Marshall riposted that,

> Let the nature and objects of our Union be considered; let the great fundamental principles on which the fabric stands be examined; and we think the result must be that there is nothing so extravagantly absurd in giving to the Court of the nation the power of revising the decisions of local tribunals on questions which affect the nation as to require that words which import this power should be restricted by a forced construction.

Roane insisted that Americans formed the Union from a compact and Congress was a "subordinate agent[s]." Therefore, one compact party could not "pass finally upon the chartered rights of another." States lost no sovereignty when they made a delegation to the federal republic because they could reclaim delegated powers and resume them.

Specifically in this ruling the Court had insisted that the states were no longer sovereign and independent by reversing a state court ruling. The government treated the supreme courts of the states "as inferior federal tribunals" thus emphasizing the loss of sovereignty. The result would be a consolidation of the states, an apparent government goal. To Roane, "it is better that liberty and state-rights should be maintained, in some states, than no where." Consequently, the Virginia state legislature must continue to protest.

The Supreme Court had assumed that the states had few rights and that their legal arguments were fanciful while its own were correct. States would never find support from that branch. Combining his fear for Virginia's lost sovereignty with this case, Roane claimed, "there is no right more clearly appertaining to sovereignty, than an exemption from being sued, in the courts of another government."

Virginia claimed sovereignty and independence with a judiciary separate from that of the Union. Despite this contention, Marshall observed that it was unsupported by any word or clause in the Constitution. After presenting many examples to support his observation, he returned to a favorite maxim. Was it not obvious that a government that exercised limited powers was supreme with respect to them? Thus, "it can, in effecting these objects, legitimately control all individuals and governments within the American territory." A state law or constitutional article "repugnant to the Constitution" was void. As a result the states belong to "one great empire" sometimes sovereign, sometimes not.

Virginia state rights men's continued resort to the Tenth Amendment must baffle readers and provoke a review. Recall, that during the debate over the Bill of Rights, Congress had refused to add the word "expressly" to it. Had not this diluted its force? If one noticed its application only once, one could argue that it was simply a rhetorical flourish. However, as our study showed, men of unquestionable intelligence applied it for decades. The Virginia Dynasty, William Branch Giles, Spencer Roane, and a host of others saw it as a constitutional beacon. Was it possible that the story of the Tenth Amendment required reexamination? The short answer is yes.

For traditionalists, the Tenth was merely a declaration, a reminder of a power that would have existed even without the Amendment's inclusion. That right fell to them through the constitutional compact. By definition, it left nondelegated powers to the people, or the state. Parsing the Amendment was a waste of time. The concept was clear, and any omission of the word "expressly" had no impact on its applicability.

As noted, protests against the Court's decision lasted almost two years. Never had a Marshall decision received such scrutiny or promulgated such heated rhetoric. Those participating in the debate over federal-state relations were often veterans of the ratifying conventions. They brought to the debate their memories, and prejudices, of that convocation. All decided their opponents would destroy the Union.

Despite the rhetoric, Virginia state rights men could not attract enough support to hamstring Marshall or amend the Constitution. This was a blow to their collective ego because they had come to believe, based on the Jeffersonian revolution, that their form of protest was bound to produce favorable results. Its failure limited their field of action. As Ray Luce had recognized, "their failure became an important element in the evolution of state rights thought from a national defense of freedom and local control to a defense of sectional interests."

The Court decision and the newspaper outpouring served to prove that the two philosophical groups — nationalist and state rights — had little in common and in fact distrusted one another. Consolidation sprang from Virginia commentators' lips due to the attack on state sovereignty and rights. The shaky nature of some Marshall arguments exacerbated this concern. For example, it was inconceivable that Virginia's ratification included permission for anyone to sue it in federal court.

Marshall had achieved four goals inimical to state rights that we had defined previously. However, his most important foray was his attack on compact theory and the elevation of another nature of the Union interpretation. The *Washington National Intelligencer* hosted a spirited exchange, one of whose contentions was that the whole people of the United States, and not the states, established the Constitution. Roane was disconsolate. The decision could "only be accounted for, from a love of power, which all history informs us, infects and corrupts all who possess it, and from which even the high and ermined judges themselves, are not exempted."

The *Richmond Enquirer*, on March 12, wrote its epitaph on the case.

> Triumph not too soon, gentlemen — the crisis is, in truth, only postponed — it has not passed away. — We hope yet to see the usurpations of the Supreme Court and of Congress itself, discountenanced by the voice of an indignant nation, roused to a just sense of its rights.
> For our part we do not yet despair of the republic. The states or rather the people, will gradually awaken to the truths which Virginia has endeavored to support. She is actuated by no other consideration than an attachment to the constitution. She is yet firm to her faith. But she forbears at present pressing her opinions, and especially as the doctrines which she has most at heart, are not without their advocates in other quarters.

The Dynasty supported Roane's cause. Madison harshly criticized Marshall's decision and tactics. "It is to be regretted," he wrote, "that the Court is so much in the practice of mingling with their judgments pronounced, comments & reasonings of a scope beyond them; and that there is often an apparent disposition to amplify the authorities of the Union at the expence (sic) of those of the States." Marshall had ignored the plain language of the Constitution and particularly the Eleventh Amendment without reference to the original debates on them. Did not the Eleventh specifically introduce exceptions? Moreover, the "projectile capacity" of the District law was ridiculous. Madison repeated his definition of a compact and stressed it was not between governments.

The House of Delegates leapt into the fray on February 22, 1822. Spencer Roane had prepared five potential Constitutional amendments that would simultaneously curb congressional power and limit Court jurisdiction. Because of their content, Roane knew that they would never pass. Since his target was to influence the Senate deliberations, he was satisfied to make them public. Strangely, the house voted against postponing debate but tabled, and forgot them. The Senate followed the same course. There was no appetite for a messy Constitutional fight.[2]

Transitions

From 1800 to 1824, federal-state disputes shifted from a Federalist-Republican power struggle to a North-South contest and abolition rhetoric accelerated. However, one must be clear that, within the period, two dynamics operated. In Washington, the Republican Virginia Dynasty, with its emphasis on nationalistic programs ruled. For example, it was clear to it that despite earlier national bank fears, all parties had agreed on its importance to American economic prosperity. Toward the end of the second decade, driven by the Panic of 1819, Virginia's policy-sublimated state rights men reestablished dominance within the Republican party due to their certitude that questionable Bank policy had been the Panic's basis.

Due to its prominence in Virginia political thought, codifying state rights was natural. St. George Tucker chose to define the Union's nature by employing *Blackstone's Commentaries* as a foil. This tactic legitimized the effort because everyone acknowledged that Sir William Blackstone was that era's preeminent legal commentator. Importantly, one Tucker goal was to distinguish traditional state rights characteristics from those of its competitor for Virginians' fealty. It promoted dual compacts, and the important role strict construction played protecting individual rights. Its fundamental position was that the state consisted of the people acting in their highest sovereign capacity. Unlike their competitors, traditionalists relied on elections or the courts to solve problems of usurpation. Radical sovereigntists were apt to look to secession or nullification for relief.

Obviously, sovereignty occupied a prominent place in his exposition. It reminded us that an individual's support for state sovereignty should never be the discriminator for membership as a sovereigntist. Because of their reliance on a compact, both traditional state rights men and state sovereigntists believed firmly in state sovereignty. Thus, it was a first approximation of a group's driving motivation. Other planks separated these doctrines.

Political differences were upgraded to sectional polarization. A surety that Court decisions would promote consolidation by usurping state powers and change the American understanding of the Union's nature partnered Virginia mistrust of Congress's motives. Had not Virginians noticed the nationalist tactics associated with government usurpation? Commonly, they roamed through the Constitution seeking justification by cobbling together various articles despite specific ones to the contrary. How could Virginians trust parties that relied on such a dynamic? The Convention faith in checks and balances on power, so widely touted during ratification, proved a chimera. Unfortunately, they failed to support the state rights defence of individual and property rights. As a result, Virginia Republicans and Federalists united against the Missouri Compromise. It became a test of their position on North-South affairs.

The Tallmadge Amendment changed state rights doctrinal history forever. From this date forward, it would be associated with slavery protection. Previously, Constitutional power disputes were almost predictable due to the concerns raised at the ratifying convention. Nevertheless, the Missouri debate uncovered the latent hatred some northerners had for slavery. For the first time, Virginians faced a Constitutional crisis that could seriously undermine the peculiar institution. Court disputes, until early in the country's third decade, had the aspect of a bloodless chess match. Although it had seldom supported Virginia's interests, it had inflicted no permanent economic damage. However, *McCulloch* and *Cohens* in tandem with the slavery debate during the Missouri Compromise escalated Old Dominion concerns exponentially. A combination of Supreme Court decisions and northern abolitionist propaganda might circumscribe its most important institution. Two sections with antithetical definitions of the Union's nature, previously controlled by important compromises, raced toward collision.

Chief Justice Marshall's rulings in *McCulloch* and *Cohens* exacerbated Virginia's distrust of the national government. They highlighted the continual government attacks on Virginia's sovereignty. Not only Congress but also the Court became the enemy. All hope that the latter might limit the Legislature was lost, replaced by the conviction that it would amend the original ideas of the Framers. Moreover, doubtful application of legal principles added to the unease. The complexity of Marshall's judgments and their emasculation of Virginia ideals ensured that state rights men would be suspicious of their basis. Habitually, thought Virginians, he organized snippets of Constitutional phraseology to negate plainly-written Articles. How could Marshall rule one way on an issue in one instance, and then, under the same set of circumstances, later rule the opposite? Was it just a human error when he misstated the primacy of the Hustings court? Did he purposefully ignore Section 22 of the Judiciary Act? Would its inclusion have destroyed his case? After all, had not Judge Roane's counterattacks been straightforward? It seemed to many Virginians that Marshall's intent was to imprint his notion of the Union's nature on America despite legal impediments. Perhaps the nationalistic approach of Jefferson and Madison had been a mistake.

Obviously, the northern reliance on implied powers was unlikely to be damped so self-preservation became an issue. To seek compromise, state rights men specifically emphasized that rather than just denounce implied powers fostered by the sweeping clause, they recognized that incidents could, constitutionally, associate with enumerated powers. This concession proved useless. Their sectional opponents continued to pile incident on incident as in the Madisonian example. Thus, Virginians increasingly turned to state rights and particularly the Tenth Amendment in their attempt to blunt national government action. Since they assumed that the term "expressly" was not necessary for the clause to protect reserved rights, it remained the state's most basic weapon against implication.

Virginians did learn one lesson from these differences. Richard Henry Lee's tactic of immediate state reaction to federal usurpations was no longer feasible. Yes, *Cohens* had raised a storm among a certain set, but *McCulloch* and the Missouri Compromise had failed to do so. Perhaps its local equivalent should replace state efforts at retribution on the national level.

One theoretical problem cannot be ignored. Analysts must be careful to categorize correctly supposed breaches of state rights. One might examine the Fugitive Slave Act as a sample. It was a United States statute and the Court had never declared it unconstitutional. Unfortunately, it had a sad consequence in nonslave states. It denied captured runaways their *civil* rights, especially due process. Let us examine Pennsylvania's reaction. It had passed a personal liberty law to sidestep slave catching. Should not Virginians, so adamant about state rights, support Pennsylvanians in their attack on the Act's results? If they did not, they were nothing but state rights apostates who used the doctrine if it suited their own purposes.

Examine the scenario closely. First, why would anyone expect Virginians to dispute a law based on a famous Constitutional compromise? Second, Pennsylvania had no state right to the personal liberty law because it had been ruled unconstitutional. The law failed since a state right required an argument for it within the Constitution or natural law. Since Northerners rejected the latter application, one may accuse Virginians of following their self-interest but Pennsylvania's problem was with the Supreme Court, not Virginia.

9

Andrew Jackson, Nullification, and the Nature of the Union

Events of the 1820s buffeted Carolinians. The Panic of 1819 began the decade, exerting economic pressure on its staple crop, cotton. Abolitionist attacks on slavery added to their anxiety. It crested due to a significant increase in the protective tariff. Perhaps the state had no future in the Union.

South Carolina determined that the protective tariff of 1824 discriminated against agriculture. Unfortunately, it had to purchase its manufactured goods from either Europe or the North, but exporters sent fewer products to America. Reversing the process, they were less liable to import cotton. In protest, the South Carolina Assembly denied Congress's power to pass a protective tariff. Without a firm stand, other usurpations would follow.

By 1828, South Carolina was in a ferment against the tariff. The *Charleston Mercury* ran a series of articles denouncing government tyranny, while the respected president of South Carolina College, Thomas Cooper, hinted at secession. The tariff of that year, glibly labelled "The Tariff of Abominations," increased import duties from thirty to fifty percent. In November, John C. Calhoun wrote two documents, the *South Carolina Exposition and Protest* outlining Carolina's grievances. Besides expanding on familiar concepts like compact and state sovereignty, Calhoun provided a solution to continuing government usurpation. Whenever a state and federal government disagreed on the constitutionality of an act, the state, as a party to the compact, could call a convention of its people. If it approved the state's interpretation, it could nullify the federal law within the state. The basis for a nullification policy was set.

In late 1832, South Carolina employed that process to scrutinize the tariffs of 1828 and 1832. On November 24, it declared them not binding in South Carolina and a convention applied Calhoun's protest structure. A sovereign state had identified a usurping power and, through a convention of the people, declared it void. Next, Congress would file an amendment that inserted the tariff law into the Constitution. If three-fourths of the states supported the insertion, the nation rejected the sovereign state's action. The sovereign state must either retreat from its protest or secede from the Union. Note that this agenda not only bypassed Supreme Court jurisdiction but also legitimized a basic plank of state sovereignty.

Unsurprisingly, the combative President Andrew Jackson rejected South Carolina's nullification theory and answered it in his famous Proclamation. On December 2, 1828, Virginia Governor William Branch Giles's annual message expressed concern over the federal tariff assignments that favored the northern states at the expense of the South. Giles prompted the General Assembly to take some action.

After presenting a doctrine of strict construction, the House of Delegates, on February

24, 1829, finished its deliberations by passing several resolutions. The federal Constitution was a compact between sovereign states. Because they were the parties to the compact, no other agency could arbitrate a difference between them and each could "construe the Compact for itself." However, Virginia had always respected the compact partners' opinions and a "community of attachment to the Union" would guide it. The only proviso was that its actions did not endanger Virginia's self-preservation or "Republican institutions." As a guardian of the Constitution, the assembly felt constrained to assert that the tariff laws were unconstitutional since they "are not authorized by the plain construction, true intent, and meaning of the Constitution." Because they were oppressive "to a large portion of the Union," South Carolina should repeal them.[1]

As had become habitual, celebrated Virginians accepted the duty of clarifying the issues for the people while spelling out their effects on the Commonwealth. Simultaneously, they updated and defended state rights theory. Usually, this took the form of learned exposés of nationalist rhetoric. However, for the first time, a new voice rang out. Angered at the temerity of Jackson's actions, state sovereigntists raised the flag of secession.

Littleton Waller Tazewell was born in Williamsburg on December 17, 1774. After private tuition, he entered William and Mary College and graduated in 1791. Five years later, he was admitted to the bar. From 1798 to 1836 he represented Virginia on both the state and federal levels. He was a member of the General Assembly or House of Delegates locally and the House of Representatives or the United States Senate in Washington. His last office was Governor of Virginia from 1834 to 1836.

Although Andrew Jackson's potential to the country had been unclear to Tazewell, he had supported the Tennessean initially rather than John Quincy Adams or John Calhoun. Tazewell could not digest the latter's nullification theory since it seemed that a single state could negate a congressional act. Either protest the law or secede from the Union, but do not expect to remain after vetoing a national law.

He soon regretted his decision. During the banking crisis, Tazewell spoke persuasively against Jackson's removal of the bank deposits. As governor, he sought assembly authority to correspond with other states with a view to stem the flood of abolitionist literature. When it voted to instruct the Virginia senators to expunge the Jacksonian censure, Tazewell refused to transmit the instructions because they were unconstitutional. Although his frequent clashes with Jackson led him to support some Whig notions, Tazewell was a Jeffersonian democrat who abhorred formalized political parties. Still, in 1840, he was a candidate for vice president.

Virginians highly respected Tazewell's word. The historian Henry H. Simms declared that "Tazewell was esteemed venerable by his state," while Governor John Floyd "believed it 'absolutely imperative' that they have this 'tower of strength' in the Virginia assembly" during Jackson's administration.

President Jackson's Proclamation concerning the Nullification Crisis broadcast the basic nationalist arguments on the nature of the Union. According to Tazewell, Jackson claimed that the states had delegated sufficient power to the government to constitute a single nation; the states were no longer sovereign; their citizens had transferred their allegiance to the government of the United States making it sovereign; and no state could secede from the Union. The president's shoddy reasoning and bold, unsubstantiated assertions concerning the nature of the Union offended Tazewell. He published his rebuttal, a topical series, in the *Norfolk and Portsmouth Herald*.

Tazewell carefully organized and skillfully wrote thirteen articles. Any educated reader could understand his arguments since examples often accompanied difficult concepts. Wisely, he often began an article with a brief review of previously studied concepts. This allowed a casual reader to follow his plan of attack. Although Tazewell hinted at a personal antipathy to Jackson, he did not employ invective. Still, he did suggest that the president had only a smattering of knowledge on the matter. Tazewell labelled it "political heresies."

He warmed his audience by reviewing some ideas basic to the debate. For Tazewell, both present and future generations would be effected by its outcome. Americans would soon forget the Nullification Crisis, but political philosophers would study its consequences for decades. The basic conflict between government and the people was the "struggle between Power and Right" and it was axiomatic that anyone possessing "authority will probably abuse it." The optimum condition occurred if government power protected the people's rights but could not introduce tyranny. Hopefully, a democratic government would result. One conclusion was clear, power was temporary whereas rights were eternal.

No one could logically propose a compact between the people and its agent, the government. Although a lengthier discussion will follow, one must remember that only the people were sovereign and no agent could usurp that power without force. Thus, the sovereign granted all power and, if it chose, could delegate to the government limited and defined recallable authority. With these few ideas in hand, Tazewell presented his arguments that negated, he said, the absurdities in Jackson's exposition.

Before the Revolution, no body politic called "the people" existed. During the colonial period, the American governments derived their powers from Great Britain, obviating any necessity to define it. Naturally, the Revolution dissolved the colonial governments, but, importantly, the societies remained the same. They fulfilled theory's demand for a pre-existing society upon which it could build government.

The societies exerted authority over only their own members, thus none called "the people of the United States" was to be found. Eventually, the several societies established governments, and thus became sovereign states. Because they were sovereign, they could choose to confederate with other sovereign states without damage. Nevertheless, they avoided consolidation because liberty would have been "sacrificed to the power of an interested majority."

A convention of the people declared the sovereign Commonwealth of Virginia and through their agents, they pledged themselves to it. The simultaneous dissolution of the colonial government and ordination of a new form, made Virginia a sovereign state. However, stressing that the Commonwealth of Virginia was synonymous with the people of the state was important. They were the society that overthrew the old sovereign and replaced it with themselves. In other words, in quick succession, the pre-existing society renounced its allegiance to Great Britain, "incorporated themselves into a body politic," and chose a new "corporate" name to preserve the sovereign rights taken from Great Britain for themselves. Since each colony mirrored this process, we could recognize the people of the several states but not a people of the United States. Therefore, each state had reached a level at which individuals were subject to the body politic. But if acting in a corporate sense, each was sovereign.

In contradistinction, Jackson postulated a doctrine that the states had never been sovereign. Somewhere lurked a central sovereign other than the several states. For example, Jackson's proclamation insisted that "we very early considered ourselves as connected by common interest with each other." Remember, colonies had formed leagues for common defence and, before the Declaration of Independence, many called the colonies the United Colonies of America. These joint acts declared America to be one nation.

Tazewell was unimpressed. He accused Jackson of purposefully obscuring the issue with imprecise terminology designed to invent the existence of a single nation before the blossoming of state sovereignty. The United States would be one people and they could not alter this state except "by force, or common consent." Yet, Jackson seemed unaware that Virginia, for example, had promulgated its own sovereignty before the Declaration of Independence by dissolving the previous government and declaring its own. Of course, he could sidestep this problem simply by declaring a new sovereign. However, he would have to prove its existence.

To do so required the president to demonstrate there was a pre-existing society that could lead to one nation. He must search for a community of all the people who would be the nation's subjects, and who would form its government. Jackson's first foray, claimed Tazewell, was a "flimsy pretext." "Common interest," without any reference to a society was the initial thrust. Was there a common territory, religion, institution, or any other parameter that tied all colonials? He surmised that with Jackson's methodology "one-half the People of the whole world" might consolidate.

A secondary presidential "proof" required an examination of colonial documents. True, one could interpret many as demonstrating a common interest. Nevertheless, a closer examination also showed that the colonists never intended them to establish an amalgamated nation. Instead, they invited other colonies into a temporary confederacy to ensure "distinct, independent communities."

Once Jackson's one nation proposal was in place, he had to produce its government. Since there was no evidence that, in the colonial stage, any national government existed, Jackson's only avenue was inference. He began with the common defence leagues. They required communities with governments that spoke and contracted for them. Thus, if they formed the league, its community and government must have existed. Tazewell wondered not only who formed these leagues but also with whom did they do it? Of course, he commented, it was easy to see why the president avoided these questions. No one had formed any leagues fulfilling the criteria above. Instead, those that one could identify were between sovereign and independent states. The supposed one nation theory could not stand on this argument.

The last step in Jackson's one nation proposal was to name the new entity. Before the Declaration, he argued, Americans knew the colonies as the United Colonies of America. This implied the "aggregate character" of the supposed nation. That the president could make such an inference from the arrangement of a few words amazed Tazewell. He considered it a "perversion of the meaning of words" and could find not a scintilla of evidence that the colonies had ever acted in Jackson's aggregate character. In counterpoint, one need only examine the *Journal of the First Continental Congress* that labelled the participants "several colonies." After presenting other similar examples, Tazewell concluded that "the President seems to have as little ground for bestowing this new name of the United Colonies of America upon all the revolted Colonies, or Colonists of that day, as he had to bestow upon the Colonists any such aggregate character as that under which he is supposed to assert that they were then known."

The question remained, did the Declaration of Independence consolidate the colonies into one nation? President Jackson described it as a joint action of the colonies and therefore it declared the United States to be one nation. Tazewell began with a truism. Simply because some agents cooperate did not necessarily define joint action. That possibility depended upon the intended result. In this case, the Declaration published the colonial goals to the world. Also, the signatories were not the agents of any single body politic recognized as one nation.

Nor did they have any power to bargain away their colony's rights by agreeing to a consolidated nation. Moreover, Jackson had already argued that his one nation was in place before the Declaration. Thus, not only logic but fact contradicted him since the Declaration clearly defined the colonies to be free and independent. These obvious issues must have been clear to the president, but, according to Tazewell, he solved this problem in the usual way. He simply asserted his conclusion. Luckily for Virginians, who could delve into the Declaration, the opposite of Jackson's contention was clear. Its principal role was "to declare this [free, sovereign, independent] their new condition to the world, and to justify that which it so declared."

Given the above discussion, one must agree that, except some catastrophic act, the states were still sovereign. Had the Articles of Confederation changed that state? Jackson insisted that it produced a "solemn league of several States, by which they agreed, that they would, collectively, form one nation, for the purpose of conducting some certain domestic concerns, and all foreign relations." Again, he fell into the old error of internal inconsistency. His arguments assigning one nation status to both the pre–Declaration and Declaration colonies disputed that made for the Articles era. Tazewell humorously built a scenario in which the president touched one nation with his wizard's wand to make it disappear while another took its place. Unfortunately, the president's construction did not depend on the people but on the league of states. It held "sovereignty without supremacy" and was merely "a nation created for certain purposes only."

Jackson's theory had another disconcerting effect. It set the stage for two nations, one formed for certain purposes by the Articles, and another for different goals by the Declaration. The only way to overcome this clash was to prove that the states had agreed to a new one nation concept that superceded other agreements. Again, one must examine the document forming the Articles for evidence of such a change. Did it "divest the States of the original sovereign character"?

First, the ratification dynamic proved the states were sovereign. It took place over a period of several years. Thus, the Articles did not affect the sovereignty of the states. Otherwise, the states formed a confederation with "different degrees of sovereignty." Also, direct references within the document ensured state sovereignty. The first article declared the style — not name — of the confederacy to be the United States of America, while the second was conclusive. It boldly retained the "sovereignty, freedom, and independence, and every power, jurisdiction, and right, which is not by the Confederation expressly delegated to the United States in Congress assembled" to the several states. To retain a power, the state must have held it prior to the signing of the Articles of Confederation. Importantly, the states delegated express powers to Congress, but never gave up sovereignty. The delegation to Congress rather than the United States bolstered this argument. Congress could never be considered a repository of sovereignty. The Articles established a confederacy, not one nation.

Jackson's proclamation promoted the idea that all states, according to the Articles, had to submit to the decisions of Congress. This strange conclusion seemed to contradict Article II declaring state sovereignty. Indeed, the states had merely pledged "to abide by the determination of Congress on all questions, which by that Confederation should be submitted to them." Remember, warned Tazewell, if two parties agreed to arbitrate a matter, the judge adjudicated that specific matter and no other. If he did, any *orbiter dictum* did not bind the parties. Therefore, if one examined the Articles and discovered but few questions within Congress's power — see Article IX — one must agree that no proof existed within the Articles establishing Jackson's one nation theory.

Although it was eminently clear that the states, based on Tazewell's premises, did not lose their sovereignty through the Articles historical phase, he still had to clarify their position after the Constitutional ratification. The proclamation announced "they surrendered many of their essential parts of sovereignty" and "were no longer Sovereign." He agreed immediately that if Jackson could prove that the states had surrendered one iota of sovereignty, he was correct in his grander premise.

Tazewell began by casting aside Madison's dual sovereignty scheme. He claimed that "I have high authority for the belief, that none can serve two masters at the same time." Sovereignty was supreme and indivisible, and one who possessed it could recognize no superior. A corollary to this affirmation was that sovereign states must be equal. Once one accepted these aspects, sovereignty and government were never synonymous. If it were, the result would be "unchecked Despotism." Government was a mere repository for delegated powers that could be withdrawn or altered by the sovereign. Either revolution or reform could involve changes. The former replaced one sovereign with another while the latter contemplated a change in government structure.

Who adopted the Constitution? All concurred it was the people. However, its definition eluded consensus. Jackson maintained that "the People of the United States formed the Constitution." True, they acted for their state legislatures, but they employed conventions to achieve their goal. Tazewell considered this shoddy thinking. Neither the consolidated "People of the United States" as one nation nor a majority of the consolidated mass ratified the Constitution. Instead, it was the "People of the several States acting as several distinct and independent commonwealths, each in its own separate corporate character, and each binding its own particular minority by the will of its own particular majority." To test the latter assertion quickly, one need only examine the postratification period. Neither Rhode Island nor North Carolina initially ratified, but never was either state bound by those that did ratify. Clearly, each state's decisions were independent of the others. This was crucial because "none 'but a sovereign,' could rightfully have abolished the old government formed by the Articles of Confederation and ... established this new government in its stead."

The sovereign states preserved the government formed by the Constitution. They controlled the election of the representatives, senators, president, vice president and, through them, the judiciary. Moreover, only the states could judge their federal government pledges of faith. In addition, the states, according to the Constitution, played a crucial role in amending the Constitution. It seemed sensible that if the states could create, preserve, and alter the Constitution, they must be sovereign. Arguments to the contrary inferring the states surrendered it at ratification were specious. Remember, by definition, the "right to make and to alter government when made, is Sovereignty."

According to Tazewell, Jackson's most persistent error lay in conflating sovereignty with government. For the president, the entity that wielded government power possessed sovereignty. With this basis, he could argue that because the states granted a few powers to government they could not be sovereign. The next step was the postulate that the state's citizens had transferred their sovereignty to the United States government. Tazewell had a quick rejoinder. Unless a government could somehow form itself, it could not be sovereign. Another difficulty was inherent in the Constitution. If one associated sovereignty with the powers accorded a government, one eventually reached a point at which two sovereignties clashed. In Tazewell's exposition, sovereignty was not divisible. Instead, the sovereign people delegated certain duties to its agents, but did not transfer sovereignty.

Jackson's claim that his fellow citizens had transferred allegiance to the general government particularly incensed Tazewell. "Not one word of any such transfer is found in the

Articles of Confederation.... Not one word of such a transfer is to be met in the Constitution.... Nor have the citizens of any state ever taken, or been required to take, any oath of allegiance to the United States or the government." Remember, swearing an oath to uphold the Constitution merely reaffirmed one's "fidelity to his State, which has chosen to adopt this Constitution as its supreme law, and so has made it part of its own code."

During the ratification stage, the people of various states, to codify inherent rights, suggested many amendments. When Congress winnowed these down, two, labelled the Ninth and Tenth Amendments, contained some protection. The Ninth assured that the specific recognition of some rights was not a delimiter on others. The Tenth assured the same role for state powers and those remaining to the people. Notice that the people had both rights and powers reflecting their dual nature as individuals and sovereigns. As individuals they had no political power but many rights. As a body politic, they had no natural rights but great political power. Recall, rights were eternal while political power was transient.

The Tenth Amendment, claimed Tazewell, had its basis in Article II of the Articles of Confederation. It reflected the notion that this Union of the states was a league. However, the people formed the Constitution and delegated some power to the general government. Therefore, to reflect both the original idea from the Articles and the new form, Congress had rewritten Article II. Within the Tenth Amendment was enough power to encompass all political powers not granted. Because of this contention, the word "expressly" was not necessary.

One should not conclude that a sovereign state had no obligations. The obvious one was to the Constitution. Also, the states made various pledges of faith like reciprocal pledges with their co-states according to the terms of the compact. Logically, this compact might be broken if any of the compact parties violated their pledge. At that stage, the others may either choose to ignore the violation or change the agreement to compensate for the violation. Still, that was only one scenario. It was more likely that all parties would refuse to change their positions. As a result, the violating state would revert to its precompact condition but must realize that the injured parties might resort to force.

Broken obligations "by some of the other parties" could release a state from the covenant, and might lead to secession. Note that either a single or multiple states could secede. Any argument against this power must deal with a pertinent question. If a sovereign state did not have it, what defence did the Constitution provide against a majority of the people who purposefully broke the Constitution and bound the minority to its will? Secession was always the antidote to compact violations. The Tenth Amendment reserved that power.

Some critics argued that no state could secede because it previously agreed that the Supreme Court was the final and common arbiter of constitutional disputes, but Tazewell refused this interpretation. The Supreme Court was limited to cases in law and equity that required "representations by the parties." The critics' interpretation would allow a case involving a compact party vs. the United States government. However, the government was simply an agent of the party. It was nonsensical to argue that a compact party must sue its agent in the party's court over a decision the party had already made. Where was this authority stated?

Final arbitration invoked a trust gap. The Court could be an unwitting accomplice to "the wicked will of the Legislature." Suppose Congress declared an unrighteous war. The Court could judge only the legal, not moral, aspects of the declaration. A similar situation could involve the president and senate over treaties. Or, the Court itself may be the source of evil by its decisions. How could one ask the judiciary to judge its own failings? No, Tazewell had too many reasons to allow the court to be the final and common arbiter of constitutional questions.[2]

South Carolina's appropriation of the term "interpose" drew ex–President James Madison into the debate. Its ordinance referred to his Report of 1799 as a guiding principle. He warned interpreters to be cautious when translating generalized statements from one crisis to another. Perhaps the language of the Report maneuvered them into false interpretations. To Madison, "it appears, that the proceedings of Virginia have been misconceived by those who have appealed to them." However, he could enlighten those who had misread the document.

The participants could never solve the dispute unless they understood the "true character of the Constitution." Remember, its government was partly federal, partly national. Any attempt to focus it through the lens of one aspect, but not the other, would fail. In his classic restatement, Madison reminded his audience that the states, who by definition, were "the people ... acting in their highest sovereign capacity," formed the Constitution. Necessarily, they formed both the state and federal constitutions. As a result, each had the same authority — the people — within a state while restricting each constitution within its own sphere. At this point, Madison added an interesting wrinkle. Since this Constitution, which acts within each state in its own sphere, was a compact "among the states in their highest sovereign capacity" and simultaneously acted for all the people of the United States, "it cannot be altered or amended at the will of the States individually as the constitution of a State may be at its individual will." Therefore, South Carolina had no constitutional or extraconstitutional power or right to nullify the federal law.

One should always remember the distribution of powers between the two governments. Once allocated, the powers of the federal government were at least as sovereign as those of an individual state. Thus, in cases of concurrent jurisdiction, the Constitution must arrange a mechanism to mediate any dispute. Left to the states, each could produce a myriad of outcomes and burden the Union with different interpretations. Surely, that outcome bode ill for the people. It "would be attended with delays, with inconveniences, and with expenses amounting to a prohibition of the expedient." This was a dangerous situation because each form organized a government with an armed force.

In contradistinction, the Constitution contained a Supremacy Clause that bypassed these problems. It detailed the correct relationships for solving internal disputes. Moreover, the states had several Constitutional securities protecting their interests. No one could predict the future, but if the commotion surrounding the Alien and Sedition Acts was an example, the people would soon forget the present quarrel. True, the state's decision to avoid the courts had some basis as "there have been occasional decisions from the bench, which had incurred serious and extensive disapprobation." Nevertheless, most Americans seemed to support the system. Whenever Americans identified the need for potential amendments, they knew that they must rely on the Constitutional framework.

However, one was left with the larger question. What does a state do in the face of constant abuses? One must read Madison's answer carefully. Before continuing, let us be clear that he *never* advocated secession. The last resort of the state was to make "an appeal from the cancelled obligations of the constitutional compact to original rights and self-preservation." In our case, South Carolina, a single state, appealed a power through nullification, and made it unconstitutional in that state. She appealed that decision to the other parties of the compact.

At this point, Madison switched from generalities to specifics. He claimed that South Carolina's decision had "the effect of nullifying the act of the Government of the United States, unless the decision of the State be reversed by three fourths of the parties." This assertion contemplated a Constitutional amendment based on the nullified act and success was defined according to Article V, an acceptance of three-fourths of the states. If one examined the ultimate statement of Carolina's intentions, its *Address to the People of Carolina by Their Delegates in Convention*, one found the process expressly stated.

> That upon such a convocation [convention] it should be incumbent upon the States claiming the doubtful power, to propose an amendment to the constitution giving the doubtful power, and, on failure to obtain it by a consent of three-fourths of all the States, to regard the power as never having been intended to be given.

Examine the procedure. Congress had passed an act of doubtful constitutionality, say the tariff of 1832. Some states considered it constitutional. They, or Congress, would propose a constitutional amendment asserting the power in the tariff act. The states, mirroring the amending process of Article V, would vote on that amendment. If three-fourths supported it, the law became an Article of the Constitution. If not, Congress expunged the doubtful law. Notice the *Address* did not presume the state's decision to be "valid." Instead, the states tested a "doubtful power." Moreover, the constitutional vote would be on an amendment conceived by the states *opposed* to Carolina's position.

Madison examined the interrelationship of the various Articles. It made little sense to rule on the admissibility of one divorced from the rest since the Constitution was full of compromises. Delegates often bundled and accepted Articles that might not have been palatable individually. Political strife would follow any procedure that allowed a few states to challenge and expunge individual Articles. The only path avoiding this pitfall set aside the presumption that only the parties to the constitutional compact could interpret it. Instead, the parties must agree, in some form, on a method for "expounding it" employing the Constitution. They could never "renounce" this agreement. Hedging his statement, Madison reverted to an older delimiter. If a party must "renounce the expounding provision ... it must grow out of abuses to the compact releasing the sufferers from their fealty to it."

Madison ended his essay by listing some generalities that "inferred" that he did not defend interposition. The House of Delegates' debate notes contained no reference to the topic. Of course, it did not include many topics. Perhaps the straightforward language on interposition was so clear to debaters that it required no further comment. Similarly, the published report to Virginians contained no mention of extraconstitutional action. Furthermore, one need only examine the reaction of other states to the Report. The predominant complaint was the perceived state assumption that Virginia would nullify a legislative act. It interfered with the "exclusive jurisdiction of the Supreme Court of the United States." If the resolutions had made that claim, which other states assumed it did, then "it must be presumed that it would have been a conspicuous object of their denunciations."[3]

Previously, we examined the state of the Republican party in Virginia and concluded that its members promoted differing theoretical positions. Even Federalists found a temporary home within its folds. Although few, some radical ultra state rights men joined the party. Nevertheless, moderate Republicans made up the majority. As constitutional crises followed one upon the other, the voice of the ultra was increasingly common. This emotional, often irrational, response to supposed threats became a danger to the Union.

Admittedly, the personal diary of our next commentator, Governor John Floyd, skirted the boundary of our defined subjects because it was not public knowledge. Nevertheless, Floyd's diary entries mirrored his political actions while governor. We will consider his diary as a compendium of his publically expressed opinions. Moreover, it demonstrated a particularly important shift in attitude.

John Floyd was a child of the frontier. He was born on April 24, 1783 near Louisville, Kentucky. His father was a famous Indian fighter who eventually lost his life to his enemy. He attended Dickinson College, but a bout of illness prevented his graduation. In May 1804 he married Letitia Preston, and joined that prestigious South Carolina family. His return to the University of Pennsylvania produced a medical degree and he practiced in several Virginia towns, earning a fine reputation. The outbreak of the War of 1812 found him a surgeon major in the United States army. Two years later, his district elected him to the General Assembly and after three terms, the people of Abingdon sent him to Congress.

Floyd ploughed his own furrow. Party lines never constrained him. He supported placing Virginia troops under federal orders, condemned the Treaty of Ghent as an incursion on American sovereignty, promoted frontier enterprises like the opening of the Oregon territory, and refused to criticize the Missouri Compromise. After twelve years, he retired from Congress. His explanatory letter to his constituents contained an enlightening phrase. "That portion of the sovereign power of Virginia," he proudly reminded them, "which you confided to me, is returned to you uninjured and undiminished." His behavior reminded Virginians of two oft-forgotten truisms. In time of national crisis, the state rights man warehoused his localist tendencies and actively supported the national government. This was a natural reaction to the different spheres of constitutional authority. Moreover, Floyd and others like him, had long fought for both the people's sovereignty and its centrality in American government. The agent did not get it perpetually. At regular intervals, he returned it to the people.

Perhaps instigated by Floyd, most of the family were strict construction sovereigntists. It was the only check, according to Floyd, on national government consolidation. Although he accepted the Missouri Compromise, the furor over the state's constitution raised concern. Recall, it contained a clause that forbade free Negroes or mulattoes from settling in the state. Although an early supporter of gradual abolition — he had stated "I will not rest until slavery is abolished in Virginia"— the demands of state sovereignty overcame this sympathetic view. Missouri was a sovereign state, equally protected under the Constitution as an original. How long would it be before Congress encroached on its rights? Unless sovereignty theory became universal "this confederacy cannot long last."

The election of 1828 proved pivotal to Floyd's career. He explained his present opposition to the tariff that began a five-year tirade against the administration.

> At this moment [1828] came the direful struggle between the great parties in Congress founded upon the claim which the majority ... from the north of the Potomac made to the right to lay any tax upon the importations into the United States which was intended to act as a protection to northern manufacturers by excluding foreign fabrics of the same kind. Hence all the states to the south of the Potomac became dependent upon the Northern States for a supply of whatever thing they might want, and in this way the South was compelled to sell its products low and buy from the North all articles it needed from twenty-five to one hundred and twenty-five per cent higher than from France to England.... At this juncture the southern party brought out Jackson.

Floyd had left Congress, some said, because he expected his Jackson support to earn him a cabinet position. Later, he claimed that such had been the case but he had refused Jackson's offer. Nevertheless, it provided an initial motivation for Floyd's eventual contempt for President Jackson. Of course, the tariff issue and nullification played a primary role in Floyd's reaction. We saw above its effects on Virginia. Many, including Floyd, had concluded that only a southern president like Jackson could repair the inequities promulgated by Henry Clay and John Quincy Adams. In 1830, he became governor of Virginia and in a moment of despair, Floyd decided to keep a diary of events that could help future generations understand the Jackson administration's undermining of self-government.

Floyd's scathing comments left the reader no latitude in deciding his personal hatred of Jackson's administration. He introduced every mention with a pejorative term. Cabinet members were wretches, depraved, profligate, ignorant, blackguards, and filthy, ignorant, beasts. Jackson was vulgar, feeble, ignorant, vindictive, intractable, conceited, unprincipled, without intellect, and author of an imbecilic government. Perhaps the entry from Floyd's diary for December 26, 1832 would define the depth of Floyd's hostility.

> I have often said and here state that Jackson is the worst man in the Union, a scoundrel in private life, devoid of patriotism and a tyrant withal, and is only capable of using power that he may have the gratification of seeing himself obeyed by every human being. He speaks the language ungrammatically, writes it worse and is exceedingly ignorant, but strange to tell, he is feared and most all seem disposed to give up their liberty rather than displease him, who is now so popular that many fear to encounter his frown and many, very many, seem willing to let him rule, the arbitrary despot, provided they can obtain office. Thus office and a base love for gold and power have mainly contributed to enslave us by a brutal, ignorant soldier.

One need only examine Jackson's reaction during the dreadful Eaton affair to conclude he could not govern. Still, Americans reelected Jackson in 1832 despite Floyd's support for John C. Calhoun.

After Floyd's stirring prosovereignty annual messages of 1831 and 1832, it was not surprising that Jackson's Proclamation in response to South Carolina's tariff nullification outraged him. Did it not make war inevitable?

> It concentrates all power in the President and denounces all meetings in any states, as treason if to call in question the constitutionality of any act passed by Congress, denies the States to be sovereign or this to be a confederacy, and acknowledges no authority but that vested in the President ... I think I shall be able to check him.

To this end, he presented the Ordinance of South Carolina to the Virginia General Assembly in a favorable light. After all, nullification was a reserved right of the state and it had been confirmed in the Virginia Resolutions of 1798. Ominously, he believed that civil war would accompany any presidential incursion into South Carolina.

In January 1833, the House of Delegates debated federal-state relations. One theory presented incensed Floyd. It proposed that a single state had the right to judge violations of a "compact, treaty, or Constitution" and secede. Yet, the others had the same right to judge, and if they concluded that the government had violated no Articles, they could coerce the first state back into the Union. Although the president currently did not have the power to order this action, Congress could pass a law to subdue South Carolina. Obviously, some delegates sustained Jackson's solution.

On January 15, the debate ended and several resolutions passed by a majority of one vote. Eleven days later, the General Assembly prepared an answer to South Carolina's nullification proclamation. Its basis was an "ardent desire to preserve the peace and harmony of our common country." The assembly was sure that the other states would reconsider the tariff bill and placate the South. Congress would surely revisit its imposts and relieve South Carolina's burden.

Carolina would never follow through with disunion sentiment if the government could find some accommodation. Since Virginia felt compelled to mediate the dispute, it provided five resolutions as a settlement basis. South Carolina should rescind the ordinance, Congress must modify the tariff acts on "foreign commodities," and each side must refrain from acts "calculated to disturb the tranquility of the country, or endanger the existence of the Union." To ensure understanding, the assembly also resolved that the doctrines of state sovereignty and rights as defined in the 1798 resolutions and Madison's Report outlined the basis of Union. Still, this interpretation disagreed with both South Carolina's ordinance and the expansive powers claimed by Jackson in his proclamation. To ensure no interpretative errors, Virginia would trust it to a commissioner who would transmit it to the South Carolina legislature.

Later that year, Floyd, despairing of the effects of Jackson's popularity, moaned that,

> I am no longer surprised that the republics of Greece and Rome were overthrown by popular men. The multitude are ignorant and neither understand their rights or have learning enough to pursue them. They huzza for their leader and never believe anything which is told them except what he says nor is there any hope for support of liberty from a very large proportion of the learned and intellectual, because many are scoundrels and are soon bought up, many are cowards and cannot act; and a still greater number are mean and take any position which will give them office or pelf. As for power, the multitude seem to care nothing. Their idea of power and of kings is that to be a king and to have power one must have a crown on his head and a scepter in his hand. Without these, they cannot believe any man is a king or can have power.

Floyd's remarks echoed the uncertainty of human nature postulated years earlier by the anti-ratification Antifederalists.[4]

Floyd was not the only sovereignty activist publicizing his theory in Virginia. Nathaniel Beverley Tucker, the son of distinguished parents, St. George Tucker and Francis Bland Randolph Tucker, was born on September 6, 1784, in Matoax, Virginia. His early influences were George Wythe of William and Mary College and John Randolph of Roanoke, his maternal half-brother. They exposed him to agrarianism and the Principles of '98.

After serving in the United States Army from 1813 to 1815, he moved to Missouri and eventually became a judge. Politically, he opposed the Compromise and its debate persuaded him that secession was an important sovereigntist weapon. Originally, he opposed Calhoun but by 1828 he reversed his position and supported nullification and secession since it made little sense to be a member of the Union but claim to disobey its laws. Secession was the sensible option.

President Jackson's Proclamation during the Nullification Crisis solidified Tucker's radical sovereigntist tendencies. Upon John Randolph's death, Tucker returned to Virginia as a professor at William and Mary and remained there until 1851. Both his genuine hatred of the North and a personal disdain for southern politicians were palpable. He compared northern manners to those of a "badly-trained dog, who comes to you with his tail tucked, and his ears back to neck, and is no sooner relieved of his fear of being kicked, then he paws you with his dirty foot." Moreover, northerners were "vile mercenary rabble." Similarly, his own southern politicians could not be trusted because they had concluded that their personal futures were better secured by remaining in the Union. Had not the Nullification Crisis provided the perfect springboard to secession which they had ignored? For our purposes, his most important work was the novel *The Partisan Leader.*

Tucker's theoretical expositions offered few new ideas. His importance, like that of John Floyd, was his passionate — some might say bombastic — defence of state sovereignty. His concurrent hatred of Andrew Jackson and Martin Van Buren as representatives of a decadent North added a personal motivation. Unlike moderate state rights men, he concluded that divided sovereignty was nonsensical. Thus, the states had never surrendered any to the government. He extended his theory to the notion of the people. The individual states of the Union contained separate body politics of the people. They formed a league — the Union — but did not form a new body politic. Thus, he recognized no concept called "the people of the United States." One of *The Partisan Leader's* reviewers, Abel P. Upshur, remarked that Tucker's strong opinions did not currently match those of many Virginians. Instead, his book would earn him the enmity of the proponents of Union.

The melodrama mentioned above portrayed Virginia a decade in the future. A league of states, called the southern confederacy, had formed due to constant federal power usurpations. Virginia had indicated that it might join its brethren, but President Martin Van Buren, running for a fourth term, had suborned the state legislature against it. As a pretext to insert federal troops into Virginia, Van Buren had argued that the southern confederacy might invade. Therefore, the government had dispatched an "army of observation" to the Old Dominion and Virginia became a province of the United States in which Yankee troops acted as invaders rather than protectors. They controlled the state legislature by force and threats. Thus, Van Buren chose to dominate Virginia by keeping its citizens poor and maintaining the form of suffrage without the substance. Not only did he invent a special court to deal with Virginia crimes but also he corrupted its existing judiciary. Slowly, desperate rebel groups began to form in the West.

As one might expect, some Virginians either actively supported Van Buren or simply maintained their usual routine. One typical example was a member of the lesser gentry described as "a coarse, strong man, with a brain-fed look, plainly, cheaply, and untastefully dressed, in clothes which, by their substantial goodness, indicated at once the wearer's prudence and the length of his purse." He talked loudly and was self-impressed, interested only in "corn and tobacco."

The mass of rebels did not match this portrait. They were simple folk, rustic farmers who held Old Virginia and the Principles of '98 in high esteem. They were an independent lot and at one stage made it clear that their leader would remain so "as long as we choose." However, the rebel leaders were universally from the gentry.

The book was a series of vignettes acting as essays on politics and morality. The story itself proved secondary to the propagation of state sovereignty. As many had done before him, Tucker sought to warn Virginians about the dangers of government consolidation. Secession was in the wind. One source of discontent was the corrupt courts, whose philosophy was "that the necessity of the case should overrule all constitutional scruples." The reader did not have to search for Tucker's themes. He conveniently wrote them in italics.

The principal rebel characters in *The Partisan Leader* were planter aristocrats and each was associated with a Virginia political group. Hugh Trevor was a moderate state rights man who had supported President Andrew Jackson but inveighed against government usurpation. However, Jackson's Force Bill compelled him to reexamine his position although he denied the nullifying doctrine. He recognized a right to secession but could not contemplate resorting to it. If Virginia did secede, it could expect the general government to coerce it back into the Union. Trevor supported Van Buren, and his surrogate Thomas Ritchie of the *Richmond Enquirer*, because he was certain that Union, rather than no Union, was better for Virginia.

Tucker described him as a man who, for thirty years "had been sacrificing the *substance* of liberty and prosperity to the *form* of a constitution devised to secure, but perverted to destroy them."

His brother Bernard opposed these sentiments. He preached secession and would never sacrifice sovereignty to preserve the Union. Hugh's sons, Owen and Douglas, continued the dichotomy of generations. Both attended West Point, but Van Buren became Owen's mentor and the president quickly promoted him. In conversation, he criticized Virginia's principles and derided state sovereignty. His sibling, Douglas, had visited and been impressed by South Carolina's constitutional contentions. He would stand with Virginia.

Critics attempted to associate Tucker's fictional characters with actual participants. Bernard Trevor seemed to model John Randolph while his brother Hugh resembled Henry St. George Tucker. Perhaps Tucker saw himself as the partisan leader, Douglas Trevor, but this association was unclear. Despite the interest in this activity, the truth was that none of the characters matched exactly.

A student of the era would be interested in Tucker's portrayal of slavery. Slaves, over time, eventually became comfortable with their lot. Masters treated house slaves particularly well and looked after and liked them. Characters called one "my good old friend," and another his children's "daddy." The latter was "a graceful and gentlemanly old man." Immediately, Tucker contrasted him with northern servants, who were "ferocious" and "hostile." During the most dangerous action, Bernard Trevor trusted his life to a slave. This prompted Tucker to make a crucial proposal. In case of war, Virginia would arm its slaves because they were "faithful creatures." The supposed southern weakness became a strength, because the slave had a "staunch loyalty and heart-felt devotion ... to his master."

Virginians could learn several lessons from Tucker's fiction. For example, his popular characters were always truthful on moral issues. This required one to trust his own motivation rather than that of government officials. They were without honor. Also, events could push even Union men like Hugh Trevor to contemplate secession.

Politically, "the usurper's claim to a dominion, unchecked by the authority of the state" was unsupportable. Highlighting their basic value, Bernard swore that Virginians must rely on its "RIGHTS" and "SOVEREIGNTY." A resort to the courts wasted time because its members were corrupt.

The tariff evoked comment. Readers had to understand that the protective tariff affected Virginia's farmers inequitably. It was unconstitutional and by itself should force Virginians to consider secession. On the other hand, lower imposts or even free trade would energize them. If the present system persisted, Virginia would be in constant bondage to the North. The South Carolina nullifiers offered a relief roadmap and Virginians should applaud them.

The novel's progression of events showed that tyranny could provoke every Virginian to secession. Hugh Trevor, moderate Republican, eventually cast his lot with the rebels. Secondarily, Tucker reminded his readers that if one sought to understand any man's motives, one need only consult his self-interest.[5]

✠

This section's last commentator, Abel Parker Upshur, returned us to the voice of reason. As had Tazewell, he combined state rights and the nature of the Union to prove the nationalist organic view unconstitutional. He was an Eastern Shore conservative politician, planter and judge who had held positions at both local and national levels and eventually became

Secretary of the Navy in John Tyler's administration. An explosion of one of the *Princeton's* guns during a demonstration tragically killed him.

Upshur promoted many basic state rights beliefs during his review of Tucker's *Partisan Leader*. First, Americans must understand that Virginians loved the Union, but they insisted on original interpretations. The United States was a confederation protecting liberty for its citizens; the compact that bound them made the country stronger as long as politicians maintained their pledges; states were sovereign and government was their creation; and the people of the states delegated government's limited powers and expressly enumerated any necessary incidents. He added specifics arising from the tariff debate. Jackson's response was a "monstrous violation[s]" of the Constitution and state sovereignty; South Carolina's ordinance would prompt other states to defend their rights; the Force Bill, if carried out, would begin civil war; and the North sought to destroy slavery.

His inquiry into Justice Joseph Story's *Commentaries on the Constitution of the United States* highlighted his brief writing career. Using Story's book as a benchmark, Upshur wrote a highly readable exposition debunking the Justice's interpretations while simultaneously presenting his own. They were apt to be more reasonable since he had both the benefit of past criticisms and Story's organization.

Because the concentration was on the nature of the Union, four topics were mandatory. The emphasis was on the people, sovereignty, state rights, and compact. For good measure, Upshur added germane comments about the jurisdiction and authority of the Supreme Court.

Story had adopted a specific plan of attack to elevate "one people" to "the people of the United States." He began his argument by positing that the colonies, for many objects, were one people. After 1776, the Declaration of Independence made them one nation. Finally, one people formed the Constitution.

According to Story, the people of the colonies could, for some important but unstated reasons, be considered as one people. Upshur countered that this interpretation failed because all important colonial functions and relationships were with the mother country rather than one another since the colonies were settled separately. Moreover, they had distinctive governments and political backgrounds. England held a separate sovereignty over each colony and never declared joint sovereignty over the group. How could separate parts of an empire constitute one people? To make his position clear, Upshur offered his definition of the word. Start with a "political corporation." The people of this construct were those with an "allegiance to a common sovereignty" and political interest. They were bound only by the laws of the sovereign and could "exert no sovereign power except in the name of the whole." Such a definition would be useful for adherents of the compact theory.

Story's conclusions, if based on the above definition, baffled Upshur. He could not find "the people of the United States." Where did they live? How did they relate to each other politically? Where was their sovereignty? To whom did they hold allegiance? He awaited Story's response.

Perhaps, as Story argued, the Declaration of Independence introduced the idea of one people who, in turn, defined a nation. Upshur doubted that "united in one purpose" was synonymous with "one nation." It seemed far-fetched that an announcement of independence might lead any revolutionaries to second Story's insinuation. Instead, it was more likely that the Declaration "was simply their joint expression of their separate wills; each expressing its own will, and not that of any other; each bound by its own act and not responsible for the act of any other." In other words, it was "a joint expression of their separate identities." Moreover, the Continental Congress had no power to "league" the colonies. If one examined its output, one noticed it took the form of resolutions, not laws. It offered suggestions but never commanded. One might conclude that it was not a government at all. Never did it act directly on the people and always it required the states to secure its ends. A numerical majority of the people was never fundamental to its decisions. Importantly, Congress did not receive its few powers from any recognized grant. It merely assumed them. Historically, it exercised a power, and due to that exercise, others assumed some agency had granted it.

For Story, the Preamble to the Constitution proved that one people, not those of the several states, had ratified it. After all, it began "We, the people of the United States, do ordain and establish this Constitution." Upshur made particular note that "the people do ordain and establish not contract and stipulate with each other." History had proven Story wrong. Everyone knew the Constitution was a compact.

Obviously, the Preamble only announced a few intentions. Unless the Constitutional Convention represented one people, which it did not, then it had no power to assume or act as if it did, particularly if another power had called it. Moreover, the Committee on Style had edited the preceding version for effect. The original, on August 6, began with a list of all the states after the phrase "We, the people." The style committee edited out the list, illegally according to Upshur, and replaced it with a final version. Because there were no substantial revisions, one could correctly assume that Story's application of "We, the people" was unfortunate and secondarily, similar arguments were incorrect.

Another line of reasoning blunted Story's conclusions. The draft Constitution required nine states for ratification. Which nine was problematic. Perhaps eleven would do so. Therefore, the style committee adopted a mechanism that "applied to those who should ratify the Constitution and not to those who should refuse to do so." The choice reflected "We, the people of the States who have united for that purpose" rather than "We, the people of the United States."

According to Upshur, the Preamble contained all the words necessary for an introduction to the Constitution. They just needed reordering. Since the "people of the United States ... neither appointed the convention, nor ratified their act, nor otherwise adopted it as obligatory upon them," then "We, the people of the United States" should be interpreted as "We, the people of the States united." Such a construction would comport with the original intention of the Preamble.

Upshur's compact theory commentary was based on his fundamental rule of the Union's nature. "The Constitution of the United States was to be considered," he noted, "as a compact or confederation between free, independent, and sovereign States, and is to be construed as such, in all cases where its language is doubtful." Story translated this assertion for the nationalists.

> The cardinal conclusions for which this doctrine of a compact has been, with much ingenuity and ability, forced into the language of the Constitution, (for the latter no where alludes to it), is avowedly to establish that, in construing the Constitution there is no common umpire; but that each State, nay, each department of the government of each State, is the supreme judge for itself, of the powers and rights and duties arising under that instrument.

Instead, the Constitution was

> not a contract imposing mutual obligations, and contemplating the permanent subsistence of parties having an independent right to construe, control, and judge its obligations. If in this latter sense, it is to be deemed a compact, it must be either because it contains, on its face, stipulations to that effect, or because it is necessarily implied, from the nature and objects of the frame of government.

Story emphasized one aspect. Political scientists commonly discussed compacts. Did it not make sense that the Framers would have expressly included a descriptive phrase defining the Constitution as a compact? Upshur elected to highlight another. Lawyers realized that categorizing a document involved an examination of its clause's effects on the constituency. Here, the Constitutional provisions insured that it was a compact.

Upshur acknowledged that the national government, within its Constitutional sphere, was superior to those of the states in some instances, and coordinate in others. Citizens, commanded by their own states through ratification, must recognize the federal government's power and authority. Moreover, both citizens and states must refrain from construing the obligations of ratification. But, a state did have the power to "judge of its own obligations, and ... those of the Federal Government, so far as they relate to such State itself, and no further" because some questions of federal power were not conducive to Supreme Court scrutiny. This power followed naturally from state sovereignty. Their creature, the government, could not judge the states since the compact parties need not obey government usurpation. As sovereign states, they interacted through a compact, in this case the Constitution.

Nullification was an example of state sovereignty in action. Its adherents sought only to prevent a Constitutional usurpation. As a party to the compact, South Carolina had executed its power to stop government usurpation. This decision did not include any suspension of the compact. Secessionists based their argument on a state's power to withdraw from the Union at will, but did not claim that this abrogated or suspended the Constitution for the other states. It would merely revoke the seceding state's membership in the compact. Furthermore, the other parties could not coerce it to return or treat it as an enemy.

Justice Story had constructed a tiered power scheme for the interpretation of the Constitution and laws. Because the Constitution was a law — the supreme law — the Court could interpret it. Logically, it took precedence over those of a state, making its interpreter, the Supreme Court, the final arbiter if a case were within its jurisdiction. Article III and the Eleventh Amendment listed this jurisdiction clearly. Cases and parties to controversies were well defined. "Beyond these cases," interjected Upshur, "they [Justices] have no jurisdiction." Usually cases arising under the Constitution were based on a restraint of some Constitutional right while those under the law also involved the Legislature. These powers were not exotic. They were a direct product of the compact between the states. Therefore, the federal judiciary, "the common tribunals of all the States" could adjudicate them, Clearly, powers assigned by the parties to the compact were limited and circumscribed by restrictions.

The states had agreed to Court authority under certain conditions. However, if it usurped power through its decisions by ignoring jurisdiction or the definition of eligible litigants, the compact parties could ignore its decision because it had broken the agreement. Within the Constitution, "the judges are the interpreters of the Constitution, [and] there is nothing to prevent them from interpreting in favor of any power which they may claim." This included cases and jurisdiction not expressed within the Constitution. Was there an antidote to this usurpation?

According to Upshur, the Tenth Amendment took effect when the judiciary overstepped its boundaries. It reserved the state's powers from the federal government, and its departments in particular. At this point, Upshur made a novel interpretation. The Amendment reserved power to the states "respectively; that is to each State separately and distinctly" because any power held by an independent state must be sovereign. The independent state could exercise it without reference to another. One example of this power would be nullification of a usurping federal statute.

Story considered the Tenth Amendment mere window dressing. Without it, government powers would remain unchanged. Upshur countered this assertion. The Tenth Amendment's role was to bind the government's power to select its own means. The sweeping clause applied only to Congress and The Tenth acted as a buffer against its undue power assumptions.

One must always insist, said Upshur, that the federal government was not a compact party. It was merely a state construct, designed to accomplish certain legislative, executive, and judicial tasks. Was it sensible that the agent judged the powers of its master without reference to the other parties? If the answer was positive, the written Constitution had no value. It would ignore express powers and trample on the rights and liberties of the people. Eventually, one department would insist that it could rule the others, an intolerable situation. No, the sovereign states must retain the right to interpret their own compacts without interference. For example, one might decide that an extension of a Court power destroyed an enumerated power and refuse to obey its ruling. Another would be the blatant jurisdictional acceptance of a case denied by the Eleventh Amendment. Many Constitutional cases did not assign jurisdiction to the Court.

We know that the Supreme Court, if it had jurisdiction and the parties were well defined, was the ultimate arbiter of the constitutionality of a law. Suppose a case arose between a citizen and the United States. If the Court had jurisdiction and ruled against the United States, the decision was acceptable. However, if a citizen lost the decision, the courts of his own state would tender any relief. He must obey only those federal decisions that his state accepted. The question became, "did the state agree to the passage of the law in question?" If yes, the individual found no relief. Otherwise, the law under which it convicted him was a usurpation and his state might, or might not, interpose for his benefit. The case, originally between the state and a citizen, transmuted to one between a state and the United States. As usual, the United States could not judge the actions of a party to the compact. The state would adjudicate and its ruling would be binding.

Some may conclude that the above scenario usurped Court power. Upshur did not agree. He was sure that judiciaries throughout the world operated under similar restrictions. He lectured,

> It is their [Court] proper province to interpret the laws, but their decisions are not binding, except between the parties litigant and their privies. So far as they may claim the force of authority, they are not conclusive, even upon those who pronounce them, and certainly are not so beyond the sphere of their own government.

The states created the government and its departments and therefore the Court could not require them to seek its guidance unless their obligations stated it explicitly.

Naturally, sovereignty, strict construction, and implication came under review. Sovereignty did not reside in the government because it was subject to the power of those that created it. Within states, the people were obviously sovereign. Similarly, if the "people of the United States" existed, it would have sovereignty over the Constitution. Still, one cannot divide sovereignty. It could never simultaneously reside in the people and government. Thus, sovereignty must reside in the people of the states, that is the states. Government, as shown earlier, was simply an agent designed to "exert" the sovereign's power.

Judge Story demanded a liberal interpretation of the Constitution, particularly regarding implication. Upshur argued that "a strict construction of the Constitution will give to the Federal Government all the power which it could beneficially exert, all that is necessary for her to possess, and all that its framers ever designed to confer on it." Each sovereign state received and gave what they defined in the contract. Of course, its exposition must contain a restriction on any liberal interpretation since each state, as grantor of power, "would give exactly as much as it would take away. The only mode ... by which we may be certain to do no injustice to the intentions of the parties, is by taking their words as the true exponents of their meaning."

Implication, as usual, was a provocation to state rights men if the addition of the sweeping clause provided for an unwarranted extension of the enumerated powers. Yet, for the Tenth Amendment to come into play, should not the Framers have included the word "expressly"? Upshur thought not. If "expressly" had been added, Congress could not have enacted necessary incidents. For example, Congress could provide for a Navy but could not build a dry dock though it was a "necessary and proper means for providing a Navy." By eliminating "expressly" one received the best of two worlds. It allowed necessary incidents but curtailed congressional power. As a natural extension of this interpretation, Upshur concluded, as had John Marshall for the opposition, that incidental powers did not exist. The Constitution granted all powers and implied none.

Story rejected this line of reasoning. Harkening to Alexander Hamilton's defense of a national bank, he stated "that every power vested in the government was, in its nature, sovereign, and included by the force of the term, a right to employ all the means requisite, and fairly applicable to the attainment of the end of such power." Upshur also returned to original thinking. He reminded his readers that Story's argument was tantamount to that objected to by Patrick Henry during the ratification debate. He had warned that Federalists would claim that the Constitution granted every power unless it was specifically exempted. Recalling an earlier Marshall decision, Upshur declared, "the means must be *consistent with the letter and spirit of the instrument* [Constitution]" if Story's locus of power was to be minimally acceptable.

It was evident to Upshur that Story's omnipotent government powers resided in an unrestricted majority of the people. They had, unchecked, the numbers to decide as they pleased. Certainly, homogeneous governments, like those of a state, could operate effectively under this condition. Nevertheless, a huge heterogeneous country like America would develop the problem of large minorities and tyranny could follow. Justice Story's America provided no solution. The Court was a department of his government and had displayed little impartiality thus damaging minority rights. Despotism of the majority would accompany a government that justified "its excesses under the name of republican liberty." Lately, this had been the result of government consolidation, "the government of an irresponsible majority."

What role did state rights play? Governments constantly attempted to increase their power. For its part, the state rights "school of politics" believed strongly that its precepts were the only "effective check upon the Federal Government." At some point in time, unless restrained, government power would be unrecognizable from that originally designed by the Framers. State rights men fought this tendency because they loved the Constitution and Union. Insuring the rights of the states translated to confining government usurpation and preventing tyranny.

Unfortunately, Americans often misunderstood state rights. For example, no one had ever argued that the Constitution expressed state interposition. That right was a function of sovereignty, not constitutionality. To argue, as did Story, that its believers "forced this principle into the language of the instrument" was dishonest. In the same vein, state rights men had never asserted that no common body could construe the Constitution nor that any state department had "a right to judge for itself, of the powers, rights and duties, arising under" the Constitution.

According to state rights dogma, the states had created the Union. Therefore, it seemed strange to Upshur that some Americans accused them of planning its destruction. After investing it with powers to benefit the people, why would the states hamstring those powers? The answer lay in history. "The danger is, not that the States," warned Upshur, "will interpose too often, but that they will rather submit to federal usurpations.... Flagrant abuses alone, and such as public liberty cannot ensure, will ever call into action this salutary and conservative power of the States."[6]

We now have enough data to compare and contrast, circa 1850, the two state rights subclasses, traditionalist and sovereigntist. To do so requires an imposition of specific categories driven by the ideology. The critical element was sovereignty, the basis of the compact theories and in turn state rights. Once this trio has been developed, we can move to their effect on government.

Disciples of each variation agreed on the origin of sovereignty. Because of the Revolution, Virginians had reverted to a state of nature but retained their sovereignty. The Declaration of Independence separated the state from Great Britain but failed to divide its citizens. The identical political society, based on a social compact, existed both before and after the Declaration. Since it was Virginians' primary allegiance, they could forgo the lesser one to Great Britain. Of course, sovereigntists interpreted this dynamic as a transfer of sovereignty from the king to the state. The next step was to agree on a new social compact.

In their "highest sovereign capacity" Virginians agreed to a state constitution outlining the power disposition between the people and government. Madison described this compact to his kinsman Nicholas Trist. "The original compact," he explained, "is the one implied or presumed, but no where reduced to writing, by which the people agreed to form one society." Interestingly, powers not directly assigned to the people were delegated to the state government. This assignment introduced an interpretive difference. Although each variety of state rights agreed that the state, that is the people of the state, was sovereign due to the delegation of sovereign powers, sovereigntists added that the people had no power left to distribute to a central government.

The necessity for a central government to bind the states required another political compact for state rights men. The Constitution, as a compact, described a temporal transfer of authority from the state to the general government. Again, sovereignty came into play. The radical sovereigntists assigned the states complete authority and its government was but its agent. The opposition traditionalists adopted dual sovereignty at ratification delegating some recallable sovereign powers to the government and the remainder to the states. As a result, they could argue that the Constitution was created by both the people and the states and generated two compacts mirroring dual sovereignty. In counterpoint, radicals assigned that task to only the states. So, although the two subgroups agreed that the United States was a confederation of states, they differed substantially on its basis.

Not surprisingly, the above discussion might lead one to conclude that the two state rights variations would lead to differing government relations. Sovereignty evolved from interposition and nullification to a position at which it demanded government sanction for southern rights. During this era, traditionalists maintained their affinity for limited government. Of course, sovereigntists argued that the central government was only an agent of the sovereign states and as such could not direct the parties to the constitutional compact. Any attempt by the government to increase its power without state permission could be checked.

Traditionalists emphasized the state's reserved rights through a constant resort to the Tenth Amendment. Usually, each side saw these rights as an extension of natural rights, but sovereigntists eventually stressed state independence and sovereignty both before and after ratification.

Due to radical theory, there was always a possibility that the Union would split. In the first few decades of the nation's existence, radical Southerners had been strong supporters of the American System, but by the 1830s their faith in a strong central government had been replaced by that of a strong state government. Disputes between different government levels must meet the tests laid out by radicals. On the other hand, traditionalists would use petitions, state appeals, Supreme Court decisions, or new elections to solve these problems. Their adherents could not find any basis for Jeffersonian democracy in the radical dogma.

Traditionalists rejected the idea of single state secession because of their affinity for dual sovereignty and compacts. But, sovereigntists had no difficulty advocating it due to their belief in state sovereignty. Unhappily for future events, there was one condition upon which both sides agreed. The central government could not coerce a state. Madison predicted the sequel to its application.

> The use of force agst. a state, would look more like a declaration of war, than an infliction of punishment, and would probably be considered by the party attacked as a dissolution of all previous compacts by which it might be bound.[7]

10

The Culmination of the State Rights Doctrines

In August 1846, President James Polk requested $2,000,000 to purchase land from Mexico, currently at war with the United States. When the appropriation reached the House of Representatives, David Wilmot, an antislavery, high tariff, Pennsylvania Democrat, proposed a bombshell amendment. Modeling the Northwest Ordinance of 1787, he demanded,

> that as an express and fundamental condition to the acquisition of any territory from the Republic of Mexico by the United States by virtue of any treaty which may be negotiated between them, and to the use by the Executive of the money herein appropriated, neither slavery nor involuntary servitude shall ever exist in any part of said territory except for crime, whereof the party shall first be duly convicted.

This powerful antislavery proposal channeled all sectional debate for the next fourteen years and set the stage for southern secession. Although it passed the House several times, the Senate always rejected it. Still, it lay bare before the nation the chasm between its two societies.

For our purposes, this chapter amalgamated the Proviso's effect with those of the Compromise of 1850 and the Kansas-Nebraska Act to demonstrate changes to state rights doctrines wrought by the territorial dispute. The result was publicized in the Virginia secession convention of 1861.

✠

Virginia's delegates made the first legislative protest against the proviso. On February 17, 1847, Lewis E. Harvie, a state sovereigntist, introduced several strong resolutions that the house slightly edited and published on March 8. They became a template for southern reaction — often called the Platform of the South — to the proviso. Because the assembly considered it "destructive of the compromises of the constitution of the United States, and an attack on the dearest rights of the south, as well as a dangerous and alarming usurpation by the federal government," it favored Harvie's resolutions. The government of the United States did not control slavery. If it attempted to do so, it usurped power by interfering with the "internal organization" of the sovereign state that created it. Northerners seemed to forget that the public domain was the "joint and common property" of all the states. Within it, each had equal rights and any federal law that prevented Virginia's citizens from emigrating to a territory was discriminatory and a violation of the Constitution "and the rights of the states from which citizens emigrated." If Congress ignored the spirit of the Missouri Compromise, then Virginia might choose an alternative path to Union. The last resolution called for united action by "every slaveholding state ... to take firm, united and concerted action in this emergency." From our previous study, we noticed that states usually acted alone as befit a compact party. From this time forward, the phrase "southern rights" began to replace "state rights" in debate. The South considered itself one political unit.

Following another House passage of the proviso, the assembly issued a second set of resolutions that R. M. T. Hunter eventually introduced to the federal Senate. However, the house was not ready for confrontation and smoothed over the radical sections. Originally, Governor John B. Floyd, in his annual message, pronounced that if the proviso ever passed, "then indeed the day of compromise will have past [sic], and the dissolution of our great and glorious Union will become necessary and inevitable." Nevertheless, a united South could prevent this catastrophe. The Constitution protected slavery and Virginians would never submit to any federal law abridging it. To defend against such a federal proposal, the governor would call a national convention to seek solutions to its passage. After nearly one month, the assembly passed and sent more moderate resolutions to Hunter. They reaffirmed the 1847 resolutions, announced that any law abolishing slavery or the trade was "a direct attack upon the institutions of the southern states" and predicted a resistance to their implementation. The passage of the proviso would result in an extra session of the Legislature to plot Virginia's course. These replacement resolutions were clear indicators that moderate Virginians were still in control and that saber rattling, but not action, was the result.[1]

Establishing the correct interpretation of previous territorial acquisitions and applications for statehood was crucial for House Virginians. Thomas H. Bayly, tempestuous future Chairman of the House Ways and Means Committee, offered one hint from the past. One needed only examine Great Britain's methodology and the Patriots' reaction to establish a parallel situation. Had not the Revolutionaries refused Parliament's authority over its territories in the same fashion that the southern states denied Congress's authority to legislate for the American territories? Also, the proviso's proponents would find no authority in the Northwest Ordinance of 1787. Not only did the Articles of Confederation assign the Continental Congress few powers, but also the one required to pass the Ordinance was nonexistent. Congress realized this usurpation, so it had labelled it a compact. On at least two occasions, Congress had defeated attempts to insert a "no slave" article. But, it did form territorial self-government, including the power to alter congressional laws. Thus, the Legislature had enacted for the territories, who, in turn, could repeal the law. Did this not indicate that Congress was organizing new states?

Now, if it were creating a compact to accept new states, who were the partners? Surely the state delegates had no power to act on this issue. No, said Bayly, "if this ordinance is to be considered a legislative act, it was always null and void ... because the Congress of 1787 had no authority to pass it as such." James Madison in *The Federalist* No. 38 supported him in his contention. After describing Congress's actions, Madison added, "and all this has been done, and done without the least color of constitutional authority." Therefore, the article prohibiting slavery was a nullity. James McDowell agreed that the Ordinance was unconstitutional, and added a vital fact. Congress held the territories relinquished by Virginia "for the common use and benefit" of the United States, including Virginia. Because of this enduring, but faulty, understanding of Ordinance constitutionality, "the Territories [were left] without any regular territorial government at all — to distract our national councils with agitation, and to bring the different sections of our great Union into an inflamed and dangerous state of irritation and contest with each other."

Bayly cited Madison in another instance. On August 18, 1788, Madison proposed Legislative powers to the Committee of Detail, "to dispose of the unappropriated lands of the United States" and "to institute temporary governments for the new States arising therein." The Convention adopted the first in form. The second was lost to posterity. One could infer that the Convention loathed assigning this power to Congress. Thus, the only territory in existence had its own temporary government with the power to make any alterations to its own charter.

Were northerners, asked the soft-spoken James Seddon, willing to ignore the compromises solemnly agreed to by both sections during the Convention? One of the "sacred compromises" concerned slavery. Its stability was the focus of the fugitive slave clause that assured the master's rights to his property. Senator James M. Mason reminded his colleagues that when slaves toiled in the North, representatives of their white masters "conceded to the slaveholding States important privileges and advantages ... for which they derived ample equivalents." They agreed to a system by which fugitive slaves would be "delivered up" to their owners. Also, southern suffrage rights were based on the institution. Attacks on all these, claimed Bayly, proved the abolitionists were intent on a "war upon slavery" despite constitutional guarantees. "When the South insisted upon safeguards and guarantees in one part of the constitution," he asked, "as a condition of their adopting it, can anyone believe they would have conceded in other parts powers which would make them all nugatory?" To Virginians, a deal was a deal.

The Compromise, "the great pacific settlement of the Missouri question," was cast aside as a benchmark. Even some Virginians refused to employ it as a basis for further compromise. William B. Preston, who eventually offered Virginia's ordinance of secession, refused to extend the 36°30' line. How would Virginia's slaveholders react if they transported their property to a supposed slave territory, but, several years later, immigration reversed territorial opinion? The fight over slavery would begin again, because a state could judge its own institutions. Bayly supported this position. The "South had voted against the Missouri compromise" because the "strict constructionists never admitted the right of Congress" to "adopt fundamental legislation for the territories." Despite this objection, "it was forced upon us by the North." Still, Bayly warned that proviso implementation would prove northern bad faith. If the 36°30' line was acceptable in 1820, why was it not so now? Senator Mason firmly advocated its extension to the Pacific and he claimed that the Virginia legislature supported him. He could not guess what other compromises might be necessary to accomplish this goal, but they would include "terms similar to those adopted in 1820, on the occasion of the admission of the State of Missouri." If all else failed, perhaps the judiciary ought to adjudicate the problem. Nevertheless, an extended compromise must both define the boundaries of Texas and prescribe territorial governments in the part of California below the 36°30' line. Robert M. T. Hunter considered the Missouri Compromise as a template for future territorial division. If any territory were unavailable to all, then Congress should divide it between the sections.

Surely, Mexican law would come into play. According to Senator Mason, "it [slavery] never has been prohibited by the Mexican Congress in California" except during government dictatorship. Although there had been acts of emancipation, there had never been one of prohibition.[2]

✠

As might be expected, opponents hurled harsh accusations concerning perceived motivation. According to James Seddon and James McDowell, some northern colleagues, who did not support the war, sought to label it as one of slave territory acquisition. If they could incite southern "disgust" for the proviso, perhaps the latter would end their participation. This scenario was invalid. Seddon himself was not a proponent of the Mexican invasion, but army preservation in the face of the enemy had forced him to support a bill to supply the troops. Slowly the conflict had drawn him to its defense. Upon reflection, he concluded that "we had been subjected to a repetition of insult and injury from her [Mexico]" and support was inevitable. Considering this train of events, the charge that the war was one "of acquisition with a view to the extension of slavery and the aggrandizement of the South, falls hurtless and pointless." Except the "rightful" acquisition of Texas, Seddon had no territorial ambitions. However, he realized that a Mexican defeat meant it would have to cede territory to the United States. He suggested New Mexico and California. These were national, not sectional goals.

The southern view of northern motivation was clear. "The majority of those who represent the people of the United States in Congress," one declared, "have a right by law, to prohibit the people of the southern States from taking one species of property into their territory; and ... there is nothing in the constitution to prevent it." R. M. T. Hunter took it a step farther. He accused the North of planning "to denationalize the institution of slavery ... that is, to place it beyond the protection of the General Government."

Northerners amazed Virginia representatives by their determined support of the proviso. "Is it done," questioned McDowell, "to try the strength of our political system, and to see from actual proof what the agencies are that can tear it apart?" "Does the North suspect the loyalty of the South?" What would the North gain by successful passage of the proviso? Obviously, the "moral and social, if not the political unity of your country will be broken up and destroyed." Despite this puzzlement, "it is due from Virginia to make every effort to save both the Union and the indispensable rights of the people."

Expansion of the American borders had always involved Virginian blood and treasure. "Is there a sod of soil, a strip of territory won by the unaided valor, or purchased by the separate treasure of northern men?" queried James Seddon. Still, northern fanatics would deny Virginians the right to emigrate there with their "guaranteed" property despite the southern predominance in the conquering army. Surely concluding that southern efforts at nation building would always result in their prohibition from the new territory was easy for them. Such would be the case because freesoilers could occupy it before slaveholders could organize. The territories would all become free.

Virginians suggested several other disparate motivations behind the proviso. The abolition movement was the "prompting of the British nation" who had "aggressions on us"; politicians would make "the slavery question ... the prominent issue in all the Congressional elections"; uncaring demagogues ignored both the unconstitutional issues and the inexpediency of the proviso considering that fourteen of the thirty states opposed it; unethical abolitionists had spread a false message about the proviso since it "does not emancipate a slave, or make one of a person now free"; and America would be better off if the South had more power to protect its rights. Senator Mason, disenchanted by the process, demanded that the government print various resolutions for southern distribution. Their damning language would educate Virginians to the true state of slavery agitation in the North. "I think ... it is absolutely necessary to the preservation of our rights," he said, "that we should have this knowledge."[3]

The principal constitutional arguments, pro and con, ran the gamut of possibilities. It included forays into congressional power, federal protection of slavery, republican equality, popular sovereignty, and, of course, slavery. Each came armed with its own prediction of the results of congressional action.

"Not from timidity or weakness," explained James Seddon, "but from prudence and choice, we plant ourselves on the constitution and its solemn compromises." Yet, legal manipulations alone did not drive Virginia's attack on the proviso. That resolution, said Seddon, was an outrage against the spirit of the Constitution "and subversive of the very basis of its being." Thomas Bayly agreed. While discussing Congress's power to legislate for the territories, he exclaimed, "I maintain that not only no such authority is delegated by any provision of the constitution, but [also] that it is in direct conflict with some of them, and with the spirit of the federal instrument." Republican governments simply did not act in this fashion.

An examination of Article I, Section 2, clause 3 would convince anyone that it linked republican government and slavery since it apportioned both representation and taxation among the states. Did this not mean that the Constitution not only provided for future states but also provided for future slave states? "This proves conclusively," insisted Bayly, "that the framers of the constitution contemplated the future admission of slave states." Obviously, Congress would carve most of them from the territories.

Because the Constitution promised republican government to the states, it also pledged self-government, one of its "fundamental principles." If a territory were subjected to the laws of Congress, in which it had no voice, then it could safely claim that it was the subject of tyranny. Surprisingly, northerners "professing to being republicans come here, and not only claim the right to legislate for people without consulting them, but absolutely to make that legislation irreversible."

Northern insistence that Congress could legislate for the territories cast it in the role of supporting an unconstitutional act. Moreover, every territory that it had organized had been done so illegally. Everyone recognized that the people delegated limited powers to Congress. Now, it, in turn, claimed the power to redelegate some of them to a territory. According to authority and the Constitution, the Legislature cannot delegate its delegated powers. A glance at post territorial organization would prove this allegation. Each of these "temporary governments" was unconstitutional.

The proviso was unconstitutional because it violated the equal rights of the states and their citizens. Whenever congressional law exempted a citizen "with respect to his internal affairs," then it did not divest him of this right upon his emigration to a territory. If so, he was subject to an unconstitutional law. "Although he was exempt in his State from the tyranny of being governed by laws which did not operate at all upon the majority which passed them," argued one Virginian, "yet by going to a Territory, he would be compelled to live under laws, in the enactment of which the precise portion of the people who would be subject to them would be the only portion which could have no hand."[4]

The main question associated with the proviso was whether Congress had the power to prohibit slavery in the territories. Of course, Virginians tried to influence the question negatively. First, they sought to define their terms. The singular use of the word "territory" in the Constitution convinced them that the Framers meant land, not jurisdiction, in Article IV. Thus, the correct relationship between the territories and government was one of the soil and did not extend to any attempt to regulate people or their personal property. If Congress could rule on property within a state, then it could legislate for slavery there. Since this was unconstitutional, it seemed logical that it could not rule on property in the territories. Congress could pass laws required by the infant territory, but none should restrict slavery.

What tethers did Virginians snake around Congress's powers? Of course, they began as usual. Congress could apply only powers delegated by the states and those did not include territorial exclusion of slaves. Nor was it an incident of the power to acquire territories. Therefore, Congress had no power to legislate for the domestic affairs of a territory. If the proviso allowed Congress to legislate within a territory, an incipient state, the federal government would ignore the general welfare. Remember, it held the territories in trust for all the states and should not abuse it. Southerners must have free access with their property to all the territories. Congressional authority ended after it proposed a form of government.

Congress also scrutinized territorial government power. Suppose the government abolished slavery from California and New Mexico and, by extension, other territories under the proviso. No one could challenge it "even if a law was passed creating the institution or repealing the statute already written." Congress would refuse the will of the people. Clearly, said Mason, it must wade through the legal swamp surrounding slavery in the territories before considering any free state application from California.

Never had there been any attempt to restrict slavery in the territories, except the unconstitutional language in the Northwest Ordinance. Even the Missouri Compromise offered a palliative to southern fears. Always, Congress had given the territory legislative powers, although possibly, that was unconstitutional. Moreover, it usually appointed territorial officers, which infringed on the president's appointing power. Nevertheless, it did suggest an acceptance of the territorial government's power to control its own institutions.[5]

Many Virginia legislators did an about-face on the application of federal power. Recall, it was a fundamental precept with moderate republicans that government should adopt, as far as possible, a hands-off policy toward state rights. Southerners knew best how to organize the institution of slavery. This policy changed for radical state rights men during the debate over territorial expansion. James Seddon exhorted the federal government to protect southern property "which it is under the most solemn obligations to conserve and maintain." He linked this demand to "the basis of equality and mutual privilege." Congress must protect territories "in their chrysalis stage." The Calhounite, James M. Mason, reminded the Senate that the Constitution, federal law, and Supreme Court decisions, required northern states to provide "for the capture and surrender of fugitive slaves." However, the nonslave states would evidently not cooperate. "We must have federal officers," claimed the senator, "because the States affected will not permit their own officers to execute a law of this Government." Mason agreed with Seddon that since territories were the property of the United States, southerners had the right to emigrate there with their property "and to enjoy it under the protection of the Constitution." The federal government must take positive steps "to interpose to remove such hindrance." Constitutionally, the president, "as the head of the Government," insured that it "faithfully executed" all laws, particularly those of property. R. M. T. Hunter added that territorial governments must protect slave property if it existed there. Moreover, said James McDowell, to participate in territorial expansion, the slaveholder should not have to give up rights assigned to him by both the federal and state constitutions. Instead, they should protect those rights. A slaveholder had "the very same right to call upon that Government to protect it [slavery] that he would have to call upon the State to do so."

This doctrinal variation did not pass without comment. Senator Henry Foote of Mississippi, a compromiser on popular sovereignty, chided Virginians on its sudden appearance.

A Senator from the Old Dominion herself [Hunter], of a State-Rights Strict-Construction school, formerly a zealous non-interventionist, now cries out for intervention ... I am most seriously mortified that this claim of "protection" for a great constitutional right by act of Congress emanates from a Senator from my native state.... Sir, is this standing upon the rock of the Constitution? Is this an appeal "to the great principles of justice, the Constitution, and self-government"? ... Why, Sir, does he not discover that he is warring most mischievously upon State rights and State dignity? Indeed, I fear that all the doctrines once so highly venerated, of the State-rights school of Virginia, are about to fall into contempt and oblivion.

In short bursts, state sovereigntists had expanded their doctrine. They borrowed the notion of nullification from the Report of 1799 and appended the right of secession to it during the Nullification Crisis. In the 1840s, many returned to the concept that sovereignty was indivisible and combined it with the basis positions of sovereignty, compact, limited government, and strict construction. Still, the moderate state rights version appealed to a wider audience from 1800 to 1846. Coincident with the territorial slavery dispute, sovereigntists recast their theory and captured a significant minority opinion. They based it on the need to disprove the constitutionality of northern territorial claims. Success in this effort required a new paradigm. Fortunately for our purposes, Arthur Bestor, in 1961, wrote the seminal article on state sovereignty. We will follow his guide.

According to Bestor, most students of state rights associated local autonomy, decentralization, and interposition with state sovereignty. Unfortunately for them, these assertions may have had currency before 1846, but afterward they proved less applicable. For, if they were precursors to secession, one would be hard pressed to explain the South's actions. From 1846 onward, slavers expected the Union to continue. As Senator Foote told us, some Virginians looked to the Constitution and federal government to protect slavery. Not until other forces intervened in 1861 did sovereigntists judge the Constitution to be badly flawed. Frequent southern cries for protection promoted consolidation, not decentralization, and weakened arguments for local autonomy. Moreover, their actions put a crimp in the basic notions of nullification and interposition.

Due to the nature of the Fugitive Slave Law, slave owners could argue that they could apply a state law outside their borders. If that were true, could other instances follow? Might they transfer to the territories? All these examples promoted the notion that the states required federal government protection for slavery in the west. Bestor concluded that rather than the defensive posture associated with traditional state rights, state sovereignty was an aggressive doctrine of power and command. As a corollary, all its demands proved that the sovereigntists recognized that the national government was supreme.

They offered five planks for slavery protection. A sovereign authority — that eliminated the territorial people — was necessary to exercise power; the Tenth Amendment precluded any attempt by Congress to wield a police power over a territory; no sovereign had delegated Congress power over a territory; local police powers belonged to the sovereign states; and the federal government was the agent of the states. As a group, these planks elevated the states into the position of sovereign, while the last would lead to broad, not strict, construction of the Constitution. Moreover, it hinted at a nationalistic, not localist, approach.

Whereas moderate state rights protected individual and minority rights, state sovereignty did little. Moreover, the former had a shaky relationship with the judiciary, while the latter embraced it as a defender of southern territorial rights. One can see why traditional state rights men held this naked power doctrine in such low esteem.[6]

The sense that southerners had become second-class citizens was a dominant theme of territorial debate. Every speaker worked it into his message. The Framers had designed the Constitution to protect liberty and individual rights for all Americans. If it could not do so, they should tear it up. Equality could also mean equality of choice. Unfortunately, the proviso interdicted this process. No longer would the property rights of one section be as valuable as those of another. The situation reminded James Seddon that his Revolutionary forbearers had faced a similar charge of inferiority from the haughty British. It forced him to conclude that once a section allowed a law denoting its citizens' inequality and inferiority, others were likely to follow. Had not the process begun already with the slaveholder condemnation? Did not "these northern gentlemen make it one of the chief objects of this Government to stigmatize the institutions and deprecate and impair the labor and property of the people of one-half the States of the Confederacy"?

One must understand that the Constitution defined a "Confederacy of equals," both on the state and individual levels, because "it makes no invidious distinction between States or citizens." Inequity would be the result of recognizing disparate rights for different species of citizens and Virginians would "protect the rights of her sons" by any legitimate means. For example, the equality of "immunities and privileges" could never be protected if Mexican law influenced that of the acquired territory. Remember, colonial Americans had insisted on representative government despite Parliament's habit of meddling in their domestic affairs. By dividing the nation into unequal classes, northerners increased the likelihood of conflict.

When citizens emigrated to a territory, "they carry with them all their rights, the most important of which is the right to self-government." It followed naturally that "all the States of the Union are tenants in common; and that it is common property ... on all the vacant territory of the United States." All Americans, despite geography, shared this right equally. If the government prevented a territory from selecting its own government, its citizens lost the equality they had enjoyed before emigration. As a last resort, southerners had a right to a partition of it or at least access. This had been the American experience since 1820 but the proviso destroyed the equal enjoyment of the public domain.

It was interesting that every other form of property, except slaves, could be transported to a new territory. Because of this discrimination, the proviso treated immigrants from different sections unequally. Of course, this was antithetical to the notion of a right "that can be enjoyed unmolested, undiminished, and freely." Moreover, the proviso acted against the slaveholder in another way. Nonslaveholding became a condition of immigration and was in place before the master prepared to emigrate. Using the same principles, was it far fetched to claim that Congress might refuse to apply funds from the sale of territorial land to the slave states unless they renounced slavery? "If the territories are ... common property," argued James McDowell, "then the exclusion from their use of any part of the people by conditions not affecting all of them alike, is clearly and offensively unequal." It seemed incongruent that immigrants of all kinds, including foreigners and criminals, were welcomed, but southerners with their property were not.[7]

Seeking an alternative to the harsh reality of the Wilmot proviso, worried representatives began to support the notion of popular sovereignty, also known as squatter sovereignty or nonintervention. Overall, it suggested that emigrants from each section could enter a territory and in either the state or territorial phase, they would choose their institutions.

Timing was crucial. If popular sovereignty included the territorial power to exclude slavery, no slaveholders would emigrate. On the other hand, if a law postponed the slavery decision to the state constitution phase, slaveholders and their property could emigrate and influence the choice from within the territory. Robert R. Russel, an investigator of the Compromise of 1850, claimed that "informed people of the day used the term 'squatter sovereignty' or 'popular sovereignty' [when] they meant the right of a *territory* (not a state) to decide for itself what to do with regard to slavery during the *territorial stage*."

Virginia representatives appended conflicting corollaries to the general idea. Southerners should not demand, declared one, the establishment of slavery in the territorial phase. Let the "climate and soil" be the final discriminators. Yet others insisted that they must not reject slaves from the territories or organize territorial governments immediately without reference to slavery.

Senator Mason reminded Congress that at the Baltimore Democratic Convention, his northern colleagues had agreed that Congress would not intervene in territorial slavery. To do so would damage both state equality and individual rights. Unfortunately, for those faithful to an extension of the 36°30' line, this might be an unacceptable delimiter. The line's historical and constitutional precedents swayed them.

As we have noted, the Patriots had rejected Parliament's claim that it could legislate America's domestic affairs. Nor did the Constitution authorize Congress to enforce republican government in a territory/state. Its only task was to furnish a form of government. American citizens had the absolute right to judge a territory's institutions. One cannot escape the conclusion that opponents of the proviso found disparate reasons to favor either popular sovereignty or an extension of the Missouri Compromise line. However, usually the latter group took the fallback position of the former.

Repeatedly, the people as sovereign highlighted the debate. It was a "fundamental principle of American law" that only the people could establish domestic institutions. Thomas Bayly took the debate on Congress and republican government in another direction. He proposed that the Constitutional clause on that subject did not allow Congress to interfere in a state constitution because "to say that we may prescribe is to declare that the people shall not create a constitution themselves." Remember, authority for territorial government comes from its people, not Congress. Interference was tantamount to unrepublican government.

Although many Virginians viewed popular sovereignty as an alternative to the proviso, they recognized some important weaknesses. To Bayly, its acceptance introduced associated conundrums. Suppose the United States acquired property in which slavery existed. Did that mean that it automatically legalized bondage? Could the people of such a territory, through their legislature, "prohibit slavery in the event of the first question being decided one way or legalize it in the event it was decided the other"? In short, could a territory establish its own institutions? Perhaps the courts could adjudicate this question.

No concession of self-government was unlimited. It must pass the test of protecting a citizen's "life, liberty, and property." For example, the territories had no authority to pass a law preventing slaveholders from taking their property there. Unfortunately, a rump convention in California had taken steps in that direction. The first comers to that territory had legislated in a way that affected individual rights without congressional restraint. This was an unhappy situation because Congress, the trustees of all the people and the true owners of California, had accepted the result. Now, immigrants who had lived there for two years or less had extended its southern boundary below the Missouri Compromise line. Moreover, non-slaveholders would fill California and eventually they might carve three states from it. Clearly, those who preferred the extension of the 36°30' line had reason for their chilly support of nonintervention.

State opinion against the proviso matched that in Congress. Richmond Democrats strongly supported favorable resolutions offered by Representative Daniel Dickenson (New York) because of the "true constitutional spirit they evince." The proviso was "a gross outrage upon the rights of the South and an ... open violation both of the letter and spirit of the constitution."[8]

According to both James Seddon and R. M. T. Hunter, slaves were usually considered property. Even the Supreme Court had ruled that "you have a right to carry slaves and to be protected in your property through free States, to some other slave State." Thus, slavery in the territories was not a new issue.

Some territories were apparently not conducive to slavery expansion. In one instance it was a matter of timing. Southerners could never resurrect California as a slave state because it had already shown that it would not do so. New Mexico was not prepared for organization said some, but they wrapped that conclusion in demagoguery, presidential politics, and sectional advantage. Interestingly, Virginians failed to present an argument that slaves would not be productive in the territories. Perhaps this was due to its position as the preeminent slave broker.

They offered many reasons for their role in the slavery debate. Slave states were best qualified to manage it; not one slave would be set free nor a free black made slave by this proviso; the article controlling the slave trade in the District was not a template for the territories because it had power over a place not people; and they were only responding to another attempt at northern political advantage.

The Fugitive Slave Law was crucial to Virginia's representatives. Its author was Senator James M. Mason and he made the bulk of remarks on its history and future. Unfortunately, northern states had chosen to ignore the current law. It laid out the process by which states were to help slave catchers reclaim runaways. Even the Supreme Court in *Prigg v. Pennsylvania* had insisted that Congress must legislate their return. Because states refused their own officials permission to perform this duty, Congress should provide federal functionaries to take over the task. This act of nullification could have onerous effects on constitutional law. "I fear ... that the legislative bodies of the non-slaveholding States," he predicted, "and the spirit of their people, had inflicted a wound upon the Constitution which will prove itself" irremediable. Otherwise, there was no current method to ensure they obeyed the law. As parties to the federal compact, to which northern states had assented, Virginia had a right to expect the federal government to do its duty. Northerners must promptly return fugitive slaves to their masters.[9]

Several alternative dangers loomed. As we have noted, Thomas Bayly regarded the issues to be so conflicting that he might send the question concerning Congress's power to legislate in the territories to the judiciary. Just how he would accomplish this was not made clear. James Seddon could not understand why northerners could constantly assert that slaves and free labor could not coexist and the former must give way. On what basis did they make such an assertion? "Are they better men, wiser, purer, or greater men," he asked? Such an assumption labeled all southerners to be inferior. James McDowell suggested that northerners just let slavery alone. His inference was that it would live or die on its merits and utility. Seddon was not willing to turn the other cheek but he did not mind turning the tables. Was it not true, he asked, that a representative could propose a proviso that would exclude all citizens from the territories unless they brought slave property with them? "Yet were [this] our proposition," he intoned, "...how loud and with what manifest justice would [be] the outcry of the North against our rapacity and our gross outrage on the common charter of the Confederacy."

One might expect the slight against southern honor inherent in the proviso to draw attention. James Seddon warned that,

> To do so [accept the proviso] would be to argue us unworthy of our ancestry and their heritage of fame and freedom, and would exhibit us as but too ready to be degraded and oppressed, meriting richly the dishonor and exactions we would by slow degrees but soon inevitably realize.

Associate Justice Peter V. Daniel emphasized the northern assumption that its society was superior to that of the decadent South.

> There is another aspect of this pretension which exhibits it as fraught with dangers far greater than any that can flow from mere calculation of political influence, or of profit arising from a distribution of territory. It is that view of the case which pretends to an insulting exclusiveness or superiority on the one hand, and denounces a degrading, inequality or inferiority on the other; which says in effect to the Southern man, Avaunt! you are not my equal, and hence are to be excluded as carrying a moral taint with you. Here is at once the extinction of all fraternity, of all sympathy, of all endurance even; the creation of animosity fierce, implacable, undying. It is the unmitigated outrage which I venture to say, there is no true Southron from the schoolboy to the octogenarian, who is not prepared for any extremity in order to repel it.

William B. Preston recognized the importance of honor to some Virginians but he was intent on solutions. Because of this attitude, he presented a compromise plan for the territories.

Congress would ensure a republican government in the Mexican acquisition. On October 1, 1849, it would accept the whole California territory ceded to the United States as one state and its people would write their own constitution. Thus, he recognized the great principle of, "supremacy and popular government." Furthermore, this stratagem might avoid any proviso attachment because California would enter as a state. By persuasion he could avoid its deleterious effects. Unfortunately, he was wrong, and the proviso's proponents killed his potential compromise.[10]

Virginians proposed disparate state reactions to territorial restrictions. Obviously, the threat of less slave territory accompanying any adjustment of Texas's borders was worrisome. The "territorial prison" that would envelop the South if the proviso applied to all future territories dismayed James McDowell. No matter what choice a Virginian made, the proviso would punish him. If he emigrated without his property, the slave/master ratio in Virginia would increase producing a dangerous situation. Eventually, slaves would "absorb" every trade craft, force more emigration, and continue the deadly spiral of black concentration. Naturally, this prediction contained warnings about the economic future for masters that remained. Thus, it would adversely affect property and security.

Perhaps the most important long term result was Virginia's heightened lack of trust in the North's motivations for change and a concomitant shift toward secession rhetoric.

McDowell eloquently reminded the House that Virginians considered themselves "wronged, aggrieved, and outraged" by the offensive contents of both the proviso and northern criticism. The likelihood of secession would take another step down its dangerous path. R. M. T. Hunter warned of "the fearful proclivity with which we are proceeding in the downward race of concession and submission," while McDowell labelled the proviso "a first measure for the dissolution of the Union." Seddon also announced that "the ultimate issue of the conflict may involve the dissolution of the Union." He foresaw "a mangled Constitution and dismembered Union." "I utter this," he warned, "in no spirit of bravado or menace; I know the people of the South and believe it." Henry Bedinger, who seldom entered debate, clearly announced, "But the time is coming, sir, the first blast upon that trumpet has been blown; the first mutterings of that thunder have been heard in the distance — the first threatenings of that storm which I fear is destined to shake this Union to its firm foundations." The southern states, according to James M. Mason, "just as cordially as they came into this Union, so will they go out of it when they are satisfied that the bonds of Union are regarded by the majority only for the purpose of oppression."[11]

Although the Compromise of 1850, Kansas-Nebraska Act, and Dred Scott decision provided solace to many Virginians, the sudden rise of the proslavery Republican party challenged it. In April 1860, the Democratic party gathered in Baltimore to select its presidential candidate and build a competitive political platform. Southerners demanded territorial slavery protection while western Democrats opted for a compromising statement that could smooth party differences. They could either send slavery questions to the Supreme Court or endorse popular sovereignty. After the convention adopted the western approach, the cotton state delegates withdrew. The remainder chose Stephen A. Douglas, but he could not muster the required two-thirds majority. The Democracy decided to try again in June.

Again, the attending southern delegates walked out. They met in Richmond and selected John C. Breckenridge of Kentucky, rending the party North and South. It was a dramatic precursor of future events.

Old line Whigs, conservative by nature, nominated John Bell of Tennessee to support the Constitution, Union, and obedience to the law. Still, it was the burgeoning Republican party that offered the principal Democratic competition. It chose Abraham Lincoln as its candidate and endorsed platform planks on the tariff, internal improvements, homesteading, and a Pacific railroad. Although it would not attack slavery in the southern states, Republicans still opposed any expansion in the territories.

Lincoln's election hastened deep South secession. On December 20, 1860, South Carolina left the Union. By February, six others joined it to form the Confederate States of America. At President Buchanan's urging, Congress appointed committees to seek a reunion compromise. Senator John J. Crittenden of Kentucky proposed a series of constitutional amendments guaranteeing slavery within the states and meeting demands concerning both runaway slaves and District slavery. Most important, he suggested that the 36°30' line extend westward with respect to all territories then held or afterwards acquired. Republicans rejected Crittenden's proposal.

Virginia attempted compromise. The legislature invited delegates to Washington to discuss solutions. During February 1861, they worked assiduously for a solution, but its resemblance to Crittenden's plan predicted a certainty. The Senate again refused to countenance it.

Meanwhile, Virginians prepared to debate the fate of the Union. On January 8, 1861, both houses had passed resolutions decrying coercion of a seceding state. Later, the assembly provided for convention delegate election on February 4. Those elected would meet in Richmond nine days later to consider Virginia's future.

Differentiating between the doctrinal views of convention delegates was difficult. James C. McGregor in *The Disruption of Virginia*, identified three categories. They were "avowed Secessionists, avowed Unionists, and those who would 'preserve the Union if it could be done with honor.'" Henry T. Shanks, in his seminal *The Secession Movement in Virginia, 1847–1861*, was individually more discriminating. Of the 152 delegates, about eighty-five had favored the Whig John Bell, forty-seven had voted for the northern Democrat Stephen H. Douglas, while thirty supported the southern Democrat John Breckenridge. Like McGregor, Shanks delineated three distinct groups murky at the borders. They were secessionists, moderates, and Unionists. Members of the first group were usually from the Tidewater, Piedmont, or Southwest and assumed secession was a right, sure that Virginia interests mirrored those of the cotton states, and unbending that it should join them soon. Perhaps, some thought, good tactics suggested waiting for the results of the Virginia-sponsored peace conference. Lewis E. Harvie (Amelia and Nottoway) and Henry A. Wise (Princess Anne) provided the leadership.

The moderates, usually state rights Whigs plus a few Douglas and Breckenridge men, also recognized the right of secession. Nevertheless, Virginia should attempt compromise beforehand. Robert Y. Conrad (Frederick), Robert E. Scott (Fauquier), and William Ballard Preston (Montgomery) provided its leadership. They pinned their hopes on a border state convention to provide solutions to any disunion problems.

The Unionists, led by George W. Summers (Kanawha), John S. Carlile (Harrison), and A. H. H. Stuart (Augusta), were mainly national Whigs or Douglas Democrats. Located principally in the Valley and Northwest, they denied any secession right, but refused to extend federal law enforcement to a seceded state because it was both unconstitutional and inexpedient. Although secession was not acceptable, any people could revolt if conditions became unbearable. They should actively seek compromise, but if it failed, dissolution at this time was not the result.

Convention delegates provided little information on its divisions. Lewis Harvie recognized that his party was in a distinct minority. J. G. Holladay (Norfolk County) found only two parties, the secessionists and those demanding constitutional guarantees while perpetuating the Union. Robert L. Montague (Matthews and Middlesex), a secessionist, reverted to the MacGregor-Shanks model. Humorously, he called the factions "extreme secession," a middle party defined by Preston, and a third "a little farther down [Unionists]." The main difficulty with this division was at the edges and with the moderates. No one could fail to categorize Harvie, Montague, or Carlile, but many adopted one or more tenets of a faction but not others. Party switches like that of James Barbour, who converted from moderate to secessionist during the debate, complicated matters. Still, the MacGregor-Shanks model may be most accurate, and we will follow it except in special circumstances.

On the third day of the convention, the delegates appointed a select twenty-one member committee called the Committee on Federal Relations. Its task was to organize specific resolutions to act as a touchstone for debate on important issues. Meanwhile, the conventioneers established their positions.[12]

One issue that produced no party or sectional dissent was the efficacy of slavery. Whether Piedmont planter surrounded by slaves or Northwestern farmer energetically ploughing his own fields, slavery found no detractors. Delegates declared it a boon not an evil, "one of God's institutions," and "a blessing alike to the master and the slave." According to the secessionist George W. Randolph (Richmond City), Virginia had to protect its institution now. "We must have not only immunity from attack," he acknowledged, "but [also] rest from the ever wearing agitation of the slavery question." His colleague Henry A. Wise agreed, and to facilitate this protection, he wrote a minority report containing several constitutional amendments.

The Federal Relations report included fifteen "guarantees and assurances" that the North must accept. Most involved slavery protection. James P. Holcombe (Albemarle) added a further crucial parameter. Without room to expand, slavery would die and one could expect southern slave revolts. Perhaps William G. Brown (Preston), a northwesterner, vocalized Virginia opinion on the institution's role. "I am not only interested directly in the institution of slavery," he enunciated, "but have vindicated it as one highly conservative; one that is ordained of God himself for the purpose of redeeming the African race from barbarism."

Randolph offered an interesting aside. He was sure that future Republican judges would be the catalysts for deciding the locality of slavery, whether within a state or territory. He did not trust this future. Experience had taught him that the opposition habitually found alternative ways of interpreting laws and the Constitution deleterious to the South.

Unionist delegates did not recognize any beneficial aspects of secession on the institution. Virginians must remind themselves that they had supported every slavery measure since ratification of the Constitution. This record did not convince one that Virginia should secede over the results. Moreover, secession failed the practicality test. Everyone knew that losses due to runaway slaves were negligible. Also, if secession avoided war, masters would transfer their slaves from northern Virginia to the rich cotton lands further south. Yankees, hostile to slavery, would quickly move into these areas, undermining its white basis. The result would be civil war. Virginia would require a "cordon of military posts" lining its northern border. What would it gain through separation? Instead, it must calmly assess the issues before blindly leaping into the secession quagmire.[13]

Slavery in the territories raised a new set of questions. According to the Dred Scott decision, said most Virginians, southerners could now participate equally in the territories because they could migrate to them with their slaves. However, Abraham Lincoln's Cooper Union speech plus the Republican platform raised doubts about the Scott decision's longevity. One plank asserted, "And we deny the authority of Congress or a Territorial Legislature or of any individuals to give legal existence to slavery in a Territory of the United States." Unionists, like George W. Summers and secessionists like Jeremiah Morton (Greene and Orange) agreed that such a plank bode ill for Virginia. Summers considered acceptance of the Dred Scott decision an abandonment of the Missouri Compromise line in return for supposed equal access. If Virginia could not trust the North to accept the decision, perhaps it should protect itself by demanding a partition of any territory. Morton disagreed with those who considered the 36°30' line to be one of equality. Surely, that word implied equal access. Nevertheless, northerners could migrate both north or south of the line while it restricted southerners with their property below the line. "I would not give up," he intoned, "the perfect equality of the North with the South, that is established by the Dred Scott decision."

Considering the lack of current territory that it would affect, Morton may have been attempting to establish a principal that they might apply to acquisitions further south.

The radical Franklin P. Turner (Jackson and Roane) offered several suggestions. Virginia must stop using euphemisms for slavery in its reports. Also, the government must explicitly protect slave property in the territories; extend the 36°30' line to the Pacific; and require a concurrent majority of slave and nonslave states for the acquisition of new territory.

Unionists like John B. Baldwin (Augusta) and Hugh M. Nelson (Clarke), were sure these territorial demands were nonsensical. Secession, at least temporarily, would obviously cut off Virginia from the territories. Would it not have a better chance of access by working within the Union? Also, the remaining territories were not conducive to slave labor and Virginia had no surplus slaves to send west. If true, Virginia could expect an "Africanization of the South." Baldwin summed up the Unionist argument by reminding the convention "that the question of extending slavery into them is one purely abstract, that they are not adapted to slave labor, and that no sane man, having regard for the prudent investment of his money ... would ever think of carrying slave property into these Territories."[14]

Initially some delegates were confused about the motivation behind a rumored border state convention. For example, James B. Mallory (Brunswick) assumed its purpose was to unite a "Central Confederacy." When appraised of its true nature, he agreed that the border slave states should meet only to affect a united strategy. Most moderates agreed with this conclusion. William A. Goggin (Bedford) considered it a vehicle for influencing other states and James A. Cox (Chesterfield), George W. Best (Amelia), John B. Baldwin and Robert E. Scott agreed. They named Frankfort, Kentucky as a likely venue. Still, Goggin and Best had other considerations. Best viewed a conference as a natural place to gather potential amendments for any future ultimatum to the North. Otherwise, Virginia should just turn south. Goggin made no direct comment on Best's conclusion but he did remind his colleagues to look to their roots. Scott was the most optimistic about the outcome of the border conference. He assured the convention that it "will avoid war."

Surprisingly, the secessionist leader Lewis Harvie took his party's most compromising position. He accepted the notion, but would never let other states decide Virginia's fate. His partners uniformly dismissed the idea. James C. Bruce (Halifax), Henry A. Wise, Thomas F. Goode (Mecklenburg), Thomas S. Flournoy (Halifax), and Franklin P. Turner labeled it a waste of time. One had only to look at other conferences to predict the result. Disagreements between potential allies would ultimately lead to "animosities and hatreds." Surely, argued Wise, this was just a moderate tactic to delay eventual secession. Since the government had shown no inclination to compromise, a border slave conference was questionable. Virginia should forget this useless tactic and immediately join the cotton states.[15]

During the debate on the federal relations report, the ultra, Robert M. Montague, offered an incendiary amendment clarifying one conception of the Union's nature. He claimed that Virginia was independent and sovereign. William H. McFarland soon enunciated the crucial questions. "While Virginia acknowledges her obligations to the Union," could it simultaneously be out of it? While it was within the Union, were its delegated powers "hers in fact"?

One might expect that this query would elicit different definitions of the word sovereignty. Few considered one germane. William C. Scott (Cumberland and Powhatan) said it was synonymous with "supremacy." Angus R. Blakey (Madison) thought it a "primitive, original power." As Scott inferred, most members were unconcerned about the word's definition although they were vitally interested in its nature.

Unionists and moderates led the charge against Montague's amendment. History, according to John Carlile and Timothy Rives (Prince George and Surry) offered evidence that Montague's amendment did not fit the facts. An examination of the ratification article would persuade a reader that it was "binding upon the said people" not the people of the several states. After all, the Declaration of Independence did not list the separate states individually which "sufficiently confutes ... the doctrine of the individual sovereignty and independence of the several States." It was "never thought of by the enlightened patriots who formed this Declaration.... Let us then consider all attempts to weaken this Union by maintaining that each State is separately and individually independent, as a species of political heresy." To counteract the Articles reference to sovereignty and independence, Carlile raised the ghost of James Madison. "Some contend that states are sovereign," Madison had stated, "when in fact they are only political societies.... The states never possessed the essential rights of sovereignty. These were always invested in Congress."

When challenged, Carlile retreated to Madison's dual sovereignty model. Although sovereignty rested with the people of the several states, they "have agreed one with the other that certain sovereign powers shall be exercised for the benefit of all." Constitutional amendments bound all the states, even the minority not in favor.

Clearly, an absence of essential powers was tantamount to a lack of sovereignty. Robert Scott remarked that Montague's amendment was just an error of fact. One need not look far to find essential powers that the states had delegated to Congress. George Baylor mused that the phrase "the powers not delegated" implied that they had delegated some powers. Moreover, denying that the states delegated powers was impossible if one argued that the Union was a compact. According to Rives, Virginia could never confer sovereign powers on Congress and still claim to be "*entirely sovereign*" and "*independent.*" Continuing this concentration on lost sovereignty, William C. Scott maintained "I hold that the State of Virginia, and other States, are not sovereign so far as regards the powers that are granted." William McFarland was sure that the American confederacy deprived its members of "essential and important attributes" so they could not be sovereign.

One could not examine sovereignty without including the Supremacy Clause. Both Rives and George Baylor held that its power was discriminating. It insured that a federal act superseded any state equivalent upon the same subject. Baylor, parting from some of his colleagues, insisted that sovereignty was not divisible. The concurrence of this assertion and the Clause resulted in a lack of sovereignty and independence in Virginia.

An examination of some likely effects associated with Montague's resolution might persuade one to reject it. J. G. Holladay associated it with a power to secede from the Union. Rives claimed that such an interpretation would allow the government to set up a monarchy despite the article on republican government. Considering these criticisms, prounion sentiment insisted that Virginia was not sovereign within the Union. Interestingly, the state could reassert sovereignty by reclaiming its delegated powers. Unfortunately, as McFarland noted, secession might be the result.

It was evident to radical state rights men that no consolidated American people ever existed. "It was never true," claimed Miers Fisher (Northampton), "that the people of the States of this Confederacy associated with each other as people." Instead, said Wise, the people of Virginia were "her organized legal voters" because the State was an organized people. If so, how could there be an American sovereignty? Radicals, to their satisfaction, skewered consolidation on this ground. Wise put it nicely. "I knew ... that your report [Federal Relations] would bring up the fundamental principles that have guided us in this State, at least from 1800 down to this time. It is impossible to keep them down. The old strict construction of the States Rights principle meet an antagonism here."

Historically, the Constitution merely expanded the ideas of the Articles of Confederation. It was noteworthy that Virginia, throughout the Constitution building phase, followed the steps one expected of a sovereign and independent state intent on forming a compact with its peers. According to Henry Wise, these compact parties could merge their sovereignties and each would then be a "united sovereign, independent power." Through this compact, Virginia could wage war or apply other delegated powers. Even if the national government declared war in the face of Virginia's objection, the state would remain sovereign because her obligation to the compact overrode a temporary disagreement. Within the document, the Preamble, before an unwarranted edit by a convention committee, listed all the states individually. Did this not infer sovereignty and independence?

The states granted certain nonpermanent powers to the general government and Virginia retained these powers. Wise grounded this opinion on an interesting interpretation. "It is not true in political law," he lectured, "that nothing can be above a sovereignty; a sovereignty recognized *de facto* and *de jure*." Dozens of nations had given up vital sovereignty to others but were still considered sovereign.

Angus R. Blakey invented an interesting path avoiding the issue of delegated sovereignty. Recall, he claimed that sovereignty was a primitive power and the people spoke through their state. However, if it delegated a power to Congress, it did not transmit the primitive power. Instead, it delegated a derivative power, a copy, which Congress might apply, but was never sovereign.[16]

The Virginia legislature, on January 8, 1861, by an almost unanimous vote, had condemned the principle of state coercion. The vote was a solid predictor of the convention's attitude. All three factions fell into line behind the assembly.

Walter D. Leake (Goochland) and James W. Sheffey (Smyth) gave the delegates a working knowledge of coercion. The federal government could not forcibly retake the occupied forts nor collect any revenues on imports within seceded states. Speaker after speaker reprehended the policy. It was just a pretext to consolidate the government; no constitutional power allowed it; an "impairment of their [cotton states] safety is a danger to our own"; it was nonsensical that the agent of a compact party could act against it; it was "a declaration of war"; and the Eleventh Amendment and *Chisholm vs. Georgia* prevented federal coercion were a few of the complaints. Any coercion "into reunion or submission" would result in civil war because "the people of Virginia will never be coerced." According to Sheffey, "the sword of coercion will be raised over our beloved Union" if Virginia did not resist.

The eminent historians Henry Shanks and Daniel W. Crofts supplied students of the era with several interesting motives for Virginia's firm stand. If allowed, coercion would change the nature of the Union and subjugate the state. Because it would affect her economic system, Virginia faced the humiliation of a conquered state denied the fundamental right of equality. Moreover, it would force the Old Dominion to take sides against its fellow slave states. Inevitably, coercion forced an agonizing question on a slave state. If it did not resist now, what other catastrophe would follow?

Because of the North's relentless succession of broken promises, it was likely that Virginia would resist the federal government. If it persisted, "an identity of interests and of wrongs with the seceded States" would send Virginia's forces to aid "in resisting such aggression." Also, joining a powerful southern confederacy would better serve Virginia because the government would be less likely to attack a united South. James P. Holcome (Albemarle) left us with a ringing tribute to state rights: "Infinitely would I rather see her [Virginia] fall in a glorious struggle for her own rights, and the rights of her sister States, and leave to future history the memorable response in her behalf, 'dead upon the field of honor.'"[17]

Delegates offered various scenarios leading to secession. Radicals uncovered several proximate causes. Henry Wise claimed that the South had always kept her bargain, but the "Black Republicans" had broken "every constitutional obligation and every constitutional right which the South holds dear." Lincoln's election alerted George W. Randolph to the South's precarious position. Since it did not "violate the forms of the Constitution," it proved that the document could no longer protect the minority South.

Some delegates tried to blunt a stampede to secession by contradicting commonly held beliefs. No one should claim that Lincoln's election was *prima facia* evidence for secession. Virginians overemphasized its importance. After all, he represented only one branch of government. Do not forget, it was the abominable political tactics of the Democratic South that led to Lincoln's election. One need only examine the vote tallies to understand that the president could never cause secession. However, Lincoln's Inaugural Address elicited fears of coercion among Virginians despite George W. Brent's claim that it contained the Principles of '98.

Historians could write chapters about the effect of equality, honor, and humiliation on secession motivation. Perhaps, we should let the participants speak for themselves. George W. Richardson (Hanover): "Neither individuals or nations can submit ... to insult and indignity ... I, for one, will never consent to live or hold intercourse with men who claim that I am socially their inferior." Jeremiah Morton: "Is the Northern man a better or purer man than the slaveholder from the Southern States? I think not." James P. Holcombe: "There is yet another feature of this sectional ascendancy ... the element of humiliation; not only the iron hand of oppression, but the insolent spurn of contempt." John B. Baldwin: "Sir, I stand here to demand, under all circumstances, to demand against all opposers full equality — aye, for protection, for all the institutions of the South."

Delegates debated various secession options. According to the ultra Walter D. Leake, his colleagues had only two choices, go North or South. Others discriminated between restoring the old Union or joining the new confederacy. Jeremiah Morton would restore the old Union only "upon terms of safety and honor to all its members." In what must be a surprise to many readers, Henry Wise proclaimed that the real goal of secession must be to unite the old confederacy while Lewis Harvie partially supported him. He proclaimed, as one might expect, that Virginia must "make a common destiny with the Cotton States and to break up this Union," but added, "unless these States come back." Although the Gulf Squadron was out of the Union, it had the power to treat with the United States for possible restoration.

Even secessionists considering a new union usually advocated exhausting all methods before going South. Virginians "would not hesitate to unite with her sister States of the South," but radical Virginians must remember that the Union was a compact and only the parties could solve this problem. On the other hand, ultras like James C. Bruce (Halifax), demanded "what has this Confederacy done for us?"

Moderates were not immune to restoration of the old Union. They adopted a position that an apparent tough stance might force the North to rethink its position. Perhaps Virginia should "cling to the Union" as long as possible while working for reunion. It should threaten to secede, resume old Union property rights, convene with the other border states and recognize the Confederate States of America. Hugh M. Nelson suggested that the Old Dominion must stop slavery agitation by constitutional amendment. Restoration required an unrepealable extension of the 36°30' line across the continent, a guarantee that the North would give up fugitive slaves, and pledges that Congress must get the consent of all states before interfering in the territories. Otherwise, Virginia would secede "upon equitable terms and conditions, and for a proper division of the common property." The *Report on Federal Relations* contained a notice that Virginia should work to restore the Union, but if such were not achieved, it would resume its reserved powers. The threat of secession did not sit well with Goggin. "I do not believe ... the doctrine of the right of a State to secede," he declared, "as a remedy under the Constitution, or as existing by compact; but I believe it to exist only by the action of the people in Convention, but only as a right, which, for good cause, our fathers acted upon when they declared themselves independent of England." Revolution, not secession, was the answer.

The Unionist majority wanted "compromise, conciliation, a settlement" and sought only vague "assurances" for restoration. The South, for the last fifteen years, had prospered so secession was unfathomable, merely a "political idea" and if Virginia remained in the Union, this prosperity was bound to continue. Secession was a precursor to civil war and was nothing but "political suicide" and, "the direst calamity that could befall a people." In another vein, Virginia could never support any state that claimed federal property. Of course, most northwesterners supported the Unionist faction, that generally had little inclination to protect slavery. Moreover, its border counties would be the first to feel the federal boot.

One large delegate contingent did not specify Virginia's destination. Some preferred to "appeal to the God of battles" unless Virginia could remain in the Union "upon terms of honor." For them, it was mandatory that all its rights and equality be constitutionally secured. Hopefully, these changes would "preserve and adjust [the] proper equilibrium between the sections." There could be no "lasting peace or permanent security" unless one amendment prevented the government "from using its authority ... to the prejudice of their [southern states] institutions."

Another group specified that the cotton states were Virginia's natural home. Security for her institutions lay there because Virginia faced identical dangers. The moderate William Goggin specified that, without concessions, Virginia must join the confederacy. In any case, according to the radical Walter D. Leake, his state should never go hat-in-hand like some mendicant north with ideas to save the Union. Let it solve the problem, and if it could not, Virginia would go south.

This latter plan did not satisfy Unionists. It particularly incensed Samuel McD. Moore (Rockbridge). Prior to their secession, the cotton states had neglected to share their plans. Why would Virginia join them now? Its vital interests differed from those of the confederacy and Virginia had lost many fugitive slaves while they had lost virtually none. Moreover, they were unlikely to promote a tariff, declare for free trade, and impose direct taxes. The absence of these policies worked against a new government's revenue requirements and would be "absolutely ruinous to Virginia." Perhaps most loathsome to Moore, was the strong possibility that the confederate states would restart the slave trade. He could never accept it. Thomas Branch (Petersburg) echoed Moore's anger at the deep South's unilateral action regarding secession. It had thrust the commonwealth into a very delicate position without consultation. He might consider a border state confederacy but would never go south. George W. Brent (Alexandria) could not see any advantage to union with the cotton states. As noted earlier, Virginia would have to seal off her northern border to contain runaways. John B. Baldwin seemed to enunciate the general Unionist opinion. The Gulf Squadron had not earned the right to dictate Virginia's policy and it should not receive the chance to do so.

Most Unionists would not consider secession. "I ... denounce it as being the most absurd and ridiculous notion that was ever presented" declared Moore. Waitman T. Willey (Monongalia) declared that he was not there "to break up this government" although the South had suffered many grievances. Secession was not constitutional, and historically, the famous Report of 1799 had never included it as an option. Logan Osborn (Jefferson) agreed. Secession required unanimous approval. The Northwestern Unionist John Carlile announced that "the Union is mine and it shall go ... to my children to be handed down to them." Could anyone believe that the Framers, the most brilliant men in the country, had "expressly provided in the Constitution for its dissolution." No one could break up "a more perfect union" and to do so was equivalent to war.

Brent theorized that secession under certain terms was legal, but here he saw only expediency because the motivations preferred for it were spurious. Those who argued that the election of Lincoln was proof of future aggression could not satisfy South Carolina's commissioners' repudiation of their argument. Similarly, inequity and the South's exclusion from the territories may have been a defensible philosophy, but fell on the horns of practicality. No remaining American territory could support slave labor profitably. Last, did any conventioneer believe that South Carolina and the cotton states had been injured by northern personal liberty laws?

Of course, the radicals knew that "the people of Virginia recognized the American principle that government is founded in the consent of the governed." By extension, a state could secede from the Union. Virginians first allegiance was to their state and it could be "lawfully withdrawn by her whenever she may deem it her duty to do so." The federal government played no role in this decision because only the compact parties had the prerogative. As a corollary, the United States government could not operate within a seceded state. However, the convention identified an important theme that the old Union was gone and her citizens must concentrate on their own self-preservation.

A notable contention in the secessionist argument was Virginia's claim that it could resume its delegated powers. According to L. S. Hall (Wetzel), "Virginia has the legal right at any time to return to herself the powers that she heretofore granted to the Federal Government." James Boisseau (Dinwiddie), Thomas F. Goode, James W. Sheffey, and Benjamin F. Wysor (Pulaski) supported this position. J. R. Chambliss (Greensville and Sussex) supplied the theory behind it. The people of the several states "acting for themselves" were the people that reserved the right to resume their powers. No others had it. Logically, it could not be the people of the whole United States "for there could be no oppression of the whole with their own consent ... and it could not have entered into the conception of the convention that the power granted could not be resumed until the oppresser himself united in such a plan."

Benjamin Wilson (Harrison) provided another similar explanation.

> To my mind, it is clear that the right to resume rests in each State to be exercised by its Convention possessing sovereign powers, subject only to the action of the people.... If this were not so, and the right to resume depended upon the will of the majority of the people ... it

would place it in the power of the majority to "pervert the government to the injury and oppression" of the minority, and give to that minority no other right but that of revolution.

Unionists could never accept these interpretations. Within the reservation, the people mentioned were the people of the United States, not the people of Virginia. Surely, if the Convention had meant the people to be those of Virginia, it would have specified it. Secession was not constitutional or legal.[18]

News from Washington shuffled aside all diverse opinions. Once the convention confirmed that Fort Sumter had been fired upon, secession was inevitable. Even the staunch Unionist, Robert E. Scott, agreed that "we must disconnect ourselves with this Federal Government." Lincoln's call for 75,000 troops, confirmed by Henry Wise on April 15, merely hardened the established opinion. The next day, the convention went into secret session and William Ballard Preston, a moderate, presented an ordinance of secession based upon Virginia's reserved right of June 25, 1788. On April 17, 1861, by a vote of 88–55, Virginia's delegates seceded from the Union. The state rights doctrines were complete.[19]

One wondered if war were inevitable. Surely each section's ideology led to that conclusion. Because they were founded on mutually exclusive bases, the sections talked past each other in critical situations. True, the several states had signed famous compromises over the decades, but they had few lasting effects. Instead, they acted as a stopgap before the next vituperative round because the North relied on its Constitutional, or favorable Supreme Court, interpretations while Virginians were apt to elevate extra-constitutional ideals based on sovereignty, the social compact, and reserved rights to explain their position. The Tenth Amendment's interpretation was a perfect example. Northerners, activated by the Supremacy Clause and its partner the sweeping clause, considered it mere window dressing because the Constitution had not assigned any irrevocable power in the amendment. Virginians riposted that, due to the Constitutional compact, "expressly" was unnecessary in a statement that simply declared a power understood to be a reserved right. Even if the Constitution had omitted the Tenth, that argument was germane. Since most northerners would not accept Virginia's reliance on compact, discussion and compromise were fruitless. Practically, the events of the secession winter proved that interpretation. Each side was determined to force its ideology on the other. The above remarks, in conjunction with the numerous disputes studied in this work, make it clear that Virginia's lack of trust in the North's motivation for power accumulation was a major contributor to the eventual split.

Brilliant historians over the last century have offered ingenious explanations for civil war causation. They made their task difficult by the scope of their task — to account for the action of many states. This study has narrower goals. Given the accumulated information, the possibilities in Virginia reduce to three, defenses of slavery or state rights or their combination.

Undoubtedly, today most historians favor slavery as the primary cause of the Civil War. Let us stipulate that conclusion for the deep South. If such were the case, then an interpreter must explain the time lapse between the Gulf Squadron's secession and that of Virginia. The clear answer was that it did not have the same fealty to the institution as had her sister states. However, that conclusion did not infer that it had little interest in slavery protection.

Our examination of the secession convention demonstrated that the radicals could not convince the traditionalists or Unionists to sunder the nation. State slavery was a constitutionally protected state right, so it seemed unlikely that defending the existing institution was at secession's core. Still, we can extend our baseline by including slavery in the territories as a motivator. Certainly, Virginia's state sovereigntists would fight for southern and property rights over their territorial exclusion. However, they were badly outnumbered by the moderates and Unionists.

Events at the secession convention provided our answer. Remember, sovereigntist attempts to stampede Virginia toward secession had failed. Nevertheless, myriad Supreme Court and congressional constitutional interpretations still rankled. It was in this milieu that Lincoln's demand for 75,000 troops to coerce the Gulf Squadron back into the Union recalled for moderates the Madisonian, and state rights, pledge that a republican government could never coerce a state. Liberty must be defended. Virginian distrust of the northern majority, stewing for decades, exploded and produced secession. To stress that point, Governor John Letcher couched his refusal to take part in a coercive action by referring to the long held and oft quoted Virginia reservation of 1788 that concentrated on reserved rights. The above discussion suggested that any historian interested in Virginia civil war causation must begin with its adherence to state rights and add a spoonful of distrust, keeping in mind that state controlled slavery was a state right's plank.

The latter conclusion raised another question. If state rights, and not just its plank, state controlled slavery, was the underlying cause of the Civil War, why did so many southern commentators focus on slavery in their denunciations of northern motives? For example, Congressional attempts to avoid war in the secession winter coupled with the various state secession ordinances might convince one that slavery divorced from state rights was the cause of Virginia's secession. Two explanations were germane.

As demonstrated herein, a significant number of Virginians had proved their state rights fealty through the decades. How would one uncouple the plank from the doctrine whose basis was the Constitution? Was it not logical to assume that a Virginian promoting slavery did so because of its relation to state rights?

A second sister motivation was based on regional interplay from 1820 to 1861. Overwhelmingly, for Virginians, northern attacks on slavery were the principal friction points between the sections. Was there any doubt that northern abolitionists kept up a steady drum beat against the institution? Given this assumption, it was understandable that Virginians couched their responses in the terms defined by the attacks. Logically, arguments against slavery elicited its defense despite its relation to state rights.

Transitions

Throughout the antebellum period, traditional moderate state rights was the preferred Virginia doctrine. Nevertheless, beginning with South Carolina's nullifying adoption, and continuing with the feisty debate over territorial slavery, state sovereigntists exerted increasing influence. Now influential conservatives like Littleton Tazewell and Abel Upshur publically contradicted the notion of one nation while simultaneously casting off Madison's dual sovereignty. Based on the Tenth Amendment, they concluded that a single state, since it was a compact party, could secede from the Union. Upshur even agreed with John Marshall that the sweeping clause did not imply incidental power. As the Chief Justice had proposed, incidental power did not exist, thus no implication was inherent within the sweeping clause.

Moderates maintained their usual fidelity to compact theory and strict construction, but events in the territories forced them to adopt new planks. They returned to the classical republican tenet of equality as a corporate goal. Also, they continued the thrust toward individual rights established during the 1790s. Still, their distrust of human nature overall, and the federal government in particular, hamstrung their view. If one contemplated state coercion, what other tyranny would follow?

Was it possible that the sovereigntist power doctrine could protect slavery, whereas moderate state rights could not? After all, many Virginians had concluded that the debate over slavery camouflaged a naked power grab. Despite this unease, moderates could not accept their opponents' philosophy. In a worst-case scenario, coerced moderates would adopt the state sovereigntist' ends but skip the means. Instead, they would persevere with Madison's Convention assertion. A republican government could never coerce a sovereign state.

Surprisingly, one would find relatively few debate references to liberty in this period, but given the circumstances and the doctrine's reliance on self-preservation, perhaps they were unnecessary. To sovereigntists, secession would produce liberty through reunion with the cotton states, while moderates seemed unsure of their destiny. They preferred Union, but realized state coercion would push them toward secession. Unionists maintained that they had found liberty within the United States' fold.

The main question facing sovereigntists and some moderates concerned timing. Could they trust the northern states to eschew coercion and not threaten liberty while they struggled with this critical decision? In addition, they were not sure if northern abolitionists would protect southern rights and institutions. Until late in the convention debate, the pressure applied by the sovereigntists to secede failed. However, with the call for troops, coercion trumped caution. For moderates, Lincoln's action confirmed that they could not trust the North.

As usual, historical imperative produced changes in state rights dogma. Because each party to the compact could construe it, often states stood alone in constitutional controversies. However, by approximately 1848, individual state power began to give way to a united southern coalition. Popularly, the phrase "southern rights" often replaced "state rights" in debate and newspaper columns. Two decades of abolitionist pressure had succeeded in psychologically uniting previously separate states.

Still, the core traditional state rights tenets remained firm. Their reliance on state sovereignty, the centrality of the compact, limited government, strict construction, the power of the Tenth Amendment, the primacy of the Union in times of stress, and the contention that the states had built a Union became more prominent after political reorganization in 1824. The emergent national Democratic party platform from 1840 onward specifically announced some plank supporting state rights. Yet, one trend was evident. Even moderates began to revert to the original notion of undivided sovereignty. If it became universal, the specter of a dismantled Union ratcheted up a notch. Madison's dual sovereignty had been an important aspect of the relationship between the federal government and the states.

The dispute over the nature of the Union produced new clarity. Debate over original interpretation versus a living document, "one people" versus "the people of the United States" and organic growth versus planned Union under a compact were more immediate than disputes over implication. In addition, radicals began to emphasize the Convention notion that the federal government could not coerce a state.

Perhaps the most disheartening aspect of the debate for Unionists was the increasingly vituperative aspect of specific allegations. One cannot read Governor Floyd or Beverley Tucker without recognizing their naked hatred for Jackson and Van Buren and by symbiosis, the North, in their allegations. It was one thing to have a staid legal debate, but another to consider openly, or to promote, disunion. Perhaps these rabble rousers were comfortable in the knowledge that their methodology mirrored that of abolition extremists. Still, with each section harboring ultras, hatred and mistrust challenged the Union.

Chapter Notes

Chapter 1

1. Lance Banning, "Jeffersonian Ideology Revisited: Liberal and Classical Ideas in the New American Republic," *William and Mary Quarterly*, 3rd ser., 43 (1986), 6 and "The Republican Interpretation: Retrospect and Prospect," in Milton M. Klein, Richard D. Brown, and John B. Hench (eds.), *The Republican Synthesis Revisited: Essays in Honor of George Athan Billias* (Worcester, MA: American Antiquarian Society, 1992), 95, 102 and *The Jeffersonian Persuasion: Evolution of a Party Ideology* (Ithaca: Cornell University Press, 1978), 55, 107 and *The Sacred Fire of Liberty: James Madison & the Founding Fathers of the Federal Republic* (Ithaca: Cornell University Press, 1995), 216; Gordon Wood, *The Creation of the American Republic* (Chapel Hill: University of North Carolina Press, 1969), 11, 16, 49, 59, 152, 282, 356, 499, 610, and "Afterword," in Klein et al., *The Republican Synthesis Revisited*, 146 and *The Radicalism of the American Revolution* (New York: Alfred A. Knopf, 1992), 13, 57, 97; Bernard Bailyn, *The Ideological Origins of the American Revolution* (Cambridge, MA: The Belknap Press, 1967), 27, 36, 43, 44, 45, 86, 164; Gerald Stourzh, *Alexander Hamilton and the Idea of Republican Government* (Stanford: Stanford University Press, 1970), 35, 64, 66, 67, 71, 90, 96, 228n93; Joyce Appleby, "What is Still American in the Political Philosophy of Thomas Jefferson?," *William and Mary Quarterly*, 3rd ser., 39 (April 1982), 288; Charles Louis Secondat, Baron de Montesquieu, *The Spirit of Laws*, Anne M. Cohler et al. (eds.) (New York: Cambridge University Press, 1989), 7–10, 156–57; John Patrick Diggins, *The Lost Soul of American Politics: Virtue, Self-Interest, and the Foundations of Liberalism* (New York: Basic Books, 1984), 101; Drew E. McCoy, *The Elusive Republic: Political Economy in Jeffersonian America* (Chapel Hill: University of North Carolina Press, 1980), 77; Kurt T. Lash, "James Madison's Celebrated Report of 1800: The Transformation of the Tenth Amendment," *George Washington Law Review*, 74 (January 2006), 165.

2. Thomas Hobbes, *Leviathan*, Edwin Corley (ed.) (Indianapolis: Hackett Publishing Company, Inc., 1994), viii, xvii, 22–27, 63–76, 80, 82, 106, 109, 112, 133, 245; John Locke, *Two Treatises on Government*, Peter Laslett (ed.) (New York: Cambridge University Press, 1988), Book II, Section 4, 269; Section 6, 269–71;

Section 7, 271–72; Section 12, 274–75; Section 13, 275; Section 15, 277–78; Section 21, 282; Section 23, 284; Section 89, 325; Section 96, 331–32; Section 97, 332; Section 119, 347–48; Section 121, 349; Section 123, 350; Section 124, 350–51; Section 132, 354; Section 134, 355–57; Section 135, 357–58; Section 141, 362–63; Section 143, 364; Section 144, 364–65; Section 149, 366–67; Section 153, 369–70; Section 171, 381–82; Section 172, 382–83; Section 192, 394; Section 197, 397; Section 198, 397–98; Section 199, 398–99; Section 201, 400; Section 212, 407–408; Section 220, 411; Section 221, 412; Section 222, 412–14; Section 223, 414; Section 227, 416; Section 228, 416–17; Section 242, 427; Section 243, 427–28; Paul C. Nagel, *One Nation Indivisible: The Union in American Thought, 1776–1861* (Westport, CT: Greenwood Press, 1964), 134–37; Wood, *The Radicalism of the American Revolution*, 149 and *The Creation of the American Republic*, 14, 268, 290, 541; Herman Belz, "The South and the American Constitutional Tradition at the Bicentennial," in Kermit L. Hall and James W. Ely (eds.), *An Uncertain Tradition: Constitutionalism and the History of the South* (Athens: The University of Georgia Press, 1989), 24–25; Thad Tate, "The Social Contract in America: Revolutionary Theory as a Conservative Instrument," *William and Mary Quarterly*, 3rd ser., 22 (1965), 341, 375, 376; Bailyn, *The Ideological Origins of the American Revolution*, 27, 30, 58; Banning, *The Sacred Fire of Liberty*, 133 and *The Jeffersonian Persuasion*, 72; Stourzh, *Alexander Hamilton and the Idea of Republican Government*, 18, 73; Harry V. Jaffa, "'Partly Federal, Partly National': On the Political Theory of the Civil War," in Robert A. Goldwin (ed.), *A Nation of States: Essays on the American Federal System* (2nd ed., Chicago: Rand McNally College Publishing Company, 1974), 122; Kurt T. Lash, "'Tucker's Rule': St. George Tucker and the Limited Construction of Federal Power," *William and Mary Law Review*, 47 (February 2006), 1349–50; Chad Vanderford, "Rights of Humans, Rights of States: The Academic Legacy of St. George Tucker in Nineteenth-Century Virginia," (unpublished Ph.D. dissertation, Louisiana State University, 2005), 11, 12; Forrest McDonald, *Novus Ordo Seclorum: The Intellectual Origins of the Constitution* (Lawrence: University Press of Kansas, 1985), 145. Several years later, some Kentuckians proposed to join the Union. As an argument they claimed that the Revolution had returned them to a state of nature and thus

251

their territory was no longer part of Virginia. Madison disagreed. He argued that the social compact between the people was intact and the political society with it. See McDonald, *Novus Ordo Seclorum*, 146.

3. Adam Smith, *An Inquiry into the Nature and Causes of the Wealth of Nations*, Edwin Cannan (ed.) (Chicago: University of Chicago Press, 1976), i, I, I, 10; i, I, II, 19; i, I, VI, 60; i, I, XI, 276–78; i, II, III, 363, 364, 367; i, III, I, 402; i, III, IV, 345, 432; i, IV, II, 477, 478; ii, II, VII, 127; ii, IV, V, 23, 49; ii, IV, IX, 188; ii, V, I, 231–35, 243–44; Joyce Appleby, *Capitalism and a New Social Order: The Republican Vision of the 1790s* (New York: New York University Press, 1984), 32; Wood, *The Creation of the American Republic*, 268; McDonald, *Novus Ordo Seclorum*, 97, 124–25, 134. Political economy can be considered as "ideas about the policies governments should or should not pursue regarding property relations to promote the general welfare." See McDonald, *Novus Ordo Seclorum*, 128. Interestingly, Smith considered wage earners unfit for public office.

4. Wesley Gewehr, *The Great Awakening in Virginia* (Gloucester, MA: Peter Smith, 1965), 3, 9, 26–27, 29, 40–43, 53–54, 84, 101, 103–104, 126, 135, 137–38, 141–42, 152, 187–9, 194–95, 197–98; Robert Kelley, "Ideology and Political Culture from Jefferson to Nixon," *American Historical Review*, 82 (June, 1977), 534–35; Rhys Isaac, "Evangelical Revolt: The Nature of the Baptist's Challenge to the Traditional Order in Virginia, 1765 to 1775," *William and Mary Quarterly*, 3rd ser., 31 (1974), 358 and *The Transformation of Virginia, 1740–1790* (Chapel Hill: University of North Carolina Press, 1982), 148, 150–52, 155, 160, 162–63, 170, 173, 247, 260–62, 300, 311–12; Thomas E. Buckley, *Church and State in Revolutionary Virginia, 1776–1787* (Charlottesville: University Press of Virginia, 1977), 13; Appleby, *Capitalism and a New Social Order*, 8; Jack P. Greene, "Society, Ideology, and Politics: An Analysis of the Political Culture of Mid–Eighteenth Century Virginia," in Richard M. Jellison (ed.), *Society, Freedom, and Conscience: The Coming of the Revolution in Virginia, Massachusetts, and New York* (New York: W. W. Norton, 1976), 35–37. Baptists totaled about 10 percent of the population circa 1776. See Herbert Sloan and Peter Onuf, "Politics, Culture, and the Revolution in Virginia," *Virginia Magazine of History and Biography* 91 (July 1983), 270–71.

5. Arthur Link, *The Public Papers of Woodrow Wilson, 1966–1994*, 69 vols. (Princeton, NJ: Princeton University Press, 1966–1994), vol. 25, 124; Walter Hartwell Bennett, *American Theories of Federalism* (Tuscaloosa: University of Alabama Press, 1964), 33; Albert Beveridge, *The Life of John Marshall*, 4 vols. (Boston: Houghton Mifflin Company, 1929), vol. 1, 232; Gewehr, *The Great Awakening in Virginia*, 189–191.

6. Gaillard Hunt (ed.), *The Writings of James Madison*, 9 vols. (New York: G. P. Putnam's Sons, 1906), vol. 2, 361–69; Richard E. Ellis, *The Union at Risk: Jacksonian Democracy, States' Rights, and the Nullification Crisis* (New York: Oxford University Press, 1987), 2, 3; Martin Diamond, "What the Framers Meant by Federalism," in Goldwin, *A Nation of States: Essays on the*

American Federal System, 29, 31; Nagel, *One Nation Indivisible, 1776–1861*, 43; Lance Banning, "1776 and 1787: Patrick Henry, James Madison, the Constitution, and the Revolution," in Neal York (ed.), *Toward a More Perfect Union: Six Essays on the Constitution* (Provo: Brigham Young University Press, 1988), 69 and *The Sacred Fire of Liberty*, 14, 16, 117, 140; Wood, *The Creation of the American Republic*, 12, 525–26; Beveridge, *The Life of John Marshall*, vol. 1, 252; Alpheus Thomas Mason, *The States Right Debate: Antifederalism and the Constitution* (Englewood Cliffs, NJ: Prentice-Hall, Inc., 1964), 10, 14, 15, 21, 23; Joseph Lynch, *Negotiating the Constitution: The Earliest Debates Over Original Intent* (Ithaca: Cornell University Press, 1999), 11; Jaffa, "Partly Federal, Partly National," 13; John P. Kaminsky et al., *The Documentary History of the Ratification of the Constitution, Ratification of the Constitution by the States: Virginia*, 19 vols. (Madison: State Historical Society of Wisconsin, 1988), vol. 8, xxiii, 71 (hereinafter cited as *DHRC* with an appended volume number, for example *DHRC8* in this case).

7. *Melancton Smith's Diary*, Edward Carrington to James Madison, September 23, 1787, Richard Henry Lee to Elbridge Gerry, September 29, 1787, James Madison to George Washington, September 30, 1787, Richard Henry Lee to George Mason, October 1, 1787, in Paul H. Smith et al. (eds.), *Letters of Delegates to Congress, 1774–1789*, 25 vols. (Washington, D.C.: Library of Congress, 1976–2000), vol. 24, 438–44, 435–36, 452–54, 456–57, 458, respectively (hereinafter cited as *LDC*). Also, Arthur Lee to Samuel Adams, October 3, 1787, Richard Henry Lee to Samuel Adams, October 5, 1787, *Richard Henry Lee and the Constitution*, Richard Henry Lee to Edmund Randolph, October 16, 1787, Edward Carrington to Thomas Jefferson, October 23, 1787, *DHRC8*, 34, 36, 59–60, 64, 93, respectively. See also Worthington C. Ford et al. (eds.), *Journals of the Continental Congress, 1774–1789*, 34 vols. (Washington, D.C.: Library of Congress, 1904–37), vol. 33, 540–44, 549 (hereinafter cited as *JCC*).

8. Edmund Randolph to James Madison, September 30, 1787, James Monroe to James Madison, October 13, 1787, *The General Assembly Receives the Constitution*, October 15–16, *The General Assembly Calls a State Convention, 25–31 October, DHRC8*, 25, 51, 57, 110 respectively; *DHRC9*, 788–90, 811–13.

Chapter 2

1. Many correspondents effected descriptive pseudonyms. Several have been identified. *Winchester Virginia Gazette*, February 29, 1788, *DHRC9*, 440 (Alexander White); *Kentucky Gazette*, March 1, 1788, *DHRC8*, 447–49; *Virginia Independent Chronicle*, January 30, 1778, *DHRC8*, 335 (Civis Rusticus), February 20, 1788, *DHRC8*, 397 (An Old Planter); Jacob E. Cooke (ed.), *The Federalist* (Middletown, CT: Wesleyan University Press, 1961), No. 53, 360–65; No. 54, 369; No. 55, 374–76; No. 57, 379, 384–85, No. 62, 418; No. 63, 424; Morton Borden (ed.), *The Antifederalist Papers* (Lansing: Michigan State University Press, 1965), 97, 158–65, 170, 171, 178–80, 184, 185, 207; Paul Leicester

Ford (ed.), *Pamphlets on the Constitution of the United States* (New York: Da Capo Press, 1968), 288, 292, 295, 297, 319; Richard Henry Lee to Samuel Adams, October 5, 1787; Richard Henry Lee to Edmund Randolph, October 16, 1787; James McClurg to James Madison, October 31, 1787; George Lee Turberville to James Madison, December 11, 1787; Thomas Jefferson to James Madison, December 20, 1787; Joseph Spencer to James Madison, February 28, 1788, *DHRC8*, 37, 66, 137, 233, 250, 425, respectively; Edmund Pendleton to Richard Henry Lee, June 14, 1788, in David John Mays, *The Letters and Papers of Edmund Pendleton, 1774–1803,* 2 vols. (Charlottesville: University Press of Virginia, 1967), vol. 2, 534; *A Native of Virginia: Observations upon the Proposed Plan of Federal Government,* April 2, 1788, *DHRC9,* 661, 667–69, 694.

2. *Virginia Independent Chronicle,* February 20, 1788, March 5, 1788, *DHRC8,* 395 (An Old Planter), 462 (An Impartial Examiner I), respectively; *Winchester Virginia Gazette,* February 22, 1788, *DHRC8,* 406 (Alexander White); Cooke, *The Federalist,* No. 40, 262; No. 41, 269; No. 45, 311, 313–14; Jon Kukla, "A Spectrum of Sentiments: Virginia's Federalists, Antifederalists, and 'Federalists Who Are for Amendments,'" *Virginia Magazine of History and Biography,* 96 (July 1988), 292; Ford, *Pamphlets on the Constitution of the United States,* 318 (The Federal Farmer); Peter Onuf, "Constitutional Politics: States, Sections, and National Interest," in York, *Toward a More Perfect Union,* 45; Banning, *The Sacred Fire of Liberty,* 282; Wood, *The Creation of the American Republic,* 542, 545, 546 and "The Political Ideology of the Founders," in York (ed.), *Toward a More Perfect Union,* 22; Mason, *The States Right Debate,* 3; Reverend James Madison to James Madison, October 1, 1787, Richard Henry Lee to William Shippen Jr., October 12, 1787, Benjamin Harrison to George Washington, October 4, 1787, Richard Henry Lee to Samuel Adams, October 8, 1787, George Lee Turberville to Arthur Lee, October 28, 1787, William Grayson to William Short, November 10, 1787, *A True Friend,* Broadside, December 6, 1787, William Russell to William Fleming, January 25, 1788, George Nicholas to [Unknown], February 16, 1788, Harry Innes to John Brown, February 28, 1788, *DHRC8,* 32, 36, 37, 128, 150, 217, 324, 369 and 373, 387, respectively; *A Native of Virginia: Observations upon the Proposed Plan of Federal Government, 2 April, DHRC9,* 692; Edmund Pendleton to Richard Henry Lee, June 14, 1788, in Mays, *Letters and Papers of Edmund Pendleton,* vol. 2, 533–34. Throughout this section the Federal Farmer has been treated as a Virginian. For years it was assumed that he was, in reality, R. H. Lee. Suspicion has been cast on this interpretation by at least two authors. However, their arguments are not conclusive although highly suggestive. Thus, the Farmer has been included herein not to claim that he was Lee, but only to elicit a possible Virginia opinion. See Gordon Wood, "The Authorship of the Letters from the Federal Farmer," *William and Mary Quarterly,* 3rd ser., 23 (April 1974), 299–308 and Robert H. Webking, "Melancton Smith and the *Letters from the Federal Farmer,*" *William and Mary Quarterly,* 3rd ser., 44 (July 1987), 510–28.

3. *Kentucky Gazette,* March 1, 1788, *DHRC8,* 449;

Virginia Independent Chronicle, December 5, 1787, *DHRC8,* 203; *Petersburg Virginia Gazette,* February 28, 1788, *DHRC8,* 429 (An Impartial Citizen V); Borden, *The Antifederalist Papers,* 202, 208 (Republicus); Arthur Lee to John Adams, October 3, 1787, *George Mason's Objections to the Constitution of Government Formed by the Convention,* Edward Carrington to Thomas Jefferson, October 23, 1787, James Madison to Thomas Jefferson, October 24 and November 1, 1787, Thomas Jefferson to James Madison, December 20, 1787, Edmund Randolph to the Speaker of the House of Delegates, October 10, 1787, *DHRC8,* 34, 44, 95, 100–105, 250, 273, respectively; *A Native of Virginia: Observations upon the Proposed Plan of Federal Government, 2 April, DHRC9,* 669, 681.

4. *Kentucky Gazette,* March 1, 1788, *DHRC8,* 446–48 (Republicus); *Virginia Independent Chronicle,* December 19, 1787, January 30, 1788, *DHRC8,* 245–46 (Americanis II), 335 (Civis Rusticus), respectively; *Virginia Journal,* December 6, 1787, *DHRC8,* 214–15; *Winchester Virginia Gazette,* February 29, 1788, *DHRC8,* 440 (Alexander White); Banning, *The Sacred Fire of Liberty,* 147; Cooke, *The Federalist,* No. 62, 415, 416, 418; No. 63, 424; Borden, *The Antifederalist Papers,* 187 (The Federal Farmer) and 208 (Republicus); Ford, *Pamphlets on the Constitution of the United States,* 297 (The Federal Farmer); Arthur Lee to John Adams, October 3, 1787; *George Mason's Objections to the Constitution of Government Formed by the Convention;* Edward Carrington to Thomas Jefferson, October 23, 1787, James Madison to Thomas Jefferson, October 24 and November 1, 1787, George Lee Turberville to Arthur Lee, October 28, 1787, Joseph Jones to James Madison, October 29, 1787, Arthur Lee to Edward Rutledge, October 29, 1787, James McClurg to James Madison, October 31, 1787, William Grayson to William Short, November 10, 1787, Edmund Randolph to the Speaker of the House of Delegates, October 10, 1787, Joseph Spencer to James Madison, February 28, 1788, *DHRC8,* 34, 43–44, 95, 99, 127, 129, 131, 137, 151, 273, 425, respectively; *A Native of Virginia: Observations upon the Proposed Plan of Federal Government, 2 April, DHRC9,* 663–64; Edmund Pendleton to Richard Henry Lee, June 14, 1788, in Mays, *Letters and Papers of Edmund Pendleton,* vol. 2, 534.

5. David Thomas Konig, "Country Justice: The Rural Roots of Constitutionalism in Colonial Virginia," in Hall and Ely, *An Uncertain Tradition,* 75–76; Cooke, *The Federalist,* No. 39, 256; No. 44, 305; No. 45, 313; Richard Ellis, "The Path Not Taken: Virginia and the Supreme Court, 1789–1821," in A. E. Dick Howard and Melvin Urofsky (eds.), *Virginia and the Constitution* (Charlottesville: Virginia Commission on the Bicentennial of the United States, 1992), 27; Ford, *Pamphlets on the Constitution of the United States,* 289–90, 298 (The Federal Farmer); Borden, *The Antifederalist Papers,* 81 (Cato Uticensis — George Mason); *Virginia Independent Chronicle,* October 17, 1787, January 16, 1788, February 27, 1788, February 29, 1788, March 19, 1788, *DHRC8,* 73–74 (Cato Uticensis — George Mason), 305 (The State Soldier I — George Nicholas?), 336 (Civis Rusticus), 423, 510 (The State Soldier IV — George

Nicholas?) respectively; *Winchester Virginia Gazette, DHRC8*, 443 (Alexander White); Arthur Lee to John Adams, October 3, 1787, Benjamin Harrison to George Washington, October 4, 1787, Richard Henry Lee to Edmund Randolph, October 16, 1787, Joseph Jones to James Madison, October 29, 1787, William Grayson to William Short, November 10, 1787, George Lee Turberville to James Madison, December 11, 1787, Edmund Randolph to the Speaker of the House of Delegates, October 10, 1787, George Nicholas to [Unknown], February 16, 1788, Harry Innes to John Brown, February 28, 1788, *DHRC8*, 34, 36, 63, 130, 151, 233, 273, 371, 387, respectively; *A Native of Virginia: Observations upon the Proposed Plan of Federal Government, 2 April*, Richard Henry Lee to George Mason, May 7, 1788, *DHRC9*, 683–85, 786, respectively; Edmund Pendleton to Richard Henry Lee, June 14, 1788, in Mays, *Letters and Papers of Edmund Pendleton*, vol. 2, 535; Richard Henry Lee to Samuel Adams, October 5, 1787, in *LDC*, vol. 24, 466.

6. Arthur Lee to John Adams, October 3, 1787, *George Mason's Objections to the Constitution of the Government Formed by the Convention*, Richard Henry Lee to Edmund Randolph, October 16, 1787, George Lee Turberville to James Madison, December 11, 1787, *DHRC8*, 34, 44, 65–66, 232, respectively; *A Native of Virginia: Observations upon the Proposed Plan of Federal Government, 2 April, DHRC9*, 679; *Virginia Independent Chronicle, To Richard Henry Lee Esquire*, April 9, 1788, *DHRC9*, 718 (Cassius II).

7. *Winchester Virginia Gazette*, February 29, 1788, *DHRC8*, 441–42 (Alexander White); Edmund Pendleton to Richard Henry Lee, June 14, 1788, in Mays, *Letters and Papers of Edmund Pendleton*, vol. 2, 535; George Lee Turberville to James Madison, December 11, 1787, Joseph Spencer to James Madison, February 28, 1788, *DHRC8*, 234, 425, respectively; *A Native of Virginia: Observations upon the Proposed Plan of Federal Government, 2 April, DHRC9*, 673–74, 688, 690.

8. *Virginia Independent Chronicle,* January 30, 1788, *DHRC8*, 338 (Civis Rusticus); *Kentucky Gazette*, March 1, 1788, *DHRC8*, 450; Kukla, "A Spectrum of Sentiments," 293; Cooke, *The Federalist,* No. 54, 367–68; *George Mason's Objections to the Constitution of Government Formed by the Convention*, George Lee Turberville to James Madison, December 11, 1787, George Nicholas to [Unknown], February 16, 1788, *DHRC8*, 45, 233, 371–72, respectively; *A Native of Virginia: Observations upon the Proposed Plan of Federal Government, 2 April, DHRC9*, 675.

9. *Virginia Independent Chronicle*, October 31, February 20, 1788, *DHRC8*, 138, 389–90 and 393 (The Impartial Examiner I), *To Richard Henry Lee Esquire,* April 9, 1788, *DHRC9*, 715 (Cassius II); *Winchester Virginia Gazette*, January 18, 1788, February 22, 1788, *DHRC8*, 311 (An Independent Freeholder — Alexander White?), 404 (Alexander White) respectively; *Virginia Journal*, December 6, 1787, *DHRC8*, 212–13 (Brutus — Tobias Lear); Ford, *Pamphlets on the Constitution of the United States*, 155–56, 313 (The Federal Farmer); Thomas Jefferson to James Madison, December 20, 1787, *DHRC8*, 250; Edmund Pendleton to Richard Henry Lee, June 14, 1788, in Mays, *Letters and Papers of Edmund Pendleton*, vol. 2, 532.

10. Kukla, "A Spectrum of Sentiments," 293; Joseph Lynch, *Negotiating the Constitution*, 5, 32–33; Ford, *Pamphlets on the Constitution of the United States*, 312–13 (The Federal Farmer); Cooke, *The Federalist,* No. 14, 86; No. 41, 277; No. 44, 303–305; Mason, *The States Right Debate*, 79; *Petersburg Virginia Gazette*, February 28, 1788, *DHRC8*, 431 (An Impartial Citizen V); *Virginia Independent Chronicle*, April 19, 1788, *DHRC9*, 714; *George Mason's Objections to the Constitution of Government formed by the Constitution*, William Grayson to William Short, November 10, 1787, George Lee Turberville to James Madison, December 11, 1787, Edmund Randolph to the Speaker of the House of Delegates, October 10, 1787; William Russell to William Fleming, January 25, 1788, *DHRC8*, 45, 150, 233, 273, 324, respectively; *A Native of Virginia: Observations upon the Proposed Plan of Federal Government, 2 April, DHRC9*, 675.

11. Ellis, "The Path Not Taken," 26; Borden, *The Antifederalist Papers*, 80–81, 96–97, 117 (Cato Uticensis-George Mason); Ford, *Pamphlets on the Constitution of the United States*, 301 (The Federal Farmer); *Virginia Independent Chronicle*, October 17, 1787, December 19, 1787, January 16, 1788, February 20, 1788, *DHRC8*, 73 (Cato Uticensis-George Mason), 248 (Americanis II), 305 (The State Soldier I-George Nicholas?), 396 (An Old Planter); *Winchester Virginia Gazette,* February 29, 1788, *DHRC8*, 439 (Alexander White); Benjamin Harrison to George Washington, October 4, 1787, Thomas Jefferson to James Madison, December 20, 1787, George Nicholas to [Unknown], February 16, 1788, *DHRC8*, 36, 250, 372, respectively.

12. *Virginia Independent Chronicle, To Richard Henry Lee Esquire,* April 9, 1788, *DHRC9*, 716–17 (Cassius II); Kukla, "A Spectrum of Sentiments," 289; Cooke, *The Federalist,* No. 42, 283; Ford, *Pamphlets on the Constitution of the United States*, 319 (The Federal Farmer); Benjamin Harrison to George Washington, October 4, 1787, *George Mason's Objections to the Constitution of Government formed by the Constitution*, Richard Henry Lee to Edmund Randolph, October 16, 1787, Martin Oster to the Maréchal de Castries, October 19, 1787, Edward Carrington to Thomas Jefferson, October 23, 1787, *DHRC8*, 36, 45, 63 and 66, 83, 94, respectively; *A Native of Virginia: Observations upon the Proposed Plan of Federal Government, 2 April*, Caleb Wallace to William Fleming, May 3, 1788, Richard Henry Lee to George Mason, May 7, 1788, *DHRC9*, 671–72, 783, 786, respectively.

13. *Winchester Virginia Gazette*, February 29, 1788, *DHRC8*, 441–42 (Alexander White); *Virginia Independent Chronicle*, April 9, 1788 (Extraordinary), *DHRC9*, 720 (A Freeholder); Ford, *Pamphlets on the Constitution of the United States*, 279, 299 (The Federal Farmer); Borden, *The Antifederalist Papers*, 170 (The Federal Farmer); Cooke, *The Federalist,* No. 47, 324–25; No. 48, 332–338; No. 51, 347, 349–50; *George Mason's Objections to the Constitution of Government Formed by the Convention,* Richard Henry Lee to Edmund Pendleton, October 16, 1787, Joseph Spencer to James Madi-

son, February 28, 1788, *DHRC8*, 44, 61, 425, respectively.

14. Cooke, *The Federalist*, No. 51, 351; Wood, *The Creation of the American Republic*, 537, 539; Ford, *Pamphlets on the Constitution of the United States*, 290 (The Federal Farmer); Charlene Bangs Bickford and Kenneth R. Bowling, *Birth of a Nation: The First Federal Congress, 1789–1791* (Madison, WI: Madison House Publishers, 1989), 51; Mason, *The States Right Debate*, 87; *Virginia Journal*, December 6, 1787, *DHRC8*, 212–13 (Brutus—Tobias Lear); *Winchester Virginia Gazette*, January 18, 1788, February 29, 1788, *DHRC8*, 311, 438 (Alexander White), respectively; *Virginia Independent Chronicle*, January 30, 1788, February 20, 1788, *DHRC8*, 334 (Civis Rusticus), 393 (The Impartial Examiner I), respectively; *To Richard Henry Lee Esquire*, April 9, 1788, *DHRC9*, 714–15 (Cassius II); Arthur Lee to John Adams, October 3, 1787, Richard Henry Lee to Samuel Adams, October 5, 1787, *George Mason's Objections to the Constitution of Government Formed by the Convention*, Richard Henry Lee to Edmund Randolph, October 16, 1787, Joseph Jones to James Madison, October 29, 1787, Arthur Lee to Edward Rutledge, October 29, 1787, William Grayson to William Short, November 10, 1787, *To the Advocates for the Federal Constitution: and to their Antagonists*, December 6, 1787, Broadside, George Lee Turberville to James Madison, December 11, 1787, Thomas Jefferson to James Madison, December 20, 1787, and Alexander Donald, February 7, 1788, Joseph Spencer to James Madison, February 28, 1788, *DHRC8*, 34, 37, 43, 62, 130, 131, 151, 220 (A True Friend), 243, 250, 353, 425, respectively; *A Native of Virginia: Observations upon the Proposed Plan of Federal Government, 2 April*, Richard Henry Lee to Edmund Pendleton, May 26, 1788, *DHRC9*, 658–61, 878–79, respectively; Edmund Pendleton to Richard Henry Lee, June 14, 1788, in Mays, *Letters and Papers of Edmund Pendleton*, vol. 2, 531–32.

15. *Virginia Independent Chronicle*, January 30, 1788, *DHRC8*, 357 (Civis Rusticus); *To Richard Henry Lee Esquire*, April 9, 1788, *DHRC9*, 715 (Cassius II); *Winchester Virginia Gazette*, February 22, 1788, *DHRC8*, 404–405 (Alexander White); Arthur Lee to John Adams, October 3, 1787, Richard Henry Lee to Samuel Adams, October 5, 1787, *George Mason's Objections to the Constitution of Government formed by the Convention*, William Grayson to William Short, November 10, 1787, George Lee Turberville to James Madison, December 11, 1787, Joseph Spencer to James Madison, February 28, 1788, *DHRC8*, 34, 37, 45, 151, 233, 425 respectively; *A Native of Virginia: Observations upon the Proposed Plan of Federal Government, 2 April*, Richard Henry Lee to George Mason, May 7, 1788, *DHRC9*, 685–86 and 691, 786, respectively.

16. Cooke, *The Federalist*, No. 45, 311, 313; No. 54, 369; No. 62, 417; Richard E. Ellis, *The Union at Risk*, 4.

17. Cooke, *The Federalist*, No. 39, 254; No. 40, 263; No. 43, 296; Forrest McDonald, *States' Rights and the Union: Imperium in Imperio, 1776–1876* (Lawrence: University Press of Kansas, 2000), 19; Ford, *Pamphlets on the Constitution of the United States*, 322 (The Federal Farmer); *Petersburg Virginia Gazette*, January 10,

1788, *DHRC8*, 297 (An Impartial Citizen); *Virginia Independent Chronicle*, February 6, 1788, *DHRC8*, 346 (A State Soldier II); Richard Henry Lee to George Mason, October 1, 1787, Richard Henry Lee to George Washington, October 11, 1787, George Washington to Edmund Randolph, January 8, 1788, Richard Henry Lee to James Gordon Jr., February 26, 1788, Cyrus Griffin to Thomas Fitzsimmons, March 3, 1788, James Madison to George Washington, March 3, 1788, *DHRC8*, 29, 51, 286, 419, 453, 454, respectively; George Washington to John Armstrong Sr., April 23, 1788, George Mason to Thomas Jefferson, May 26, 1788, *DHRC9*, 759, 883, respectively.

18. James Madison to Thomas Jefferson, October 24, 1787, December 9, 1787, Edmund Randolph to the Speaker of the House of Delegates, October 10, 1787, *DHRC8*, 111, 226, 271, respectively; Ford, *Pamphlets on the Constitution of the United States*, 324 (The Federal Farmer); Kukla, "A Spectrum of Sentiments," 289; *Petersburg Virginia Gazette*, January 10, 1788, *DHRC8*, 297.

19. Banning, *The Jeffersonian Persuasion*, 112; Kukla, "A Spectrum of Sentiments," 285; Ford, *Pamphlets on the Constitution of the United States*, 320 (The Federal Farmer); Reverend James Madison to James Madison, February 9, 1787, George Nicholas to [Unknown], February 16, 1788, *DHRC8*, 358, 374, respectively; *Baltimore Maryland Gazette*, April 4, 1788, *DHRC9*, 701–702; *A Native of Virginia: Observations upon the Proposed Plan of Federal Government, 2 April*, George Washington to John Armstrong Sr., April 25, 1788, *DHRC9*, 689, 759, respectively; Edmund Pendleton to Richard Henry Lee, June 14, 1788, in Mays, *Letters and Papers of Edmund Pendleton*, vol. 2, 531.

20. Cooke, *The Federalist*, No. 38, 246; Banning, *The Jeffersonian Persuasion*, 112; *Petersburg Virginia Gazette*, January 10, 1787, *DHRC8*, 297 (An Impartial Citizen); Richard Henry Lee to George Mason, October 1, 1787, and Samuel Adams, October 5, 1787, George Mason to George Washington, October 7, 1787, Richard Henry Lee to George Washington, October 11, 1787, and Edmund Randolph, October 16, 1787, James Madison to Edmund Randolph, November 18, 1787, January 10, 1788, *DHRC8*, 29, 38, 43, 51, 61, 166–67, 290, respectively; Edmund Pendleton to Richard Henry Lee, June 14, 1788, in Mays, *Letters and Papers of Edmund Pendleton*, vol. 2, 531; *A Native of Virginia: Observations upon the Proposed Plan of Federal Government, 2 April*, James Madison to George Nicholas, April 8, 1788, James Madison to Edmund Randolph, April 10, 1788, James Madison to Thomas Jefferson, April 22, 1788, Caleb Wallace to William Fleming, May 3, 1788, *DHRC9*, 689, 708, 731, 745, 783, respectively.

21. Kukla, "A Spectrum of Sentiments," 287; Edmund Pendleton to Richard Henry Lee, June 14, 1788, in Mays, *Letters and Papers of Edmund Pendleton*, vol. 2, 531; Joseph Jones to James Madison, February 14, 1788, *DHRC8*, 368; James Madison to Edmund Randolph, April 10, 1788, Richard Henry Lee to Samuel Adams, April 28, 1788, George Mason to Thomas Jefferson, May 26, 1788, *DHRC9*, 731, 765, 883, respectively.

22. Edmund Pendleton to Richard Henry Lee, June

14, 1788, in Mays, *Letters and Papers of Edmund Pendleton*, vol. 2, 530–31.

23. Reverend James Madison to James Madison, October 1, 1787, *A True Friend*, Broadside, December 6, 1787, *DHRC8*, 32, 219, respectively.

24. *Virginia Independent Chronicle*, October 7, 1787, March 5, 1788, DHRC8, 75 (Cato Uticensis — George Mason?), 460 (The Impartial Examiner I), respectively. Cooke, *The Federalist*, No. 10, 57, 65; No. 37, 234; No. 46, 320; No. 63, 428; Diggins, "Recovering 'First Principles,'" 120; Kukla, "A Spectrum of Sentiments," 290; Martin Oster to the Maréchal de Castries, October 19, 1787, *To the Advocates for the New Federal Constitution: and to their Antagonists*, December 6, 1787, Broadside (A True Friend); Joseph Spencer to James Madison, February 28, 1788, *DHRC8*, 83, 217–18, 425, respectively.

25. *Virginia Independent Chronicle*, October 17, 1787, November 14, 1787, December 5, 1787, February 20, 1788, February 28, 1788, March 19, 1788, *DHRC8*, 75 (Cato Uticensis — George Mason?), 163, 200 (Americanis I), 392 (The Impartial Examiner I), 392–93, 511 and 513–14 (A State Soldier IV-George Nicholas), respectively; April 9 (Extraordinary), 1788, *To Richard Henry Lee, Esquire*, April 23, 1788, *DHRC9*, 720 (A Freeholder), 750 (Cassius III), respectively; *Petersburg Virginia Gazette*, October 25, 1787, *DHRC8*, 96; *Virginia Journal*, December 6, 1787, *DHRC8*, 214 (Brutus); *Winchester Virginia Gazette*, February 29, 1788, March 7, 1788, March 19, 1788, *DHRC8*, 438 and 442, 470 (A Virginia Planter), 507 (A Ploughman), respectively; *Frederick County Meeting*, October 22, 1787, James Madison to Thomas Jefferson, October 24 and November 1, 1787, George Washington to Bushrod Washington, November 10, 1787, Reverend James Madison to James Madison, February 9, 1788, George Nicholas to [Unknown], February 16, 1788, *DHRC8*, 92, 98 and 101–102 and 105, 154, 357–58, 369 and 373, respectively; Caleb Wallace to William Fleming, May 3, 1788; *James Monroe: Some Observations on the Constitution, c. May 25, 1788*; Richard Henry Lee to Edmund Pendleton, May 26, 1788, *DHRC9*, 783, 845 and 852–58, 879, respectively.

Chapter 3

1. Jackson T. Main, "Sections and Politics in Virginia, 1781–1787," *William and Mary Quarterly*, 3rd ser., 12 (January 1955), 97–106; Sloan and Onuf, "Politics, Culture, and the Revolution in Virginia," 280; Forrest McDonald, *E Pluribus Unum* (New York: Cambridge University Press, 1965), 129 and *We the People: The Economic Origins of the Constitution* (Chicago: University of Chicago Press, 1958), 263, 265; Dice Robins Anderson, *William Branch Giles: A Study in the Politics of Virginia and the Nation from 1790 to 1830* (Gloucester, MA: Peter Smith, 1965), 7; Banning, *The Sacred Fire of Liberty*, 255, 258; Norman K. Risjord, "The Virginia Federalists," *Journal of Southern History*, 33 (1967), 500; *DHRC8*, xxvii–xviii, 173; *DHRC9*, 935, 946, 978, 1034, 1107, 1129, 1138n10, 1138n11; *DHRC10*, 1411n11, 1522; Archibald Stuart to John Breckenridge, October 21,

1787, Edmund Randolph to James Madison, October 29, 1787, John Pierce to Henry Knox, November 19, 1787, Joseph Jones to James Madison, November 22, 1787, *DHRC8*, 89 and 90n4, 133, 168, 173, respectively.

2. Greene, "Society, Ideology, and Politics," 22, 24, 25, 28, 33, 35, 47, 54–56; Jackson T. Main, *Political Parties Before the Constitution* (Chapel Hill: University of North Carolina Press, 1973), 245, 248–49, 260, 264–65 and *The Antifederalists: Critics of the Constitution, 1781–1788* (Chapel Hill: University of North Carolina Press, 1961), 28–33 and "Sections and Politics in Virginia," 97, 98n9, 98; Sloan and Onuf, "Politics, Culture, and the Revolution in Virginia," 277–80, 283; Norman K. Risjord, *Chesapeake Politics, 1781–1800* (New York: Columbia University Press, 1978), 226–27, 296–97 and "The Virginia Federalists," 501; Hugh Blair Grigsby, *The History of the Virginia Federal Convention of 1788*, 2 vols. (New York: Da Capo Press, 1969), vol. I, 338–49.

3. Max Farrand, *The Records of the Federal Convention*, 4 vols. (New Haven, CT: Yale University Press, 1966), vol. 3, 94, 95; Liste du Membres et Officiers du Congrés, in *ibid.*, 237.

4. Isaac, *The Transformation of Virginia, 1740–1790*, 267–269; Banning, "1776 and 1787," 61–64; Buckley, *Church and State in Revolutionary Virginia*, 71–72, 78; Kukla, "A Spectrum of Sentiments," 292; Stourzh, *Alexander Hamilton and the Idea of Republican Government*, 129; Grigsby, *The History of the Virginia Federal Convention of 1788*, vol. 1, 83n98, 158–61, 195–206; vol. 2, 284–98.

5. F. Claiborne Johnson Jr., "Federalist, Doubtful, and Antifederalist: A Note on the Virginia Convention of 1788," *Virginia Magazine of History and Biography*, 95 (July 1988), 333–44; McDonald, *We the People*, 257–58, 260n7; Main, *The Antifederalists*, 28, 30, 225, 226, 227, 232–33, 249, 273, 286 and *Political Parties Before the Constitution*, 244; Risjord, *Chesapeake Politics*, 296, 314; Kukla, "A Spectrum of Sentiments," 279–85; Appleby, *Capitalism and a New Social Order*, 47; Robert E. Thomas, "The Virginia Convention of 1788: A Criticism of Beard's *An Economic Interpretation of the Constitution*," *Journal of Southern History*, 19 (February 1953), 65, 66, 70, 71; Sloan and Onuf, "Politics, Culture, and the Revolution in Virginia," 270–71; Grigsby, *The History of the Virginia Federal Convention of 1788*, vol. 1, 193.

6. *DHRC9*, 945, 952–54, 965, 1029, 1038, 1064–65, 1159; *DHRC10*, 1192–93, 1524–25; Ellis, "The Path Not Taken," 26; Banning, *The Sacred Fire of Liberty*, 241; Wood, *The Creation of the American Republic*, 494; Grigsby, *The History of the Virginia Federal Convention of 1788*, vol. 1, 166n148, 247, 259, 307, 310, 319, 319n244, 334.

7. *DHRC9*, 917, 931, 945; Banning, *The Sacred Fire of Liberty*, 255; Grigsby, *The History of the Virginia Federal Convention of 1788*, vol.1, 103.

8. *DHRC9*, 931, 946, 954, 1041; *DHRC10*, 1193.

9. Banning, *The Sacred Fire of Liberty*, 237; Grigsby, *The History of the Virginia Federal Convention of 1788*, vol. 1, 67, 70, 72, 78; *DHRC9*, 897.

10. Banning, *The Sacred Fire of Liberty*, 238, 258;

DHRC9, 967–68, 988–90; Grigsby, *The History of the Virginia Federal Convention of 1788*, vol. 1, 73, 80, 207, 254, 309; McDonald, *We the People*, 259.

11. *DHRC9*, 972, 1054–56, 1059, 1166; *DHRC10*, 1214, 1253, 1354–55, 1360, 1422, 1447, 1455; Grigsby, *The History of the Virginia Federal Convention of 1788*, vol. 1, 279, 287, 289, 290; Edmund Randolph to James Madison, October 29, 1787, *DHRC8*, 133.

12. *DHRC9*, 1050–51, 1077, 1102; *DHRC10*, 1220, 1222, 1229–35, 1237, 1239, 1241, 1245, 1247, 1249; Grigsby, *The History of the Virginia Federal Convention of 1788*, vol. 1, 135, 235, 247.

13. *DHRC9*, 922–23, 926–27, 934, 937, 939–40, 946, 950, 953, 999, 1012, 1023, 1041, 1080, 1102, 1108, 1116, 1118, 1157–58, 1162; *DHRC10*, 1188, 1193, 1235, 1272, 1276, 1283, 1302–1303, 1306, 1308–10, 1316–17, 1321–22, 1341, 1417, 1470; Banning, *The Sacred Fire of Liberty*, 252 and "1776 and 1787," 69; Bernard Siegan, *The Supreme Court's Constitution: An Inquiry into Judicial Review and Its Impact on Society* (New Brunswick, NJ: Transaction Books, 1987), 1; Mason, *The States Right Debate*, 85.

14. *DHRC9*, 921–22, 1101, 1170; *DHRC10*, 1196, 1200, 1214, 1219, 1221, 1252, 1259, 1267, 1268, 1277, 1292, 1365, 1398–1407, 1409, 1412–24, 1419, 1427, 1430–31, 1438–48, 1450–52, 1454–56, 1464–66, 1469; Konig, "Country Justice," 75–76; Ellis, "The Path Not Taken," 27, 41; Walter Edgar, *South Carolina: A History* (Columbia: University of South Carolina Press, 1998), 124; Grigsby, *The History of the Virginia Federal Convention of 1788*, vol. 1, 264, 268–70, 284.

15. *DHRC9*, 1070, 1141, 1197, 1227n17; *DHRC10*, 1219, 1427, 1431, 1448; Thomas Jefferson to James Madison, December 20, 1787, *DHRC8*, 250; *Virginia Independent Chronicle*, March 9, 1788, *DHRC8*, 510 (The State Soldier IV); Charles Lee to George Washington, May 14, 1788, *DHRC9*, 797; Grigsby, *The History of the Virginia Federal Convention of 1788*, vol. 1, 227, 282; Diggins, *The Lost Soul of American Politics*, 133.

16. *DHRC9*, 50, 916, 920, 923, 930, 944–46, 951–54, 956–57, 959, 961–62, 965, 972–73, 975, 983, 987–89, 1002, 1010–12, 1026, 1035–36, 1054–55, 1060, 1079–80, 1116, 1118, 1126–28, 1155, 1158, 1162; *DHRC10*, 1193, 1195–96, 1211, 1217, 1261–64, 1266, 1276–77, 1365, 1372, 1413–23, 1438–48, 1454–64, 1477–78, 1482, 1490, 1536; Banning, "1776 and 1787," 64, 65 and *The Sacred Fire of Liberty*, 239, 240, 241, 244, 247; Grigsby, *The History of the Virginia Federal Convention of 1788*, vol. 1, 104, 115, 159, 177, 268–69; Wood, *The Creation of the American Republic*, 524; Diggins, "Recovering 'First Principles,'" 120, 122.

17. Sloan and Onuf, "Politics, Culture, and the Revolution in Virginia," 265; *DHRC9*, 927, 939, 944–45, 1061–62, 1064, 1077–78, 1163–64, 1171, 1220, 1222, 1235, 1264; *DHRC10*, 1220, 1249, 1264, 1277–78; Grigsby, *The History of the Virginia Federal Convention of 1788*, vol. 1, 209; Mason, *The States Right Debate*, 85; Charles S. Sydnor, *Gentlemen Freeholders: Political Practices in Washington's Virginia* (Chapel Hill: University of North Carolina Press, 1952), 94.

18. *DHRC9*, 956, 1002, 1010; *DHRC10*, 1372, 1482.

19. *DHRC9*, 937, 939–40, 1010, 1059, 1149–50;

Banning, *The Sacred Fire of Liberty*, 238; Wood, *The Creation of the American Republic*, 500.

20. *DHRC9*, 951, 992, 995–96, 1080; *DHRC10*, 1195–96, 1306–1307, 1403–1406; Main, *The Antifederalists*, 80; Banning, "1776 and 1787," 65, 71 and *The Sacred Fire of Liberty*, 243; Mason, *The States Right Debate*, 51; Belz, "The South and the American Constitutional Tradition at the Bicentennial," 23; Wood, *The Creation of the American Republic*, 535; Lacy K. Ford, Jr., "Inventing the Concurrent Majority: Madison, Calhoun, and the Problem of Majoritarianism in American Political Thought," *Journal of Southern History* 60 (1994), 20; Grigsby, *The History of the Virginia Federal Convention of 1788*, vol. 1, 287; Bennett, *American Theories of Federalism*, 86.

21. Nagel, *One Nation Indivisible, 1776–1861*, 33–34, 36, 64; McDonald, *States' Rights and the Union*, 19, and *Novus Ordo Seclorum*, 280; Banning, *The Sacred Fire of Liberty*, 215; Farrand, *The Records of the Federal Convention*, vol. 1, 54, 314; Tate, "The Social Contract in America," 375–77, 381, 383; Wood, *The Creation of the American Republic*, 269, 283, 284, 290, 541–42; Jaffa, "Partly Federal, Partly National," 115, 115n6, 118, 122 and *A New Birth of Freedom: Abraham Lincoln and the Coming of the Civil War* (New York: Rowman & Littlefield, 2000), 37, 38; Belz, "The South and the American Constitutional Tradition at the Bicentennial," 23–25, 27–28, 30; Paul Finkelman, "States' Rights North and South in Antebellum America," in Hall and Ely, *An Uncertain Tradition*, 125–27; Walter Berns, "The Meaning of the Tenth Amendment," in Goldwin, *A Nation of States: Essays on the American Federal System*, 142; Bailyn, *The Ideological Origins of the American Revolution*, 58; Frederick D. Drake and Lynn R. Nelson, *States' Rights and American Federalism: A Documentary History* (Westport, CT: Greenwood Press, 1999), 72; Isaac, *The Transformation of Virginia, 1740–1790*, 291–92, 310; *Virginia Independent Chronicle*, February 28, 1788, *DHRC8*, 389 (The Impartial Examiner I); Borden, *The Antifederalist Papers*, 177; Richard Henry Lee to Edmund Randolph, October 16, 1787, *DHRC8*, 65; "Secession," *Oxford English Dictionary Online*, http://dictionary.oed.com/cgi/entry/50217973?single=1&query_type=world&queryword=secession&first=1&max_to_show=10; "Secession," *Online Etymology Dictionary*, http://www.etymonline.com/~index.php?search=secession&searchmode=none (accessed January 25, 2007).

22. *DHRC9*, 945, 951, 1030; *DHRC10*, 1477; Tate, "The Social Contract in America," 375–76, 385; Wood, *The Creation of the American Republic*, 541, 542; Banning, *The Sacred Fire of Liberty*, 215 and "1776 and 1787," 64; Nagel, *One Nation Indivisible, 1776–1861*, 36.

Chapter 4

1. Banning, "1776 and 1787," 71 and *The Sacred Fire of Liberty*, 246–47; *DHRC9*, 1080; *DHRC10*, 1307, 1501–1502.

2. Grigsby, *The History of the Virginia Federal Convention of 1788*, vol. 1, 274–75; Main, *The Antifederalists*, 139; *DHRC9*, 1039; *DHRC10*, 1200, 1391, 1496.

3. *DHRC9*, 920, 936–37, 948, 962, 996, 999, 1002, 1008–1009, 1011, 1027, 1044–45, 1076, 1111, 1119, 1146–47, 1159; *DHRC10*, 1185–88, 1198–99, 1203–1204, 1210, 1215, 1221–22, 1225; Banning, *The Sacred Fire of Liberty*, 254; Farrand, *The Records of the Federal Convention*, vol. 3, 309.

4. *DHRC9*, 957–58, 992, 1074, 1102; *DHRC10*, 1269, 1276–77, 1302–11; Albert Beveridge, *The Life of John Marshall*, vol. 1, 435; Ellis, "The Path Not Taken," 26; Grigsby, *The History of the Virginia Federal Convention of 1788*, vol. 1, 259.

5. *DHRC9*, 1161; *DHRC10*, 1310, 1319–20, 1334, 1338–39, 1342, 1475–76; Grigsby, *The History of the Virginia Federal Convention of 1788*, vol. 1, 260, 309, 315.

6. *DHRC9*, 1061, 1098, 1113; *DHRC10*, 1196, 1308.

7. *DHRC9*, 918–20; *DHRC10*, 1196.

8. *DHRC9*, 919–20, 964, 1071, 1099; *DHRC10*, 1259, 1314, 1372–73, 1375.

9. *DHRC9*, 923–24, 926–27, 938–40, 945, 948–50, 968, 1000, 1012, 1024–26, 1041, 1118–19, 1128, 1149–50, 1158, 1170–71; *DHRC10*, 1187, 1196, 1198, 1209–10, 1217–18, 1225, 1241, 1263, 1275; Banning, *The Jeffersonian Persuasion*, 110; Wood, *The Radicalism of the American Revolution*, 259.

10. *DHRC9*, 944–45, 947, 959, 963, 989–92, 995, 997, 1010, 1067–69, 1171; *DHRC10*, 1194, 1219, 1221–22, 1283–84, 1401–1402, 1477, 1490; Beveridge, *The Life of John Marshall*, vol. 1, 446; Wood, *The Creation of the American Republic*, 507, 526–27; Lance Banning, "Republican Ideology and the Triumph of the Constitution, 1789 to 1793," *William and Mary Quarterly*, 3rd ser., 31 (1974), 167 and "1776 and 1787," 65 and *The Sacred Fire of Liberty*, 241, 254, 258, 262; Grigsby, *The History of the Virginia Federal Convention of 1788*, vol. 1, 81, 91–92, 103, 113, 134, 141, 156, 284; Bennett, *American Theories of Federalism*, 167.

11. *DHRC9*, 973; *DHRC10*, 1455, 1525; McDonald, *Novus Ordo Seclorum*, 280; Grigsby, *The History of the Virginia Federal Convention of 1788*, vol. 1, 87.

12. *DHRC9*, 951, 954, 1045–46, 1080, 1099, 1134–35; *DHRC10*, 1212, 1301, 1306, 1309, 1328, 1331–32, 1341, 1475, 1501–1502; Grigsby, *The History of the Virginia Federal Convention of 1788*, vol. 1, 225, 308, 317; Beveridge, *The Life of John Marshall*, vol. 1, 436, 440; Wood, *The Creation of the American Republic*, 541; Banning, *The Sacred Fire of Liberty*, 240.

13. *DHRC9*, 951, 1046, 1050, 1080, 1085–86, 1099, 1112, 1135, 1157; *DHRC10*, 1196–97, 1213, 1270–71, 1327–29, 1331, 1340, 1345, 1430–37, 1482–83; Farrand, *The Records of the Federal Convention*, vol. 3, 309; Beveridge, *The Life of John Marshall*, vol. 1, 440; Mason, *The States Right Debate*, 85, 87; Banning, "1776 and 1787," 64 and *The Sacred Fire of Liberty*, 241; Wood, *The Creation of the American Republic*, 537–42.

14. *DHRC9*, 999, 1023, 1046, 1102, 1111–12, 1134–36; *DHRC10*, 1303, 1309–10, 1321–28, 1345, 1347–48, 1353, 1430–38; Lynch, *Negotiating the Constitution*, 5; Siegan, *The Supreme Court's Constitution*, 15; Mason, *The States Right Debate*, 78; Banning, *The Sacred Fire of Liberty*, 240.

15. *DHRC9*, 1103; *DHRC10*, 1326–27, 1332, 1348, 1350, 1484.

16. *DHRC9*, 1045–46; *DHRC10*, 1305–1306, 1329, 1340, 1345, 1347–48; Beveridge, *The Life of John Marshall*, vol. 1, 452; Banning, *The Sacred Fire of Liberty*, 255; Siegan, *The Supreme Court's Constitution*, 1.

17. *DHRC9*, 926, 927, 931, 937, 945, 950, 958, 961, 999, 1074; *DHRC10*, 1187, 1307, 1327, 1338–39, 1393–94; Banning, "1776 and 1787," 71; Jaffa, "Partly Federal, Partly National," 127.

18. *DHRC10*, 1455–56, 1475, 1501–1502, 1506–1507, 1536, 1542, 1556; Grigsby, *The History of the Virginia Federal Convention of 1788*, vol. 1, 317, 342, 350–51; Richard Beeman, *The Old Dominion and the New Nation, 1788–1801* (Lexington: The University Press of Kentucky, 1972), 11–12; Ellis, "The Path Not Taken," 27; Henry T. Shanks, *The Secession Movement in Virginia, 1847–1861* (Richmond: Garrett and Massie, 1934), 18; Jaffa, "Partly Federal, Partly National," 126–27; Beveridge, *The Life of John Marshall*, vol. 4, 324n4, 463; McDonald, *Novus Ordo Seclorum*, 280; James Madison to George Washington, June 23, 1788, Alexander Hamilton, June 27, 1788, Ambrose Madison, June 24, 1788, *DHRC10*, 1668, 1688, 1689–70, respectively; *New York Journal*, July 3, 1788, *DHRC10*, 1725–26; Martin Oster to Comte de la Luzerne, June 28, 1788, *DHRC10*, 1689.

19. Main, *Political Parties Before the Constitution*, 265 and *The Antifederalists*, 31, 226–27 and "Sections and Politics in Virginia," 107, 111; McDonald, *We the People*, 261, 264; Risjord, *Chesapeake Politics*, 294–95.

Chapter 5

1. *Annals of Congress*, 1 Cong., 1 Sess., 257–61 (May 5, 1789); Risjord, "The Virginia Federalists," 489; Richard Henry Lee to Patrick Henry, May 28, 1789, in William Wirt Henry, *Patrick Henry: Life, Correspondence, and Speeches*, 3 vols. (New York: Burt Franklin, 1969), vol. 3, 386.

2. *Annals of Congress*, 1 Cong., 1 Sess., 51 (July 17, 1789), 685 (July 20, 1789), 843–44 (August 29, 1789), 85 (August 31, 1789), 928–29 (September 17, 1789); Edgar S. MacLay (ed.), *Journal of William MacLay, United States Senator from Pennsylvania, 1789–1791* (New York: D. Appleton and Company, 1890), 85–87; Leonard Levy, *Original Intent and the Framers' Constitution* (New York: Macmillan, 1988), 110–11, 112, 114; Bickford and Bowling, *Birth of a Nation*, 37, 45–48; Bennett, *American Theories of Federalism*, 91, 92; William Grayson to Patrick Henry, September 29, 1789, in Henry, *Patrick Henry*, vol. 3, 406.

3. Helen E. Veit et al., *Creating the Bill of Rights: The Documentary Record from the First Federal Congress* (Baltimore: The Johns Hopkins Press, 1991), 33, 37, 47, 49, 51, 193, 197, 199, 264, 281, 282, 300, 310; James Madison to Edmund Randolph, June 15, 1789; James Madison to Tenche Cox, June 24, 1789; Richard Bland Lee to Leven Powell, June 12, 1789; Edward Carrington to James Madison, September 9, 1789; Richard Peters to James Madison, July 20, 1789, in *ibid.*, 250, 254, 249, 292, 266, respectively; Bickford and Bowling, *Birth of a Nation*, 52, 53; William Grayson to Patrick

Henry, June 12, September 29, 1789, Richard Henry Lee to Patrick Henry, May 28, September 14, September 27, 1789, in Henry, *Patrick Henry*, vol. 3, 391, 406, 386, 399, 402, respectively; Risjord, "The Virginia Federalists," 490; Adrienne Koch, *Jefferson and Madison: The Great Collaboration* (New York: Oxford University Press, 1964), 56, 57, 59n49; John C. Miller, *Alexander Hamilton: Portrait in Paradox* (New York: Harper & Row Publishers, 1959), 229; Ellis, "The Path Not Taken," 28; Kurt T. Lash, "The Original Meaning of an Omission: The Tenth Amendment, Popular Sovereignty and 'Expressly' Delegated Power," *Loyola-LA Studies Paper* (No. 2007–31, October 2007), 2–5, 8, 12, 13, 17, 22, 24, 25, 27, 36 and "Tucker's Rule," 1354–55 and "James Madison's Celebrated Report of 1800: The Transformation of the Tenth Amendment," 174–75; *Annals of Congress*, 1 Cong., 1 Sess., 446 (June 8, 1789), 730 (August 13, 1789), 790 (August 18, 1789); MacLay, *Journal of William MacLay*, 134. The lack of specificity in the movers of resolutions was due to differing reports.

4. Harold C. Syrett (ed.), *The Papers of Alexander Hamilton*, 27 vols. (New York: Columbia University Press, 1965), vol. 6, 51–168; Jacob E. Cooke, "The Compromise of 1790," *William and Mary Quarterly*, 3rd ser., 27 (1970), 526; Koch, *Jefferson and Madison*, 103–104; Miller, *Alexander Hamilton*, 230, 231, 233; Harry Ammon, "The Formation of the Republican Party in Virginia, 1789–1796," *Journal of Southern History*, 19 (August 1953), 289; Stanley Elkins and Eric McKittrick, "The Founding Fathers: Young Men of the Revolution," *Political Science Quarterly* 76 (1961), 213; Wood, *The Radicalism of the American Revolution*, 261; Bickford and Bowling, *Birth of a Nation*, 62, 64, 65, 95; E. James Ferguson, *The Power of the Purse* (Chapel Hill: University of North Carolina Press, 1961), 179–86, 191, 203–206, 251–54, 290, 292–99, 305–306, 335; McCoy, *The Elusive Republic*, 147; Theodorick Bland to Patrick Henry, March 9, 1790, Richard Henry Lee to Patrick Henry, June 10, 1790, in Henry, *Patrick Henry*, vol. 3, 418, 421, respectively; Edmund Pendleton to George Washington, September 11, 1793, in Mays, *The Letters and Papers of Edmund Pendleton*, vol. 2, 613–14; *Annals of Congress*, 1 Cong., 2 Sess., 1234, 1236–38 (February 11, 1790), 1273, 1277, 1280–81 (February 16, 1790), 1284 (February 17, 1790), 1308, 1333 (February 18, 1790), 1343, 1346 (February 22, 1790), 1387 (February 24, 1790), 1389, 1391, 1395–96, 1403–1404 (February 25, 1790), 1437, 1439 (March 1, 1790), 1548–51 (March 31, 1790), 1562 (April 1, 1790), 1741 (July 21, 1790); MacLay, *Journal of William MacLay*, 199, 296; David McCarrell, "The Formation of the Jeffersonian Party in Virginia," (unpublished Ph.D. dissertation, Duke University, 1937), 78.

5. Alexander Hamilton to John Jay, November 13, 1790, John Jay to Alexander Hamilton, November 28, 1790, Benjamin Lincoln to Alexander Hamilton, December 4, 1790, William Short to Alexander Hamilton, December 30, 1790, in Syrett, *The Papers of Alexander Hamilton*, vol. 7, 149–50, 166–67, 196–98, 392–96, respectively; MacLay, *Journal of William MacLay*, 297; Lynch, *Negotiating the Constitution* 71, 74–75; Bickford and Bowling, *Birth of a Nation*, 65–67; Ferguson, *The*

Power of the Purse, 180–84, 187, 203, 206, 208, 211, 218, 307–309, 312–15, 317; Stanley Elkins and Eric McKittrick, *The Age of Federalism* (Oxford University Press, 1993), 234, 265; Richard Henry Lee to Patrick Henry, September 14, 1789, and June 10, 1790, Theodorick Bland to Patrick Henry, March 9, 1790, in Henry, *Patrick Henry*, vol. 3, 399, 421, 418, respectively; William Waller Hening, *The Statutes at Large: Being a Collection of All the Laws of Virginia from the First Session of the Legislature, in the Year 1619*, 13 vols. (Philadelphia: Thomas DeSilver, 1823), vol. 13, 234–35, 237–39; Herman V. Ames, *State Documents on Federal Relations: The States and the United States* (New York: Da Capo Press, 1970), 4–7; *Annals of Congress*, 1 Cong., 2 Sess., 1396 (February 25, 1790), 1443–44 (March 1, 1790), 1462 (March 3, 1790), 1532–33, 1544 (March 30, 1790), 1587–88, 1592 (April 22, 1790).

6. Syrett, *Papers of Alexander Hamilton*, vol. 8, 63–164; Julian P. Boyd (ed.), *The Papers of Thomas Jefferson*, 32 vols. (Princeton: Princeton University Press, 1974), vol. 19, 275–80; Bickford and Bowling, *Birth of a Nation*, 73; Anderson, *William Branch Giles*, 11, 12, 14; Elkins and McKittrick, *The Age of Federalism*, 224–33; Risjord, "The Virginia Federalists," 490; Benjamin B. Klubes, "The First Federal Congress and the First National Bank: A Case Study in Constitutional Interpretation," *Journal of the Early Republic*, 10 (1990), 19–20, 20n2, 22–23, 25–27, 29, 31–38; Ammon, "The Formation of the Republican Party in Virginia," 289, 293; Koch, *Jefferson and Madison*, 35, 37–46, 104–14; Miller, *Alexander Hamilton*, 260, 262, 264–66, 311; Banning, *The Sacred Fire of Liberty*, 295 and "Republican Ideology and the Triumph of the Constitution," 180, 183n33; Harry V. Jaffa, *A New Birth of Freedom*, 30–31; Edmund Pendleton to George Washington, September 11, 1793, in Mays, *The Letters and Papers of Edmund Pendleton*, vol. 2, 614; Siegan, *The Supreme Court's Constitution*, 9; Ellis, "The Path Not Taken," 29; *Annals of Congress*, 1 Cong., 3 Sess., 1845 (December 16, 1790), 1944–52 (February 2, 1791), 1989–97 (February 7, 1791), 2008–2112 (February 9, 1791); 2 Cong., 1 Sess., 179 (November 14, 1791); McDonald, *Novus Ordo Seclorum*, 267; MacLay, *Journal of William MacLay*, 374; Jesse T. Carpenter, *The South as a Conscious Minority, 1789–1861: A Study in Political Thought* (Gloucester, MA: Peter Smith, 1963), 41–42; Ralph Ketchum, *James Madison: A Biography* (New York: The Macmillan Company, 1971), 314–15, 319–20; William Sterne Randall, *Thomas Jefferson: A Life* (New York: Henry Hill and Company, 1993), 506; David G. Smith, *The Convention and the Constitution: The Political Ideas of The Founding Fathers, Young Men of the Revolution* (New York: St. Martin's Press, 1965), 82, 83n14; Stourzh, *Alexander Hamilton and the Idea of Republican Government*, 166; Cooke, *The Federalist*, No. 23, 151; No. 28, 178; No. 29, 182–83; Robert E. Shalhope, "Thomas Jefferson's Republicanism and Antebellum Southern Thought," *Journal of Southern History*, 42 (November 1976), 545.

7. Syrett, *Papers of Alexander Hamilton*, vol. 10, 23–340; *Annals of Congress*, 1 Cong., 2 Sess., 1094–95 (January 15, 1790); 2 Cong., 1 Sess., 362–65 (February 3, 1792), 386–89 (February 6, 1792), 391–96

(February 7, 1792), 397–400 (February 8, 1792), Appendix, 971–1034 (n.d., 1790); McCoy, *The Elusive Republic*, 154; Miller, *Alexander Hamilton*, 282, 286–87, 289, 296–98, 297n*; Edmund Pendleton to George Washington, September 11, 1793, in Mays, *The Letters and Papers of Edmund Pendleton*, vol. 2, 614; James Madison to Andrew Stevenson, November 17, 1830, in Farrand, *The Records of the Federal Convention*, vol. 3, 483; Thomas Jefferson to Edward Carrington, August 4, 1787, in Carpenter, *The South as a Conscious Minority*, 35.

8. For biographies with different foci, read Robert Shalhope, *John Taylor of Caroline: Pastoral Republican* (Columbia: University of South Carolina Press, 1980) and Eugene Tenbroeck Mudge, *The Social Philosophy of John Taylor of Caroline: A Study in Jeffersonian Democracy* (New York: Columbia University Press, 1939); John Taylor, *An Enquiry into the Principles and Tendency of Certain Public Measures* (Philadelphia: Thomas Dobson, 1794), 1–11, 13–19, 22–32, 34, 36–37, 39, 41–44, 46–55, 58, 61–68, 85–92.

Chapter 6

1. McCarrell, "The Formation of the Jeffersonian Party in Virginia," 166–67; Anderson, *William Branch Giles*, 36–38, 41–43, 45; Risjord, "The Virginia Federalists," 500, 502; Ammon, "The Formation of the Republican Party in Virginia," 305; Ellis, "The Path Not Taken," 29; *Annals of Congress*, 3 Cong., Appendix, 855 (June 8, 1795); 4 Cong., 1 Sess., 160–61 (December 23, 1795), 394 (March 1, 1796), 426–27 (March 2, 1796), 437 (March 7, 1796), 444–48 (March 8, 1796), 501, 503–509, 512, 555–56 (March 11, 1796), 556–57, 560–64 (March 15, 1796), 759 (March 24, 1796), 760–62 (March 30, 1796), 771–72 (March 31, 1796), 773–74, 777, 781 (April 6, 1796), 976–77, 979–87 (April 15, 1796), 1004–1009, 1011 (April 16, 1796), 1061, 1064–65 (April 19, 1796), 1097–98 (April 20, 1796), 1121 (April 21, 1796), 1229, 1231–34, 1236–37 (April 28, 1796).

2. Gaillard Hunt (ed.), *The Writings of James Madison*, 9 vols. (New York: G. P. Putnam's Sons, 1906), vol. 6, 67–123; Thomas Jefferson to George Washington, May 23, 1792, in Boyd, *The Papers of Thomas Jefferson*, vol. 23, 535–40; Ammon, "The Formation of the Republican Party in Virginia," 285, 295–97, 301, 305, 309–310 and "The Jeffersonian Republicans in Virginia," *Virginia Magazine of History and Biography*, 71 (1963), 153–59, 161–65, 167; Banning, *The Jeffersonian Persuasion*, 13, 113, 162; Risjord, "The Virginia Federalists," 486–90, 496, 496n46, 497–502; Wood, *The Radicalism of the American Revolution*, 262; Bickford and Bowling, *Birth of a Nation*, 93, 95, 97; Ferguson, *The Power of the Purse*, 297–99; McCoy, *The Elusive Republic*, 153; Noble E. Cunningham, Jr., *The Jeffersonian Republicans: The Formation of Party Organization* (Chapel Hill: University of North Carolina Press, 1957), 8, 41, 49, 144–45, 256; Beeman, *The Old Dominion and the New Nation*, xii, 67, 114–15, 120–21; Ford, "Inventing the Concurrent Majority," 31, 35, 41; Elkins and McKitrick, *The Age of Federalism*, 263–64, 266, 268; James M. Banner, *To the Hartford Convention: The Federalists*

and the Origin of Party Politics in Massachusetts, 1789–1815 (New York: Alfred A. Knopf, 1970), 29.

3. McCarrell, "The Formation of the Jeffersonian Party in Virginia," 198, 220; Boyd, *The Papers of Thomas Jefferson*, vol. 30, 529–56; Hunt, *The Writings of James Madison*, vol. 6, 326–31; Beveridge, *The Life of John Marshall*, vol. 2, 397, 404–405; Don Fehrenbacher, *The South and Three Sectional Crises* (Baton Rouge: Louisiana State University Press, 1980), 11; Beeman, *The Old Dominion and the New Nation*, 184; Banning, *The Sacred Fire of Liberty*, 386–87, 394 and "Republican Ideology and the Triumph of the Constitution," 186n41 and *The Jeffersonian Persuasion*, 71, 256, 260; Ellis, "The Path Not Taken," 29–31; Ford, "Inventing the Concurrent Majority," 35; Adrienne Koch and Harry Ammon, "The Virginia and Kentucky Resolutions: An Episode in Jefferson's and Madison's Defense of Civil Liberties," *William and Mary Quarterly*, 3rd ser., 5 (April 1948), 146–47, 151–52, 156–57, 160–67, 170; Ammon, "The Jeffersonian Republicans in Virginia," 159; Berns, "The Meaning of the Tenth Amendment," 142; Anderson, *William Branch Giles*, 61, 62n185; Elkins and McKitrick, *The Age of Federalism*, 700; Jaffa, "Partly Federal, Partly National," 118, 132, 133 and *A New Birth of Freedom*, 35; Risjord, "The Virginia Federalists," 503; Lash, "James Madison's Celebrated Report of 1800," 180, 180n121, 181; Bennett, *American Theories of Federalism*, 93–94.

4. *The Virginia Report of 1799–1800, Touching the Alien and Sedition Laws; Together With the Virginia Resolutions of December 21, 1798, the Debate and Proceedings Thereon in the House of Delegates of Virginia and Several Other Documents Illustrative of the Report and Resolutions* (New York: Da Capo Press, 1970), passim; Risjord, "The Virginia Federalists," 503–504.

5. *Address of the General Assembly to the People of the Commonwealth of Virginia*, *Journal of the House of Delegates*, January 22, 1799, 88–96; Beveridge, *The Life of John Marshall*, vol. 2, 389, 401–402; Hunt, *The Writings of James Madison*, vol. 6, 332–40; Lash, "The Original Meaning of an Omission," 39 and "Minority Report: John Marshall and the Defense of the Alien and Sedition Acts," *Ohio State Law Journal*, 68 (no. 2, 2007), 442, 453, 455–56, 457, 497–98, 507 and "James Madison's Celebrated Report of 1800," 181; James Madison to George Washington, October 18, 1787, in Farrand, *The Records of the Federal Convention*, vol. 3, 130; James Madison to Peter S. Duponceau, August [no date], 1824, in Farrand, *The Records of the Federal Convention*, Supplement, 314; Lynch, *Negotiating the Constitution*, 188; *Annals of Congress*, 5 Cong., 2 Sess., 2145–47 (July 10, 1798); 6 Cong., 1 Sess., 411–14 (January 23, 1800); Vanderford, "Rights of Humans, Rights of States," 81, 94–96; Cunningham, *The Jeffersonian Republicans*, 133. In a letter to Edmund Randolph, Spencer Roane repeated the Virginia opinion on the introduction of common law to the Constitution. "I have no hesitation ... to say that I have always entirely concurred with you in opinion, as to the erroneousness and mischief of that theory which sets up the common law as a part of the Code of the United States." See Spencer Roane to Edmund Randolph, August 18, 1799,

in "Roane Correspondence," *John P. Branch Historical Papers of Randolph-Macon College*, 2 (1905), 124.

6. *The Virginia Report of 1799–1800*, 170–77; Bennett, *American Theories of Federalism*, 97; Koch and Ammon, "The Virginia and Kentucky Resolutions," 147, 164; Anderson, *William Branch Giles*, 61; Risjord, "The Virginia Federalists," 530.

7. Hunt, *The Writings of James Madison*, vol. 6, 341–406; Banning, *The Sacred Fire of Liberty*, 390; Belz, "The South and the American Constitutional Tradition at the Bicentennial," 24; Jaffa, "Partly Federal, Partly National," 127; Koch and Ammon, "The Virginia and Kentucky Resolutions," 165, 169, 172–73; Ford, "Inventing the Concurrent Majority," 53; Bennett, *American Theories of Federalism*, 100. For a negative view on Madison's doctrinal inconsistencies see Kevin R, Gutzman, "A Troublesome Legacy: James Madison and the 'Principles of '98,'" *Journal of the Early Republic*, 15 (Winter 1995), 569–89.

8. Jaffa, "Partly Federal, Partly National," 116, 118, 122, 126, 131 and *A New Birth of Freedom*, 37–39; Belz, "The South and the American Constitutional Tradition at the Bicentennial," 23–25; Nagel, *One Nation Indivisible, 1776–1861*, 33–34; Berns, "The Meaning of the Tenth Amendment," 142.

9. Banning, "Republican Ideology and the Triumph of the Constitution," 168, 175, 177–78 and *The Jeffersonian Persuasion*, 105, 113, 117, 201–202; Ammon, "The Jeffersonian Republicans in Virginia," 158.

10. Ellis, *The Union at Risk*, 4; Banning, "Republican Ideology and the Triumph of the Constitution," 178–80, 184–85, 186n41; Ammon, "The Formation of the Republican Party in Virginia," 292; Jaffa, *A New Birth of Freedom*, 33.

11. Jaffa, "Partly Federal, Partly National," 115 and *A New Birth of Freedom*, 33; Onuf, "Constitutional Politics," 48; Cooke, *The Federalist*, No. 45, 313; Arthur Bestor, "State Sovereignty and Slavery: A Reinterpretation of Proslavery Constitutional Doctrine, 1848–1860," *Journal of the Illinois State Historical Society*, 54 (1961), 143–46; Hall and Ely, "The South and the American Constitution," 9–10; Ellis, *The Union at Risk*, 3; Finkelman, "States' Rights North and South in Antebellum America," 125, 127.

12. Thomas Jefferson to James Madison, November 26, 1799, in Boyd, *The Papers of Thomas Jefferson*, vol. 31, 243–44; Koch and Ammon, "The Virginia and Kentucky Resolutions," 170; Robert E. Shalhope, "Thomas Jefferson's Republicanism and Antebellum Southern Thought," 537; David John Mays, *Edmund Pendleton, 1721–1803: A Biography*, 2 vols. (Cambridge: MA: Harvard University Press, 1952), vol. 2, 329–31.

13. Banning, *The Jeffersonian Persuasion*, 14, 117n48, 126–28, 140, 146 and "Republican Ideology and the Triumph of the Constitution," 184–85; Belz, "The South and the American Constitutional Tradition at the Bicentennial," 29–30; Koch and Ammon, "The Virginia and Kentucky Resolutions," 173. For information about the early Republican party and its relations to conservative sovereigntists see McCarrell, "The Formation of the Jeffersonian Party in Virginia," 133; Richard E. Ellis,

The Jeffersonian Crisis: Courts and Politics in the Young Republic (New York: Oxford University Press, 1971), 19–24; Appleby, *Capitalism and a New Social Order*, 5.

Chapter 7

1. Mays, *The Letters and Papers of Edmund Pendleton, 1734–1803*, vol. 2, 695–99.

2. Charles T. Cullen, "St. George Tucker, John Marshall, and Constitutionalism in the Post-Revolutionary South," *Vanderbilt Law Review*, 32 (1979), 342; St. George Tucker (ed.), *Blackstone's Commentaries: With Notes of Reference to the Constitution and Laws of the Federal Government of the United States and of the Commonwealth of Virginia*, 5 vols. (Philadelphia: William Young Birch and Abraham Small, 1803; reprint, South Hackensack, NJ: Augustus M. Kelly, Rothman Reprints Inc., 1969), vol. 1, Appendix, 8, 31, 53, 75–76, 151, 153, 169, 170, 322.

3. Tucker, *Blackstone's Commentaries*, vol. 1, Appendix, 5, 8–9, 10, 13–15, 17, 19–21, 25–29, 33–36, 37, 38, 40, 55, 65, 70, 73, 75, 78.

4. *Ibid.*, 140, 141, 143–45, 146, 150, 153–54, 173–74, 176, 187, 287; Lash, "The Original Meaning of an Omission," 2, 4, 5, 14, 15, 30, 35, 41, 44, 54 and "Tucker's Rule," 1347–48, 1350–51, 1358–60, 1362–73 and "James Madison's Celebrated Report of 1800," 171–72, 182, 185–86, 198; Vanderford, "Rights of Humans, Rights of States," 2, 30, 65, 81, 93, 97, 99, 101. For an interesting interpretation of St. George Tucker's political philosophy see David Thomas Konig, "St. George Tucker and the Limits of States' Rights Constitutionalism: Understanding the Federal Compact in the Early Republic," *William and Mary Law Review*, 47 (February 2006), 1279–1341.

5. Ellis, *The Jeffersonian Crisis*, 14; Beveridge, *The Life of John Marshall*, vol. 3, 55–56; McDonald, *States' Rights and the Union*, 54–55; *Annals of Congress*, 7 Cong., 2 Sess., 362 (January 4, 1802), 23 (January 6, 1802), 59–70 (January 13, 1802), 520 (February 15, 1802), 546–54 (February 17, 1802), 580–602 (February 18, 1802), 650–63 (February 20, 1802), 666 (February 23, 1802), 768 (February 25, 1802), 958–68 (March 3, 1802), 1361 (February 16, 1820); 8 Cong., 1 Sess., 18 (October 22, 1803), 387–89, 406–417 (October 24, 1803), 414, 434–37, 444, 457, 487 (October 25, 1803), 49–52 (November 3, 1803); Appleby, *Capitalism and a New Social Order*, 94; Banning, "Jeffersonian Ideology Revisited," 6; Curtius [John Taylor], *A Defence of the Measures of the Administration of Thomas Jefferson: Taken from the National Intelligencer* (Washington, D.C.: S. H. Smith, 1804; reprint, Union, NJ: The Lawbook Exchange Ltd., 1999), 129–36. The latter pamphlet was a campaign tract designed to further Thomas Jefferson's case before the people in the 1804 election. Thus, his audience was the American common folk so there was little constitutionalism within it. Instead, Taylor lauded the future benefits to the United States of the Purchase.

6. Tucker, *Blackstone's Commentaries*, vol. 2, Appendix, 31, 34, 41–43, 52–53, 68–73, 76, 78–79; *Annals of Congress*, 15 Cong., 2 Sess., 1188–89 (February 15, 1819); 16 Cong., 1 Sess., 1219, 1240 (February 10, 1820).

For a summary of Virginia's slave property laws see Tucker, *Blackstone's Commentaries*, vol. 3, Appendix, 73–97.

7. For the story of the compromises see Glover Moore, *The Missouri Controversy, 1819–1821* (Gloucester, MA: Peter Smith, 1967); Don E. Fehrenbacher, *The South and Three Sectional Crises*, 9–23; and William J. Cooper, *Liberty and Slavery: Southern Politics to 1860* (New York: Alfred A. Knopf, 1983), 134–42; *Annals of Congress*, 15 Cong., 2 Sess., 1166 (February 13, 1819), 1180, 1184–91, 1205 (February 15, 1819); 16 Cong., 1 Sess., 1218–41 (February 10, 1820), 1265–89 (February 12, 1820), 1356–73 (February 16, 1820), 1382–94 (February 17, 1820); 16 Cong., 2 Sess., 543–54 (December 8, 1820), 555–65 (December 9, 1820), 580–95 (December 11, 1820), 736–37 (January 4, 1821), 990–94 (January 30, 1821), 1022–25 (February 2, 1821), 1118–20 (February 13, 1821); James Madison to James Monroe, February 10 and February 23, 1820 in Hunt, *The Writings of James Madison*, vol. 9, 21–24; James Monroe to Thomas Jefferson, February 7 and February 19, 1820, in Stanislaus Murray Hamilton (ed.), *The Writings of James Monroe Including a Collection of his Public and Private Papers and Correspondence Now for the First Time Printed*, 7 vols. (New York: AMS, 1960), vol. 6, 114–16; Spencer Roane to James Monroe, February 16, 1820, in "Letters of Spencer Roane, 1788–1822," *Bulletin of the New York Public Library*, 10 (March 1906), 174–75.

Chapter 8

1. *Richmond Enquirer*, June 11, 15, 18, 22, 1819; and Gerald Gunther (ed.), *John Marshall's Defense of McCulloch vs. Maryland* (Stanford, CA: Stanford University Press, 1969), 1–11, 13–14, 17–20, 23, 25–30, 32–34, 36–39, 40–44, 46–47, 49, 52–55, 57–61, 64–67, 70–85, 87–89, 90–97, 99, 101, 106, 108–118, 121–29, 130–35, 138–39, 140–42, 145–47, 149, 150, 152–54, 156, 158–59, 162–63, 167–68, 170–73, 176–77, 179, 180, 182–87, 191, 194–95, 197–98, 200–203, 210–14; Eric Tscheschlok, "Mistaken Identity: Spencer Roane and the 'Amphictyon' Letters of 1819," *Virginia Magazine of History and Biography*, 106 (Spring 1998), 201–12; Ellis, "The Path Not Taken," 25–26, 32–33; Timothy S. Huebner, "The Consolidation of State Judicial Power: Spencer Roane, Virginia Legal Culture, and the Southern Judicial Tradition," *Virginia Magazine of History and Biography*, 102 (January 1994), 47–72; Beveridge, *The Life of John Marshall*, vol. 1, 52; McDonald, *States' Rights and the Union*, 78; F. Thornton Miller, "John Marshall Versus Spencer Roane: A Reevaluation of Martin vs. Hunter's Lessee," *Virginia Magazine of History and Biography*, 96 (July 1988), 297–314; R. Kent Newmyer, "John Marshall and the Southern Constitutional Tradition," in Hall and Ely, *An Uncertain Tradition*, 108–111; William W. Wiecek, "'Old Times There Are Not Forgotten': The Distinctiveness of the Southern Constitutional Experience," in Hall and Ely, *An Uncertain Tradition*, 163; James Madison to Judge Roane, September 2, 1819, in Farrand, *The Records of the Federal Convention*, vol. 3, 435; Belz, "The South and the American Constitutional Tradition at the Bicenten-

nial," 26–27; Berns, "The Meaning of the Tenth Amendment," 150; William E. Dodd, "Chief Justice Marshall and Virginia, 1813–1821," *American Historical Review*, 12 (July 1907), 776, 777–79, 781, 784; Thomas Jefferson to Spencer Roane, September 6, 1819 in Paul Leicester Ford (ed.), *The Writings of Thomas Jefferson*, 12 vols. (New York: G. P. Putnam's Sons, 1892–99), vol. 12, 135–37; James Madison to Spencer Roane, September 2, 1819, in Hunt, *The Writings of James Madison*, vol. 8, 447–53; Spencer Roane to James Monroe, August 22, 1819, in "Letters of Spencer Roane, 1788–1822," 173; Lash, "Minority Report," 496, 497–98 and "The Original Meaning of an Omission," 1, 45, 47; Ames, *State Documents on Federal Relations*, 103–104.

2. The best exposition of the Junto exaggeration is F. Thornton Miller, "The Richmond Junto: Secret All-powerful Club — or Myth," *Virginia Magazine of History and Biography*, 99 (January 1991), 63–80. William E. Dodd, "Chief Justice Marshall and Virginia, 1813–1821," 783–86; James Madison to Spencer Roane, May 6 and June 29, 1821 in Hunt, *The Writings of James Madison*, vol. 9, 55–63, 65–68, respectively; Spencer Roane to James Monroe, June 20, 1821 in "Letters of Spencer Roane, 1788–1822," 174–75; Spencer Roane to Archibald Thweatt, December 24, 1821, in "Roane Correspondence," 141; *Richmond Enquirer*, May 25, 29, June 1, 5, 8, 1821; Ray W. Luce, *Cohens v. Virginia: The Supreme Court and State Rights, A Reevaluation of Influences and Impacts* (New York: Taylor & Francis, 1990), xiii–xvi, 1–2, 25, 29, 31, 35–43, 47–52, 54–56, 75, 118, 122–30, 132–37, 140–47, 149, 155, 157, 168, 183–85, 193, 195, 200, 206–207, 210, 212–13, 215, 218–19, 233–34, 240–41, 243–44, 246–47.

Chapter 9

1. Ames, *State Documents on Federal Relations*, 24–25.

2. Norma Lois Peterson, *Littleton Waller Tazewell* (Charlottesville: University Press of Virginia, 1983), 147, 200, 217; Littleton Waller Tazewell, *A Review of the Proclamation of President Jackson of the 10th of December, 1832 in a Series of Numbers Originally Published in the Norfolk and Portsmouth Herald Under the Signature of "A Virginian,"* (Norfolk: J.D. Ghiselin, 1888), 3–112; *Register of Debates*, 22 Cong., 2 Sess., Appendix, 145–55, 180–87 (January 16, 1833); Henry H. Simms, *The Rise of the Whigs in Virginia, 1824–1840* (Richmond: The William Byrd Press, Inc., 1929), 71, 81, 103, 155; William G. Shade, *Democratizing the Old Dominion: Virginia and the Second Party System* (Charlottesville: The University Press of Virginia, 1996), 244.

3. James Madison, "The Right of a State to Nullify an Act of Congress," *North American Review*, 31 (October 1830), 537–46; Edgar, *South Carolina: A History*, 330–32; *Register of Debates*, 22 Cong., 2 Sess., Appendix, 167 (January 16, 1832); Ulrich Bonnell Phillips, *Georgia and State Rights* (Washington, D.C.: Government Printing Office, 1902; reprint, Macon: Mercer University Press, 1984), 123–24.

4. Charles H. Ambler (ed.), *The Life and Diary of John Floyd, Governor of Virginia, an Apostle of Secession, and the*

Father of the Oregon Country (Richmond: Richmond Press, Inc., Printers, 1918), 8–9, 31, 34–37, 43, 47–49, 51, 78–80, 82, 85, 95, 97–100, 103, 109–10, 113–14, 123–25, 133–36, 142–43, 147–48, 154–55, 170–73, 175, 184, 186–87, 200–203, 206–209, 212, 214, 225, 233; Ames, *State Documents on Federal Relations*, 53–56.

5. Beverley Tucker, *The Partisan Leader: A Tale of the Future* (New York: Rudd & Carleton, 1861; reprint Chapel Hill: The University of North Carolina Press, 1971), vii–x, xx, xxii, 1–5, 8, 10–11, 13–14, 18, 22, 37–42, 46–48, 50, 65, 78, 80, 97–99, 108, 123, 144, 151, 155–56, 159, 170–71, 174, 177, 183, 190, 202–205, 224, 228, 238–39, 250–52, 266, 323, 365; Abel P. Upshur, "A Review of Edward William Sydney [pseudonym for Nathaniel Beverley Tucker], *The Partisan Leader: A Tale of the Future*" *Southern Literary Messenger*, 3 (January 1837), 73; Vanderford, "Rights of Humans, Rights of States," 141, 152, 159, 186–88; Bennett, *American Theories of Federalism*, 156–58.

6. Claude H. Hall, *Abel Parker Upshur: Conservative Virginian, 1790–1844* (Stevens Point, WI: Worzalla Publishing Company, 1964), 5, 97–105; Abel P. Upshur, *A Brief Inquiry into the True Nature of Our Federal Government: Being a Review of Judge Story's 'Commentaries on the Constitution of the United States,'* (Petersburg, VA: Edmund and Julian C. Ruffin, 1840; reprint, New York: Da Capo Press, 1971), 9–12, 14, 16, 19, 23, 27–28, 30, 36, 39–41, 45, 47, 49–53, 55, 57, 60–66, 68–69, 71, 80–82, 84–90, 93–94, 98–101, 125, 128, 131; Abel P. Upshur, "A Review of Edward William Sydney [pseudonym for Nathaniel Beverley Tucker], *The Partisan Leader: A Tale of the Future*," 76–81; Lash, "The Original Meaning of an Omission," 2, 46n192, 48, 48n203 and "Tucker's Rule," 1343–44; Vanderford, "Rights of Humans, Rights of States," 163; Bennett, *American Theories of Federalism*, 155–56.

7. Ellis, *The Union at Risk*, 8–11; *Annals of Congress*, 1 Cong., 1 Sess., 420–23 (May 22, 1789); James Madison to Nicholas P. Trist, February 15, 1830, in Hunt, *The Writings of James Madison*, vol. 9, 354–58; Farrand, *The Records of the Federal Convention*, vol.1, 54; *Madison's Report of 1799, Virginia House of Delegates*, January 7, 1800, 3.

Chapter 10

1. Shanks, *The Secession Movement in Virginia*, 15, 22–23, 26; Charles Pinnegar, *Brand of Infamy: A Biography of John Buchanan Floyd* (Westport, CT: Greenwood Press, 2002), 28; Chaplain W. Morrison, *Democratic Politics and Sectionalism: The Wilmot Controversy* (Chapel Hill: The University of North Carolina Press, 1967), 18, 48; Ames, *State Documents on Federal Relations*, 244–47; *Congressional Globe*, 30 Cong., 2 Sess., 440 (February 5, 1849).

2. *Congressional Globe*, 29 Cong., 2 Sess., Appendix, 77 (January 7, 1847); 30 Cong., 1 Sess., Appendix, 572–75 (May 16, 1848), 1084 (August 3, 1848); 30 Cong., 2 Sess., 478 (February 7, 1849); 31 Cong., 1 Sess., 234 (January 28, 1850), 249 (January 29, 1850), Appendix, 650, 654 (May 27, 1850), Appendix, 1384 (July 18, 1850), Appendix, 1679–80 (Septem-

ber 3, 1850); Shanks, *The Secession Movement in Virginia*, 201; Morrison, *Democratic Politics and Sectionalism*, 16–17; Holman Hamilton, *Prologue to Conflict: The Crisis and Compromise of 1850* (Lexington: University of Kentucky Press, 1964), 121.

3. *Congressional Globe*, 29 Cong., 2 Sess., Appendix, 77–79 (January 7, 1847); 30 Cong., 1 Sess., 659 (April 21, 1848), Appendix, 1082, 1085 (August 3, 1848); 30 Cong., 2 Sess., 311–12 (January 22, 1849), 440 (February 5, 1849); 31 Cong., 1 Sess., 650 (April 5, 1850), Appendix, 1387 (July 18, 1850), Appendix, 1678, 1682 (September 3, 1850); Pinnegar, *Brand of Infamy*, 29; Hamilton, *Prologue to Conflict*, 49.

4. *Congressional Globe*, 29 Cong., 2 Sess., Appendix, 76 (January 7, 1847); 30 Cong., 1 Sess., Appendix, 573, 576, 578 (May 16, 1848), Appendix, 1083 (August 3, 1848); 31 Cong., 1 Sess., Appendix, 1678, 1683 (September 3, 1850).

5. *Ibid.*, 30 Cong., 1 Sess., Appendix, 572–76, 578 (May 16, 1848), Appendix, 1082–83 (August 3, 1848); 31 Cong., 1 Sess., 248 (January 20, 1850), Appendix, 649–50 (May 27, 1850), Appendix, 1679–80 (September 3, 1850).

6. *Ibid.*, 29 Cong., 2 Sess., Appendix, 77–78 (January 7, 1847); 31 Cong., 1 Sess., 234–35 (January 28, 1850), 650 (April 5, 1850), Appendix, 650–51 (May 27, 1850), Appendix, 1389 (July 18, 1850), Appendix, 1384 (July 18, 1850); Appendix, 1680–81 (September 3, 1850); Hamilton, *Prologue to Conflict*, 32–34; Bestor, "State Sovereignty and Slavery," 118–21, 128, 130–31, 145–47, 158, 161, 163, 165–66, 180.

7. *Congressional Globe*, 29 Cong., 2 Sess., Appendix, 76–77, 79 (January 7, 1847); 30 Cong., 1 Sess., Appendix, 514 (May 16, 1848), 1084 (August 3, 1848); 30 Cong., 2 Sess., 312 (January 22, 1849), 440 (February 5, 1849); 31 Cong., 1 Sess., 249 (January 28, 1850), 650 (April 5, 1850), Appendix, 1384 (July 18, 1850), Appendix, 1678–81 (September 3, 1850).

8. *Ibid.*, 29 Cong., 2 Sess., Appendix, 78 (January 7, 1847); 30 Cong., 1 Sess., Appendix, 572, 578 (May 16, 1848), Appendix, 1083–84 (August 3, 1848); 30 Cong., 2 Sess., 478–79 (February 7, 1849); 31 Cong., 1 Sess., 248–49 (January 29, 1850), Appendix, 651 (May 27, 1850), Appendix, 915 (June 18, 1850), Appendix, 1384 (July 18, 1850), Appendix, 1473 (July 31, 1850), Appendix, 1510 (August 6, 1850); Hamilton, *Prologue to Conflict*, 173; Morrison, *Democratic Politics and Sectionalism*, 129, 138–39.

9. *Congressional Globe*, 29 Cong., 2 Sess., Appendix, 77, 79 (January 7, 1847); 30 Cong., 1 Sess., Appendix, 572 (May 16, 1848); 30 Cong., 2 Sess., 480 (February 7, 1849); 31 Cong., 1 Sess., 233–35 (January 28, 1850), 249 (January 29, 1850), Appendix, 650 (May 27, 1850), Appendix, 914 (June 18, 1850), Appendix, 1583 (August 19, 1850), Appendix, 1604, 1607 (August 21, 1850), Appendix, 1678 (September 3, 1850).

10. *Ibid.*, 29 Cong., 2 Sess., Appendix, 77 (January 7, 1847); 30 Cong., 1 Sess., Appendix, 1084 (August 3, 1848); 30 Cong., 2 Sess., 477–80 (February 7, 1849); 31 Cong., 1 Sess., Appendix, 1678 (September 3, 1850); Shade, *Democratizing the Old Dominion*, 255; Morrison, *Democratic Politics and Sectionalism*, 65.

11. *Congressional Globe*, 29 Cong., 2 Sess., Appendix, 86 (January 6, 1847), Appendix, 76, 79 (January 7, 1847); 31 Cong., 1 Sess., 651 (April 5, 1850), Appendix, 1383 (July 18, 1850), Appendix, 1682 (September 3, 1850); Hamilton, *Prologue to Conflict*, 40.

12. George H. Reese (ed.), *Proceedings of the Virginia State Convention of 1861*, 4 vols. (Richmond: Virginia State Library, 1965), Appendix C, 783–87; vol. 1, 24, 304; vol. 2, 458; vol. 3, 352; Shanks, *The Secession Movement in Virginia*, 158–60, James C. McGregor, *The Disruption of Virginia* (New York: The Macmillan Company, 1922), 114.

13. Reese, *Proceedings of the Virginia State Convention of 1861*, vol. 1, 251, 278, 498–99, 502–503, 534, 731–33; vol. 2, 6, 78, 82–83, 142–43, 346–47, 360, 505–506; vol. 3, 37.

14. *Ibid.*, vol. 1, 551, 645; vol. 2, 210–11, 348, 389; vol. 3, 117, 143, 667.

15. *Ibid.*, vol. 1, 205–206, 276, 293, 351, 379–80, 387, 517; vol. 2, 231–32, 265, 304, 532, 596–99; vol. 3, 76, 499–501.

16. *Ibid.*, vol. 2, 56, 433, 435, 438–52, 458–60, 462–70, 474–75, 479, 513–17, 546–47, 553; vol. 3, 15–16.

17. *Ibid.*, vol. 1, 1, 41–42, 47–49, 100–101, 108, 118, 129, 194–95, 230, 234–35, 241–42, 282, 284, 385, 396, 399, 415; vol. 2, 110, 326; vol. 3, 25, 76; Shanks, *The Secession Movement in Virginia*, 191; Daniel W. Crofts, *Reluctant Confederates: Upper South Unionists in the Secession Crisis* (Chapel Hill: University of North Carolina Press, 1989), 127.

18. Reese, *Proceedings of the Virginia State Convention of 1861*, vol. 1, 43, 45, 47–48, 93, 101, 106–107, 117, 129, 151, 163–64, 173, 182, 202, 204, 241, 277, 283, 293, 338, 345, 354–58, 381, 385, 395, 403, 408, 490, 498–99, 502–503, 506, 511, 517, 543–44, 712–13, 717–18, 730; vol. 2, 6, 93, 180, 216, 243, 270, 277, 311, 315, 362, 513, 613, 617, 706–707; vol. 3, 13, 107, 117, 254, 258, 361, 412, 741.

19. *Ibid.*, vol. 3, 734, 741, 759; vol. 4, 3, 24, 26–27, 122, 144.

Bibliography

Adair, Douglass. "'That Politics May be Reduced to a Science': David Hume, James Madison, and the Tenth *Federalist.*" *Huntington Library Quarterly*, 20 (August 1957), 343–60.

Address of the General Assembly to the People of the Commonwealth of Virginia. Journal of the House of Delegates.

Ambler, Charles Henry. *Thomas Ritchie: A Study in Virginia Politics.* Richmond: Bell Book & Stationery Co., 1913.

Ames, Herman V. *State Documents on Federal Relations: The States and the United States.* New York: Da Capo Press, 1970.

Ammon, Harry. "The Formation of the Republican Party in Virginia, 1789–1796." *Journal of Southern History* 19 (August 1953), 283–310.

_____. "The Jeffersonian Republicans in Virginia." *Virginia Magazine of History and Biography* 71 (1963), 153–67.

Anderson, Dice Robins. *William Branch Giles: A Study in the Politics of Virginia and the Nation from 1790 to 1830.* Gloucester, MA: Peter Smith, 1965.

Annals of Congress. Washington, DC: Gales and Seaton, 1834–1856.

Appleby, Joyce. *Capitalism and a New Social Order: The Republican Vision of the 1790s.* New York: New York University Press, 1984.

_____. "Republicanism in Old and New Contexts." *William and Mary Quarterly* 3rd series, 43 (1986), 20–34.

_____. "What Is Still American in the Political Philosophy of Thomas Jefferson?" *William and Mary Quarterly* 39 (April 1982), 287–309.

Bailyn, Bernard. *The Ideological Origins of the American Revolution.* Cambridge, MA: The Belknap Press, 1967.

Banner, James M., Jr. *To the Hartford Convention: The Federalists and the Origins of Party Politics in Massachusetts, 1789–1815.* New York: Alfred A. Knopf, 1970.

Banning, Lance. "James Madison and the Dynamics of the Constitutional Convention." *The Political Science Reviewer* 17 (1987), 5–48.

_____. "Jeffersonian Ideology Revisited: Liberal and Classical Ideas in the New American Republic." *William and Mary Quarterly*, 3rd series, 43 (1986), 3–19.

_____. *The Jeffersonian Persuasion: Evolution Of A Party Ideology.* Ithaca, NY: Cornell University Press, 1978.

_____. "Republican Ideology and the Triumph of the Constitution, 1789 to 1793." *William and Mary Quarterly* 31 3rd Series (1974), 167–188.

_____. "The Republican Interpretation: Retrospect and Prospect." In *The Republican Synthesis Revisited: Essays in Honor of George Athan Billias*, edited by Milton M. Klein, Richard D. Brown, and John B. Hench, 91–117. Worcester, MA: American Antiquarian Society, 1992.

_____. *The Sacred Fire of Liberty: James Madison & the Founding of the Federal Republic.* Ithaca, NY: Cornell University Press, 1995.

_____. "1787 and 1776: Patrick Henry, James Madison, the Constitution, and the Revolution." In *Toward a More Perfect Union: Six Essays on the Constitution*, edited by Neil L. York, 59–89. Provo, UT: Brigham Young University Press, 1988.

Beeman, Richard. *The Old Dominion and the New Nation: 1788–1801.* Lexington: The University Press of Kentucky, 1972.

Belz, Herman. "The South and the American Constitutional Tradition at the Bicentennial." In *An Uncertain Tradition: Constitutionalism and the History of the South*, edited by Kermit L. Hall and James W. Ely, Jr., 17–59. Athens: The University of Georgia Press, 1989.

Benedict, Michael Les. "Judicial Infamy: The Black Testimony Cases." In *Virginia and the Constitution*, edited by A. E. Dick Howard and Melvin Urofsky, 53–82. Charlottesville: Virginia Commission on the Bicentennial of the United States Constitution, 1992.

Bennett, Walter Hartwell. *American Theories of Federalism.* Tuscaloosa, AL: University of Alabama Press, 1964.

Berns, Walter. "The Meaning of the Tenth Amendment." In *A Nation of States: Essays on the American Federal System*, edited by Robert A. Goldwin, 139–61. 2nd ed. Chicago: Rand McNally College Publishing Company, 1974, 139–161.

Bestor, Arthur. "State Sovereignty and Slavery: A Reinterpretation of Proslavery Constitutional Doctrine, 1848–1860." *Journal of the Illinois State Historical Society* 54 (1961), 117–180.

Beveridge, Albert. *The Life of John Marshall.* 4 vols. Boston and New York: Houghton Mifflin Company, 1929.

Bickford, Charlene Bangs, and Kenneth R. Bowling. *Birth of a Nation: The First Federal Congress, 1789–1791.* Madison, WI: Madison House Publishers, 1989.

Borden, Morton, ed. *The Antifederalist Papers.* Lansing: Michigan State University Press, 1965.

Buckley, Thomas E. *Church and State in Revolutionary Virginia, 1776–1787.* Charlottesville: The University Press of Virginia, 1977.

Carpenter, Jesse T. *The South as a Conscious Minority, 1789–1861: A Study in Political Thought.* Gloucester, MA: Peter Smith, 1963.

Chomsky, Noam. *Necessary Illusions: Thought Control in Democratic Societies.* Concord, ON: House of Anansi Press, 1989.

Congressional Globe. Washington, DC: Blair & Rives, 1834–1873.

Cooke, Jacob E. "The Compromise of 1790." *William and Mary Quarterly*, 3rd series, 27 (1970), 523–45.

_____, ed. *The Federalist.* Middletown, CT: Wesleyan University Press, 1961.

Cooper, William J., Jr. *The South and the Politics of Slavery, 1828–1856.* Baton Rouge: Louisiana State University Press, 1978.

_____. *Liberty and Slavery: Southern Politics to 1860.* New York: Alfred A. Knopf, 1983.

Crofts, Daniel W. *Reluctant Confederates: Upper South Unionists in the Secession Crisis.* Chapel Hill: University of North Carolina Press, 1989.

Cullen, Charles T. "St. George Tucker, John Marshall, and Constitutionalism in the Post-Revolutionary South." *Vanderbilt Law Review* 32 (1979), 341–45.

Cunningham, Noble E., Jr. *The Jeffersonian Republicans: The Formation of Party Organization.* Chapel Hill: University of North Carolina Press, 1957.

Curtius [John Taylor]. *A Defence of the Measures of the Administration of Thomas Jefferson: Taken from the National Intelligencer.* Washington, D.C.: S. H. Smith, 1804. Reprint, Union, NJ: The Lawbook Exchange Ltd., 1999.

Dent, Lynwood M., Jr. "The Virginia Democratic Party, 1824–1847." Unpublished Ph.D. dissertation, Louisiana State University, 1971.

Diamond, Martin. "What the Framers Meant by Federalism." In *A Nation of States: Essays on the American Federal System*, edited by Robert A. Goldwin, 25–42. 2nd ed. Chicago: Rand McNally College Publishing Company, 1974.

Diggins, John Patrick. *The Lost Soul of American Politics: Virtue, Self-Interest, and the Foundations of Liberalism.* New York: Basic Books, 1984.

_____. "Recovering 'First Principles': Critical Perspectives on the Constitution and the Fate of Classical Republicanism." In *Toward a More Perfect Union: Six Essays on the Constitution*, edited by Neil L. York, 119–43. Provo, UT: Brigham Young University Press, 1988.

Dodd, William E. "Chief Justice Marshall and Virginia, 1813–1821." *American Historical Review* 12 (July 1907), 776–87.

Drake, Frederick D., and Lynn R. Nelson, eds. *States' Rights and American Federalism: A Documentary History.* Westport, CT: Greenwood Press, 1999.

Edgar, Walter. *South Carolina: A History.* Columbia: University of South Carolina Press, 1998.

Elkins, Stanley, and Eric McKitrick. *The Age of Federalism.* New York: Oxford University Press, 1993.

_____. "The Founding Fathers: Young Men of the Revolution." *Political Science Quarterly* 76 (1961), 181–216.

Elliot, Jonathan, comp. *The Debates in the Several State Conventions on the Adoption of the Federal Constitution, as Recommended by the General Convention at Philadelphia, in 1787, Together With the Journal of the Federal Convention, Luther Martin's Letter, Yates' Minutes, Congressional Opinions, Virginia and Kentucky Resolutions of '98–99, and Other Illustrations of the Constitution.* 5 vols. New York: B. Franklin, 1836.

Ellis, Richard E. *The Jeffersonian Crisis: Courts and Politics in the Young Republic.* New York: Oxford University Press, 1971.

_____. "The Path Not Taken: Virginia and the Supreme Court, 1789–1821." In *Virginia and the Constitu-*

tion, edited by A. E. Dick Howard and Melvin Urofsky, 24–52. Charlottesville: Virginia Commission on the Bicentennial of the United States Constitution, 1992.

_____. *The Union at Risk: Jacksonian Democracy, States' Rights, and the Nullification Crisis*. New York: Oxford University Press, 1987.

Farrand, Max, ed. *The Records of the Federal Convention*. 4 vols. New Haven: Yale University Press, 1937.

Fehrenbacher, Don E. *The South and Three Sectional Crises*. Baton Rouge: Louisiana State University Press, 1980.

Ferguson, E. James. *The Power of the Purse*. Chapel Hill: University of North Carolina Press, 1961.

Finkelman, Paul. "Slavery and the Constitutional Convention: Making a Covenant with Death." In *Beyond Confederation: Origins of the Constitution and American National Identity*, edited by Richard Beeman et al., 188–225. Chapel Hill: University of North Carolina Press, 1987.

_____. "States' Rights North and South in Antebellum America." In *An Uncertain Tradition: Constitutionalism and the History of the South*, edited by Kermit L. Hall and James W. Ely, Jr., 125–58. Athens: The University of Georgia Press, 1989.

Floyd, John. *The Life and Diary of John Floyd, Governor of Virginia, an Apostle of Secession, and the Father of the Oregon Country*. Edited by Charles Henry Ambler. Richmond: Richmond Press, Inc., Printers, 1918.

Ford, Lacy K., Jr. "Inventing the Concurrent Majority: Madison, Calhoun, and the Problem of Majoritarianism in American Political Thought." *Journal of Southern History* 60 (1994), 19–58.

Ford, Paul Leicester, ed. *Pamphlets on the Constitution of the United States*. New York: Da Capo Press, 1968.

_____, ed. *The Writings of Thomas Jefferson*. 12 vols. New York: G. P. Putnam's Sons, 1892–99.

Ford, Worthington C., et al., eds. *Journals of the Continental Congress, 1774–1789*. 34 vols. Washington, DC: Library of Congress, 1904–37.

Gewehr, Wesley M. *The Great Awakening in Virginia*. Gloucester, MA: Peter Smith, 1965.

Greene, Jack P. "Society, Ideology, and Politics: An Analysis of the Political Culture of Mid–Eighteenth Century Virginia." In *Society, Freedom, and Conscience: The Coming of the Revolution in Virginia, Massachusetts, and New York*, edited by Richard M. Jellison et al., 14–76. New York: W. W. Norton, 1976.

Grigsby, Hugh Blair. *The History of the Virginia Federal Convention of 1788*. 2 vols., New York: Da Capo Press, 1969.

Gunther, Gerald, ed. *John Marshall's Defense of McCulloch vs. Maryland*. Stanford: Stanford University Press, 1969.

Gutzman, Kevin R. "A Troublesome Legacy: James Madison and the 'Principles of '98.'" *Journal of the Early Republic* 15 (Winter 1995), 569–89.

_____. "The Virginia and Kentucky Resolutions Reconsidered: 'An Appeal to the *Real Laws* of Our Country.'" *Journal of Southern History* 66 (August 2000), 473–96.

Hall, Claude H. *Abel Parker Upshur: Conservative Virginian, 1790–1844*. Stevens Point, WI: Worzalla Publishing Company, 1964.

Hall, Kermit L., and James W. Ely, Jr. "The South and the American Constitution." In *An Uncertain Tradition: Constitutionalism and the History of the South*, edited by Kermit L. Hall and James W. Ely, Jr., 3–16. Athens: The University of Georgia Press, 1989.

Hamilton, Alexander. *The Papers of Alexander Hamilton*. Edited by Harold C. Syrett. 27 vols. New York: Columbia University Press, 1962.

Hamilton, Holman. *Prologue to Conflict: The Crisis and Compromise of 1850*. Lexington: University of Kentucky Press, 1964.

Hening, William Waller, comp. *The Statutes at Large: Being a Collection of All the Laws of Virginia from the First Session of the Legislature, in the Year 1619*. 13 vols. Philadelphia: Thomas DeSilver, 1823.

Henry, Patrick. *Patrick Henry: Life, Correspondence, and Speeches*. Edited by William Wirt Henry. 3 vols. New York: Burt Franklin, 1969.

Hobbes, Thomas. *Leviathan*. Edited by Edwin Corley. Indianapolis: Hackett Publishing Company, Inc., 1994.

Huebner, Timothy S. "The Consolidation of State Judicial Power: Spencer Roane, Virginia Legal Culture, and the Southern Judicial Tradition." *Virginia Magazine of History and Biography* 102 (January 1994), 47–72.

Isaac, Rhys. "Dramatizing the Ideology of Revolution: Popular Mobilization in Virginia, 1774 to 1776." *William and Mary Quarterly* 3rd series, 33 (1976), 357–385.

_____. *The Transformation of Virginia, 1740–1790*. Chapel Hill: University of North Carolina Press, 1982.

_____. "Evangelical Revolt: The Nature of the Baptists' Challenge to the Traditional Order in Virginia, 1765 to 1775." *William and Mary Quarterly*, 3rd series, 31 (1974), 345–368.

Jaffa, Henry V. *A New Birth of Freedom: Abraham Lincoln and the Coming of the Civil War*. New York: Rowman & Littlefield, 2000.

_____. "'Partly Federal, Partly National': On the Political Theory of the Civil War." In *A Nation of States: Essays on the American Federal System*, edited by Robert A. Goldwin, 109–37. 2nd ed. Chicago: Rand McNally College Publishing Company, 1974.

Jefferson, Thomas. *The Papers of Thomas Jefferson*. Edited by Julian P. Boyd. 32 vols. Princeton: Princeton University Press, 1974.

Johnson, F. Claiborne, Jr. "Federalist, Doubtful, and Antifederalist: A Note on the Virginia Convention of 1788." *Virginia Magazine of History and Biography* 96 (July 1988), 333–344.

Journal of the Virginia House of Delegates.

Kaminski, John P., et al., eds. *Ratification of the Constitution by States: Virginia.* 19 vols. Madison: State Historical Society of Wisconsin, 1988.

Kelley, Robert. "Ideology and Political Culture From Jefferson to Nixon." *American Historical Review* 82 (June 1977), 531–582.

Ketchum, Ralph. *James Madison: A Biography.* New York: The Macmillan Company, 1971.

Klubes, Benjamin B. "The First Federal Congress and the First National Bank: A Case Study in Constitutional Interpretation." *Journal of the Early Republic* 10 (1990), 19–41.

Koch, Adrienne. *Jefferson and Madison: The Great Collaboration.* New York: Oxford University Press, 1964.

_____, and Harry Ammon. "The Virginia and Kentucky Resolutions: An Episode in Jefferson's and Madison's Defense of Civil Liberties." *William and Mary Quarterly* 3rd series, 5 (April 1948), 145–76.

Konig, David Thomas. "Country Justice: The Rural Roots of Constitutionalism in Colonial Virginia." In *An Uncertain Tradition: Constitutionalism and the History of the South*, edited by Kermit L. Hall and James W. Ely, Jr., 63–82. Athens: The University of Georgia Press, 1989.

_____. "St. George Tucker and the Limits of States' Rights Constitutionalism: Understanding the Federal Compact in the Early Republic." *William and Mary Law Review*, 47 (February 2006), 1279–1341.

Kramnick, Isaac. "Republicanism Revisited: The Case of James Burgh." In *The Republican Synthesis Revisited: Essays in Honor of George Athan Billias*, edited by Milton M. Klein, Richard D. Brown, and John B. Hench, 19–36. Worcester: American Antiquarian Society, 1992.

Kukla, Jon. "A Spectrum of Sentiments: Virginia's Federalists, Antifederalists, and 'Federalists Who Are For Amendments,' 1787–1788." *Virginia Magazine of History and Biography* 96 (July 1988), 277–296.

Lash, Kurt T. "James Madison's Celebrated Report of 1800: The Transformation of the Tenth Amendment." *George Washington Law Review*, 74 (January 2006), 165–200.

_____. "Minority Report: John Marshall and the Defense of the Alien and Sedition Acts." *Ohio State Law Journal*, 68 (no. 2, 2007), 435–516.

_____. "The Original Meaning of an Omission: The Tenth Amendment, Popular Sovereignty and 'Expressly' Delegated Power." *Loyola-LA Studies Paper* (October 2007), 1–55. Available at http://ssrn.com/abstract =1000087.

_____. "'Tucker's Rule': St. George Tucker and the Limited Construction of Federal Power." *William and Mary Law Review*, 47 (February 2006), 1343–91.

"Letters of Spencer Roane, 1788–1822." *Bulletin of the New York Public Library* 10 (March 1906), 167–80.

Levy, Leonard. *Original Intent and the Framers' Constitution.* New York: Macmillan, 1988.

Locke, John. *Two Treatises on Government.* Edited by Peter Laslett. New York: Cambridge University Press, 1988.

Luce, Ray W. *Cohens v. Virginia: The Supreme Court and State Rights, A Reevaluation of Influences and Impacts.* New York: Taylor & Francis, 1990.

Lynch, Joseph M. *Negotiating The Constitution: The Earliest Debates Over Original Intent.* Ithaca: Cornell University Press, 1999.

MacLay, Edgar S., ed. *Journal of William MacLay, United States Senator from Pennsylvania, 1789–1791.* New York: D. Appleton and Company, 1890.

Madison, James. "The Right of a State to Nullify an Act of Congress." *North American Review* 31 (October 1830), 537–46.

_____. *The Writings of James Madison.* Edited by Gaillard Hunt. 9 vols. New York: G. P. Putnam's Sons, 1906.

Main, Jackson T. *The Antifederalists: Critics of the Constitution, 1781–1788.* Chapel Hill: University of North Carolina Press, 1961.

_____. *Political Parties Before the Constitution.* Chapel Hill: University of North Carolina Press, 1973.

_____. "Sections and Politics in Virginia, 1781–1787." *William and Mary Quarterly* 3rd series, 12 (January 1955), 96–112.

Mason, Alpheus Thomas. *The States Rights Debate: Antifederalism and the Constitution.* Englewood Cliffs, NJ: Prentice-Hall, 1964.

Mason, George. *The Papers of George Mason, 1725–1792.* Edited by Robert R. Rutland. 3 vols. Chapel Hill: University of North Carolina Press, 1970.

Mayer, David M. "Of Principles and Men: The Correspondence of John Taylor of Caroline with Wilson Cary Nicholas, 1806–1808." *Virginia Magazine of History and Biography* 96 (July 1988), 345–88.

Mays, David John. *Edmund Pendleton, 1721–1803: A Biography.* 2 vols. Cambridge, MA: Harvard University Press, 1952.

_____. *The Letters and Papers of Edmund Pendleton, 1774–1803.* 2 vols. Charlottesville: University Press of Virginia, 1967.

McCarrel, David K. "The Formation of the Jeffersonian Party in Virginia." Unpublished Ph.D. dissertation, Duke University, 1937.

McCoy, Drew E. *The Elusive Republic: Political Economy in Jeffersonian America.* Chapel Hill: University of North Carolina Press, 1980.

McDonald, Forrest. *E Pluribus Unum.* New York: Cambridge University Press, 1965.

_____. *Novus Ordo Seclorum: The Intellectual Origins of the Constitution.* Lawrence: University Press of Kansas, 1985.

_____. *We the People: The Economic Origins of the Constitution.* Chicago: University of Chicago Press, 1958.

_____. *States' Rights and the Union: Imperium in Imperio, 1776–1876.* Lawrence: University Press of Kansas, 2000.

McGregor, James C. *The Disruption of Virginia.* New York: The Macmillan Company, 1922.

Miller, F. Thornton. "John Marshall Versus Spencer Roane: A Reevaluation of Martin Versus Hunter's Lessee." *Virginia Magazine of History and Biography* 96 (July 1988), 297–314.

_____. "The Richmond Junto: Secret All-powerful Club — or Myth." *Virginia Magazine of History and Biography* 99 (January 1991), 63–80.

Miller, John C. *Alexander Hamilton: Portrait in Paradox.* New York: Harper & Row, 1959.

Monroe, James. *The Writings of James Monroe Including a Collection of his Public and Private Papers and Correspondence Now for the First Time Printed.* Edited by Stanislaus Murray Hamilton. 7 vols. New York: AMS, 1960.

Moore, Glover. *The Missouri Controversy, 1819–1821.* Gloucester, MA: Peter Smith, 1967.

Morgan, Edmund S. "*The Puritan Ethic and the American Revolution.*" *William and Mary Quarterly* 3d. series, 24 (1967), 3–43.

Morrison, Chaplain W. *Democratic Politics and Sectionalism: The Wilmot Controversy.* Chapel Hill: The University of North Carolina Press, 1967.

Mudge, Eugene Tenbroeck. *The Social Philosophy of John Taylor of Caroline: A Study in Jeffersonian Democracy.* New York: Columbia University Press, 1939.

Nagel, Paul C. *One Nation Indivisible: The Union In American Thought, 1776–1861.* Westport, CT: Greenwood Press, 1964.

Newmyer, R. Kent. "John Marshall and the Southern Constitutional Tradition." In *An Uncertain Tradition: Constitutionalism and the History of the South,* edited by Kermit L. Hall and James W. Ely, Jr., 105–24. Athens: The University of Georgia Press, 1989.

Onuf, Peter S. "Constitutional Politics: States, Sections, and National Interest." In *Toward a More Perfect Union: Six Essays on the Constitution,*" edited by Neil L. York, 29–57. Provo, UT: Brigham Young University Press, 1988.

_____, and Cathy Matson. "Republicanism and Federalism in the Constitutional Decade." In *The Republican Synthesis Revisited: Essays in Honor of George Athan Billias,* edited by Milton M. Klein, Richard D. Brown, and John B. Hench, 119–41. Worcester, MA: American Antiquarian Society, 1992.

Padover, Saul K., ed. *The Complete Jefferson: Containing His Major Writings, Published and Unpublished, Except His Letters.* New York: Duell, Sloan & Pearce, Inc., 1943.

Peterson, Norma Lois. *Littleton Waller Tazewell.* Charlottesville: University Press of Virginia, 1983.

Phillips, Ulrich B. *Georgia and State Rights.* Macon, GA: Mercer University Press, 1983.

Pinnegar, Charles. *Brand of Infamy: A Biography of John Buchanan Floyd.* Westport, CT: Greenwood Press, 2002.

Randall, William Sterne. *Thomas Jefferson: A Life.* New York: Henry Hill and Company, 1993.

Rawle, William. *A View of the Constitution of the United States of America.* Reprint 2d ed. New York: Da Capo Press, 1970. Philadelphia: Philip H. Nicklin, Law Bookseller, 1829.

Reese, George H., ed. *Proceedings of the Virginia State Convention of 1861.* 4 vols. Richmond: Virginia State Library, 1965.

Richmond Enquirer.

Risjord, Norman K. *Chesapeake Politics, 1781–1800.* New York: Columbia University Press, 1978.

_____. *The Old Republicans: Southern Conservatives in the Age of Jefferson.* New York: Columbia University Press, 1965.

_____. "The Virginia Federalists." *Journal of Southern History* 33 (1967), 486–517.

_____. "Virginians and the Constitution: A Multivariate Analysis." *William and Mary Quarterly* 3rd series, 31 (1974), 613–32.

_____, and Gordon den Boer. "The Evolution of Political Parties in Virginia, 1782–1800." *Journal of American History* 60 (1974), 961–84.

"Roane Correspondence." *John P. Branch Historical Papers of Randolph-Macon College* 2 (1905).

Rosen, Gary. *American Compact: James Madison and the Problem of Founding*. Lawrence: University Press of Kansas, 1999.

Secondat, Charles Louis, Baron de Montesquieu. *The Spirit of Laws*. Edited by Anne M. Cohler, et al. New York: Cambridge University Press, 1989.

Shade, William G. *Democratizing the Old Dominion: Virginia and the Second Party System, 1824–1861*. Charlottesville: The University Press of Virginia, 1996.

Shalhope, Robert E. *John Taylor of Caroline: Pastoral Republican*. Columbia: University of South Carolina Press, 1980.

_____. "Republicanism, Liberalism, and Democracy: Political Culture in the Early Republic." In *The Republican Synthesis Revisited: Essays in Honor of George Athan Billias*, edited by Milton M. Klein, Richard D. Brown, and John B. Hench, 37–90. Worcester, MA: American Antiquarian Society, 1992.

_____. "Thomas Jefferson's Republicanism and Antebellum Southern Thought." *Journal of Southern History* 42 (November 1976), 529–56.

Shanks, Henry T. *The Secession Movement in Virginia, 1847–1861*. Richmond: Garrett and Massie, 1934.

Siegan, Bernard H. *The Supreme Court's Constitution: An Inquiry Into Judicial Review and Its Impact on Society*. New Brunswick, NJ: Transaction Books, 1987.

Simms, Henry H. *The Rise of the Whigs in Virginia*. Richmond: The William Byrd Press, 1929.

Sloan, Herbert, and Peter Onuf. "Politics, Culture, and the Revolution in Virginia." *Virginia Magazine of History and Biography* 91 (July 1983), 259–84.

Smith, Adam. *An Inquiry into the Nature and Causes of the Wealth of Nations*. Edited by Edward Canaan. 2 vols. Chicago: University of Chicago Press, 1976.

Smith, David G. *The Convention and the Constitution: The Political Ideas of The Founding Fathers, Young Men of the Revolution*. New York: St. Martin's Press, 1965.

Smith, Paul H., et al., eds. *Letters of Delegates to Congress, 1774–1789*. 25 vols. Washington, DC: Library of Congress, 1976–2000.

Stourzh, Gerald. *Alexander Hamilton And The Idea Of Republican Government*. Stanford: Stanford University Press, 1970.

Sydnor, Charles. *Gentlemen Freeholders: Political Practices in Washington's Virginia*. Chapel Hill: University of North Carolina Press, 1952.

Tate, Thad W. "The Social Contract in America, 1774–1787: Revolutionary Theory as a Conservative Instrument." *William and Mary Quarterly* 3rd series, 22 (1965), 375–91.

Taylor, John. *An Enquiry into the Principles and Tendency of Certain Public Measures*. Philadelphia: Thomas Dobson, 1794.

Tazewell, Littleton Waller. *A Review of the Proclamation of President Jackson of the 10th of December, 1832 in a Series of Numbers Originally Published in the Norfolk and Portsmouth Herald Under the Signature of "A Virginian."* Norfolk: J.D. Ghiselin, 1888.

Tscheschlok, Eric. "Mistaken Identity: Spencer Roane and the 'Amphictyon' Letters of 1819." *Virginia Magazine of History and Biography* 106 (Spring 1998), 201–12.

Thomas, Robert E. "The Virginia Convention of 1788: A Criticism of Beard's An Economic Interpretation of the Constitution." *Journal of Southern History* 19 (February 1953), 63–72.

Tucker, Nathaniel Beverley. *The Partisan Leader: A Tale of the Future*. Reprint Chapel Hill: The University of North Carolina Press, 1971. Sydney, Edward William. pseudo. Beverley Tucker. *The Partisan Leader: A Tale of the Future*. New York: Rudd & Carleton, 1861.

Tucker, St. George, ed. *Blackstone's Commentaries: With Notes of Reference to the Constitution and Laws of the Federal Government of the United States and of the Commonwealth of Virginia*. 5 vols. Philadelphia: William Young Birch and Abraham Small, 1803. Reprint, South Hackensack, NJ: Augustus M. Kelly, Rothman Reprints Inc., 1969.

United States Statutes.

Upshur, Abel P. *A Brief Inquiry into the True Nature of Our Federal Government: Being a Review of Judge Story's 'Commentaries on the Constitution of the United States.'* Petersburg, VA: Edmund and Julian C. Ruffin, 1840. Reprint, New York: Da Capo Press, 1971.

_____. "A Review of Edward William Sydney (pseudonym for Nathaniel Beverley Tucker), *The Partisan Leader: A Tale of the Future*." *Southern Literary Messenger* 3 (January 1837), 73–89.

Vanderford, Chad. "Rights of Humans, Rights of States: The Academic Legacy of St. George Tucker in Nineteenth-Century Virginia." Unpublished Ph.D. dissertation, Louisiana State University, 2005.

Veit, Helen E. et al., eds. *Creating the Bill of Rights: The Documentary Record from the First Federal Congress.* Baltimore: The Johns Hopkins Press, 1991.

Vetterli, Richard, and Gary C. Bryner. "Religion, Public Virtue, and the Founding of the American Republic." In *Toward a More Perfect Union: Six Essays on the Constitution,* edited by Neil L. York, 91–117. Provo, UT: Brigham Young University Press, 1988.

The Virginia Report of 1799–1800, Touching the Alien and Sedition Laws; Together With the Virginia Resolutions of December 21, 1798, the Debate and Proceedings Thereon in the House of Delegates of Virginia and Several Other Documents Illustrative of the Report and Resolutions. New York: Da Capo Press, 1970.

Webking, Robert H. "Melancton Smith and the *Letters from the Federal Farmer.*" *William and Mary Quarterly* 3rd series, 44 (July 1987), 510–28.

Wiecek, William M. "'Old Times There Are Not Forgotten': The Distinctiveness of the Southern Constitutional Experience." In *An Uncertain Tradition: Constitutionalism and the History of the South,* edited by Kermit L. Hall and James W. Ely, Jr., 159–97. Athens: The University of Georgia Press, 1989.

Wood, Gordon S. "Afterword." In *The Republican Synthesis Revisited: Essays in Honor of George Athan Billias,* edited by Milton M. Klein, Richard D. Brown, and John B. Hench, 143–51. Worcester, MA: American Antiquarian Society, 1992.

_____. "The Authorship of the Letters from the Federal Farmer." *William and Mary Quarterly* 3rd series, 23 (April 1974), 299–308.

_____. *The Creation of the American Republic, 1776–1787.* Chapel Hill: University of North Carolina Press, 1969.

_____. "Ideology and the Origins of Liberal America." *William and Mary Quarterly,* 3rd series, 44 (July 1987), 628–638.

_____. "The Political Ideology of the Founders." In *Toward a More Perfect Union: Six Essays on the Constitution,* edited by Neil L. York, 7–25. Provo, UT: Brigham Young University Press, 1988.

_____. *The Radicalism of the American Revolution.* New York: Alfred A. Knopf, 1992.

Yarbrough, Jean M. *American Virtues: Thomas Jefferson on the Character of a Free People.* Lawrence: University Press of Kansas, 1998.

Index